ADMINISTRATION

- Samba Essentials for Windows Administrators
  Wilson

- Tuning and Sizing Windows 2000
  for Maximum Performance
  Aubley

- Windows 2000 Cluster Server Guidebook
  Libertone

- Windows 2000 Hardware and Disk Management
  Simmons

- Windows 2000 Server: Management and Control,
  Third Edition
  Spencer, Goncalves

- Creating Active Directory Infrastructures
  Simmons

- Windows 2000 Registry
  Sanna

- Configuring Windows 2000 Server
  Simmons

- Supporting Windows NT and 2000 Workstation
  and Server
  Mohr

- Zero Administration Kit for Windows
  McInerney

- Windows NT 4.0 Server Security Guide
  Goncalves

- Windows NT Security
  McInerney

CERTIFICATION

- Core MCSE: Windows 2000 Edition
  Dell

- Core MCSE: Designing a Windows 2000 Directory
  Services Infrastructure
  Simmons

- MCSE: Implementing and Supporting Windows 98
  Dell

- Core MCSE
  Dell

- Core MCSE: Networking Essentials
  Keogh

- MCSE: Administering Microsoft SQL Server 7
  Byrne

- MCSE: Implementing and Supporting Microsoft
  Exchange Server 5.5
  Goncalves

- MCSE: Internetworking with Microsoft TCP/IP
  Ryvkin, Houde, Hoffman

- MCSE: Implementing and Supporting Microsoft Proxy
  Server 2.0
  Ryvkin, Hoffman

- MCSE: Implementing and Supporting Microsoft SNA
  Server 4.0
  Mariscal

- MCSE: Implementing and Supporting Microsoft Internet
  Information Server 4
  Dell

- MCSE: Implementing and Supporting Web Sites Using
  Microsoft Site Server 3
  Goncalves

- MCSE: Microsoft System Management Server 2
  Jewett

- MCSE: Implementing and Supporting Internet Explorer 5
  Dell

- Core MCSD: Designing and Implementing Desktop
  Applications with Microsoft Visual Basic 6
  Holzner

- MCSD: Planning and Implementing SQL Server 7
  Vacca

- MCSD: Designing and Implementing Web Sites with
  Microsoft FrontPage 98
  Karlins

PRENTICE HALL SERIES ON MICROSOFT® TECHNOLOGIES

Samba Essentials for Windows® Administrators

Gary Wilson

Prentice Hall PTR, Upper Saddle River, NJ 07458
www.phptr.com

Library of Congress Cataloging-in-Publication Data

Wilson, Gary, B. A.
    Samba essentials for Windows administrators / Gary Wilson.
      p. cm. -- (Prentice Hall PTR Microsoft technologies series)
    ISBN 0-13-040942-1 (alk. paper)
     1. Client/server computing. 2. Samba (Computer file). 3. Microsoft Windows (Computer file) I. Title. II.
Series.

QA76.9.C55 W54 2001
005.4'476--dc21

                                                    2001033921

Production Supervisor: Wil Mara
Acquisitions Editor: Mike Meehan
Editorial Assistant: Linda Ramagnano
Marketing Manager: Debby van Dijk
Manufacturing Manager: Alexis Heydt
Buyer: Maura Zaldivar
Cover Designer: Talar Boorujy

© 2002 Gary Wilson
Published by Prentice-Hall, Inc.
Upper Saddle River, NJ 07458

The publisher offers discounts on this book when ordered in bulk quantities. For more information contact:
Corporate Sales Department, Prentice Hall PTR, One Lake Street, Upper Saddle River, NJ 07458. Phone: 800-382-3419; FAX: 201-236-7141; E-mail: corpsales@prenhall.com

Printed in the United States of America

10 9 8 7 6 5 4 3 2 1

ISBN 0-13-040942-1

Pearson Education LTD.
Pearson Education Australia PTY, Limited
Pearson Education Singapore, Pte. Ltd
Pearson Education North Asia Ltd
Pearson Education Canada, Ltd.
Pearson Educación de Mexico, S.A. de C.V.
Pearson Education—Japan
Pearson Education Malaysia, Pte. Ltd
Pearson Education, Upper Saddle River, New Jersey

CONTENTS

Acknowledgements   *xix*

Preface   *xxi*

Foreword   *xxv*

▼ ONE   Samba and Windows   1

The Secret to Free High-Quality Software   *2*

Samba Put Free Software onto Office Networks   3

Why Is It Called Samba?   3

The History of Samba   4

Comparing Samba and Windows   *5*

Samba's Strengths   5

Lower Costs for Software and Hardware   *6*

Open Source Licensing   *6*

Vendor Independence   *7*

Improved Network Security   *7*

Web-Based Administration   *7*

Linux's Legendary Stability   *8*

Where Samba and Windows conflict   8

Microsoft Sets Its Own Standards   *9*

Samba is Like NT 4, not Windows 2000   *9*

Windows Servers Are Best for Domain Controllers   *9*

Windows Has Finer Access Control   *10*

Samba Requires Additional Skills   *10*

Windows Has More Hardware Support   *10*

Linux and Windows   *11*

Linux is Case-Sensitive   *11*

Linux Uses the Forward Slash   *11*

Linux Has no Unerase Feature   *12*

Linux Doesn't Require File Extensions   *12*

Linux Doesn't Use Drive Letters   *12*

Some Common Linux Questions   *13*

▼ TWO   Installing and Configuring Samba   17

Checking Whether Samba Is Installed   *17*

How to See Whether Samba Is Installed   17

When to Use the Installed Version   18

Samba Versions   *18*

When to Update   20

How to Get the Samba Software   *20*

Updating Linux   21

Using Webmin to Install Updates   *22*

Compiling Samba   23

Matching Red Hat's configuration   26

A Look at What's Installed   27

Administering Samba with Webmin and SWAT   *30*

Setting up Webmin for Samba administration   31

Using SWAT   34

The SWAT options   37

Home   *37*

Globals   *37*

Shares   *38*

Printers   *39*

Status   *39*

View   *39*

Password   *39*

Initial Configuration   *39*

Base Settings   40

Samba's Configuration Variables   40

Security Settings   41

The Security Parameter   *41*

The Encrypt Passwords Option   *42*

Guest Accounts   *42*

Tuning Settings   43

Dead Time   *43*

Socket Options   *43*

Starting Samba Services   *43*

Joining a Domain   *44*

Create a Computer Account on the Domain Controller   44

Update the Samba Configuration   44

Join the Domain   45

User Management   46

Matching Windows and Linux Usernames   48

Getting Help   50

Help on SWAT's Home Page   50

The Online Manual   50

Help on Configuration Pages   51

Samba's Email Help Lists   51

Commercial Support   51

▼ THREE   The Samba File Server   53

The Homes Share   54

Securing the Homes Share   56

Setting Up Linux Directories for Sharing   58

Linux File Permissions   58

Setting Permissions from Windows   61

Creating Directories for Samba Shares   61

Linux Settings for a Share for a Single User   63

Linux Settings for a Share for a Group of Users   65

Linux Settings for a Public Share   65

A Shortcut to Creating a Share in Samba   65

Setting Up Shares   68

The Basic Group Share   68

Security Options   69

Invalid Users and Valid Users   *69*

Admin Users   *69*

Read List and Write List   *70*

Force User and Force Group   *70*

Read Only   *71*

Create Mask and Directory Mask   *71*

Force Create Mode and Force Directory Mode   *71*

Hosts Allow and Hosts Deny   *71*

Filename Handling Options   72

Browsing Options   73
File Locking Options   73
Miscellaneous Options   74
The Basic Group Share, Short Version   75
Adding Features to Homes Share   76

A Secure Group Share   76
A Public Directory   77
A Basic Public Directory   78
A Limited Public Directory   78
A Secured Public Directory   78
Adding Guest Access   79
Guest Account   79

Sharing CD-ROMs and Removable Devices   80
A CD-ROM Share   80
A Removable Device Share   82

Sharing a Microsoft Access Database   82
Application Sharing   84

▼ FOUR   The Samba Print Server   85
How Samba Print Sharing Works   86
Set Spool Permissions   86

Configuring Printer Sharing   88
Webmin's Printer Administration Tool Settings   88
Step 1: Name the Printer Share   90
Step 2: Choose a Connection   91
Step 3: Create the Spool Directory   91
Configuring Samba for Printer Support   92
Customizing Individual Printers   94

Accessing Samba Print Shares from Windows   96
Installing Printers Using the Add Printer Wizard   96
Installing Printers from the Network Neighborhood/
My Network Places   97

Automatic Printer Driver Installation   98
Configure Samba for Automatic Printer Services   98

Add a Printer Administrator   98

Create a Printers *Directory   98*

Set Permissions   99

Create a Print$ Share   99

Install Printers and Drivers   100

Install the Printer   101

Upload the Drivers   101

Configure the Printers   101

▼ FIVE Advanced Topics   103

Using Samba as a Logon Server   104

Configure Samba for Network Logon Support   104

Add a Netlogon Share   105

Configure a WINS Server   106

The lmhosts *Alternative   106*

Add Profile Support   106

Add System Policies   107

Add Logon Scripts   109

Advanced Logon Scripts   109

Using Samba Over SSL   111

Install OpenSSL   112

Compile Samba for SSL Support   113

Set Up the Proxy Server   113

Create a Certificate for the Samba Server   114

Become a Certificate Authority   114

Create a Server Certificate   115

Configure Samba's SSL Options   116

Start the SSL Proxy Server   117

Configure the Windows Machine   117

Samba Virtual Servers   118

Internationalization   122

The Client Code Page Option   123

The Code Page Directory Option   123

The Character Set option   124

The Coding System Option   124

The Valid Chars Option   124

The Samba Time Server   *126*

Set Up the Samba Server As a Time Server   126

Set the Time on Windows Clients   128

The Samba Fax Server   *128*

Select the Right Modem   129

Set Up the Fax Server Software   129

Set Up a Fax Printer in Samba   130

Set Up the Windows Clients   130

Samba, Windows, and Cross-Subnet Browsing   *131*

▼ SIX   Configuring Windows 9x/Me/NT/2000   133

NetBIOS and TCP/IP Networking   *133*

Different Naming Services: WINS and DNS   135

LMHOSTS and HOSTS   136

Setting Up Windows 9x/Me   *137*

Enable Multiuser Profiles   137

Configure TCP/IP Networking   138

IP Address and DHCP   *141*

WINS Configuration and LMHOSTS   *142*

Gateway and DNS Settings   *143*

Configure the Client for Microsoft Windows   144

Choose Machine and Workgroup Names   145

Choose Security and Access Control Settings   146

User-Level Security   *147*

Share-Level Security   *147*

Check the Connection   147

Ping   *147*

Setting Up Windows NT   *150*

Configure TCP/IP networking   151

Assign the NetBIOS name   *151*

Check the CIFS client   *151*

Install and Set Up TCP/IP   *152*

Set the IP Address   *152*

Check the Connection   153

Setting Up Windows 2000   155

Configure TCP/IP Networking   155

Assign the NetBIOS Name   156

Configure the CIFS Client and TCP/IP   157

WINS and NetBIOS Compatibility   158

Check the Connection   158

Browsing, Accessing, and Mapping   160

Accessing Samba File Shares   163

Mapping File Shares   163

▼ SEVEN   Troubleshooting   169

Problems Connecting to a New Server   169

Check Networking   170

Check the Samba Configuration   170

A General Guide for Troubleshooting   172

Four Quick Things to Check   172

Check the Network Wiring   172

Restart the Workstation   172

Check the Windows Client Configuration   173

Check the Logs   173

Problems With the Network Connection   174

Is the Network Configured Properly?   174

Can You Reach Other Computers on the Network?   176

Are the WINS and DNS Name Services Working?   178

Windows Reports a Problem   178

Why Isn't the Samba Server in the Network Neighborhood/
Computers Near Me?   178

You Haven't Waited Long Enough   178

No Shares are Available   179

*The Workstation and the Samba Server are in Different
Workgroups   179*

The WINS Server is Not Reachable   179

There is No Guest Account on the Samba Server   179

Samba Isn't Running   179

*The Workstation or the Samba Server Isn't Connected
to the Network   180*

There is No Master Browser on Your Network   180

More Than One Computer is Set to be the Master Browser   180

The Samba Server is on a Different Subnet   181

The Samba Server Blocks Browsing and Says "Invalid Password" or "Not Authorized"   181

There is More than One Domain Controller on the Network   181

Why Are There Problems Accessing Files or Folders on the Samba Server?   182

The Drive Letter Has Disappeared   182

The Share Name Was Not Found   182

The Network Path Was Not Found   182

You Must Supply a Password to Make This Connection   183

The Password is Invalid   183

The Network is Busy   184

Access is Denied   184

Connection Refused   184

Session Request Failed   184

Why Are There Logon Problems?   185

The Logon Script Does Not Run   185

No Domain Server is Available to Validate Your Password   185

The Password You Supplied Was Incorrect   186

Samba-Related Problems   **186**

Samba is not running   186

The Samba Services Did Not Start   187

Samba Has Not Been Configured   187

What Do the Logs Say?   188

SWAT Can't Be Opened   189

Printer Problems   **191**

▼ EIGHT   Linux System Administration Essentials   195

Understanding Linux Distributions   **196**

Xwindows and Terminals   **196**

KDE and GNOME   197

Reasons Not to Use Xwindows   197

Using Webmin   **198**

Managing Bootup Options   201

Managing Users and Groups   202
Samba Configuration   205
Printer Administration   206
Software Management   208
Other Webmin Modules   208

Using the Nongraphical Terminal   211
The File System   213
Text Editors   215
Basic Functions on a Nongraphical Terminal   217
Copying Files   218

Security Tips   221

Handling Emergencies   225

▼ NINE   Optimizing Performance   227

Performance Issues   228
Monitoring Performance   229

Maximizing Your Hardware   232
Network Infrastructure   232
ATA, SCSI, and RAID   233
ATA Disk Drives   234
SCSI Disk Drives   236
RAID Disk Drive Controllers   237
Filesystem   238
Memory Requirements   239
CPUs and SMP   240

Optimizing the Linux Server   241

Fine-Tuning the Samba Configuration   247
Fine-Tuning Logging Options   248
Fine-Tuning Protocol Options   248
Fine-Tuning Tuning Options   249
Fine-Tuning Filename Handling   253
Fine-Tuning Locking Options   253
Oplocks   253
Level 2 Oplocks   254
Strict Locking   254

Write Cache Size   255

Fine-Tuning Miscellaneous Options   255

Wide Links   255

▼ TEN   Replacing Windows with Samba   257

Replacing a Windows File Server   258

Step 1: Get the User, Group, File, and Printer Sharing Information   259

Step 2: Create User and Group Accounts on the Samba Server   260

Adding Users With the Webmin Utility   261

Adding Users Without the Webmin Utility   263

Step 3: Configure the Samba Server   265

Adding Group Directories Without Webmin   266

Configuring Shares on Samba   266

Step 4: Test the Samba Server   267

Step 5: Move Files to the Samba Server   268

Setting Up a Samba Domain Controller   268

Configure Samba   269

Set Up Netlogon   270

Create Machine Accounts   270

▼ APPENDIX A   Samba Command and Configuration Option Reference   273

The Samba Suite   273

Daemons   273

smbd   273

nmbd   274

winbindd   275

Client Tools   275

Diagnostic Utilities   276

Configuration Options   277

Globals   278

Base Options   278

Security Options   280

Logging Options   286

Protocol Options   287

Tuning Options   289

Printing Options   291

Filename Handling   293

Domain Options   295

Logon Options   296

Browse Options   297

WINS Options   298

Locking Options   299

SSL Options   300

Miscellaneous Options   301

VFS Options   304

Winbind Options   305

Shares   **305**

Base Options   305

Security Options   306

Logging Options   309

Tuning Options   309

Filename Handling   309

Browse Options   311

Locking Options   312

Miscellaneous Options   313

VFS Options   315

Printers   315

Base Options   315

Security Options   316

Logging Options   316

Tuning Options   316

Printing Options   317

Browse Options   318

Miscellaneous Options   319

▼ APPENDIX B   Finding Help   321

Samba's Complete Documentation   321

Help on the Web   322

Samba Help   322

The Samba Headquarters   322

Samba Lists   322

Samba Newsgroup   323

Free Software Foundation   323

Webmin   323

Red Hat Linux   323

Caldera OpenLinux   323

Debian GNU/Linux   324

Other Linux Sites   324

Commercial Support   325

Publications   326

▼ APPENDIX C   Linux Backup Procedures   327

What to Back Up   327

Backing Up from a Windows System   329

Add Backup Operators to a Share   329

Create Separate Backup Shares   329

A Linux-Windows Solution   330

Backing Up from a Linux System   331

Snapshot Partitions   332

Back Up to Tape With Tar   333

Creating a Tape Backup   334

Restoring from a Tape Backup   335

▼ APPENDIX D   The GNU General Public License   337

Text of the License   337

End of Terms and Conditions   342

Applying These Terms to Your New Programs   342

Index   345

ACKNOWLEDGEMENTS

Samba and free software exists because of the volunteer contributions of hundreds and thousands of developers, testers, document writers, complainers, and others who won't settle for anything but the best. The contributors, who come from all around the world, are too many to name.

At the top of the list must go the Samba team. At the time this book was being written this included: Andrew Tridgell, Jeremy Allison, John Terpstra, Chris Hertel, John Blair, Gerald Carter, Michael Warfield, Brian Roberson, Jean Francois Micouleau, Richard Sharpe, Eckart Meyer, Herb Lewis, Dan Shearer, David Fenwick, Paul Blackman, Volker Lendecke, Alexandre Oliva, Tim Potter, Matt Chapman, David Bannon, John Reilly, Simo Sorce, and Andrew Bartlett.

Many members of the Samba team regularly volunteer their time to answer questions and help others, particularly through the Samba email discussion lists. They have more than once answered my questions about particular features.

A special thanks goes to Jaime Cameron, the primary developer of the open source Webmin program for system administrators. That's not just because Webmin is the best system administration tool available for Linux systems. Jaime took time from his busy schedule to answer all of my questions.

Samba, Linux, and the other fine open source software owe a great deal to Richard Stallman and the Free Software Foundation he started. The Free Software Foundation's General Public License is the copyright that keeps much of the open source software free and accessible.

Mike Meehan, the book's acquisitions editor, deserves special thanks for pulling it altogether. He was always reachable, an uncommon trait, and had numerous good suggestions that improved the content.

Mike's executive assistant, Linda Ramagnano, kept the production flowing and probably did much more than I know about.

The production editor, Wil Mara, gets thanks for his sympathetic ear to writers' problems and for putting up with all of the "little" things I kept throwing at him. Those little things can add up quickly.

Kathryn Graehl caught many errors in copyediting, for which I am grateful. Any errors that remain are my own.

Claudette Moore of the Moore Literary Agency is a wizard. She turned a proposal into reality and could always be counted on for good ideas and suggestions. Her assistant, Debbie McKenna, kept the wheels turning.

My life partner, Lallan Schoenstein, deserves more than thanks for her patience, encouragement, and understanding.

And, of course, there's my mom and dad, who made it all possible.

Samba is inherently dynamic. Like all successful open source software, it is in a constant state of change. Developers never stop working on the software, fixing problems or improving the code, and adding new features. Any official release of the program is merely a stage of the constantly developing program. In fact, during the course of development of Samba, the Samba team will regularly release "snapshots" of the code under development for testing.

This book, too, might be seen as a snapshot of the currently available version of Samba, though it differs in many ways from a code snapshot. A big part of Samba's development involves fixing problems, no matter how small or obscure. Many hours are also spent in making Samba work on all of the many different platforms it supiports, the different versions of Unix as well as Linux. This work can take much more time than adding new features. The snapshot covered by this book will last much longer than a code snapshot.

Who This Book Is For

This book is designed to assist a Windows administrator who wants to get a Samba server up and running reliably with a minimum of fuss. The book describes how to do this by running Samba on a Linux server, the second most popular server platform after Windows.

The success of Linux is not just a reflection of its low price. Linux is successful because it is a remarkably stable system that gives server-class performance on inexpensive Intel-compatible systems. For anyone working with a tight budget, and that's almost every network administrator, Linux is an attractive solution.

Samba, however, is not limited to Linux. Samba can be run on almost any Unix-based system from IBM's AIX to Sun's Solaris. Hewlett-Packard even packages its own version of Samba called CIFS/9000 that is included with its HP-UX. Samba will also run on any version of BSD, such as FreeBSD, though it will not run on the new Macintosh OSX, which is based on FreeBSD.

For the most part, any reference in this book to Linux can also be read as a reference to Unix in general. However, the specifics may vary. If you are not using Linux, make sure to check for the correct procedures and command syntax for the version of Unix you are using.

Linux itself has some variations between its different distributions. Throughout the book, Red Hat Linux is used for the examples. Two other major distributions are Caldera OpenLinux and Debian GNU/Linux. In most cases, the information for these two distributions is included as well.

Any of the Linux distributions will work with Samba. Red Hat Linux is the most popular distribution. Caldera OpenLinux has focused on building a wide distribution primarily on business systems. Debian GNU/Linux is a completely noncommercial distribution and, like Samba and the Linux kernel, is maintained by volunteers.

The Samba Headquarters at *www.samba.org* is run on a Debian GNU/Linux server that is provided by VA Linux Systems (*www.valinux.com*) on the Sourceforge open source developers network (*www.sourceforge.net*).

For more detailed information on the three major Linux distributions and complete documentation for each one, go to the following Web sites—

- **Red Hat Linux**   *www.redhat.com*
- **Caldera OpenLinux**   *www.caldera.com*
- **Debian GNU/Linux**   *www.debian.org*

Organization of This Book

CHAPTER 1: SAMBA AND WINDOWS

This chapter introduces Samba, for those who are new to the program, and gives some background to its development, its place in history. The chapter compares Samba with Windows NT/2000. It also details what Samba can and cannot do; this section should be read by anyone thinking about adding a Samba server to a Windows network. Finally, the chapter introduces Linux terms and concepts for Windows users.

CHAPTER 2: INSTALLING AND CONFIGURING SAMBA

Samba installation might look difficult to someone who knows only Windows because there are so many possible steps and options. This chapter shows how the standard installation option is as easy as installing an application on a Windows system. It also explains the more complicated possibilities for those who want a totally customized server. This option involves compiling Samba from the source code. Compiling software is part of working with open source software like Samba. The basics of compiling—only the basics are needed to create a customized version of Samba—are easy to learn even without expertise in C or any other computer language.

CHAPTER 3: THE SAMBA FILE SERVER

This chapter steps through the process for configuring file services on a Samba server. Samba works with a configuration file that can be simple or complex, depending on the need. There is nothing equivalent to the configuration file on a Windows server. However, the process offers great flexibility and has the advantage that the configuration of Samba can be handled remotely, that is, from another computer on the network, using Webmin and SWAT, Web-based tools for remote Samba system administration. Changes and updates can be easily made without having to directly sit at the server and without rebooting the system. For the most part, Windows servers cannot be configured and updated remotely, or without rebooting when making updates.

CHAPTER 4: THE SAMBA PRINT SERVER

The Samba print server is almost as popular as the Samba file server. Cisco Systems, for example, has 300 print servers running Samba and Linux, handling more than 6,000 printers worldwide. Cisco replaced a combination of Windows NT and Sun servers handling printer sharing with Intel-based PCs and found that the Samba-Linux solution was not only more stable but also more flexible. Setting up a print server is no more difficult than setting up a file server.

CHAPTER 5: ADVANCED TOPICS

This chapter takes up advanced networking issues, including using Samba as a logon sever, using Samba as an application server, setting up virtual file servers, and using SSL for secure file transfers on a wide area Samba network. This chapter also covers Samba and browsing across multiple subnets, as well as WINS Service.

CHAPTER 6: CONFIGURING WINDOWS 9X/ME/NT/2000

A chapter on setting up Windows computers to connect to Samba servers may seem unnecessary in a book for Windows administrators. After all, the steps are exactly the same for connecting to a Windows NT/2000 server. However, it's a good idea to go over everything, especially for those who administer a Windows network as part of several other responsibilities on the job. Although the next chapter is about troubleshooting, the steps outlined in this chapter can help to find and fix problems on a Samba network.

CHAPTER 7: TROUBLESHOOTING

Samba servers won't give you a General Protection Fault blue screen. That doesn't mean, however, that Samba is trouble-free. This chapter includes general procedures for troubleshooting Samba problems, along with common solutions for specific Windows error messages.

CHAPTER 8: LINUX SYSTEM ADMINISTRATION ESSENTIALS

Most Samba servers are running on Linux. This chapter is a short course on Linux system administration, including starting up, shutting down, user and group management, and other tasks involved in administrating a server. The chapter shows how Linux system administration can be handled using the Webmin browser-based software package for Linux system administrators. The chapter also introduces the Linux file system and the tools that Linux system administrators use to maintain it.

CHAPTER 9: OPTIMIZING PERFORMANCE

For administrators who want to eke out the best possible results, this chapter discusses advanced techniques for optimizing the performance of a Samba server.

CHAPTER 10: REPLACING WINDOWS WITH SAMBA

Samba lives very happily as one part of a bigger Windows network. In fact, it performs so well that many system administrators decide to convert their entire networks to Samba servers. This chapter covers some of the issues involved and some steps an administrator should take in order to convert to an all-Samba environment. Included in this chapter is the procedure for setting up Samba as a domain controller.

APPENDIX A: SAMBA COMMAND AND CONFIGURATION OPTION REFERENCE

This appendix is a listing of the Samba applications and the configuration options.

APPENDIX B: FINDING HELP

This appendix includes information on how you can find help with Samba as well as Linux.

APPENDIX C: LINUX BACKUP PROCEDURES

Although files on a Samba server can be backed up along with your regular Windows server backups, the Linux system should also be backed up. This appendix describes what needs to be backed up on a Linux server.

APPENDIX D: THE GNU GENERAL PUBLIC LICENSE

The GNU General Public License covers both Samba and the Linux operating system.

FOREWORD

Samba has come a long way over the last ten years—from a system that only the most adventurous would try during the early days of its development, to something that has become a common component of many Unix sysadmins' toolbox.

This book takes the next step by making the world of Samba accessible to sysadmins more familiar with the world of Microsoft Windows. I was delighted to see the clear, task-oriented format that this book presents, and I am sure that Windows administrators will find it an excellent introduction to the possibilities offered by making Samba part of their network.

Andrew Tridgell
Samba creator
June 2001

Samba and Windows

*W*indows® *network administrators have heard about Samba®. It's the free software that makes a Linux® or Unix® computer look like a Windows server on a network. As a network administrator, maybe you've decided to try it out and quietly slip a Linux server running Samba onto the local network. That's already been done with thousands of Linux servers. On the other hand, setting up a Samba server may not be your idea. Maybe your boss just asked why you aren't using one of those free Linux servers everyone is talking about.*

Whatever the reason, the time has come to set up and run a Samba server.

Increasingly, system administrators are seeking out open source software like Samba and Linux because it is hassle-free. There's no complicated licensing to maintain and no additional paperwork involved when adding users or upgrading systems. For a busy administrator this is no small advantage.

Also, Samba can be installed on an older computer that would be too slow for a Windows 2000 server, but would give excellent performance running Linux. This kind of savings on hardware costs is another reason for Samba's popularity.

In this chapter we'll go over some of the advantages of free software like Samba and Linux and the reasons for Samba's legendary stability. Also, we'll compare Samba and Windows, seeing what is similar and what is different. What's different is important because there are some things that a Samba server just can't do. If you only skim through this chapter, make sure you read this part and make sure that there isn't a limitation that prevents you from using Samba.

1

The Secret to Free High-Quality Software

Samba, like the Linux operating system, is licensed under the GNU General Public License, often shortened to GPL. This is a software license established in 1984 by the Free Software Foundation. A copy of the license can be found in Appendix D

The license basically says that Samba can be freely distributed by anyone without restriction. The code is freely available to read, change, fix, give away, or sell as long as nothing is done that would restrict any of these rights. However, Andrew Tridgell, the original developer of Samba, and others who have contributed to its development retain the copyright to the Samba code.

Few network administrators will ever look at the Samba source code. So you might wonder why you should care whether the code is openly available or not.

While you may not ever look at the code, there are those who can and will look at the code, particularly if they are having a problem and they know enough to be able to fix it. Once a fix has been written, it can be made available to everyone else who is using the software. There is nothing new in this. IBM's most stable systems were originally built this way, and most computer software was developed the same way until fairly recently. Bug fixes and enhancements were freely exchanged, making possible the rapid development of very stable software.

Without shared code, software development would have taken much, much longer. The Free Software Foundation's open source licensing is designed to encourage this kind of software development so that progress isn't throttled.

The integrity and stability of open source software are enhanced by the peer review process, the same process that underlies the reliability of all scientific research. Open source software must stand up to the most demanding public scrutiny. All code is available for anyone to examine, verify, and use. Buggy code is either fixed or discarded. Innovations are added based on the suggestions of users. This kind of testing can be more extensive than is possible in the closed environment of proprietary software development.

In fact, closed software development often hinders the process of debugging software. Testing is often limited so that confidential developments are not revealed.

The open source development model makes it almost impossible to hide defects in software, and open source software will never be able to secretly collect information from users' computer systems. Open source prevents a software developer with a vested interest in the product from also being responsible for testing the software's capabilities and then verifying its usability.

The Internet itself is proof that open source works. The Internet is built on open source applications from the TCP/IP networking protocol—used by every Microsoft Windows computer on a network—to the Apache Web server software, used on more than half the Web servers in the world.

Samba Put Free Software onto Office Networks

Samba and Linux have grown up together. The quality and reliability of Linux made free open source software a viable alternative in computer operating systems. An operating system, however, is only as useful as the software applications available to run on it. Would Microsoft's operating system have been as successful without the Microsoft Office suite of applications? Bill Gates certainly doesn't think so.

Linux owes its success, in part, to two free open source applications: Samba and the Apache Web server. Samba's role was often hidden in the early use of Linux servers. Samba was quietly being installed by system administrators on Intel-based computers running Linux. To the users on the network, these servers looked just like Windows servers.

Word quietly spread that older computers could be set up with Samba and become a seamless part of a Windows network. This was an exciting development, especially for cash-strapped institutions like universities and public schools. Educational institutions became the proving grounds for Samba servers. These servers were put to the test. In many respects, the demands of a university computer network can be more exacting than those of a corporate network. Academic uses can be more varied, and students tend to be more abusive of the system than business users. Samba met this test.

Samba file and print servers have won the endorsement of computing giants like IBM and Hewlett-Packard. Samba servers have also won over the bean counters. That's because Samba makes management look smart. Managers can choose the top-rated technology and still protect the bottom line. Samba servers eliminate the need to spend money on client licenses. Running Windows 2000 Advanced Server with 100 client licenses costs about $9,400. In contrast, a Linux server running Samba with unlimited users costs about $50.

Why Is It Called Samba?

Commercial software companies can spend a bundle of money audience-testing names for a new product. They want just the right name that will enhance sales.

The names used for free software, on the other hand, are not market-tested. Free software often follows the hacker tradition creating a play on words or a recursive acronym. The Free Software Foundation's GNU software license uses such a recursive acronym. GNU stands for GNU's Not Unix.

Samba is not a recursive acronym, and the name was never market-tested. Samba was originally called SMBserver, a utilitarian name. SMB is the Windows networking protocol. Microsoft has enhanced the original SMB protocol and calls the enhanced version CIFS (Common Internet File System), but it is still the SMB protocol. So SMBserver was a logical choice for the name. However, it turned out that the name had already been trademarked by a company that makes a competing product. When Andrew Tridgell got an email message telling him that he had to stop using the name, he needed to find a new name quickly. With no idea what to call the program, Tridgell ran a search through the dictionary on his computer for every word that started with the letter "s" and included the letters "m" and "b."

From the list of words that he got, Tridgell chose Samba. The name may not have been market tested, but it works at least as well as the ambiguous Windows NT or the even stranger Millennium Edition (Windows Me).

The History of Samba

Samba was developed beginning in 1991 as a solution to a problem Tridgell had while he was a graduate student at the Australian National University. He had a PC, but he needed to access some disk space on a Unix server using the Pathworks protocol from Digital Equipment Corporation (DEC). The problem was, there was no Pathworks client for his DOS-based PC. Being a skilled programmer, Tridgell studied the problem and then hacked together some code to do the job. With his code he could access the Unix server as if it were another PC DOS computer.

That was version 0.1 of Samba. The Pathworks protocol, it turned out, is the same SMB protocol used for Windows networks.

Tridgell has written a short account of the beginnings of Samba, which can be found in the document named *history* included with the standard installation of Samba. The document can be read on the Web at *http://us1.samba.org/samba/ftp/docs/history*.

Tridgell released the code over the Internet in 1992. A few months and a few fixes later, version 1.0 was released. The code remained unchanged for the next two years. Then, Tridgell discovered Linux. He wanted to link his wife's Windows PC to his Linux PC. There was no easy way to do this without purchasing additional software for the Windows PC. He decided to try the early Samba code and was amazed to find that it worked.

At about this same time, the version 1.0 code was being discovered by Linux users. Tridgell started getting email from Linux users around the world who wanted to use the Samba code to connect Linux and Windows computers. Soon volunteer programmers were offering to help develop the code. There was a spurt of development, the major bugs were worked out, and within two years Samba running on Linux matched the performance of any of the commercial server products that were available for networking Unix systems with Windows.

Today, Samba is found on computer networks around the world, from simple home networks to sophisticated corporate networks. Samba has been accepted by almost every major Unix vendor as a standard for Unix-Windows connectivity. Hewlett-Packard (HP) has gone even further.

HP is distributing Samba with its HP-UX operating system. HP's Samba distribution is called CIFS/9000. According to a statement from Hewlett-Packard, not only is "CIFS/9000 based on open source Samba, [but] HP is committed to submitting CIFS/9000 enhancements back to the open source community." This has already happened, and Samba now includes enhancements developed by HP's programmers. This is an important endorsement of both Samba and free open source software.

Similarly, IBM has embraced Samba and Linux. The company has already earmarked over $1 billion for Linux development, and it is developing an open source version of its JFS filesystem for Linux. All of IBM's Linux servers use Samba for connecting with Windows systems.

As for Microsoft, it may not officially endorse Samba, but several of its developers helped make Samba a success. A Samba document named *thanks* expresses Andrew Tridgell's appreciation to people who did not write code or make bug reports, but who made significant contributions to the development of Samba. His thanks begin with a list of five Microsoft employees who were "very helpful and supportive of the development of Samba" over many years. The document can be read on the Web at *http://us1.samba.org/samba/ftp/docs/THANKS*.

Comparing Samba and Windows

Samba is designed to be run on a Linux computer or on almost any of the Unix systems. It is a Unix implementation of the Windows networking protocol. This blend introduces differences that can be desirable for your network as well as some that you may not want. Running a Linux server can put additional demands on network administration and may add costs for training and implementation. On the other hand, the overall cost of adding a Linux server running Samba to your network, including training, may be lower than the cost of adding a Windows 2000 server. After all, using the example cited earlier, a $3,000 training course in Linux system administration is a third of the cost of $9,400 for the Windows 2000 server software and client licenses for 100 users. In addition, a Samba server has some strengths that aren't available on Windows systems.

Here's a breakdown of some things to consider when deciding whether Samba is the right choice for your network.

Samba's Strengths

Samba has a lot going for it. It is a stable, proven platform for providing file and print services on a local area network. The cost for a Samba server is low and administration is simplified. Adding a Samba server will also increase the security of your network.

LOWER COSTS FOR SOFTWARE AND HARDWARE

There is no base cost for Samba. It is included with every Linux distribution. Prices start at about $50 for a CD with the operating system and all the additional software you'll need, plus a basic user's manual. If you purchase a computer system with Linux already installed, Samba is usually included. If not, all the Samba software can be downloaded for free over the Internet from the Samba Headquarters at *http://www.samba.org* or from any site that has Linux software.

A Linux server has lower hardware requirements than a Windows server. Linux can even be run on older systems that will not support Windows 2000. Because Linux does not require a graphical interface and can be run in terminal mode, an old Pentium 100 system with 32 megabytes (Mb) of random-access memory (RAM) can make an excellent file and print server for a small workgroup that needs its own server. The graphical interface is a resource hog that uses not only video memory but also system memory and virtual memory. Even on a top-of-the-line server, Linux can exceed the performance of a Windows server. Some controversial tests commissioned by Microsoft concluded that on single-processor systems, a Linux server running Samba will outperform a Windows NT 4 server. The same tests showed that Windows servers outperform Linux on multiprocessor systems. The Linux 2.4 kernel that was released in January 2001 has significantly improved multiprocessor support.

Of course, software and hardware are not the only costs involved in maintaining a network, and you wouldn't choose Samba over Windows just on that basis. But Samba is lower in cost even when you consider technical support agreements, the price of upgrades and service packs, downtime costs, and personnel costs for system administrators.

OPEN SOURCE LICENSING

The GNU public license is extraordinarily simple to comply with. No paperwork is involved, and there are no records to keep. It doesn't matter if your Samba server has one user or 10,000; no per-user or per-workstation licenses are involved.

This is good news for network administrators. There has been an increased burden on administrators as software licensing for most operating systems and applications has become more complex.

In order to make sure that there are no violations of software license terms, administrators are too often tied down with the paperwork involved with manual tracking of licenses. Most administrators work to keep their systems within the law, but that can be a time-consuming task, and time is the one thing most administrators don't have. The alternative is expensive license-tracking software.

VENDOR INDEPENDENCE

With an all-Windows network, you are locked into total reliance on Microsoft. That's not all bad. Microsoft has set standards, and standards are welcomed by most network administrators. The software standards greatly reduce the learning curve for any new software, and the hardware standards improve reliability and compatibility.

Yet there are problems with this reliance on a single company. For example, when something isn't working right with an application, users have to pay a service fee to Microsoft even if it is just to learn that there is a known problem with the software. The Justice Department, in its case against Microsoft, has shown some of the downside of Microsoft's total domination. Left out of the legal dispute are Microsoft's plan to start charging yearly fees for software use as well as the company's monopoly pricing practices.

Using the combination of Samba and Linux gives a network administrator independence from a single software monopoly without sacrificing standards. Linux follows the same Unix-based standards that the Internet is built on and that Microsoft has been adopting to a great degree. Support is available from a number of vendors. For example, both IBM and Hewlett-Packard offer 24/7 service support for Linux and Samba.

IMPROVED NETWORK SECURITY

Security is a big concern for all network administrators. No system is invulnerable, including both Windows and Linux. Having a single operating system throughout your network makes you much more vulnerable.

Just as biological diversity in the environment prevents the transmission of viruses between species, systems diversity blocks the spread of computer viruses and the like between systems. Most attacks on systems rely on vulnerabilities of a single operating system. Mixing up the operating systems thwarts some of the most common forms of attack.

In fact, Microsoft uses systems diversity to protect its software. In the document *How Microsoft Ensures Virus-Free Software,* which can be read at *http://support.microsoft.com/support/kb/articles/Q80/5/20.ASP,* Microsoft says: "Disks are duplicated on a variety of industrial strength, quality focused systems. Most of these systems are Unix-based. The Unix-based duplication systems used in manufacturing are impervious to MS-DOS-based, Windows-based, and Macintosh-based viruses."

Take a tip from Microsoft and diversify. Mix some Samba servers with your Windows servers and give your network greater security.

WEB-BASED ADMINISTRATION

Remote administration is an expensive add-on for a Windows NT server. Windows 2000 includes a telnet server that allows remote access, but command-line administration of a Windows 2000 server isn't easy or pretty.

A Samba server can be securely administered through Web-based applications that are included with many Linux distributions or available for free over the Internet. Samba system administration is possibly even easier than administering a Windows NT server. You can sit at one terminal and administer one or a hundred Samba servers all from the same workstation. You can even do Samba and Linux management securely from home over a simple 56K dialup connection to the Internet.

Two applications—the Samba Web Administration Tool (SWAT) and Webmin—will give you everything you need in the way of system administration tools. You'll find all the details on how to use them in this book.

The only way you can do the same job with Windows servers is to purchase expensive third-party software, most of it requiring a high-bandwidth connection to use.

LINUX'S LEGENDARY STABILITY

Overall system performance is mostly determined by hardware, but stability and reliability are based on the operating system. The Linux operating system is legendary for its stability and reliability.

Linux inherits its stability and reliability from its Unix roots. Because of the Unix architecture, Linux rarely crashes, becomes unstable, or loses or corrupts data. The Unix architecture is completely modular, that is, its software components are clearly separated, with well-defined interfaces between components. The modular architecture not only makes it easier to debug code but makes it much harder for a bug in one component to affect other components or to crash the whole system. With this design, a single point of failure does not translate into a failure of the whole system.

The Linux system kernel is completely independent of the user interface. This independence reduces the likelihood of needing to reboot the system when there is a problem with the video interface. The Linux graphical interface, called Xwindows, is a separate server module that can be independently rebooted if necessary without rebooting the operating system itself.

In addition, the Linux architecture makes it easy to eliminate unnecessary overhead. If you don't need the graphical user interface (GUI), which is unnecessary on a Samba server, you don't have to run it, and RAM and disk space that would normally be required to support the interface can be made available for running what you do need, like Samba services.

Where Samba and Windows conflict

This is not a Samba versus Windows comparison. Just as there are reasons to choose Samba, there are reasons why it may not be the right choice for you. Open source software is successful because it is based on the principle that one size does not fit all. Free software is about freedom of choice. There are many reasons to choose Microsoft, even if "there's no other choice" shouldn't be one of them.

Microsoft sets the standards for Windows servers, and Samba is always behind in adding any new features. If you need to have the latest features from Microsoft as soon as possible, then choose a Windows server. Also, consider the additional skills required to support both Windows and Samba before choosing to add a Samba server to your network.

MICROSOFT SETS ITS OWN STANDARDS

Microsoft regularly updates its products, including incremental service packs for both server systems and applications. These updates often introduce new features. Sometimes the new features might be exactly what you need for your network.

Samba can only play catch-up because Microsoft sets its own standards and defines the new features to be added to a Windows network. There is always a lag time between anything new Microsoft has introduced and the availability of that feature in Samba. It is even possible that some feature may not be added to Samba. If you must always have the latest features that Microsoft offers, then Samba is not be the right choice for you.

SAMBA IS LIKE NT 4, NOT WINDOWS 2000

Think of Samba as a Windows NT 4 file and print server. Some of the features found on a Windows 2000 server are not supported by Samba, such as the Active Directory. Active Directory is based on Lightweight Directory Access Protocol (LDAP) but uses its own access control system and replication methods. Like an NT 4 client or server, Samba cannot participate in Active Directory user management, and the Active Directory tools on a Windows 2000 server can't be used to administer a Samba server. This will change with the development of Linux LDAP and Windows Active Directory interoperability, which is being done by another open source team, the OpenLDAP project (see *http://www.OpenLDAP.org*).

Another feature on a Windows 2000 Server that isn't directly supported by Samba is the Kerberos security key system for user authentication and authorization. Although the Kerberos system originated on Unix systems, the Microsoft implementation is not compatible with Linux or Unix systems. You can't use a Windows 2000 server to authenticate Linux users or servers, and you can't use a Linux Kerberos server to authenticate Windows 2000 servers or users. Work is also being done to develop a version that will make a Linux Kerberos server compatible with Windows 2000.

WINDOWS SERVERS ARE BEST FOR DOMAIN CONTROLLERS

A Samba server is seen as an NT 4 server by a Windows 2000 server. The Samba server cannot be a domain controller on a network that includes Windows 2000 domain controllers. If you already have a Windows domain controller, there is no reason to switch to a Samba domain controller. You should switch to a Samba domain controller only if you are removing all of your Windows servers and replacing them with some other operating system, such as Linux. In general, if you need a Windows domain controller you should use a Windows server.

WINDOWS HAS FINER ACCESS CONTROL

There is no way to directly translate Windows security IDs and access control lists (ACLs) to the user account and file permissions system that Linux uses.

The Windows NTFS filesystem supports much finer control over who can do what than is possible on a standard Linux system. Windows ACLs treat users as individuals who can be given rights to files and directories in any combination. Groups can contain individuals or other groups. Windows has six access rights that can be defined for the user, for a group, or for everyone. These rights are Read, Write, Execute, Delete, Take Ownership, and Change Permission. For example, a file can be set to be viewed by two users in a group and both viewed and modified by a third user in the group, while a fourth user is denied all access to the file.

The Linux *ext2* filesystem does not include ACL support. The Linux filesystem defines Read, Write, and Execute permissions for the user, the group, and others. A number of options are available to add ACL support on Linux systems, but there is no standard implementation. No Linux distribution includes this feature in its standard kernel. On systems with ACL support compiled into the kernel, Samba will recognize the extended ACL rights. This setup gives permission rights similar to those used on Windows servers, but the ACLs are not directly translatable from one system to the other.

SAMBA REQUIRES ADDITIONAL SKILLS

If you or someone on your staff doesn't already know how to support Linux, then adding a Samba server means there is a new system to learn and support. The most difficult part of supporting a Samba server is the initial installation of Linux and the configuration of Samba. Once the server is set up, it is as easy to maintain as a Windows server, including basic troubleshooting. Dealing with any complex problems that might arise, however, can be difficult without Linux or Unix experience.

WINDOWS HAS MORE HARDWARE SUPPORT

There is a vast array of hardware choices for Intel-based PCs. All vendors make sure to include any necessary software drivers for Windows systems with hardware. Linux drivers, on the other hand, are not always available. If you have special hardware needs, check to make sure that it is supported by

Linux if you need to have it on your Samba server. For example, there are no Linux drivers for digital video disk (DVD) drives because of legal prohibitions. If you need to have a shareable DVD drive on your file server, this can only be done from a Windows system.

Linux and Windows

The differences between Linux and Windows are often exaggerated. Both are operating systems working on the same computer hardware. Both must carry out essentially the same or similar tasks.

To successfully integrate a Samba server into a Windows network requires some familiarity with the Linux operating system. You'll be surprised at how many Windows administration skills work in the same or a similar way on Linux. Many Linux terms and concepts have Windows equivalents. For example, the ominous-sounding Linux daemons are similar to services on a Windows server. In fact, system administration isn't really operating system–specific.

Following are descriptions of some Linux features and terms, with explanations. Where appropriate, Windows equivalents are given.

LINUX IS CASE-SENSITIVE

The Linux operating system is case-sensitive: for example, *letter.txt* is different from *letter.TXT*. Windows NT/2000 recognizes case and preserves it but is case-insensitive. Using Windows, you could request a file named *LETTER.TXT* and get *letter.txt* and *letter.TXT*, but using Linux you'd get a "File Not Found" error. Case sensitivity is one of the biggest differences between the two operating systems when it comes to file naming.

LINUX USES THE FORWARD SLASH

On a Linux system you don't use the backslash as a file seperator, you use the forward slash. Windows is built on DOS, which borrowed many features from the old CP/M operating system that used the backslash as its file separator. Linux is written in the C language, which uses the backslash for another purpose and uses the forward slash for its file separator. For example, at a command prompt in Windows you might enter `cd \personal\letters` and on Linux you would enter `cd /personal/letters`. In Linux (and the C language), the backslash indicates that a character is to be used literally. Thus, entering the same command on Linux using a backslash, `cd \personal\letters` would be interpreted to mean `cd personalletters`. The forward slash is also the default file separator on all Web pages because the Internet was initially built on Unix systems.

LINUX HAS NO UNERASE FEATURE

On a Linux system, if you delete a file it is gone with no possibility of retrieving it. After a file is deleted its free space is immediately made available for something else. This improves multiuser performance but sacrifices the convenience of retrieving deleted files. Users of Windows systems won't expect this behavior.

LINUX DOESN'T REQUIRE FILE EXTENSIONS

File extensions are optional on Linux and are used mainly for ease of identification. A file extension on Linux does not affect whether the file is executable or any other possible aspect of a file. This fact also means that file types aren't associated with extensions. The window managers in Linux, such as the K Desktop Environment (KDE) and Gnome let you define MIME types that associate file extensions so that clicking on a file with a certain extension will automatically open the associated application. This function is not, however, built into the Linux filesystem and has to be individually defined. As with Windows, file associations in KDE and Gnome don't always work correctly, and there can be conflicts when more than one application uses the same extension.

LINUX DOESN'T USE DRIVE LETTERS

Windows uses drive letters to indicate disk drives, partitions, and shares on servers or other Windows workstations. Samba lets you map a share on a Linux server and assign it to a drive letter on a Windows machine. But Linux does not use drive letters at all. On a Linux system everything appears to stem off a single directory hierarchy. Rather than mapping to a drive letter, disk drives, partitions, and shares on other servers are mapped to a mount point that is part of the overall directory structure. (The terms "mounting" and "mount point" used on Linux and Unix systems come from older systems that used tape reels that had to be mounted before files could be accessed.)

     Devices such as hard drives, network cards, and video cards also show up on Linux as part of the directory structure. These devices all look like files in the directory named *dev*. For example, the first primary disk drive on an ATA controller is a file named *hda* in the *dev* directory. This is usually written out as */dev/hda;* the second disk drive is named */dev/hdb*. On Windows, these might be the C and D drives. If you divide the first drive into two partitions, on Windows you might then have C and D on the first drive and E on the second drive. On Linux these would be */dev/hda1,* for the first partition of the first drive, and */dev/hda2* for the second partition. The second drive, if partitioned as a single drive, is named */dev/hdb1*. Table 1-1 lists the Linux

Table 1-1	Common device names in Linux

Device	Linux name
Floppy disk	*/dev/fd0* or */dev/floppy*
First drive on primary AT Attachment (ATA) interface	*/dev/hda*
First partition on first drive on primary ATA interface	*/dev/hda1*
Second partition on first drive on primary ATA interface	*/dev/hda2*
Second drive on primary ATA interface	*/dev/hdb*
First drive on secondary ATA interface	*/dev/hdc*
Second drive on secondaryATA interface	*/dev/hdd*
First Small Computer System Interface (SCSI) drive	*/dev/sda*
Second SCSI drive	*/dev/sdb*
SCSI tape drive (rewinding)	*/dev/st0*
SCSI tape drive (nonrewinding)	*/dev/nst0*
CD-ROM	*/dev/cdrom* or the ATA/SCSI name such as */dev/hdb* or */dev/sda*

names for several common devices. The device names are standard on the Linux 2.2 kernel. These names are also supported by the 2.4 kernel, although a new naming convention is being adopted to allow for enhanced support of USB devices.

SOME COMMON LINUX QUESTIONS

HOW DO YOU GET ADMINISTRATOR ACCESS? • The administrator logon name for Linux is "root." Unlike Windows, there is no equivalent of the Administrators group that gives administrator privileges to individual users. Linux has only one administrator account, which means that multiple users with administrative responsibilities usually must know the administrator's password.

WHAT ARE LINUX DAEMONS? • Linux daemons, which function similarly to Windows services, are services that are activated at system startup and run until the system is shut down or rebooted. The name comes from Greek mythology: daemons were guardian spirits, and Linux daemons work in the background as service guardians. Each daemon has its own configuration file or command-line options, or both. As with Windows, each service has its own daemon. The typical daemons started by Linux include a print spooler, a mail handler, system loggers, a task scheduler, and various network services. Samba is typically run as a daemon on a Linux server.

WHERE ARE THE LINUX STARTUP FILES? • Most Linux systems run an initialization script at startup to start the daemons. There are usually several different scripts, one for each runlevel. The six runlevels used by most Linux distributions can be compared to the levels shown on Windows startup when you press the F8 key. Windows runlevels include DOS, Safe Mode, Safe Mode with Networking, and so on. Linux runlevel 1 is like DOS; no daemons are started. This is a level used only for system maintenance. Runlevel 2 is like Safe Mode; some but not all daemons are started. Level 3 might be likened to Safe Mode with Networking, though it is much more than that. This is the full system running and is the mode used for many servers. Not only is networking started, but all of the daemons as well. Finally, runlevel 5 is the full Windows mode. The only difference between levels 3 and 5 is the GUI that is automatically started at runlevel 5.

WHERE IS THE LINUX TASK MANAGER? • Linux does not have a single tool that performs all the tasks of the Windows Task Manager. Linux has individual tools for every task. These tools are all accessible through a single interface, the Webmin software. Webmin is a Web-based administration interface for Linux. It can be used to start or stop a service, to monitor service status and resource usage, or to alter the priority of a service.

WHERE IS THE LINUX USER MANAGER? • As with the task manager, Linux does not have a single tool that is the user manager. However, all the tools for creating and maintaining user and group accounts as well as permissions can be accessed through the Webmin system administration software.

WHERE'S THE REGISTRY? • Linux does not have a system registry. Some of what is found in the Windows registry can be accessed on the Linux */proc* filesystem. This is not a true filesystem, but rather an interface into the kernel and the currently running processes. As in the Windows registry, changes can be made to the */proc* filesystem, but the changes are effective only on the currently running system. When the system is shut down or rebooted, the changes are lost. To make a change to */proc* occur on each startup, the administrator must include it in the initialization scripts. Some registry-type settings can also be made through the system configuration files found in the */etc* directory. Many of these configuration changes can be made through Webmin; some changes can only be made by using a text editor and putting them into the configuration file manually. Windows also stores passwords and group information in the registry, which are found in the */etc/passwd, /etc/shadow,* and */etc/group* configuration files on Linux.

WHERE IS THE EVENT VIEWER? • The Linux Syslog daemon starts at boot time and keeps logs of all system messages. The log records are similar to the system events shown by the Windows Event Viewer. All the logs are saved in the */var/log* directory and can be viewed through Webmin or by using a text viewer.

HOW DO YOU DEFRAGMENT LINUX DRIVES? • Windows administrators, who are used to dealing with fragmentation issues on their servers, will be glad to know that fragmentation is kept low on Linux hard drives and defragmentation is seldom necessary. When Windows NTFS writes a file, it can be broken up into multiple clusters and spread across the hard drive. This approach can speed disk writes because writing can begin with the first available space. However, it also fragments the file contents and can make access inefficient. Defragmentation, the process of putting the pieces of all the files together so that each file is located on a single continuous series of clusters, can often significantly improve performance.

The Linux *ext2* filesystem uses a different approach. It keeps a list of all empty blocks on the hard drive. When blocks are needed to write a file, *ext2* looks at the list and finds a contiguous set of free blocks that can hold the entire file, if one is available.

Over time, however, all filesystems tend to become fragmented. Full drives and busy network drives can become fragmented on a Linux system. The usual method for defragmenting a Linux hard drive is to do a complete backup, reformat the partition, and then restore the files from backup. When the files are restored, they are written in contiguous blocks.

HOW DO YOU CREATE SHORTCUTS IN LINUX? • Shortcuts in Linux are called links. Links can be created from the command prompt or by using one of the file managers. The command is `ln`. For example, to create a simple link from a database in the finances directory to a directory named projects, enter this command:

```
ln -s /finances/expenses.db /projects/expenses.db
```

This command creates a shortcut in the projects directory called *expenses.db*. The *-s* flag indicates that it is a symbolic link, that is, a link that points to the location of the actual file. It works in many ways like a Windows shortcut, with some exceptions. One of the limitations of links is the restrictions imposed by permissions. In order to access a linked file you must have permission not in the directory where the link is found, but in the directory where the actual file is located.

WHERE ARE THE HIDDEN FILES IN LINUX? • The Linux filesystem doesn't have a hidden file attribute. Instead, filenames that begin with a dot, such as *.profile*, are interpreted as hidden by most applications when displaying a list of files. This is similar to the Windows Explorer setting of not displaying any files with system file extensions, such as *.dll* or *.sys*. Linux file managers have settings to indicate whether or not to display hidden files. Samba also has a configuration option to indicate whether or not Linux's hidden files should be seen as hidden files by Windows.

Installing and Configuring Samba

The initial setup of a Samba server is not much different from setting up a Windows server for file and printer sharing. You make sure that the shares are defined and that the service is started. Period. That's it.

The process is so easy because Samba is included with every Linux distribution and is automatically installed on any server installation. All you need to do is configure it for the shares you want to make available and then start the Samba daemon—the Windows networking service.

It's a bit more involved for other Unix systems because Samba is not usually installed already. If you are not using Linux, then you'll need to either build the Samba executables from the source code or get an executable binary from the Samba Web site or one of its mirrors, if one is available. After installation, the procedure to get basic Samba services running is easy.

Checking Whether Samba Is Installed

Your first step will be to find out if Samba is already installed on your server.

How to See Whether Samba Is Installed

If you aren't sure whether Samba is installed, use the Package Manager on the Linux server to find out. The Package Manager is a software tool that is used on Linux systems to maintain all software, from system software to applications and utilities. It can be used for installing and uninstalling software as well as for listing what's installed. The Package Manager is similar to the Add/Remove Programs tool in the Windows control panel.

The Package Manager can be accessed using the Webmin system administration software, obtained through a Web browser on your desktop system. A full description of using Webmin can be found in Chapter 8.

Typically, Webmin is accessed by opening a Web browser and entering the URL for the Samba server, adding the special port that the Webmin miniserver is running on. Also, it is best to secure Webmin with Secure Socket Layers (SSL). If you aren't sure whether Webmin is installed and set up, or whether it is configured for secure connections, then you might want to go directly to Chapter 8 and set up Webmin before proceeding with setting up and configuring Samba. There is more about using and configuring Webmin later in this chapter as well.

Open Webmin from your desktop system. Here is an example: To connect to Webmin over a secure connection to a Samba server with the IP address of 192.168.0.4, with Webmin running on port 10000 (the default port for most Webmin installations), you'd enter this URL in your Web browser:

```
https://192.168.0.4:10000/
```

In Webmin, select the System tab. In System, click on the Software Packages icon to open the Package Manager on the Linux server. In the entry form next to the Search For Package button, enter the word "Samba." Webmin checks the installed packages and will indicate if Samba is installed. If Samba is installed, the version number is shown as part of the name. Click on the package name to get more information on the installed software. Figure 2-1 shows the results of a Webmin package check.

When to Use the Installed Version

Since every Linux server already has Samba installed or available to install on the installation CD, there may be nothing more that needs to be done in the way of installation. If you have a fairly recent version of Linux, then the version of Samba is probably recent as well.

Most administrators will want Samba version 2.2 or later for network servers. This version includes support for Windows NT sever-style print services, access control lists (ACLs), and support for acting as a Windows distributed filesystem (DFS) server. Version 2.2 also has many internal changes that improve performance over previous versions. If you don't need the new features, version 2.07 was the first version of Samba to be fully compatible with Windows 2000 Professional clients.

SAMBA VERSIONS

- **Samba 1.0** Samba introduces file and printer sharing using the Windows SMB/CIFS protocol on Linux servers; this version looks just like a Windows server on a Windows network.

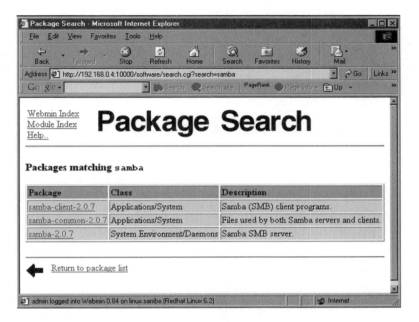

Figure 2-1	*Use Webmin's Package Search to see if Samba is installed. If it is installed, the version is shown as part of the package name. This example shows that Samba version 2.07 is installed.*

- **Samba 2.0**   Version 2.0 was a major upgrade, with emphasis on improving performance and complete compatibility with all versions of Windows. Comparison tests done with the Ziff Davis NetBench benchmark showed this version outperformed Windows NT 4 on single-processor servers. The last incremental upgrade, 2.07, is fully compatible with Windows 2000 Professional clients.
- **Samba 2.2**   Version 2.2, another major upgrade, could have been called version 3.0 because of the considerable changes introduced. The underlying code was significantly rewritten to improve performance and flexibility. Samba 2.2 adds support for Windows NT 4 server–style printer sharing, including support for downloading printer drivers to clients on demand. Previous versions used Windows 95–style printer sharing. This version adds optional support for ACLs for more robust user and group permissions than the default Unix-style permissions. It also optionally supports the Microsoft DFS, allowing a Samba server to act as a DFS server. The Winbind module adds the capability to use a Windows NT 4 domain controller for user authentication services.

- **Samba 3.0**   This version introduces full support for acting as a Windows NT 4 domain controller, fully compatible with Windows 2000 servers running in mixed mode as well as NT 4 servers. It adds support for the Unicode character set.

When to Update

Before setting up a new server, you should make sure to get the latest version of the software that is available. If you have a server that is already up and in production and you don't need any of the additional features in a new major release, the differences in performance with a newer version may not be noticeable. If you aren't sure whether the latest version has any features you want, look at the Samba Web site at *www.samba.org* to see a description of the latest version and what it includes.

Minor updates (shown with an increment in the build number, such as from 2.2.0 to 2.2.1) should generally be made as soon as reasonably possible. These upgrades usually include bug fixes as well as security updates.

Upgrading to a major new version should be approached carefully. As with any networking application, installing an upgrade takes time and can introduce unforeseen problems.

If you are using an older version on your system, however, it can be harder to find support. This may be a reason to upgrade. Most companies offering technical support offer help only with the latest version. Also, if you are having a software problem you may find that it is something that has been fixed in a newer version. If you are having problems, it is a good idea to back up your current system and install the latest version and see if that fixes the difficulty. Upgrading in that case will also make it easier to get help, either from a support company or through the Samba email support list. Details on accessing the Samba email lists can be found on the Web at *http://lists.samba.org*.

How to Get the Samba Software

Samba is included on the installation CD of every major Linux distribution. That's the first place to look for the Samba software. To find out if there is a version update, check the Samba Web site at *www.samba.org*. If there is an update that you want, get the update from your Linux distribution's maintainer.

In general, it is best to get any updates from the Linux distribution's maintainer in order to maintain complete compatibility with your current system. Each Linux distribution customizes the software in ways that can be broken if you attempt to install a software package that wasn't prepared for your

Source Code or Binaries?

The many options for software updates for Samba might be confusing to someone who has only worked with Windows systems. On Windows systems, almost all software comes ready to install and run. Sometimes updates or service packs are available, either for purchase from the vendor or from a Web site. You almost never need to compile the software.

Open source software can come ready to install and run or as source code that must be compiled before it can be used. In addition, open source software is much more frequently updated than Windows software, though you will rarely need to obtain these updates. It is even possible to get the latest development code, the code for the next major version of the software. The development code is generally unstable and should never be used on a live server.

So many options are available because of the way open source development works: the source code for the software is available to anyone. And if you can get a copy of the source code, you can use a compiler and create an executable binary. This is not possible with closed, proprietary software, like Microsoft Windows and all of Microsoft's applications, because the source code is not available. The only form of software available from Microsoft is executable binaries. That's why the difference between source and binaries is not familiar to Windows users.

If the option to compile your own software is new to you, don't worry about it. There's usually no reason to compile your own binary. In fact, the binaries for Samba available with the major Linux distributions are all that you need. Only special cases with particular needs are likely to require individual compilation from the source code.

distribution. Customization includes enabling or disabling certain options when the software was compiled, as well as creating specialized startup scripts. Not having the correct options can mean that the software won't run.

The usual way to get updates is through the Internet. The process is similar to getting software updates from Microsoft's Web site. As you would when updating Windows NT/2000 systems, you have to be logged on as the administrator—the root user on Linux—to install or update software.

Updating Linux

All Linux distributions have updates available from their Web sites. These include security updates as well as bug fixes.

Debian GNU/Linux goes further. It has the best updating features of all the Linux distributions. Debian's apt-get program will automate updates, security fixes, patches, and even adding programs. When installing any program, apt-get checks your system to see if any additional software packages are needed, and it will install them as well.

The closest thing to apt-get on Red Hat Linux is the Gnome RPM package manager. It can be used to check the Web for updates from Red Hat. It will also check for any additional software that is needed for the update to run properly. It can be started from the Gnome panel's System menu.

To install or update software, click the Install button on the icon bar. In the window that opens, click the Add button. In the file selection window that appears, locate and select the software package you want to install. Close the windows and then click on the Install button to install a new package, or the Upgrade button if you are upgrading software that is already installed.

For any Linux distribution, check the distribution's Web site for updates. Most updates can be downloaded either through the Web browser or downloaded via file transfer protocol (FTP). Usually there is a directory named Updates where you can find updated versions of Samba. Table 2-1 lists the FTP sites for several Linux distributions.

There are also fee-based systems available from both Red Hat and Caldera as well as independent vendors that will keep your Linux software up to date. Ximian's Red Carpet software management software, for those using their Gnome-based desktop, offers to keep your system current. It can be found on the Web at *http://www.ximian.com*.

USING WEBMIN TO INSTALL UPDATES

If you've downloaded a Samba update to your desktop computer or to the Linux server, you can use Webmin to install it. From your desktop system, open Webmin and select the System tab. In System, click on the Software Packages icon. Scroll to the Install a New Package section.

If the software is on the Linux computer, select the From Local File radio button. Click on the button with three dots to search the system's hard drive for the file, or type in the full path name and filename in the space provided.

If the Samba update was downloaded onto your desktop workstation, select the radio button by From Uploaded File. Click Browse to find the file on your hard drive, or type in the filename and location in the space provided.

Table 2-1	FTP sites for software updates
Red Hat Linux	*ftp://updates.redhat.com*
Caldera OpenLinux	*ftp://ftp.calderasystems.com/pub/updates*
Debian GNU/Linux	*ftp://ftp.debian.org/debian/dists*

If you know the location of the file on a Web site or an FTP server, select the From FTP or HTTP URL radio button. Enter the entire URL, including the exact file name in the space provided.

After selecting the file to install, click on the Install button. The new page that opens is shown in Figure 2-2. The name of the package to be installed is shown along with a number of options for installing or upgrading. Select the Upgrade Package option, which will work for both upgrades as well as new installs. Usually the defaults for all other options are used. Then click the Install button.

Compiling Samba

If you can't find an updated Samba binary or if you want to set up Samba with different options, you can compile and install Samba from its source code. Get the latest stable version from the Samba Web site at *www.samba.org* or one of its mirror sites, or by FTP from *ftp.samba.org*.

Compiling from source code requires some familiarity with the Linux operating system. If you aren't going to be compiling a custom version of Samba, you can skip this section.

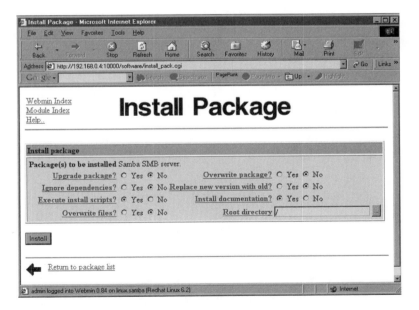

Figure 2-2   *Webmin's Software Package installer displays the name of the software to be installed and the options available when installing or upgrading.*

Samba source code is distributed as a compressed tar archive. The current stable version is always named *samba-latest.tar.gz*. Older versions are also available, with filenames that have the version number in the place of the word "latest," such as *samba-2.2.1.tar.gz*.

TIP—TAR AND GZ FILES

Although file extensions are not necessary for Linux, it is customary to add an extension that lets the user instantly see what the file type is. Files that are available for downloading often end with the extensions `.tar.gz`.

Tar, the Tape Archive utility, is a software tool on Linux that is used to combine files into one archive, and gzip is used to compress the tar file. Gzip is similar to WinZip on Windows systems.

The usual way to extract in a tar archive is to use this command:

```
tar xvf filename.tar
```

The usual way to unzip a file compressed with gzip is to use this command:

```
gunzip filename.gz
```

The version of tar that is included with Linux is the GNU tar. It can both uncompress gzipped files and expand the archive in one step. The command to do this is

```
tar xvzf filename.tar.gz
```

The version of tar that comes with Solaris and other commercial Unix versions cannot do this.

If Samba is already installed on your server, make sure to back up the configuration files and startup script, which get overwritten during installation from the source code. The names and locations of these files may vary. On Red Hat Linux, the files to back up are

smb.conf

smbpasswd (an optional password file)

smbusers (an optional map of Linux-Windows user names)

All are in the */etc/samba* directory starting with Red Hat version 7.0 and in */etc* for earlier versions of Red Hat Linux.

The smb startup script in the */etc/rc.d/init.d* directory should be backed up, and the *samba* configuration file in the */etc/pam.d* directory should be backed up as well.

After backing up the configuration files, remove the *samba* packages to avoid any conflicts with the newer version. On Red Hat Linux, enter these commands:

```
rpm -e samba
rpm -e samba-client
rpm -e samba-common
```

To compile and install the software, you must be logged in as the root user. First, uncompress and extract the source files. Copy the source archive to the */usr/src* directory, or any other directory where you want to put the source files, and change to that directory. Then unpack the archive. These are the commands:

```
cp samba-latest.tar.gz /usr/src
cd /usr/src
tar xvzf samba-latest.tar.gz
```

Tar uncompresses and extracts the files into a directory named *samba-latest*. If you've unpacked a different version of Samba, the directory will take the name of that version. Change into the new directory. In the directory, change to the *source* subdirectory. To do that with a single command, enter

```
cd samba-latest/source
```

Now you are ready to configure Samba. Running *configure* with no options installs Samba into a default location with the default settings. To do that, simply enter this command:

```
./configure
```

TIP — COMPILING

Before compiling software for the first time on Linux, make sure that all of the software you need is installed. The default server installation does not install all of the packages needed, since it is assumed that the machine is being used for production, not development. For Red Hat Linux, make sure that the following packages have been installed:

```
binutils
cpp
egcs
glibc-devel
```

After Samba has been configured by running the *configure* script, compile it with this command:

```
make
```

This process can take five minutes or more, depending on the processor's speed. (Take a coffee break.) If there were no errors, then install Samba with the command

```
make install
```

That's it.

Matching Red Hat's configuration

Samba is installed using the Samba defaults. However, Red Hat Linux and most other Linux distributions do not use the defaults; instead, they modify the configuration so that the file locations more closely match Linux standards.

You can match Red Hat's defaults by taking the following steps. This setup includes some of the options in the Red Hat Samba binary and will match file locations for Red Hat 7.0 and later versions, but it does not completely match all of the configuration changes made with the Red Hat distribution. These steps assume that you've previously installed Red Hat's Samba RPM and that you've backed up everything, as described previously, and then uninstalled Samba. First, configure Samba with these additional options:

```
./configure --prefix=/usr \
--libdir=/etc/samba \
--with-lockdir=/var/lock/samba \
--with-privatedir=/etc/samba \
--with-swatdir=/usr/share/swat \
--with-quotas \
--with-smbmount \
--with-pam \
--with-syslog \
--with-msdfs \
--with-netatalk \
--with-sambabook=/usr/share/swat/using_samba
```

After configuring with these options, follow the usual compiling commands. You can combine compiling and installing by entering this command:

```
make; make install
```

Finally, restore the configuration files that were backed up before you began compiling and installing from the source code. If you don't restore your configuration files before trying to start Samba, it won't work. Also make sure the *lock* directory is there. If */var/lock/samba* is missing, create it.

Samba is now ready to run from the Red Hat default locations.

Undoing the `make install` *command*

When a new version is installed, the old binaries are renamed with an *.old* extension. To go back to the previous version, run the command `make revert` and the old binaries will be restored. To remove all the files that were installed and not revert to a previous version, use the command `make uninstall`.

Samba can be customized in many ways using the various options available when compiling the source code. These configuration options can be selected only when compiling a binary; this process is different from configuring Samba after installation. Table 2-2 describes some of the most important configuration options. Options that affect behavior, with names that begin —*with-*, are not enabled by default and can be enabled only at the time of compiling Samba. The location options are used to change the default locations for Samba's different files.

A Look at What's Installed

Samba is modular by design, as are most Linux programs. This means that rather than being one big program that does everything, it is a suite of programs, each one designed for a specific function. This design gives the software great stability and flexibility. It means, however, that there is not a program called Samba that is run on startup. There are a number of programs. These programs can be divided into two categories: server programs and utility programs. The server programs are what you'll primarily use. There are also configuration files that are used by the server programs. The utilities include testing tools for checking the configuration and some specialized tools, many of them designed to access a Windows system from a Linux or Unix system.

Server Programs

smbd: The smbd program is the server program that enables file, folder, and printer sharing. Every time a Windows user connects to the Samba server, a new smbd daemon starts. The configuration file used by smbd is *smb.conf*. The program automatically reloads the configuration information every 30 seconds. The reloading does not affect any connections already established, while it enables any configuration changes that have been made.

nmbd: The nmbd program provides Network Basic Input/Output System (NetBIOS) name service, WINS network address and machine name

Table 2-2	The configure options for Samba
configure option	**Description**
*—prefix=***directory name**	The directory where all the Samba files are installed. The default location is */usr/local/samba*. Red Hat and most other Linux distributions put the standard binary files in */usr/bin* and the secure binaries such as *smbd* and *nmbd* in */usr/sbin*. This makes the prefix option *—prefix=/usr*.
*—libdir=***directory name**	The directory where *smb.conf, lmhosts,* and the *code pages* directory are located. The default location is */usr/local/samba/lib*. Starting with Red Hat Linux 7.0 and all versions of Debian GNU/Linux, the location is */etc/samba*. For Red Hat Linux 6.2 and older, it is */etc*. For Caldera OpenLinux, the location is */etc/samba.d*.
—with-smbmount	Including this will add the smbmount program, which lets you mount Windows file shares on a Linux system. This program works only with Linux and not with any of the commercial Unix systems.
—with-pam	Includes support for Pluggable Authentication Modules (PAMs), a secure system used on Linux systems to authenticate users and permit access.
—with-syslog	Includes support for using the syslog utility to save messages generated by the Samba server into log files.
—with-netatalk	Includes support for the AppleTalk network protocol used by Macintosh computers, using Netatalk on the Samba server. Netatalk is a Linux implementation of AppleTalk. For full details see the Netatalk Web page at *www.umich.edu/~rsug/netatalk/*.
—with-quotas	Includes support for user disk quotas. To use it, Disk Quotas must be enabled in the operating system used on the Samba server.
—with-msdfs	Includes support for acting as a Microsoft DFS server.
—with-privatedir= **directory name**	The directory for Samba's security information, including the file with encrypted user passwords (*smbpasswd*). The default location is */usr/local/samba/private*. Starting with Red Hat Linux 7.0 and all versions of Debian GNU/Linux, the location is */etc/samba*. For Red Hat Linux 6.2 and older, it is */etc*. For Caldera OpenLinux, the location is */etc/samba.d*.
—with-lockdir= **directory name**	The location for lock files used for some file access control features. This directory must be writeable. The default location is */usr/local/samba/var/locks*. For Red Hat Linux and Debian GNU/Linux, the location is */var/lock/samba*. For Caldera OpenLinux, the location is */var/lock/samba.d*.
—with-swatdir= **directory name**	The location for help files used by the Samba Web Administration Tool (SWAT). SWAT is used to administer Samba through a Web browser. The default location is */usr/local/samba/swat*. Red Hat Linux and most Linux distributions use */usr/share/swat*.
—with-sambabook= **directory name**	The location for the *Using Samba* book, accessible through SWAT. The default location is */usr/local/samba/swat/using_samba*. Red Hat Linux and most Linux distributions use */usr/share/swat/using_samba*.

translation, and network browsing support. The configuration file used by nmbd is *smb.conf.*

winbindd: The `winbindd` program is used to resolve user and group information from a Windows domain controller rather than from the Linux server's user database. This design eliminates the need to maintain two user account structures, one on the Windows domain controller and a separate one on the Linux server. Winbind is new with Samba 2.2 and is still experimental. It is not installed by default.

Configuration Files

smb.conf: This is the primary configuration file for the Samba program suite. It is a text file that can be maintained using a text editor on the Samba server or through a Web browser using the SWAT program.

smbpasswd: This file contains encrypted user passwords. Every user must have a Linux user account and a matching Samba user account, though the accounts can have different passwords and mapping can be used for different user names. This configuration file is not necessary if you are not using encrypted passwords (a security vulnerability that should be avoided) or if you are using Winbind for user authentication.

smbusers: This optional configuration file can be used to map Windows user names to user names on the Linux server. It is used primarily to fix problems with user names that work on Windows but not on Linux.

lmhosts: Like the *lmhosts* on a Windows computer, this configuration file provides a map of Windows computer names (NetBIOS names) to Internet Protocol (IP) addresses. To use *lmhosts,* the option must be enabled in *smb.conf,* which can be done through SWAT.

Utility Programs

SWAT: A program used to configure and administer Samba through a Web browser. SWAT can be accessed with any Web browser. It includes help links for all the configurable options in Samba.

testparm: A program to make a check of the syntax in the Samba configuration file. This program is used if you are using a text editor to enter changes into the Samba configuration file. It is not necessary to run testparm if you are using SWAT, which does not allow incorrect syntax in the configuration. Both testparm and SWAT make sure the syntax is correct, but neither can check to make sure that the file or printer shares you create will work correctly.

smbpasswd: The smbpasswd program is used to add users or change passwords for users on a Samba server. If you use Webmin for system administration, it can be set to automatically update Samba users as part of general user administration. If you do that, the smbpasswd program does not have to be run every time a new user is added. See the section on managing users with Webmin, found later in this chapter. It is not necessary to use smbpasswd if you are using Winbind for user authentication. If you are using the Samba server as a domain controller, smbpasswd is used to create and maintain machine accounts.

smbstatus: A program that shows current connections to the Samba server and locked files.

nmblookup: A tool to get information on clients and servers in My Network Places/Network Neighborhood. Use nmblookup to get the IP addresses of Windows clients or to find the Master Browser on a subnet.

Internationalization

All versions of Samba prior to 3.0 did not use Unicode, the universal character set that supports all scripts. On Samba 2.2 and earlier versions, Windows code pages are used to support characters that aren't part of the standard ASCII character set. The code page files are installed in the */code pages* directory and can be set in SWAT.

Administering Samba with Webmin and SWAT

Once Samba is installed, the configuration and administration can be handled through a Web browser. SWAT is the most common way to administer a Samba server. The other Web-based Samba administration tool is Webmin. Webmin is more than just a Samba administration tool; it is a complete system administration package. However, Webmin's Samba tools are not as complete as those available in SWAT. That's why a link to SWAT is included as one of the Webmin tools.

Using SWAT through Webmin has several additional advantages. First, this procedure makes using SWAT completely secure. The standard SWAT installation does not use a secure connection, whereas Webmin can be installed to use SSL for secure connections and that security is maintained when you access SWAT through Webmin. A second advantage is that you'll already be using Webmin for all your other system administration tasks, so it simplifies your work to have all of the tools in one place. A third advantage is that this setup eliminates the need to configure services on the Samba server to make SWAT work. Several Linux distributions, including most versions of Red Hat Linux, install Samba with SWAT disabled. This may be because the standard SWAT installation runs a mini–Web server on port 901 that is insecure and leaves open a possible hole for crackers. Using Webmin exclusively and closing access to SWAT on port 901 closes this hole.

Setting up Webmin for Samba administration

Webmin is installed by default on some Linux distributions, such as Caldera OpenLinux. For Red Hat Linux and other distributions that don't include Webmin, the program is available to download on the Web at *www.webmin. com*. Red Hat recommends that you use Webmin rather than linuxconf for remote system administration on Red Hat systems.

Chapter 8 details installing Webmin on systems that don't include it. Make sure that SSL security is installed with Webmin.

Linux uses OpenSSL, a free, open source version of SSL that can also be found on the Web at *www.openssl.org*. It is included with most Linux distributions and can usually be found on the distribution CD if it hasn't been installed.

The standard Webmin installation runs a mini–Web server that listens on port 10000. The Caldera OpenLinux Webmin package uses port 1000. To access Webmin on a Samba server with the IP address of 192.168.0.4 with Webmin running on the default port of 10000, you'd enter this URL:

```
https://192.168.0.4:10000/
```

Make sure to include the "s" in "https" for the secure port. The first message you get will probably be a warning that you are making a secure connection with a server that has a certificate that is not recognized. That's because this method uses a private OpenSSL certificate and not one of the commercial certificates recognized by default by Microsoft's Internet Explorer or Netscape's Navigator. Figure 2-3 shows the warning message from Internet Explorer; Navigator gives a similar message. Either browser requires that you choose to accept the security certificate as valid before proceeding.

The encryption level used by Webmin is the highest available, RC4 with a 128-bit secret key.

After accepting the Webmin security certificate, a username and password authorization box opens. Figure 2-4 shows the Webmin login page. The default username is "admin" and the password is the root password. One exception is Caldera OpenLinux, which uses "root" as the default username. After entering the username and password, you'll have full access to Webmin's system administration tools.

After you are logged in the first time, the main Webmin configuration page opens. You can choose from five tabs:

- **Webmin,** where Webmin options are configured
- **System,** where general system administration is managed, including users and groups

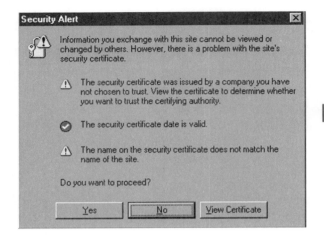

Figure 2-3

A security alert shows that you are accessing Webmin through a secure connection using the free OpenSSL security certificate, which is not automatically recognized as valid by Internet Explorer or Navigator. Just click Yes to accept the certificate.

- **Servers,** where you manage server programs on the system, including Samba
- **Hardware,** where the network configuration, printers, and other hardware are managed
- **Other,** for system status information, a file manager, and telnet access to the server

If you aren't using Winbind to get user authentication from a Windows domain controller for your Samba server, you should use Webmin to manage user accounts on the Samba server. Webmin can be configured to automatically synchronize Linux and Samba user accounts. Otherwise, managing accounts is a multistep process: unless you are using Winbind, every Samba user must also have a user account on the Linux server. See the section called "User Management" later in this chapter for information about using Webmin to synchronize Linux and Samba user accounts.

Login to Webmin

You must enter a username and password to login to the Webmin server on 192.168.0.4.

Username   root

Password   ********

Login   Clear

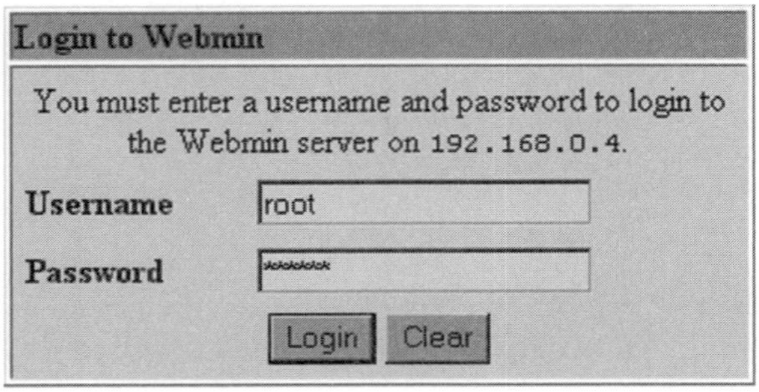

Figure 2-4

Webmin requires you to log in before you are granted access.

Winbind for Windows Domain Authentication

The Winbind system uses Windows domain servers for user authentication services. The version available with the first release of Samba 2.2 is still experimental. If you want to use Winbind, make sure you have the latest version available.

With Winbind, a Linux server can become a full member of a Windows domain, and user authentication is handled by a Windows domain controller. That means Windows users and groups are seen on the Linux server as if they are native Linux users and groups. There is no need to have the user information entered into the Samba and Linux user database on the Linux server, as it is on systems not using Winbind.

Winbind has three components: the Winbind daemon, a Pluggable Authentication Module (PAM), and a Name Service Switch (NSS) module.

All configuration can be done through SWAT. There are settings for the default home directory for users on the Linux server, the range of user and groups IDs that are allocated by Winbind, and other parameters. You can start with the default configuration options unless you know you need to make a change. Home directories may be located differently than the default. For example, Caldera OpenLinux 3.1 puts Samba home directories in a Samba subdirectory of the user's home directory.

The PAM modules are configured through control files in the */etc/pam.d/* directory. Each service that will use Winbind for user authentication must have its PAM control file updated. Winbind is not limited to Samba and can be used for any service on a Linux server. The default PAM control file for Samba in */etc/pam.d* without Winbind is

```
auth      required    /lib/security/pam_pwdb.so shadow nullok
account   required    /lib/security/pam_pwdb.so
```

With Winbind the configuration is

```
auth      sufficient  /lib/security/pam_winbind.so
auth      required    /lib/security/pam_pwbd.so shadow nullok
account   sufficient  /lib/security/pam_winbind.so
account   required    /lib/security/pam_pwdb.so
```

The NSS is an application programming interface that lets Winbind hook into the operating system and present itself as the source of system information when resolving usernames and groups. The */etc/nsswitch.conf* file needs to include the following:

```
passwd:   files winbind
group:    files winbind
```

These lines specify that when user or group information is being sought, the system should first try the user or group database file and then try Winbind.

The final step is to join the domain. This is done from the Linux server using the samedit program that installed as part of the Samba suite. For example, if your domain is named *gotham* and the machine name is *honcho,* then you'll enter this command:

```
samedit -S '*' -W GOTHAM -UAdministrator
```

This opens a `samedit` session. While in `samedit` enter this command:

```
createuser HONCHO$ -j GOTHAM -L
```

Remember to make sure that you have the latest version available from Samba. As is common with open source software, the program is constantly being updated. On new software like Winbind, the updates usually include important bug and security fixes. Also check the documentation with any new version. Configuration options can change or be added, and the installation steps can change. And, like the first version of any software, Winbind should be used with caution on production servers.

After configuring Webmin for user synchronization, you are ready to go to SWAT to configure the behavior of Samba as well as file and printer sharing. See Chapter 8 for more details on using Webmin for system administration, including managing user accounts.

Using SWAT

To access SWAT, simply click on the SWAT icon in Webmin's Samba Share Manager. If you aren't using Webmin, then SWAT is accessed through port 901 on your Samba server. For example, if your server were named *bigserver.samba.linux,* you'd open the URL *http://bigserver.samba.linux:901/* in your Web browser. The IP address would also work, as in *http://192.168. 0.4:901/.* You'd then be prompted to enter a username and password. Log in as root.

After you've logged in, you'll see the SWAT home page, shown in Figure 2-5. The icons across the page are links to different options.

- **Home,** the SWAT home page
- **Globals,** for setting Samba's global parameters
- **Shares,** for managing file shares on the Samba server
- **Printers,** for managing printers that are being shared through the Samba server
- **Status,** to see if Samba is running, with the active connections and open files
- **View,** to see the current *smb.conf* file
- **Password,** an alternative way to manage the Samba password file

What to Do when SWAT Won't Open on Port 901

If the SWAT page doesn't display when you try to open it on port 901, check the network configuration files on the Samba server.

For Red Hat version 7.0 and above, check the settings used by the Internet services daemon xinetd. For Red Hat 6.2 and earlier, as well as most other Linux distributions, a different program is used as an Internet services daemon called inetd.

For xinetd in Red Hat 7.0 and above, there is a configuration file in the `/etc/xinetd.d` directory for SWAT. Check the file named `swat` and make sure it has the correct settings:

```
service swat
{
        port = 901
        socket_type = stream
        wait = no
        only_from = localhost
        user = root
        server = /usr/sbin/swat
        log_on_failure += USERID
        disable = no
}
```

Use a text editor to make any changes, if needed. Also, these settings allow connections only from the Samba server and not from client machines on the network. To enable client connections to SWAT, add the subnet IP address for your local network. For example, on a local network that is on subnet 192.168.0.0, the `only_from` setting should be changed to read

```
only_from = localhost 192.168.0.1/24
```

After making any changes, make sure to restart xinetd. The command is

```
/etc/rc.d/init.d/xinetd restart
```

For Red Hat 6.2 and earlier, as well as most other Linux systems that use inetd and TCP wrappers, first check the */etc/services* configuration file. The services file is a list of programs and the TCP/IP ports they use. Make sure that SWAT is listed and that its port is 901. There should be a line that reads

```
swat    901/tcp
```

If it's not there, open the *services* file in a text editor and add it.

Then check the inetd configuration. The inetd daemon is an alternative way to run services on a Linux server. It is used for services that don't need to be run continuously from startup. When a request for a specific service that isn't already running is received, such as starting up SWAT or the FTP server, the inetd daemon checks its configuration file and automatically starts the service if it is found in the daemon's list. Leaving a service out of inetd's configuration list effectively disables the service and makes it unavailable.

Inetd options are set either in a file named */etc/inetd.conf* or with individual configuration files in the */etc/inet.d* directory. To enable SWAT services, make sure that the */etc/inetd.conf* file includes a line for SWAT. For Red Hat Linux and most Linux distributions, this line should read

```
swat   stream tcp  nowait.400  root  /usr/sbin/swat swat
```

If SWAT is already listed and the configuration indicates */usr/sbin/tcpd* rather than */usr/sbin/swat,* that's acceptable. Don't change it. Tcpd is the TCP wrapper that can be used for extra security when running a service. If your server uses individual inetd configuration files, there should be a file named *swat* in the */etc/inet.d* directory. The *swat* file should have a single line in it that should look like the line above.

On systems using TCP wrappers, check to see whether access is being allowed. The default is to deny access over the network by putting an entry in the *hosts.deny* file in the */etc* directory that reads

```
swat: ALL EXCEPT 127.0.0.1
```

Add the IP addresses of any additional machines necessary.

If you've made any changes, the inetd daemon must be restarted. This can be done on Red Hat Linux and Caldera OpenLinux using the following command:

```
/etc/rc.d/inet.d/inet restart
```

On Debian GNU/Linux the command is

```
/etc/inet.d/inet restart
```

Check the PAM configuration file for the Samba service. There should be a file in the */etc/pam.d* directory named *samba.* The contents of the file should read

```
auth      required  /lib/security/pam_pwdg.so shadow nullok
account   required  /lib/security/pam_pwdb.so
```

If it is not there, then create it.

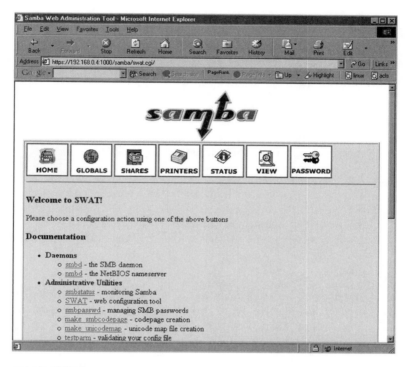

Figure 2-5   *The SWAT home page.*

If you are not using Webmin and are accessing SWAT through port 901 and the SWAT page does not open, check to make sure that SWAT has been configured for network access. The default installation on most Linux distributions is to block network access.

Following is a short tour of the SWAT options.

The SWAT options

HOME

SWAT's home page has a row of icons across the top with links to all of the options. This row of icons appears on every SWAT page. Below the icons are links to all of Samba's help documents, including the *Using Samba* book.

GLOBALS

The Globals page is where Samba's global configuration options are set. These are generally options that determine Samba's overall behavior.

On the Globals page below the row of navigation icons are three buttons:

- **Commit Changes** works like the Apply button used when configuring Windows programs. Any time you make a change, you must click this button or the change will not be made. If you move to another Web page before clicking this button, the changes will be lost.
- **Reset Values** reloads the saved version of the current Samba configuration.
- **Advanced View** shows all the available options, with more than four times as many options as the Basic View.

Below the buttons, the Global variables are grouped into related options. The Base Options are where you set the workgroup name and the server's computer name (NetBIOS name). The Security Options are where you set the security level and where you can enable or disable encrypted passwords. The different options on the Globals page are explained throughout this book.

SHARES

File sharing is managed from the Shares page. You can create a new share or modify an existing share. To modify an existing share, click on the drop-down menu next to the Choose Share button and select the share you want to change. Then click the Choose Share button.

When you are modifying a share, you have the option of working in the Basic View, which shows the most commonly used options, or the Advanced View, which shows all available options, grouped in these sections:

- **Base Options,** primarily the path to the directory being shared
- **Security Options,** the users and groups allowed access to this share
- **Logging Options**
- **Tuning Options,** including the maximum number of connections allowed to this share
- **Filename Handling,** for settings that make Windows filenames compatible with Linux
- **Browse Options,** whether or not the share can be seen by Windows clients browsing the network in the Network Neighborhood on Windows 9x/NT systems or My Network Places on Windows Me/2000 systems
- **Locking Options,** for settings on how file locking of shared files is handled
- **Miscellaneous Options**

Each share should be configured to show the directory that is being shared, the users and groups allowed access to the share, and whether users can write to the share or if it is read-only.

PRINTERS

On the Printers page, you can manage printers that are shared through the Samba server. As with the Shares page, you can create a new printer share or modify an existing one. To modify an existing printer, click on the drop-down menu next to the Choose Printer button and select the share you want to change. Then click the Choose Printer button. There are both Basic and Advanced views of Samba's printer options.

STATUS

The Status page shows the version of Samba and shows whether the Samba daemons are running, as well as who is connected to the Samba server and what files are being accessed. Clicking on the Auto Refresh button will cause the Status page to be automatically refreshed at the interval set. Normally you would manually refresh the Status page. Auto Refresh will not work if you are accessing SWAT through Webmin.

You can start or stop the Samba daemons from the Status page.

When you view the active connections on the Status page, you can disconnect a user by clicking on the X button next to the user's connection.

VIEW

The View page shows a text listing of the Samba configuration file. The Normal View shows the current configuration file. It does not show any options that are unset, that is, those options using the default value. Clicking on Full View shows the current configuration plus all unset options with their default values. You cannot make any changes to the configuration from the View page.

PASSWORD

The Password page can be used to change passwords and add or remove Samba users. For most purposes, this page has little or no usefulness. The Password page cannot display current users, and it does not change the Linux user information. It is best to use Webmin for managing user information such as changing passwords.

Initial Configuration

Before you can start Samba, an initial configuration must be made. Some core parameters should be set up, which can be found on the Globals page in SWAT. Make sure you are using the Advanced View so that you can access all of the options. Otherwise some of these options may not appear.

Base Settings

As with a Windows server, the Samba server needs to have the computer name, workgroup or domain, and other network settings.

Workgroup

The workgroup parameter specifies the workgroup or domain that your Samba server is in.

NetBIOS Name

This option sets the computer name that appears when browsing the network in the Network Neighborhood/My Network Places. The Net-BIOS name is limited to 15 characters, so a server string can be added if more details are needed to identify the server. If you use Domain Name Service (DNS), Samba uses the server's DNS host name by default. If you leave this option blank and you aren't using DNS, Samba will use the server's host name. It is best to enter a name, even if you are using DNS and you enter the same name as the Transmission Control Protocol/Internet Protocol (TCP/IP) host name. That way you can avoid some problems that might occur if there are DNS problems or the TCP/IP name becomes misconfigured.

Server String

This is the computer description that appears in the Comment field when you are browsing the Network Neighborhood/My Network Places. The server string has three variables: *%v* for the Samba version number, *%h* for the hostname of the Samba server, and *%L* for the Net-BIOS name of the Samba server. For example, on a Samba server with the NetBIOS name set to Bigserver a server string of

```
%L running Samba %v
```

would result in a comment description in the Network Neighborhood/ Computers Near Me of

```
Bigserver running Samba 2.2
```

Samba's Configuration Variables

Samba configuration can make use of several different variables. These variables all start with the % character. Table 2-3 lists many of Samba's variables. They can be used in setting global options as well as in file share settings and printer share settings.

Security Settings

Samba has many security options, some of which are critical.

THE SECURITY PARAMETER

The **Security** parameter sets the authentication process used by the Samba server. The default is setting is User, the setting for using Samba as a stand-alone server. There are four options for the security parameter: Share, User, Server, and Domain.

The **Share** option uses the validation method used by a Windows 95 file or printer server. This means that every time a connection is requested to

Table 2-3	*Samba variables*

Variable	Definition
%a	The architecture of the client computers. Possible values are Samba, WfWg, WinNT, Win95, or UNKNOWN. Windows 98 and Me are recognized as Win95. Windows 2000 is recognized as WinNT.
%d	Process ID of the current server process
%g	Primary group of username *%u*
%G	Primary group of username *%U*
%b	The DNS name of the Samba server
%H	Home directory of username *%u*
%I	The IP address of the client computer in IP address form, e.g., 192.168.0.15
%L	The computer name (NetBIOS name) of the Samba server
%m	The computer name (NetBIOS name) of the client machine
%M	The DNS name of the client machine
%N	If you use the Unix Network Information System (NIS), the name of the NIS home directory server
%p	If you use NIS, the path to user's home directory
%P	The root directory of the current service; not a global option
%R	The SMB protocol level that was set after negotiations
%S	The name of the current service; not a global option
%T	The current date and time
%u	The username of the current service; not a global option
%U	The username requested at session startup (not always used by Samba)
%v	The Samba version number

a share on the server, Samba checks the username and password from the user database, and if a match is found, the connection is accepted.

The **User** option, Samba's default setting, uses a logon process for each client. If the user logon is authenticated, the connection is accepted. As long as the session is maintained, any additional connection requests by the client do not require that the authentication process be repeated.

The **Server** option is similar to the User option, except that the initial logon authentication is passed to a password server, usually a Windows domain controller or a Samba server acting as a domain controller. A separate configuration option, **Password Server,** identifies the authentication server. When using this option, you still need an account for the user on the Samba server.

The **Domain** option is used when the Samba server is a member of a Windows domain. The Samba server must become a member of the Windows domain. The domain controller handles user management and sees the Samba server as an NT machine. This is the most robust option. If you use the Domain option, the only local administration required on the Samba server is to create the directories needed for each share. If you aren't using Winbind, you'll also need to maintain user and group IDs on the Samba server that match those on the domain controller. See Section 2.6 on adding a Samba server to a Windows domain.

THE ENCRYPT PASSWORDS OPTION

The default setting is to not encrypt passwords. This the single biggest source of confusion and problems for new Samba administrators. This setting makes Samba look like a Windows 95 system on the network, not an NT server. Older versions of Windows used clear text passwords, while current versions use encrypted passwords. If Encrypt Passwords is set to No, all current Windows systems will be unable to connect to the Samba server. Unencrypted passwords are used by Windows for Workgroups 3.1, Windows 95 prior to OEM Service Release 2 (OSR2), and Windows NT 4 prior to Service Pack 3. Windows 95 OSR2, Windows 98, Windows Me, Windows NT 4 Service Pack 3 and later, and Windows 2000 all use encrypted passwords. *For most networks, the Encrypt Passwords setting must be changed to Yes.*

GUEST ACCOUNTS

A guest account must be defined for browsing and printing. If the guest account does not exist, Windows NT/2000 machines won't see the Samba server when browsing the Network Neighborhood/My Network Places. Printing also needs the guest account. Setting a guest account does not compromise security because it does not give guest access. Guest access is defined by the shares, not the global settings. Guest access is denied by default on all shares and can be granted only if you enable it for each individual share. The default guest account is the user "nobody." On some systems this username can cause problems. If you experience a problem, either use the username "ftp," which by default has severely restricted access rights, or create a new guest user on the Samba server.

Tuning Settings

DEAD TIME

A connection is considered to be inactive when there is no activity and there are no open files. The Dead Time option sets a limit in minutes before an inactive connection is considered to be dead and disconnected. On a busy server this option can free up resources that might otherwise be tied up by a large number of inactive connections. Reconnections are transparent to users because Windows clients have an automatic reconnect feature. The default setting is 0, which means the connection should never be dropped. For a server with more than a handful of users, set this to 15.

SOCKET OPTIONS

The Socket options are used to optimize the Samba server's network connections. The settings are specific to the operating system and are often not fully documented. Some options will significantly improve performance; others will deteriorate connections or even cause server connections to fail completely. For optimal performance on a Linux server on a local network, use the IPTOS_LOWDEALY and TCP_NODELAY options. These must be typed in.

Starting Samba Services

Normally you won't need to start, stop, or restart Samba. Samba services should start when the system starts up.

To make sure that the Samba service is set to run at startup, go to the System page on Webmin. Select the Bootup and Shutdown link on the page that opens, and scroll down to find *smb* or *samba*. Next to the name is either a Yes or a No, indicating whether Samba has been set to run at startup. If it says No, click on the name, which opens the Edit Action page. Click the Yes button next to the Startup at Boot Time? option. Then click on Save, or the change won't be applied. You can also start or stop the Samba services from this page.

Starting and stopping Samba services can also be done from the Status page on SWAT. You cannot enable starting up at boot time from SWAT, however.

Yet a third way to start or stop Samba services is from a command line on the Samba server. On Red Hat Linux, the program to do this is called *smb* and can be found in the */etc/rc.d/init.d* directory. On Caldera OpenLinux, it is called *samba* and is found in the same */etc/rc.d/init.d* directory. On Debian GNU/Linux, it is called *smb* and is in the */etc/init.d* directory.

If you have installed Samba from the Red Hat package built by the Samba team, which is available for download from the Samba Web site at *www.samba.org*, a copy of the *smb* program named *samba* is installed in the */usr/sbin* directory.

The command to start Samba on Red Hat Linux is

```
/etc/rc.d/init.d/smb start
```

On Caldera OpenLinux you type `/etc/rc.d/init.d/samba start`, and on Debian GNU/Linux you type `/etc/init.d/smb start`.

You can stop Samba using the same command, but substituting "start" with "stop":

```
/etc/rc.d/init.d/smb stop
```

The parameters that can be used are Start, Stop, Restart, and Status. Restart first stops the Samba daemons and then starts them. The Status parameter returns the names of the running Samba daemons; both nmbd and smbd should be running.

Joining a Domain

On a network with a Windows NT or 2000 domain controller, a Samba server will easily integrate into the Windows domain. Samba will join and be part of either a Windows 2000 or NT 4 domain. The Samba server will be seen as an NT 4 server. That means that on a Windows 2000 domain controller, NetBIOS and NTLMv1 must enabled.

There are just a few steps involved to joining a Windows domain. First, a computer account is created on the domain controller. Then the Samba configuration is updated to enable its domain member options. Finally, the Samba server is added to the domain.

Create a Computer Account on the Domain Controller

First, create a computer account (on Windows 2000) or a machine account (on Windows NT 4) for the Samba server on the domain controller. When creating the account on a Windows 2000 domain controller, make sure to select the option to allow pre-Windows 2000 computers to use this account.

Update the Samba Configuration

Before the Samba server can join the domain, the configuration parameters must be updated to indicate that it will now be a member of the domain. On the Globals page in SWAT, check these four parameters and make any changes necessary:

- **Workgroup:** Set the Workgroup parameter to the domain name.
- **Security:** Set the Security parameter to domain.
- **Password server:** List the domain controller as the password server.
- **Encrypt Passwords:** Make sure that the Encrypt Passwords option is set to Yes.

Join the Domain

Finally, add the Samba server to the domain. To do this, make sure that Samba is not running. On the SWAT Status page, click both buttons to stop smbd and nmbd.

Then use the smbpasswd program to join the domain. The form of the command is

```
smbpasswd -j domain_name -r domain_controller_name
```

For example, if NICK were the name of the domain and NORA the name of the domain controller, the command would be

```
smbpasswd -j NICK -r NORA
```

If this operation is successful, you will get the following message:

```
smbpasswd: joined domain NICK
```

If it is not successful, some possible error messages are as follows:

NT_Status_Access_Denied. This error message usually means that the computer account on the Windows 2000 domain controller was created without selecting the option to allow pre-Windows 2000 computers to use this account.

NT_Status_No_Trust_Sam_Account. This error message usually means that the computer or machine account on the domain controller couldn't be found. Check that the account was created properly and that the correct domain was specified in the -j option.

Can't resolve address for *domain_controller_name*. This error message means that the domain controller couldn't be found. Check that the correct name was used with the -r option and that the domain controller can be reached on the network, using a network testing tool like ping. Sometimes it helps to add the domain controller to the */etc/hosts* file on the Samba server.

User Management

Unless you are using Winbind and all management of users and groups is handled on a Windows domain controller, every Samba user must have a regular Linux account. This is true even if you are using another system as the password server for Samba.

Webmin can be used to manage user accounts on the Samba server, and it can be configured to automatically synchronize Linux and Samba user accounts. Again, managing accounts without Webmin is a multistep process.

To enable Samba-Linux user synchronization in Webmin, click on the Servers tab and open the Samba link. The Samba Share Manager page should open. Figure 2-6 shows Webmin's Samba administration page, though the user synchronizations options are not shown.

Scroll down the page to find three options for managing user and group accounts, as shown in Figure 2-7.

Figure 2-6   *Webmin's Samba administration page includes a link to SWAT, which appears here in the lower right corner.*

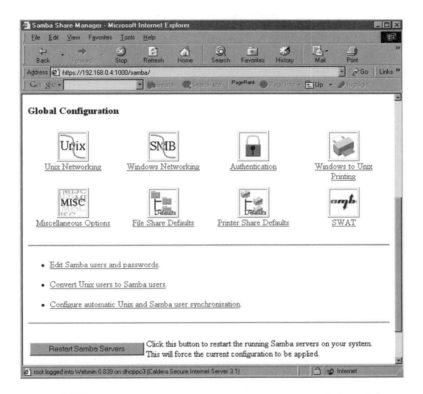

Figure 2-7   *Webmin's Samba administration page includes a link to SWAT, which appears here in the lower right corner.*

The options are as follows:

- Edit Samba Users and Passwords
- Convert Unix Users to Samba Users
- Configure Automatic Unix and Samba User Synchronization

If these options don't appear, then check the Samba configuration to make sure that use of encrypted passwords is enabled. The default installation for Samba and many Linux distributions is to have encrypted passwords disabled, for compatibility with older Windows 95 systems. If you need to enable encrypted passwords, click on the Authentication icon in Webmin. Make sure that Use Encrypted Passwords, the first item on the Passwords Options page, is set to Yes. Then save the settings. It is not necessary to restart Samba.

Select the option to configure automatic Unix and Samba user synchronization. There are three options: you can add a Samba user when a Unix user is added,change the Samba user when a Unix user is changed, or delete the Samba user when a Unix user is deleted. Normally all three options should be selected. Once you've made your selections, make sure to click the Apply button.

The link to adding existing users as Samba users can also be chosen, though the password information can't be converted this way and passwords for each user will have to be entered manually. It is best to set up synchronization before adding users to the Samba server.

With this setup, all changes made to users and groups through Webmin will automatically be updated in the Samba user database. Chapter 8 details the procedures for user and group management with Webmin.

Matching Windows and Linux Usernames

It is not always possible to match Windows usernames with Linux usernames. Windows allows more flexibility with usernames than does Linux. For example, Windows usernames can be longer, up to 255 characters, whereas Linux

---

Changing Passwords

Any changes made in user passwords on a password server or a domain controller, including a Samba server that functions as a domain controller or a password server, are transparently accepted by the Samba server. The same is true with changes users make in their Windows passwords. Samba will automatically accept the changed password. Samba will not, however, automatically update the Linux user account with the new password.

Configuring Samba to update Linux user passwords requires a few changes to the Globals settings in SWAT. These changes should work with any Linux distribution:

In SWAT, select the Advanced View and scroll down to the Security Options. Enable the Unix Password Sync so that the option is set to Yes.

Then enter the chat sequence that is used on the Linux server to change the user's password. In the Passwd Chat option type in

```
*new*password* %n\n *new*password* %n\n *changed*
```

For systems that require the old password and then the new password, type in this chat script:

```
*old*password* %o\n *new*password* %n\n *new*password* %n\n
*changed*
```

Finally, make sure that the `Passwd Program` option is set to `/bin/passwd`. You should not need to change this option.

recognizes only the first 8 characters of a username. In addition, Windows usernames can include spaces, which are not accepted in Linux usernames.

Samba has a Username Map option that can be used to map Windows usernames to Linux usernames. The Username Map option is found on the Globals page in SWAT, under Security Options.

Set the Username Map parameter to point to a file on the Samba server. The default name used by many Linux distributions is *smbusers*. You can choose any name you want, however, and some administrators like to add the extension *map* to indicate that this is not the file that has user password information. In that case, enter the name as */etc/samba/smbusers.map*. After typing in the full pathname of the file, make sure to click the Commit Changes button.

This username map file is a plain text file that can be created in any text editor. Each line in the file starts with the Linux username followed by an equals sign and then one or more Windows usernames or Linux username groups. Two or more Windows usernames can be mapped to a single Linux username by listing all the Windows usernames after the equals sign. Any Windows username that includes spaces must be enclosed in quotation marks. Lines that begin with a pound sign (#) or a semicolon (;) are treated as comments and ignored by Samba.

The contents of a *smbusers* map file might look like this:

```
jhenry = "Janet Henry"
pmadvig = "Paul Madvig" paul
nvarna = nancy
ed = "Ed Beaumont"
```

If you have just a few names to add, use Webmin to add names to the username map. On the Samba Share Manager page, select the Authentication button. In the username map table, enter the Linux username in the first column and the Windows username in the second column. After saving, some versions of Webmin do not properly display Windows usernames that were entered inside quotes, but they do properly add the names to the map file.

To add a large number of names, use a text editor to create the file on Linux or Windows and then save a copy to the */etc* directory, or whatever folder is set in the configuration. If you create the text file in a Windows editor, then make sure you convert the file to Linux text format.

TIP—CONVERTING MICROSOFT TEXT FILES TO LINUX TEXT FORMAT

Plain text files are almost the same on Linux as on Windows, but there is one significant difference in file format. The Linux operating system interprets the DOS text end-of-line character as a Ctrl-M, so if you view a DOS ASCII file in a Linux text editor, it may have a ^M at the end of each line. Conversely, if you look at a Linux text file in a Windows text editor like Notepad, the file looks like one single line with no paragraph breaks because there is no DOS end-of-line character on each line.

Converting is easy using the mcopy program, which is installed with most Linux distributions. This is a utility for copying DOS files to and from Linux. The *-t* option in mcopy is for translating the end-of-line characters from DOS to Linux. The command is

```
mcopy -t filename
```

You will prompted with a message that the file already exists, after you enter a "Y" for Yes to overwrite, the original is replaced with a file that is now in Linux text format.

To convert Word files, the word2x utility will convert files in Word 6 format to plain text. To find word2x and other Linux utility programs on the Web, go to *www.freshmeat.net*, which is a central index of Linux software.

Getting Help

The are many sources of help for Samba, from resources installed with the program to help from the Samba team to commercial help services. Also, if you're stuck, look at the troubleshooting guide in Chapter 7. It covers the most common problems on Samba servers.

Help on SWAT's Home Page

Look at the home page for SWAT.). The whole page is a list of help links. Most of these links are to the manual documents prepared by the Samba developers, usually called the "man" pages. These generally include short technical descriptions of the programs and a complete list of the program's options.

One thing to remember when using the documentation links on the SWAT home page is that they are designed to open in a second browser window. The first time you click on a link, the manual page come to the front. If you click on a different link on the home page, the contents of the second browser are changed, rather than opening up a third browser. So if you click on a link on the home page and it appears that nothing has happened, look at what's in the second browser.

The Online Manual

Installed with Samba is a copy of the technical manual *Using Samba,* written by by Robert Eckstein, David Collier-Brown, and Peter Kelly. The complete manual should already be installed on your Samba server. It is a technical guide to Samba, written mainly for Unix system administrators. It assumes a knowledge of Unix and has complete descriptions of every option available. A link to the book is on the bottom of the SWAT home page.

Help on Configuration Pages

Each option listed on the Globals, Shares, and Printers pages of SWAT includes a help link that goes to the Samba manual pages and gives a short description of the option along with all the available parameters and the default setting.

Samba's Email Help Lists

Email lists are maintained by the Samba team. These lists are very active and are used by Samba users all around the world, from Asia and Australia to Africa, Europe, and the Middle East as well as North and South America.

The email lists can often be a source of help when you have tried everything you know. Answers are freely given by experienced Samba users as well as key members of the Samba team.

There are a number of lists, most of them specialized for Samba's open development procedures. The specialized lists are, well, specialized and are not the place to ask questions unrelated to the specialized purpose. If you decide to ask a question on a Samba email list, start on the general Samba help list. It's the list just called *Samba* found on the Web at *lists.samba.org*. If your question is more appropriate for one of the specialized lists, someone is sure to tell you.

Commercial Support

There are a number of companies that provide commercial support for Samba. A list of companies around the world, sorted by country, that can help with Samba problems can be found on the Samba Web site at *www. samba.org*. Click on the Support link. Also, both Hewlett-Packard and IBM offer support for Samba on their servers.

Other soures of commercial support are the Linux vendors, such as Red Hat and Caldera, as well as the many companies that support Linux systems. Most Linux support includes support for Samba.

The Samba File Server

File sharing is the primary function for most Samba servers. While this may be Samba's most important use, file sharing is not a complex task if it is done right.

Most of the time you will follow a basic two-step procedure to set up file sharing. First you'll set up a directory on the Linux system and set its access permissions. Then you'll configure Samba to make the directory a share available on the network.

It is important to keep the two steps in mind because when there are problems, they could come from the first part, the Linux side, or the second part, the Samba side. This part of Samba administration isn't especially intuitive. Sometimes you'll think that you've checked everything, but all you've checked is the Samba configuration and it turns out that the problem is in the Linux configuration.

The user home directories are shares that are set up by default on Samba. This chapter starts with that share, both because it is there and also because it uses the basic structure that all shares are built on. The rest of the chapter then describes how to set up some of the common types of shares you may want for your network. If all you are doing is setting up a Samba server as a place where users can store their files, then everything you'll need is in this chapter. This is a popular way to use Samba, and it is used this way commercially on many Network Attached Storage (NAS) systems.

Chapter 4 describes how to set up Samba for printer services, and Chapter 5 goes into some of the advanced networking options that can be set up with Samba. Information on setting up Samba as a domain controller can be found in Chapter 10.

Let's start with bread-and-butter Samba, the basic file server.

The Homes Share

Any time a user connects to a Samba server, if the user has an account on the server, the home directory is automatically made available. This is the homes share. The configuration can be seen in SWAT by going to the Shares page and clicking on the drop-down menu next to the Choose Share button. Choose Homes and then click on the Choose Share button. Figure 3-1 shows the homes share page in SWAT with the default settings.

There are just a handful of options shown, and most of them are unchanged from the default setting. The only changes from the defaults are that a comment is added, read Read Only is set to No, and Browseable is set to No.

Comments

The first line is for comments, an optional setting. This is the message that is displayed next to the Share icon when browsing the network in Details view.

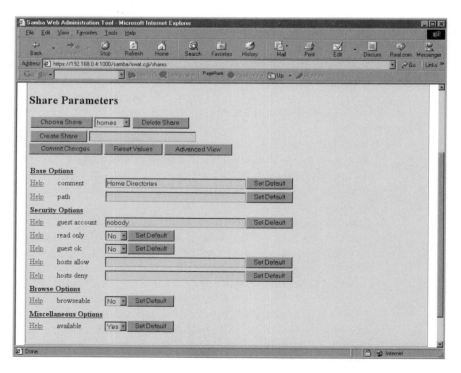

Figure 3-1   *The homes share configuration page in SWAT.*

Path

The Path option does not need to be defined for homes and can be left blank for the homes share. Any other share must have the path defined. Homes is a special share that's predefined, and the path to the user's home directory is taken from the Linux user account information.

Guest Account

The Guest Account option specifies the name to use for the guest account, if it is needed. The default name is the Linux user "nobody," a user on Linux systems that owns no files and is used for operations that require that no rights be enabled. There should be a guest account if you want to have the share appear when users are browsing the Network Neighborhood/My Network Places.

Read Only

This option sets whether or not users can write to the share. Some people find the wording of this option confusing. If Read Only is set to No, then users can write to the share. If it is set to Yes, then users will be able to read files but not modify them. If you don't want users to be able to modify files on a share, then you have to set Read Only to Yes.

Guest OK

The Guest OK option indicates whether guest users can have access to the share. The default setting for the homes share is No.

Hosts Allow

The default setting for Hosts Allow is None, which means that any host is permitted access to the share. A host can be specified by its name or IP address, and multiple hosts can be listed. To restrict access to just machines on the local network's subnet, you can enter a partial IP address. For example, entering 192.168.0. will limit access to machines on the 192.168.0.0 subnet.

Hosts Deny

This is a list of IP addresses or hostnames of systems that are to be denied access to the Samba server. The default setting is None; no hosts are denied access. The setting options are the same as those used for Hosts Allow.

Browseable

This option sets whether the share will be visible when users browse the Network Neighborhood/My Network Places. It is set to No by default for homes shares. If it is set to No, the share will appear only for a valid user. That means that when a user is browsing the network, the user's home share will appear, but not the homes of other users on the network.

Available

If a share is available, then a valid user can gain access. This option defaults to Yes. The option is there for the occasional times when you need to perform some system administration on a specific share and don't need to take the whole server off-line. Set the option to No to make sure that there is no access while you work on it and then put it back to Yes to allow access.

Securing the Homes Share

The default homes share is the most basic level of network sharing. The user can browse the Samba server and will see the home directory as a folder labeled with the user's login name. The level of security, however, is not what you might expect. The default setting is something like a shareable folder on a Windows 95 machine that is read-only, but full access to the user's folder requires a password.

Unless you make additional changes to the homes defaults, any user on the network can view the home directories of all the other home directories on the Samba server. This is not obvious to the casual user because Browseable is set to No, so the other home directories don't appear in the Network Neighborhood/My Network Places. The user will only see her or his own home directory. But if you know the login name of another user on the Samba server, you can map a drive to that user's home directory and have full read access to the directory, though you won't be able to modify any files in the directory.

For some basic workgroup servers, this may not be a problem, and it may even be a desirable feature. It is certainly similar to the security level of most Windows peer-to-peer networks.

A couple of changes to the configuration will secure the homes share in a way that is similar to that of a Windows NT server. Figure 3-2 shows the option settings in SWAT for a secure homes share.

There are three changes to make to the basic configuration to secure the homes share. To make these changes, first change to the Advance View in SWAT. Then make the following entries.

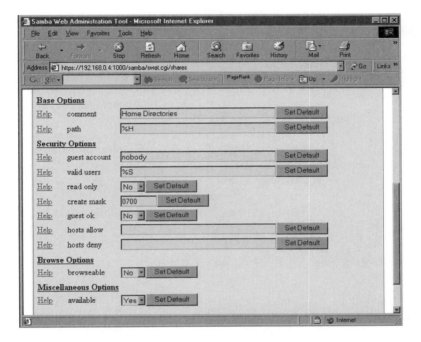

Figure 3-2   *The settings for a secure homes share.*

%H **Path**

Add a %H to the path. Remember that case matters, and don't use a lower-case "h." Because the homes directories are a special share, this is the only share for which you do not enter a path. The path is determined by the user's login name. That means, however, that the share is not restricted to a particular path. The %H variable is automatically interpreted as the user's home directory, which the Samba server gets from the Linux user account information. This procedure restricts each user's access to only his or her home directory. Mapping to another user's home directory is no longer possible.

Valid Users

This option restricts access to a share to only users shown in this list. You can type in a list of usernames, groups, or Samba variables. The %S variable is commonly used on the homes share because it expands to the name of the share, in this case the home directory. For example, for the home directory named *jhenry* the %S equals `jhenry`, so the only valid user is "jhenry."

Create Mask

The Create Mask option applies Linux file permissions settings to the share. Whenever a user creates a file, the permissions set in the Create Mask are applied to the file, overriding any other settings. Linux file permissions are explained in Section 3.2. Samba's default setting is 0744, which means that the owner of the file can read as well as modify the file in any way as well as execute the file if it is an application, and the files can be read by any group member as well as all others who can access the file even if they are not the owner or a member of the group. Changing this setting to 0700 means that only the owner of the files in the directory has access rights.

Setting Up Linux Directories for Sharing

Before a directory can become available through Samba, it must be made available in Linux. This isn't necessary for the home directories because the home directory is created when the user account is created.

Directories that will be shared by a group of users must be created in Linux, and permissions must be set so that access will be allowed or denied to the right users.

Linux File Permissions

Linux file permissions are fairly simple. The simplicity means that Linux file permissions are not hard to understand and use, but it also means that the complex permissions used on Windows servers can't be matched. On Linux each file and directory has permissions defined for the owner, for a group, and for all others. It is not possible for a file or directory to have rights set for two groups with different permission rights, as it is in Windows.

For Linux there are three possible permissions: read, write, and execute. On files, this means a user can read the file, write or modify the file, and execute the file if it is an application. On directories, the user can read the directory, write or modify files in the directory, and list (execute) the contents of a directory. Only a file's or directory's owner or the administrator ("root") can change a file's permission.

Read permission

Read permission on a file means what you'd expect, that you can read the file. Read permission is also necessary for program files if they are to be executed. Read permission on a directory is required in order to see the contents of the directory as well as to be able to create new files in it.

Write permission

Write permission on a file means that you can modify a file, but it does not mean that you can delete the file. Write permission on a directory means that you can create or delete a file or directory inside the directory.

Execute permission

Execute permission on a file means it is an executable application; in Windows that's usually a file that ends in *.exe* or *.com*. Programs on Linux must be given execute permission before they can be run. Execute permission on a directory gives the user the right to open a directory and list its contents or to move through it to other subdirectories. To do anything with a file, you must have execute permission on its directory. If a file is in a subdirectory, you must also have execute permission in the parent directory.

TIP — SAMBA AND LINUX EXECUTE PERMISSION ON DIRECTORIES

On Linux, users who do not have execute permission on a directory cannot open the directory and list its files. However, because of the way Samba and Windows handle browsing folders, execute permission does not matter for listing the contents of a directory on a Samba server when it is accessed from Windows.

These permissions are set for one owner, for one group, and for all others. The common way this is displayed on a Linux system is *-rwxrwxrwx*. If the first character is a letter "D," then it is a directory. The first trio of *rwx* is the permissions settings for the owner of the file or directory, the second trio is for the group associated with the file or directory, and the last is the permissions settings for everyone else.

You can use the *r, w,* or *x* to indicate the permission you are setting. Samba works with the octal number system, which does the same thing. The octal system uses a set of four numbers, though the first number can be omitted. The final three numbers stand for owner, group, and others. The numbers range from 0 to 7. Their values are shown in Table 3-1.

A common permission setting is 0750. The last three numbers set the permissions. The 7 means that the owner of the directory (the user) has read, write, and execute permission. The 5 for the group associated with the direc-

Table 3-1	*Permission settings by number values*
Value	**Permission**
0	No permissions
1	Execute files or list directories
2	Write
3	Write and execute files or list directories
4	Read
5	Read and execute files or list directories
6	Read and write
7	Read, write, and execute files or list directories

tory is read and execute permission, meaning that group members can display a list of files in the directory and read them but cannot create new files or modify existing ones. The final 0 means that everyone else is denied all access to the directory.

On some shares, the value of the first number will be set to something other than zero. This number sets a special set of permissions called SUID ("set user ID"), SGID ("set group ID"), and the Sticky Bit.

SGID permission on a directory means that files created in that directory will have the same group ownership as the directory itself, rather than the group of the user creating the file. This is a special permission that is used for directories that contain files shared by a group of users. SGID is commonly used on Samba file shares.

The SUID and SGID permission settings on files means that the user will have access rights or another user or group. This is used so that a file or program that would not otherwise be accessible or executable by the user can be accessed or executed as a user or group with the permissions needed for the task. If SUID is enabled and an application is launched, the program is started as if the owner of the file executed the program, rather than the user who has accessed it and has started the program. The program is then run with the permissions of the owner, not of the user executing the program. For example, the Linux password utility is used by regular users to change their Linux password. It has SUID permissions enabled so that when a regular changes his or her password, the program is executed as the root user, with the administrative access rights to change the password.

The special permissions values, set with the first number when there are four numbers used for setting permissions, are shown in Table 3-2.

Table 3-2	*Sticky Bit, SUID, and SGID settings by number values*
Value	**Permission**
0	No permissions (default if no number is specified)
1	Enable Sticky Bit
2	Enable SGID
3	Enable SGID and Sticky Bit
4	Enable SUID
5	Enable SUID and Sticky Bit
6	Enable SUID and SGID
7	Enable SUID, SGID, and Sticky Bit

Setting Permissions from Windows

Users can change permission settings on their own files or directories from Windows NT or 2000. This is done in the usual way from the Properties menu for the file or directory. Right-click on the directory or filename and select Properties. Only read, write, and execute permissions can be set or modified.

Administration changes can be made only by users with administrative access. This is a special setting in Samba that can be enabled on a per-share basis. It is one of the Security options in the Advanced View on SWAT.

Admin Users

Administrator access to a share can be granted to users listed as Admin Users for the share. If a username is listed as an Admin User, that user will be able to perform operations as the root user. In SWAT, type in the usernames for users who are to be given administrator access to the share. If you want to change the ownership of a file from Windows NT/2000, you must be listed as an Admin User.

Creating Directories for Samba Shares

To create directories in Linux, open Webmin and use the File Manager found on the Others page. Figure 3-3 shows the Webmin File Manager. Of course, there are several other ways this can be done, for example, over a telnet connection to the Linux server or by working at the terminal on the Linux server. If you are already familiar with another method, you should use it.

The Webmin File Manager can be used much like Windows Explorer, the Windows file manager.

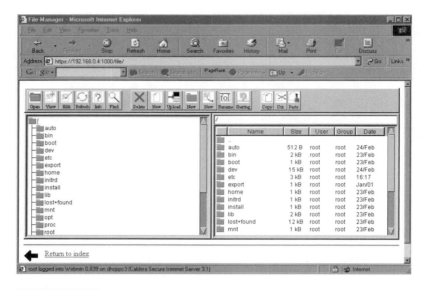

Figure 3-3   *The Webmin File Manager.*

For the Samba server, all of the directories that aren't home directories will be kept in a separate directory named *srv*. This is not a necessary step, and you can organize your server the way you want. However, putting all of the Samba shares into one directory makes management tasks easier.

To create a directory named *srv* in the Webmin File Manager, first click on the New Folder icon. A popup window opens where you can type in the name of the new directory. Type in */srv* and click on the Create button.

To see the permissions on the new directory, or to change them, find the folder in the right panel and select it. With the folder highlighted, click on the Info button on the menu bar. Figure 3-4 shows the Info window.

The permissions should show check marks for Read, Write, and List (execute) for the user. For group and others, Read and List should be selected. The user and group should both be set to "root" in the Ownership section.

Now create any directories, except for home directories, that are to be shared on the Samba server in this directory.

To create a directory in the *srv* directory, select the *srv* folder in the left panel. Then follow the same procedure used to create the *srv* directory, clicking on the Folder button with the word "new" below the folder and typing in the name for the new directory in the popup window that opens. The permissions will need to be changed, however, depending on how the share will be used.

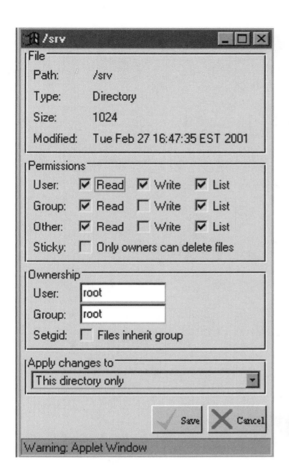

Figure 3-4

Permission settings for the srv directory, as displayed by the Webmin File Manager.

Linux Settings for a Share for a Single User

For a single user, create a directory. Then give full permissions to the user, read and list permissions to the group, and no permissions for others. Change the user and group ownership to the username and group for the user. Then select Apply Changes to This Directory and Its Files, and click on Save. Figure 3-5 shows the permissions changes for a single user named "pmadvig."

Figure 3-5   *Permission settings for a single user.*

Linux Settings for a Share for a Group of Users

Use the same procedure to create a directory that will be shared by a group of users. Then give full permissions to the group and user, no permissions to others. Leave the username as "root," but change the group ownership to the name of the group, which must be a valid group on the Linux server. Only members of the group will have full access to this directory. Check the SGID option to indicate that the files will inherit the group ID. This means that any files in the directory will be given the group ID, no matter what group ID the individual user may have. This prevents permission complications in which a user can create a file in a shared directory but no one else can access the file. Finally, select Apply Changes to This Directory and Its Files, and click on Save. Figure 3-6 shows permissions changes for a shared directory for the "accounts" group.

Linux Settings for a Public Share

To make a directory that is accessible to everyone on the local network, follow the same procedure to create a group directory. Then give full read, write, and list permissions to user, group, and others. Change the user to "nobody" and the group to "nobody." Check the SGID option to indicate that the files will inherit the group ID. Then select Apply Changes to This Directory and Its Files, and click on Save. Figure 3-7 shows a sample public directory.

A Shortcut to Creating a Share in Samba

After creating a directory in Webmin and setting the permissions, you can quickly create a share in the Webmin File Manager. To do this, in the right panel select the directory that will become a share in Samba. Then click on the Sharing button in the File Manager's menu bar. In the Windows tab in the popup window that opens, select the Windows File Sharing Enabled radio button, as shown in Figure 3-8.

This procedure will create a share in Samba with the same name as the directory's name. You can add a comment for the share, and you can choose to make it active and writable. The last option is to set guest access. The share can be set to deny guest access, allow guest, or to allow access only to guest users Click Save to add the share to your Samba configuration. If you have SWAT open when you do this, you'll have to reload SWAT before it will see the new share. That's because SWAT does not know about any changes that are made by another program. Only after you force SWAT to reload the configuration will the changes appear. If you don't reload SWAT and you make changes in SWAT and save them, then the new share configuration will be lost.

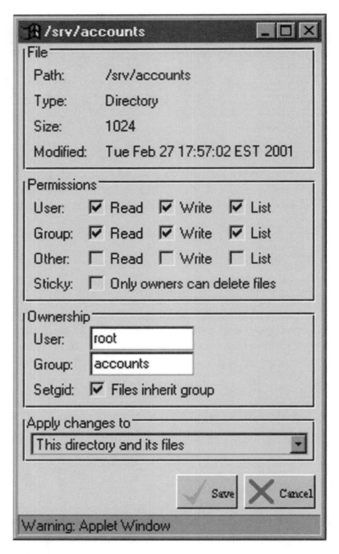

Permission settings for a shared group directory.

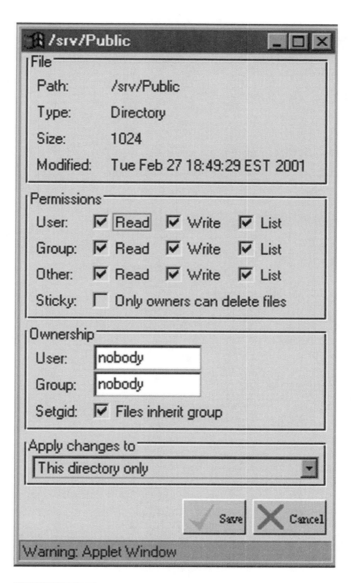

Figure 3-7   *Permission settings for a public directory.*

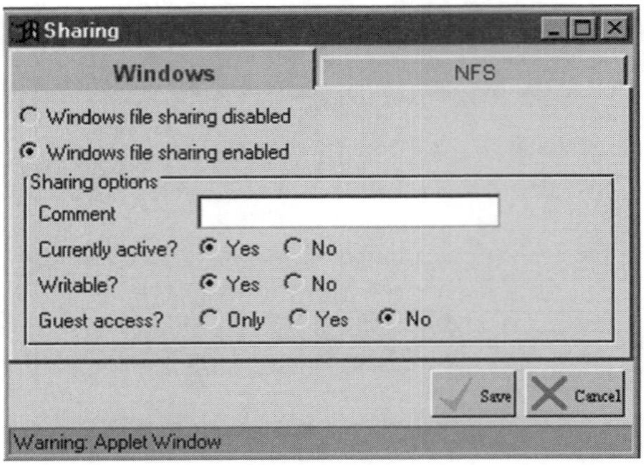

Figure 3-8

Enabling a directory for Windows file sharing in Webmin creates a file share in Samba.

Setting Up Shares

After creating the directories in Linux, the shares must be configured in Samba. If you haven't already added the basic share configuration through Webmin's File Manager using its Windows sharing tool, you should create the share in SWAT. After the share has been created, you can then configure it for the specific task it will serve.

In this section you'll find the configuration settings for a group share as well as several special-purpose shares. All of the configuration options are set in SWAT.

The Basic Group Share

The group share is the basic foundation for the Samba file server. This is the most commonly created share. After creating the necessary directory in Linux, you can create the share in Webmin or with SWAT. To create a new share in SWAT, go to the Shares page and type in a name for the share in the space next to the Create Share button. After typing in the name, click on the Create Share button.

The configuration page for the new share will then open. Check the path and read-only settings. If necessary, type in the path for the share. For example, if the share is a subdirectory named *accounts* in the *srv* directory, you will type in */srv/accounts*. If you want users to be able to save new files or modify existing files on the share, make sure that Read Only is set to No. Be sure to click the Commit Changes button, or any changes you make won't be saved.

Nothing more has to be done, though you may want to secure the share in a way similar to the homes share (see Section 3.1) and make some other changes. But the share is ready to go at this point and should be accessible on the network.

The security options can be set to limit access to a user or a group of users. Filename handling options may need to be changed for handling hidden files. The file locking options can be adjusted to improve performance. And there are several miscellaneous options, such as one to make Linux directory creation times match the Windows convention.

Because Samba has so many options, there is a tendency to skip over them and just put the share online. This is probably how the majority of shares are created. Samba's options may not need to be adjusted for every share, but making just a few changes can often improve performance and increase the security of the share. The multiple options give Samba a flexibility that's not easily matched on any other kind of network server, a mix of both Windows and Linux capabilities.

Following are some of the options that are often used to optimize Samba's file shares. These are listed here in the order in which they appear in SWAT. After the options, some examples show how they might be used.

Security Options

The security options include not only settings to control which users can and cannot access a share but also also settings to control user permissions for files and directories.

INVALID USERS AND VALID USERS

Use these options to specify a list of users who are denied or granted access. The list is a comma-separated listing of users and groups. Users *not* listed in the Invalid Users list are allowed access. The default setting is blank, meaning no user is denied access.

If there is a Valid Users list, only those users are allowed access and all others are denied access. The default is also blank, meaning that all users can have access. If a username appears in both the Invalid and Valid lists, the Invalid Users list has precedence and access is denied. Group names can be used, if the group exists on the Linux server, by putting a @ symbol before the name of the group, as in "@somegroup."

The Invalid and Valid Users options can be applied to the entire server, by enabling them in the Globals settings, or for a specific share. Setting them on a per-share basis gives the most flexibility, letting you allow or deny access to a different list of users for each share.

ADMIN USERS

This is a list of users granted complete administrative access (root user access, in Linux terms) to the share. This is one of the few Samba options that will override the permissions set on the Linux system. As on Windows servers, use great caution in allowing administrative access.

READ LIST AND WRITE LIST

The Read List is a list of users who have read-only access. This is a comma-separated list of users and groups. Group names are indicated by putting a @ symbol at the beginning of the name; the group must exist on the Linux server.

The Write List is a list of users granted write access. The Write List format is the same as the Read List. The Write List takes precedence over the Read List as well as the Read Only options. If a user appears on both the Read List and the Write List, the user will be able to write files to the share. If the share is set to Read Only but a username is in the Write List, that user will be able to write to the share.

The Write List settings cannot overcome the underlying Linux settings. If a user is in the Write List but the Linux permissions are not set to let the user write to the share, write access is denied.

The Read List will downgrade a user's rights. If a user's Linux permissions are set to allow the user to modify files on the share, but the username is in the Read List, then write access will be denied.

FORCE USER AND FORCE GROUP

This option can be set to the name of a single default user for all users accessing the share. The username must be a valid username on the Linux server. When this option is enabled, the connecting user must first provide a valid Samba username and password to access the share. Then all files and directories created on the share are owned by the user declared in the Force User parameter. The group ownership is also changed to the group of the user declared in the Force User parameter, unless the Force Group option is used to change it.

This option is used when creating a share with full access to a group of users. By creating a share with one user's name and applying the Force User option, you can give a group of users full access to read, write, create, and modify files without running into ownership permission problems. To keep files and directories tied to the user who created them, use Force Group instead.

The Force Group option works much like the Force User option. It sets the group for files created on a share. To use Force Group for giving full access to a group of users, the group permissions in Linux must be set to full read, write, and execute access. If that is done, then Force Group can be used like Force User to set up a group share. The difference is that user ownership is maintained.

READ ONLY

The Read Only option must be set to No if you want to allow anyone who can access the share to be able to create or modify files and directories on a share. Individual user and group write access can be controlled with the Read List and Write List options.

CREATE MASK AND DIRECTORY MASK

The Create Mask option is used to limit the permissions that are set when files are created. The default setting is 0744, which means that the user has full create and modify rights while everyone else is restricted to read-only permission. See the earlier section called "Setting Up Linux Directories for Sharing" for an explanation of the octal number system used to set permissions. The default setting removes write and execute permissions from new files for the group and others but preserves them for the file's owner. Set Create Mask to 0770 for shares being accessed by a group of users.

The Directory Mask option is similar to Create Mask except that it applies to directories. The default Directory Mask is 0755, which means that the owner of the directory has read, write, and execute permissions, but write permission is blocked for everyone else. For shares that are to be writable by a group of users, set this parameter to 0770.

Both Create Mask and Directory Mask set the maximum permissions for a file or directory.

FORCE CREATE MODE AND FORCE DIRECTORY MODE

These options are similar to Create Mask and Directory Mask, except that Force Create Mode and Force Directory Mode specify the permissions that must be set for any file or directory created on the share. The Force Create Mode and Force Directory Mode options will override any settings for Create Mask and Directory Mask.

For a shared directory in which users exchange files, use Force Create Mode instead of Force User to preserve usernames for file ownership. Set Force Create Mode to 0770 so that members of the same group can all create or modify files created by any member of the group.

HOSTS ALLOW AND HOSTS DENY

These options are used to specify a list of hosts or networks—by IP address or the fully qualified domain name—that you want to grant or deny access to the Samba server. For example, if the Hosts Allow parameter is set to 192.168.0.28, then only that specific host would be allowed to connect to the Samba server. Set it to 192.168.0., and any host on the 192.168.0. subnet is allowed to connect. A host can also be denied in the Hosts Allow setting. If Hosts Allow is set to

```
hosts allow = 192.168.0. EXCEPT 192.168.0.242
```

then the system will accept all hosts on the subnet except the one specified.

These options do not prevent a share from appearing when browsing, but it will block access to any host not specified. If left blank, any host that meets the other qualifications is allowed access.

Filename Handling Options

The filename handling options are used primarily to hide files or directories. On Linux, there is no hidden file attribute. Instead files are given names that begin with a dot (.)—commonly called dot files—which are then treated as hidden files. Samba hides these files so that on Windows they appear to have the DOS hidden attribute. These options let you disable this feature, which is enabled by default, as well as make other files invisible in Windows.

Hide Dot Files

This option sets the DOS hidden attribute on all dot files. The default is Yes, meaning that all dot files are hidden when viewing files on a Samba server from a Windows system.

Veto Files and Delete Veto Files

The Veto Files option is a list of filenames and directories that are marked by Samba as hidden and not accessible. If a user attempts to delete a directory that contains files that are Veto Files, the deletion will fail unless the Delete Veto Files parameter is set to Yes and the user has the correct permissions to do so. The default setting for Delete Veto Files is No. If a user complains about being unable to delete an empty directory, make sure that it does not contain any Veto Files.

Hide Files

This option is used to specify a list of files that are to be hidden by Samba. Wildcards like * and ? are allowed in filenames, as well as spaces. Separate filenames with a slash (/). The files will appear to have the DOS hidden file attribute, meaning that they are accessible in Windows only if the user knows the filename or if viewing hidden files has been enabled in Windows.

Map Archive

The Map Archive option enables Samba to map the DOS archive attribute to the owner execute bit in Linux. For the Map Archive option to work, the Create Mask option must be set to allow owner execute permissions. The default setting is Yes, and it should be left that way, particularly for compatibility with Windows backup programs. Many backup programs use the archive attribute to indicate whether a file has changed since the last backup because the archive attribute is set whenever a file is modified.

Browsing Options

There is one Browsing option. This sets whether the share will appear in the Network Neighborhood/My Network Places when a user is browsing the network.

Browseable

This option sets whether the share will appear in the list shown when the Samba server is browsed. If set to No, the share is hidden from the browse list but not unavailable.

File Locking Options

When two or more users attempt to read a file at the same time, there is no problem. If two or more users attempt to write at the same time, or even if one reads while another writes, the file is quickly corrupted. In order to prevent corruption, file locking is used to protect files when two or more users access the file. While both Windows and Linux support file locking, the implementations are different. Samba's file locking options make the two systems compatible.

Blocking Locks

The Blocking Locks option specifies how Samba is to respond when a Windows client requests a file that is blocked by a lock. The default is Yes, meaning that Samba will keep trying to open the file at regular intervals until it is successful or the attempt times out. Setting this option to No means that the attempt fails immediately and no further tries to open the file are made.

Locking

The Locking option enables partial-file locking, letting a program request a lock on only part of a file. The default is Yes and generally shouldn't be changed. One exception is for read-only shares. Because locking requires additional processing, access to read-only files is faster with locking set to No.

Oplocks

The Oplocks option sets opportunistic locks that enable a Windows client to locally cache changes made to a file. This speeds up performance on the Windows workstation because saves to the server are less frequent. When an Oplock is granted, the server can demand an update from the client at any time, which is what happens when another client attempts to read the file.

Level 2 Oplocks

Level 2 Oplocks are used by Windows NT and 2000 only. In the original Oplock, the first client loses the Oplock when a second client accesses the file. With a Level 2 Oplock, the first client is downgraded from a read-write Oplock to a read-only Oplock. The default setting is No. Setting it to Yes can improve performance for Windows NT/2000 clients.

Strict Locking

Some older Windows software is not locking-aware and will attempt to read or write to locked portions of files. Even some current Windows software does not properly check the status of locks. To protect files from these programs, Strict Locking can be enabled. When it is enabled, Samba will make a lock check on each and every read or write to the share. This procedure can slow down performance, but it protects the integrity of the files. Use this option only if necessary.

Share Modes

The Share Modes option enables whole-file locking. The default is Yes, and it should never be changed. Many Windows programs will not work properly if this option is set to No.

Miscellaneous Options

Follow Symlinks

A symbolic link on Linux is something like a shortcut in Windows. The default Follow Symlinks setting is Yes. Setting this to No can significantly degrade performance because Samba will have to check every access every time to make sure that the file is not a symbolic link.

Dont Descend

This option uses a comma-separated list of directories that Samba should not attempt to enter. If a user without the correct rights attempts to enter a directory in the list, the directory will appear to be empty.

DOS Filetimes

The DOS Filetimes option should be set to Yes if you want the timestamp on files to match the convention used by Windows. On Linux, the timestamp is updated only when the owner of the file makes a change. In Windows, any change by any user with write access updates the timestamp for the file. The default setting is No; change it to Yes so that the Samba timestamps match what Windows users expect.

DOS Filetime Resolution

The option must be set to Yes if you are using Visual C++ on a Samba file share with Oplocks. The default setting is No. When set to Yes, the timestamp of a file is rounded down to the closest two seconds when a client requests a timestamp with one-second resolution. Without this, Visual C++ erroneously reports that the file has been changed.

Delete Readonly

By default, Samba protects the DOS read-only attribute. Changing this option to Yes allows a user to delete read-only files.

Fake Directory Create Times

The default setting is No. On Linux the timestamp on a directory is the last change time; on Windows the timestamp on a directory is the creation time. If you are using Visual C++ on a Samba file share, some operations will not work properly with the Linux directory timestamp. To get around this, set this option to Yes, and all newly created directories will have a create time of midnight on 1-1-1980.

The Basic Group Share, Short Version

Though there is no single solution that fits everyone's needs, there is a common set of options from which most group shares start. Make the following changes to Samba's default settings for a basic group file share. If you have no special needs, these may be the only settings needed for your Samba file shares. Replace *somegroup* in the example with the name of the group that is to be given access to the share. Replace */full_path_name/on_Linux/server* in the example with the path information for the share, such as */srv/sales*.

```
path = /full_path_name/on_Linux_server
read only = no
valid users = @somegroup
create mask = 0770
directory mask = 0770
force group = somegroup
force create mode = 0770
force directory mode = 0770
level2 oplocks = yes
dos filetimes = yes
```

These settings create a share for a group of users that allows all users access to files created by others in the group. Access is restricted to members of the group.

ADDING FEATURES TO HOMES SHARE

The Homes share can be improved by adding these features, as follows:

```
path = %H
read only = no
valid users = %S
guest ok = no
create mask = 0700
directory mask = 0700
browseable = no
level2 oplocks = yes
dos filetimes = yes
```

Setting Create Mask and Directory Mask to 0700 limits access to the owner. This is similar to setting the permissions on a Windows share to Change for the user and No Access for Everyone or Domain Users.

A Secure Group Share

The basic group share has some security. The Valid Users option limits access to members of a particular group on the Linux server. That is enough to prevent casual browsing of a share.

For some shares, a higher level of security is needed. To create a more secure share, use the following settings:

```
path = /full_path_name/on_Linux_server
read only = no
valid users = @somegroup
hosts allow = 192.168.0. 192.168.10.233 192.168.10.166
browseable = no
create mask = 0770
directory mask = 0770
force group = somegroup
```

```
force create mode = 0770
force directory mode = 0770
level2 oplocks = yes
dos filetimes = yes
```

As you can see, a secure group share isn't much different from the basic group share. There are just a few options added

The Hosts Allow option lets you restrict access to specific machines. The list of allowed hosts includes IP addresses, a range of addresses (the 192.168.0. address in the example includes the entire subnet), or a fully qualified domain name. Samba then checks the IP address of any incoming request and accepts it only if it is in the Hosts Allow list.

Setting Browseable to No means that the share won't show up when users are browsing the network.

A Public Directory

A public directory is a share to which all users will have access. Public directories have some unique problems. After all, how much security can a share have if it is public?

There are two settings that help secure a public directory. First, set the directory so that only the owner of a file can delete that file. In addition, if necessary, the share can be set so that only the owner of each file can modify that file.

Second, prevent applications from being launched from the share. There are many difficulties with launching applications from a share. Often an application that is placed on a public share is not properly set up for network use or is in violation of the license agreement for the software. Applications should be run only from shares that have been set up for that purpose.

One other issue with public shares is that they can easily become the source for files infected with Windows vbs viruses or other similar kinds of viruses. Public shares must be regularly scanned by anti-virus software, either from your Windows workstation or from the Linux machine. Most anti-virus software, such as McAfee Anti-Virus, have a Linux version that will find Windows viruses in files on a Linux system.

The first step to create a public directory is to create a directory with the permissions set to 1666, that is, with the Sticky Bit turned on and read-write but not execute permissions for all possible users. Enabling the Sticky Bit means that only the owner of the file can delete the file. These settings can be enabled in the Webmin File Manager, as detailed in "Setting Up Shares" on using Webmin to create directories for shares. Usually a public share uses a directory named *public*. If you've set off a part of the Linux server for the Samba shares, such as a directory named *srv,* put the public directory in there. If you are using Webmin, use the Sharing button to create the share. This creates a share with the name of the directory. The share is then ready to configure.

A BASIC PUBLIC DIRECTORY

Use the following configuration options to set up a basic public directory, replacing the pathname with the correct path for your server:

```
path = /srv/Public
read only = no
create mask = 0666
directory mask = 0666
level2 oplocks = yes
dos filetimes = yes
```

The Create Mask and Directory Mask settings of 0666 remove the execute permission and therefore prevent execution of applications from the share.

A LIMITED PUBLIC DIRECTORY

To make a public directory with user read-write access and group read-only access that prevents files from being modified by anyone except the owner of the file, use these options:

```
path = /srv/Public
read only = no
create mask = 0644
directory mask = 0644
level2 oplocks = yes
dos filetimes = yes
```

Just changing the Create Mask and Directory Mask settings to 0644 means that only the owner of a file can modify it. The directory already has the Sticky Bit turned on, preventing anyone but the owner from deleting a file.

A SECURED PUBLIC DIRECTORY

A public directory can be secured by limiting access to a group like the users group. Then make sure that all the users are members of the group. These are the options for a public directory secured by membership in the users group:

```
path = /srv/Public
read only = no
valid users = @users
hosts allow = 192.168.0.
force group = users
create mask = 0640
```

```
directory mask = 0640
level2 oplocks = yes
dos filetimes = yes
```

The Valid Users option limits access to only members of the group named "users." The @ symbol in front of the name indicates that it is a group and not an individual user. The Hosts Allow option limits access to only machines on the 192.168.0. subnet. The Force Group option means that all files in the directory will be associated with the users group; it is not associated with the group of the user who created the file. The Create Mask and Directory Mask setting of 0640 means that only the owner of the file can make changes or save modifications to the file, while members of the group have read-only access. All others are denied access to the file.

Adding Guest Access

Anonymous or guest access is built into Windows networking. Some functions, such as printer sharing, require it. Other functions, such as getting usernames or share lists, also require guest access on networks without a domain controller. However, guest access for file shares is inherently insecure and should generally be avoided, though it is not always possible to do so.

Following are the Samba options that can be changed from their defaults in order to allow guest access to a file share.

On the Globals page in SWAT, change the guest account and the Map to Guest option.

GUEST ACCOUNT

This is the username that Samba uses for anonymous guest connections. This must be a valid user on the Linux server if guest access is to be allowed. The default guest user is the username "nobody." This is a default user account on Linux servers that has no access rights. A special guest account should be created that has read and write access rights. The public share directory is usually the home directory for the guest account.

Map to Guest

This is a global option that controls guest access. If it is not changed from the default setting of Never, guest access will be denied no matter how other guest options are changed. The Never setting blocks all access without a valid username and password. Change this to Bad User, which means that Samba rejects login attempts if a valid username is given but a bad password is used. If the username is invalid, Samba maps the access to the guest user.

On the Shares page in SWAT, select the share that is to have guest access, and change these options:

Guest Only

Setting this option to Yes means that only the guest user can access the share. This setting requires that Guest OK be set to Yes, or it won't be enabled.

Guest OK

Setting this option to Yes means that guest users can access the shares. Usernames and passwords will not be required for the share. The Guest OK option will not work if the Map to Guest option is set to Never.

Sharing CD-ROMs and Removable Devices

CD-ROMs and removable devices like Zip disks can be shared on a Samba server. Like a file share, sharing these media devices is a two-step process. First the device must be made accessible in Linux. Then it is made shareable in Samba.

Unlike a Windows system, a CD-ROM or Zip disk inserted into a Linux server is not immediately accessible. After the disks have been inserted into the drive, the drive has to be mounted. On most Linux desktop systems, there is an automounter utility that will perform this function automatically, as on a Windows system. On most Linux servers, mounting is a manual task. Samba gets around this restriction by executing a Mount command any time the share is accessed, so that manual mounting is not necessary.

A CD-ROM Share

Before creating a CD-ROM share in Samba, make sure that the CD-ROM is accessible to all users in Linux. On Red Hat Linux and Caldera OpenLinux, the default mount point for the CD-ROM—the directory on the Linux server where the drive is to be mounted and where users will access the drive—is /mnt/cdrom. On Debian GNU/Linux, the mount point is /cdrom.

Using the Webmin File Manager, check the permissions on the CD-ROM mount point. On a Red Hat system, for example, click on the *mnt* folder in the left panel. Select the *cdrom* folder in the right panel and click on the Info button on Webmin's menu bar. The permissions need to be set so that read and list are enabled for the user, the group, and others. Figure 3-9 shows the correct settings in the Webmin File Manager.

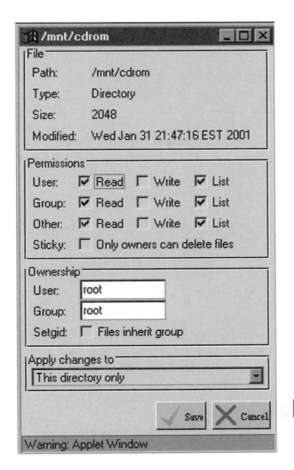

Figure 3-9 *The CD-ROM permissions should be set to enable read and list for the user, group, and others.*

In SWAT, create a new share named *cdrom*. The share needs only a few settings, including the Root Prexec and Root Postexec commands. These two options are used to specify a command that executes on the Samba server any time a user connects to or disconnects from a share. They are used to execute the Linux Mount and Umount commands. The configuration options for a CD-ROM share are

```
path = /mnt/cdrom
read-only = yes
browseable = yes
```

```
root preexec = mount /mnt/cdrom
root postexec = umount /mnt/cdrom
```

This setup works for single-user access to the CD-ROM. If multiple users access the CD-ROM with this configuration, the drive is unmounted when any user closes access to the share. If multiple users will be accessing the CD-ROM, do not use the Preexec and Postexec options, but otherwise leave the configuration the same. The disks then must be manually mounted by the system administrator. This can be done at the Linux server using the same commands: `mount /mnt/cdrom` to mount the disk and `umount /mnt/cdrom` to dismount the disk.

A Removable Device Share

For a removable device such as a Zip disk, first make sure that the disk is accessible in Linux. As with a CD-ROM, the permissions on a removable device have to be set so that all users can access the device. In addition to the read and list permissions, give write permission to the user, group, and others. The usual mount point for a Zip drive on Red Hat Linux and Caldera OpenLinux is */mnt/zip,* and on Debian GNU Linux it is */zip.* Use the Webmin File Manager to check the permissions on the mount point. If the mount point is not there, consult the documentation for the server and the version of Linux used on the server for information on making the Zip drive accessible and creating the mount point.

In SWAT, create a new share. For a Zip drive, you might want to call the share *zip* or *zip_drive.* The share settings are similar to those for a CD-ROM, including the Root Prexec and Root Postexec commands. The configuration options for a Zip drive share are

```
path = /mnt/zip
read-only = no
browseable = yes
root preexec = mount /mnt/zip
root postexec = umount /mnt/zip
```

This share has the same limitation as the CD-ROM share using the Preexec and Postexec options. It is good only for a single user. For multiuser access, remove those options and manually mount the Zip disks.

Sharing a Microsoft Access Database

Almost every office computer comes with Microsoft Access installed, and Access databases have mushroomed. Many medium-sized and smaller offices now depend on shared Access databases. With a few modifications to the basic group share, Samba can be set up for sharing an Access database. It is best to put a database on its own share because the file locking needs for a database are different than they are for word processing documents or most other kinds of files. Opportunistic locking should be turned off for a database because it will degrade performance, while Oplocks can improve performance for shared applications running from a Samba server.

The first step is to create the directory on the Linux server for the database share. Creating a directory can be done with the Webmin File Manager. If you use Webmin to create the directory on the server, use the File Manager's Sharing button to create the share. This creates a share with the name of the directory. Then proceed to configure the share in SWAT.

Access also needs to be configured. Make sure that the database is set to be opened in shared mode.

To configure a share for a database that is readable by all users but can be modified by a few users, apply the following settings to the share in SWAT:

```
path = /full_path_name/on_Linux_server
read only = yes
write list = user1 user2 @data
create mask = 0666
directory mask = 0777
force create mode = 0666
force directory mode = 0777
oplocks = no
veto oplock files = /*.mdb/*.MDB/*.ldb/*.LDB/
dos filetimes = yes
```

The path must be set to the path on the Linux server, and the share must be writable, so Read Only is set to No.

Who can modify the database is then controlled by the write list. In the example configuration, User1 and User2 have permission to modify the database, as does anyone in the "data" group. Any combination of usernames and group names can be used to finely control who is able to modify the database.

Access uses a lock file (*.ldb*) whenever someone opens the database. The lock file is created as that user. For concurrent access, when another user opens the database the lock file is updated to announce the presence of the new user. The Create Mask, Directory Mask, Force Create Mode, and Force Directory Mode settings prevent permission restrictions from interfering with updates to the lock file.

If you leave Oplocks on for an Access database, then each client will try to cache the whole database file onto its local disk. As soon as a second client connects to the database, the cache is invalidated and has to be written back to the server. The performance will significantly degrade as more users connect to the database. So turn off Oplocks. The Veto Oplock Files setting is also used to prevent Oplocks on all Access files (*.mdb*) and the lock files (*.ldb*).

This share is readable by all users on the local network. Restrictions can be added by including the Valid Users option, setting the users to a group or a list of users.

Application Sharing

Many applications can be run from a network server. This has some advantages, particularly when it comes time to upgrade a program or install a service pack. The default installation method for most software is for an individual workstation. If you are going to run an application from the server, make sure that you follow the manufacturer's instructions for a network installation. Sometimes this means getting a network edition of the software.

For most Microsoft Office products, an administrative installation onto a network drive can be used either for installing the software onto workstation clients or for running the applications from the server. Consult the documentation that came with the software for instructions on an administrative installation.

Before an administrative installation can begin, a share must be created on the Samba server. A basic group share, as detailed earlier in "Setting Up Shares," is all that is necessary for the initial installation. Make sure that the share has been allocated sufficient space, since applications like Microsoft Office can be quite large.

After the share has been created, install the software using the administrative installation process. The installation must be made before completing Samba's configuration. That's because after Samba is configured, write access will be blocked to the share.

After the administrative installation has completed, set the following options for the share in SWAT:

```
path = /full_path_name/on_Linux_server
volume = The_CD-ROM_label
read only = yes
share modes = no
locking = no
```

The CD-ROM label for Microsoft Office 2000 is *Msoffice2000*, for example. When a Windows client opens a file, it uses share modes to lock the file. This locking prevents other clients from accessing the file until the lock is released. For a shared application, locking is not only unnecessary, it breaks the system. Locking blocks all but one user from the application. With the options set to disable locking and make the share read-only, the share is ready to use either for running the application from the server or for installing the application from the server.

If you are running an application from the server, templates should be kept on a separate share. Workgroup templates can be put on a read-only share or a writable share, but user templates must be on a writable share or on the user's local machine.

The Samba Print Server

Samba print servers may be almost as widely installed as Samba file servers. Printer sharing can be run on the same server with file sharing, or on standalone print servers. Cisco Systems, for example, has 300 print servers running Samba and Linux, handling more than 6,000 printers worldwide.

Cisco replaced a combination of Windows NT and Sun servers handling printer sharing with Intel-based PCs and found that the Samba-Linux solution was not only more stable but also more flexible. The company developed its own open source management software that allows a user in any office to print to a local printer or any of the other printers in any other office worldwide. The whole story, along with the management software—the Cisco Enterprise Print System (CEPS)—can be found on the Web at *ceps.sourceforge. net*. It's a complex management system, so complex that it is probably worth the effort to learn and install only if you have several hundred printers or more to support.

Samba printer services are not that complex to install or maintain, and there is every reason to use Samba for all of your printer servers. Print services can be run from a Samba file server or from a standalone print server, as is often done when there are more than a couple of printers being shared on the network.

TIP — WINDOWS 2000 AND PRINT SERVERS

Even if your entire office is running Windows 2000, there is no necessity to have a Windows 2000 print server. The print server doesn't have to be Windows 2000–aware or interoperate with Windows 2000. There are no compatibility issues. It doesn't matter which version of Samba you use, though you'll probably prefer the advanced features introduced in Samba 2.2.

The primary factor to consider in setting up printer sharing is the expected load. Printer sharing can be on the same Samba server set up for file sharing. However, unless there are only a handful of printers to be supported, you should consider putting print services on a dedicated server. The frequent disk accesses involved in printing, particularly with large documents, can tie up a server and significantly degrade response from a file server.

A dedicated print server can be set up on any computer, even older Intel 386 or 486 systems. The speed of the hard drive and the amount of system memory (RAM) will affect performance more than the speed of the central processing unit (CPU).

Even if you use network-ready printers with built-in Ethernet connections, such as HP's JetDirect, you can improve overall printing performance with a Samba print server. Spooled printing from a Samba print server to a printer's Ethernet port can be up to 20% faster than printing directly from client workstations to the printer. That's because of the many variable factors involved when printing from a client workstation as opposed to a dedicated print server.

How Samba Print Sharing Works

Samba doesn't actually handle printing. When a Windows client prints a document to a printer that appears on a Samba print server, Samba accepts the document and then passes it along.

You don't actually set up printers in Samba, and there's little in Samba to configure for printer sharing, Samba finds printers to share from what is set up on the Linux server. Most of the configuration work is in Linux. This can be done with Webmin's printer administration tools.

What you see when printers are displayed on the Samba print server in the Network Neighborhood/My Network Places is a list of printers that are configured on the Linux system.

The Samba print server can access a printer in one of three ways. A printer can be connected directly to a printer port on the Samba server. It can be connected to a user's workstation and made available for sharing. Or a standalone printer that has its own built-in Ethernet connection, such as a Jet-Direct card, can be used.

Set Spool Permissions

Samba's printer sharing won't work if the perrmissions on the Samba spool directory are not correctly set. This is the most common reason for printer sharing problems on new Samba installations.

The spool directory must be writable by everyone, but set so that only the owner of a file can delete the file. The octal number for setting these permissions in Linux is 1777. Failure to set the correct permissions for the spool directory is one of the most common reasons for printing to fail on newly installed Samba print servers.

The permissions can be checked and corrected with the Webmin File Manager, accessed on the Others tab in Webmin. The printer spool directory for Red Hat Linux and Debian GNU Linux is */var/spool/samba*. For Caldera OpenLinux, the spool directory is */var/spool/samba.d*.

In the Webmin File Manager, select the folder for the Samba spool in the right panel. Then click the Info button on the menu bar and change the permissions so that read, write, and list access are enabled for the owner, group, and others. Check that the Sticky bit is enabled so that only owners can delete files, as shown in Figure 4-1.

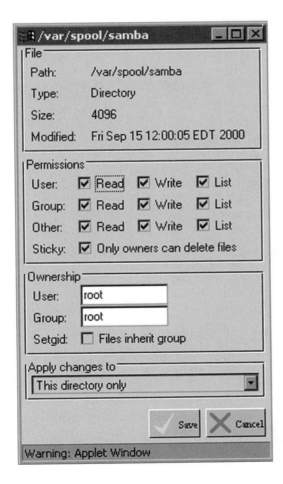

Figure 4-1   *Enable full access to the user, group, and others, and turn on the Sticky Bit.*

Configuring Printer Sharing

Whether a printer is attached to the Samba print server, to a user's workstation, or with a JetDirect connection, there are four steps to setting up a printer share. Give the printer share a name and description; tell Linux where the printer is connected; create the spool directory; and save the configuration information. All this can be done with Webmin. The printers are set up with Webmin's Printer Administration tool, and the permissions for the spool directory are set with the File Manager.

Webmin's Printer Administration Tool Settings

Before starting, check Webmin and make sure it is correctly configured for your server. In Webmin, on the Hardware tab, open the Printer Administration tool. Select the link at the top of the page labeled Module Config. Figure 4-2 shows the configuration page for the Webmin Printer Administration tool.

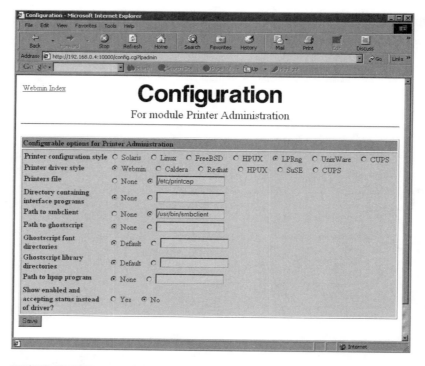

Figure 4-2   *Configuration page for Webmin's Printer Administration tool.*

Normally there should be nothing to change on the configuration. There are four settings to check: Printer Configuration Style; Printer Driver Style; Printers File; and Path to smbclient. These should all be set based on the defaults for the Linux distribution. If you've changed the server from the default configuration or changed print-spooling software, then make sure Webmin is updated for those changes.

Linux has three different print-spooling software packages. LPD is the original printer daemon. It's called BSD in Samba's configuration settings and labeled generically as Linux in Webmin. LPD is a basic print spooler with no extra features. The other two print-spooling packages—LPRng and the Common Unix Printing System (CUPS)—add many features, particularly capabilities needed for network print servers. LPRng is an enhanced version of LPD that supports multiple printers, including redirecting print queues to network printers. CUPS is a standardized printing system for all Unix systems, including Linux. It is designed in particular for use with network print servers. CUPS includes a print queue monitor that can be accessed from any Web browser.

Red Hat Linux 6.2 and older versions, as well as Debian GNU/Linux, use the original LPD software. Red Hat 7.0 and newer, as well as Caldera OpenLinux 2.4 and older versions, install LPRng as the default printing software. Newer versions of Caldera OpenLinux, starting with version 3.1, use CUPS.

Make sure that Webmin's Printer Configuration Style setting is correct for the Linux distribution you use. If you've changed the default printing software, then make sure that the Webmin settings are updated.

The Printer Driver Style setting must either match the Linux distribution or be set to Webmin. If you've changed the printer software from the default for your Linux distribution, then choose Webmin. Webmin is always a safe choice, since Linux printer drivers are not needed for Samba print queues. This setting determines the list of possible print drivers that will be displayed when adding a printer in Webmin. This is similar to the list of print drivers shown when adding a printer in Windows. Since all the printing will come from Windows clients using Windows print drivers, no Linux print drivers will be installed.

The *Printers* file is the printer configuration file on the Linux system. The default setting for LPD and LPRng is Printcap. If you are using CUPS, the *printers* file should say lpstat.

The Path to smbclient is for the Samba utility for printing from Linux on a Windows system. The smbclient utility is used when you configure a printer on the Samba print server that is connected to a Windows workstation. The location for smbclient on most Linux distributions is */usr/bin/smbclient*.

With configuration completed, Webmin is ready to use for printer installation. Select Printer Administration from the Webmin Hardware tab. Any time a new printer is added, the printer daemon on Linux must be restarted before the new printer is available, and Samba must be restarted as well. That's be-cause Samba only knows about the printers that were available when it was started up; it can't see any new printers that may have been added.

To add a printer, click on the Add a New Printer link in Webmin. The steps that follow are similar to the steps that you follow when adding a printer to a Windows system.

Step 1: Name the Printer Share

The first step in creating a printer share is to give it a name and description, as shown in Figure 4-3.

The name is the name for this printer configuration. The name is re-quired. It should be no more than eight characters and cannot include any spaces. The naming convention you use for printers can be anything from the simply functional, like printer1, printer2, and so on, to the descriptive, like HP8100 or Room424. This name is also the label that appears with the Printer

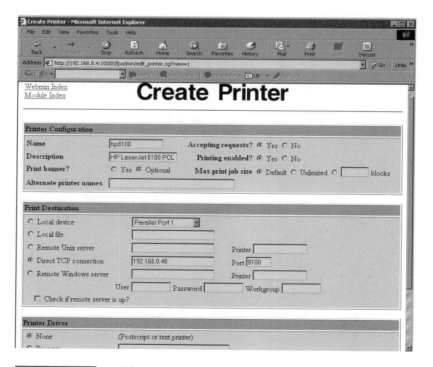

Figure 4-3   *Add a printer, starting with the name and description. Then choose the connection.*

icon when browsing the Samba server on the network, so a descriptive label is usually better.

The description, an optional setting, is what appears when you get a detailed view when browsing.

Step 2: Choose a Connection

The next step is to set how the printer is accessed. Is it a local printer connected to the server? Or is it a remote printer connected to either a Windows host or an Ethernet print-spooling device such as a JetDirect card? Select the correct setting, and then enter the configuration parameters. Figure 4-2 shows the settings for a printer with a built-in JetDirect card.

Local Device

The local device is a parallel port or serial port on the server.

Direct TCP Connection

A direct TCP connection is a printer that has a built-in JetDirect Ethernet connection or is connected to a print-spooling device such as a JetDirect box. The first parameter is the IP address of the JetDirect device. The TCP port number for the JetDirect is 9100. For JetDirect boxes with multiple ports, the first port is 9100, the second port is 9101, and so on. For similar print-spooling devices, check the manufacturer's documentation for the port number.

Remote Windows Server

For a printer connected to a Windows system on the local network, either a user's workstation or another server, use this option. It sets up a printing script that uses Samba's smbclient utility to print to the remote Windows system. The first parameter is the NetBIOS name of the machine with the printer share, the name that appears when you browse the Network Neighborhood/My Network Places. The printer name is the name of the share. A valid user, password, and workgroup for accessing the share should be entered.

Step 3: Create the Spool Directory

The third step is to confirm the configuration and save the printer configuration. This will also create the spool directory. Make sure that the Webmin configuration setting for the printer driver is set to None.

Linux printer documentation has several different names to refer to setting up a printer without a driver. It might be called a raw printer, a PostScript printer, or a text printer. All mean the same thing. There is no Linux printer driver associated with the printer. Everything is passed unchanged from the Windows client to the Linux printer spool and from there to the printer.

With the printer name and destination chosen and the printer driver set to None, click on the Create button. This saves the printer configuration, and the spool directory is created.

The printer is now created and ready to go. Test it from Webmin's Printer Administration page by selecting the List link in the Jobs category. This opens the page that shows any jobs currently in the print queue. Click on the Print Test Page button. Unless the printer is a PostScript printer, choose Plain ASCII Text and click on the Print Page button. If the page does not print, check your settings and make sure they are configured correctly.

When the printer is tested and working, restart the printer daemon on Linux. To do this, you can click on the Stop Scheduler button on the Webmin Printer Administration page and then click the Start Scheduler button. The new printer is now available in Linux. Samba won't know about it until the next time Samba starts. You can restart Samba from either the Webmin Samba Share Manager page or SWAT. When that is done, the new printer will be available to users on the network.

Configuring Samba for Printer Support

There are some options in the Globals section of SWAT that are necessary for printer support, and there is a single configuration file in the Printers section that has overall settings for the printers handled by the Samba server. In the Globals section, check the following options. For most of the options, no changes are necessary.

Printer Admin

Like the Admin Users list, this is a list of users who are granted administrator access to printer configuration. If a username is listed as a Printer Admin, that user's operations on printer shares will be performed as the root user. In SWAT, type in the usernames for users that are to be given printer administrator access.

Load Printers

This option sets whether or not all printers installed in Linux will be loaded when Samba starts up. The default setting is Yes.

Printcap Name

This option sets the name of the Linux printer definition file. For BSD and LPRng, this setting is usually */etc/printcap*. For CUPS, there isn't a configuration file; instead, a program is run that returns the printer information. The program is lpstat, which is what should be entered as the parameter for this option for CUPS printing.

Printing

This option sets the name of the printing system used on your Linux server. Although many options are shown on the drop-down menu, most of them are for other Unix systems. For Linux the most common printing systems are BSD, LPRng, and CUPS.

Starting with version 7.0, Red Hat Linux uses LPRng as its default printing software. This is also used by Caldera OpenLinux version 2.4 and older. Newer versions of Caldera OpenLinux use CUPS. Older versions of Red Hat Linux and Debian GNU/Linux use the original BSD software.

Print Command

When Samba accepts a print job, it places the job in the Samba spool directory, usually */var/spool/samba* or */var/spool/lpd/samba*. The Print command option sets the command used to send the print job to the printer. Usually this command will take the print job from the Samba spool directory and move it to the spool directory for the specified printer and then start the process of sending the file to the printer. The print command for BSD and LPRng is

```
lpr  -P%p -r %s
```

The default print command for CUPS is

```
lp -d %p -o raw %s; rm -f %s
```

lpq Command

This option sets the command to get the status of any documents in the printer queue and printing progress. The lpq command for BSD, LPRng, and CUPS is

```
lpq  -P%p
```

lprm Command

This option sets the command to remove a print job from the specified printer. The lprm command for BSD, LPRng and CUPS is

```
lprm -P%p %j
```

Overall printer configuration is set in the Printers section of SWAT. It can be accessed by selecting the Printers link in SWAT and choosing the share named Printers from the drop down menu. This is not a printer but is the configuration file for all printers handled by the Samba server.

There are several options for the Printers configuration. The defaults will probably work for most situations and won't need to be changed. Following is a description of some of the most important options.

Path

This option sets the location where files sent to Samba for printing are placed. This location must have enough disk space to accommodate as many spooled documents as you expect to handle simultaneously. The default location in Red Hat Linux is */var/spool/samba;* in Caldera Open-Linux it is */var/spool/samba.d*. In Debian GNU/Linux the default location is */var/spool/lpd/samba*.

Hosts Allow and Hosts Deny

These options are used in the same way they are used in file shares, to limit access to the printer shares to a subnet or to a few particular machines. Enter the IP address or the fully qualified domain name that you want to grant or deny access to the Samba printer shares.

Printable

This option is used to indicate that a share is a printer share, to distinguish it in the Samba configuration from a file share. The Printers share is a printer share, even though it is a unique share and not an actual printer. It should be set to Yes.

Browseable

If the printer shares are to be seen in the Network Neighborhood/My Network Places, then Browseable needs to be set to Yes.

Customizing Individual Printers

Sometimes it is necessary to modify the options for a particular printer, separate from the options set in the Printers share. For example, you may want to limit access to a printer that is used to print out confidential financial reports or personnel information, or you may want to restrict use of an expensive color laser printer.

To enter option changes for a specific printer, you can use the Webmin Samba Share Manager. Use the link to create a new printer share, and create a new share with the same name as the printer you want to modify. Figure 4-4 shows the settings for creating a new printer share that will modify the default settings for an existing share.

After entering the name of the printer, in the drop-down menu by the Unix printer setting choose the printer you want to modify. The spool directory should be the spool directory for the printer, not the Samba spool directory. The name of the directory usually matches the name of the printer.

The printer should be available. The Browseable parameter is optional. If you want to hide the printer from network browsing, set Browseable to No.

Clicking the Create button will create the modified printer configuration. The printer will appear in the shares list on the Samba Share Manager page in Webmin. Select the share by clicking on its name so that you can make any necessary modifications.

To limit access to the printer, click on the Security and Access Control button. The usual way to limit access is to list valid users. You can list individual user names or a group name, which is preceded by a @ symbol, for example, "@accounts." Make sure to save any configuration changes.

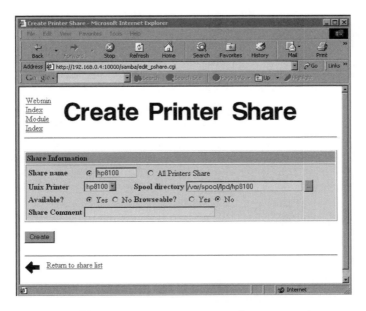

Figure 4-4   *Use Create Printer Share for customized printer settings.*

Accessing Samba Print Shares from Windows

Accessing printer shares on a Samba server from a Windows machine is like accessing standard Windows network printers. In order to print from Windows, a printer driver must be installed on the Windows client machine.

Installing Printers Using the Add Printer Wizard

The usual method for installing a printer is to use the Add Printer Wizard found on all versions of Windows from 95 to 2000. The procedure is the same for installing a printer for a Samba server or a Windows server. Follow these steps:

1. From the Windows Start button, go to Settings and select Printers.

2. Double-click on the Add Printers icon, which starts the Add Printer Wizard.

3. Click Next after the welcome message is displayed, and choose Network printer.

4. After clicking the Next button, select the option to type in the printer name or browse to find the printer on the local network. Either way, the name of the printer share will appear as shown in Figure 4-5, with a double backslash followed by the name of the server and a single backslash with the name of the printer. On Windows 9*x*/Me/NT systems, there is also an option to print from MS-DOS programs. If you have older DOS-based programs, select Yes to be able to print to this printer. The printing is redirected through a parallel port to the network printer since DOS programs don't know anything about networking and only know how to print to parallel ports. Then click Next.

5. Choose a printer driver from the list of manufacturers and printer models. When you click on Next, if a driver for that printer is already installed on the computer, you will be prompted with a message asking if you want to keep the existing driver. If you are unsure, then select Yes to keep the existing driver.

6. Name the printer. This is a name that will appear with the Printer icon in the printers folder on this computer. Click Next and choose whether to print a test page. After making your selection, click the Finish button to complete the installation.

When you click the Finish button, the Add Printer Wizard will install the driver for the printer, if the driver doesn't already exist. The driver can be installed from the Windows system installation CD or a disk with the driver on it from the manufacturer.

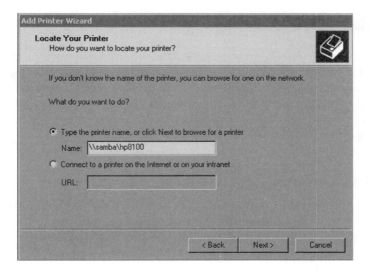

Figure 4-5	*Enter the name of the printer in the Add Printer Wizard.*

Installing Printers from the Network Neighborhood/My Network Places

Another way to install printers is to browse the Network Neighborhood/My Network Places and find the printer you want to use. Double-click on the Printer icon, and then follow these steps:

1. After selecting whether to enable printing from MS-DOS programs, click on Next. Then choose a printer driver from the list of manufacturers and printer models. When you click on Next, if a driver for that printer is already installed on the computer, you will be prompted with a message asking if you want to keep the existing driver. If you are unsure, then select Yes to keep the existing driver. The final steps are the same as for installation with the Add Printer Wizard.

2. Name the printer and click Next. Then choose whether to print a test page. After making your selection, click the Finish button to complete the installation.

Windows will install the driver for the printer, if the driver doesn't already exist. The driver can be installed from the Windows CD or a manufacturer's disk.

Automatic Printer Driver Installation

Samba version 2.2 introduced support for Windows NT printing services, in-cluding automatic printer driver installation on client machines. This feature was contributed by developers at Hewlett Packard, the company that makes many of the network printers used in offices around the world, HP's John Reilly has become a key contributor to Samba. As with any major new fea-ture, the first version has some bugs to be worked out. If you want to use this feature, make sure you have the latest version of Samba available.

Configure Samba for Automatic Printer Services

Before the automatic printer driver installation, make sure that you have a working print server with at least one working printer that users can success-fully access. To set up automatic printer driver installation, a special share will have to be created on the Samba server with its own directory on the server for holding printer drivers, and a printer administrator account will have to be assigned to handle administrative tasks.

ADD A PRINTER ADMINISTRATOR

The automatic printer services will require a printer administrator who can add the Windows drivers for installation from the Samba server and set per-missions for accessing the printer drivers. On the Globals page of SWAT, se-lect the Advanced View so that you can find Printer Admin in the Security Options section.

Enter a username or a list of names. A group can be added by preced-ing the name with a @ symbol, such as "@pradmin." Any user who is a printer administrator will have the access rights of the root user on the Linux system so that the printer drivers can be uploaded and user permissions set.

CREATE A *PRINTERS* DIRECTORY

A directory must be created that will hold the printer drivers. This directory can be anywhere that is accessible to users on your Samba server. If you are using a directory named *srv* for shared folders for groups, that would be a good location. Name the directory *printers*. You can use the Webmin File Manager to create the directory. In the next steps for setting up automatic printer services, the instructions will use a *printers* folder in the *srv* directory. If you set up your *printers* folder in another location, you will have to adjust the steps to use the location you've chosen. The path for the new *printers* folder, as set up here, is */srv/printers*.

In the *printers* directory, there must be a set of subdirectories that will hold the printer drivers. The name of each directory must exactly match the name shown here. Following are the names of the folders and a description of the driver version each will hold. You need to use only the folder for the driver versions necessary for your network.

Folder	Driver Version
W32X86	Window NT/2000 x86
WIN40	Windows 9*x*
W32ALPHA	Windows NT/2000 Alpha AXP
W32MIPS	Windows NT/2000 R4000
W32PPC	Windows NT/2000 PowerPC

SET PERMISSIONS

The *printers* folder and its subfolders must be readable by everyone and writable by the printer administrator. If there is more than one administrator, then you should create a Printer Admin group and give the group write permission for the *printers* folder. The octal number for permissions that will give write access to the owner and the group, with read access for everyone else, is 0775. Set permissions in the Webmin File Manager, selecting the *printers* folder and setting the permissions to grant read, write, and list access to the owner and group, with others set to read and list. Set the ownership at the same time, as shown in Figure 4-6, where ownership for the group is set to "pradmin," a group that was set up for printer administrators. If there is only a single printer administrator and no printer administrator's group, then set the ownership of the folder to the username for the printer administrator.

CREATE A PRINT$ SHARE

A special share is required for automatic print services. This share is named print$. It can be created in SWAT on the Shares page, not on the Printers page. This is the share that will hold the printer drivers and is not a printer. In SWAT, type in the name "print$." Make sure the name is correct; it cannot vary. After the share has been created, set the following options:

```
path = /srv/printers
guest ok = yes
browseable = yes
read only = yes
write list = @pradmin
```

Of course, use the path to your *printers* folder, if it is different. The write list should be the same as the printer administrator list. Any user listed in the write lists will be able to write to the share even though it is marked to be read-only. Write access will be needed to save drivers to the share.

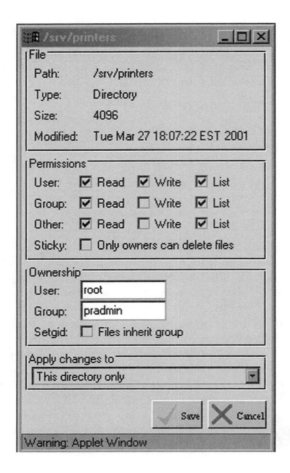

Figure 4-6   *Permission settings for a printers directory.*

Install Printers and Drivers

Once Samba has been configured for automatic printer services, then the printers must be set up and the drivers installed. This is where the printer administrator takes over. There are three basic steps for installing printers and drivers:

- Install the printers to be accessed on the Samba print server.
- Upload the drivers for the printers.
- Configure the printers.

All three steps must be completed before automatic printer services will work. This can be done one printer at a time or for several printers at once.

INSTALL THE PRINTER

Follow the steps given earlier in this chapter on installing a printer. The printer must be installed on the Linux system and working from Linux before it will be accessible in Samba. You can use Webmin to create the printer. After the printer has been created, make sure to restart the printer daemon on Linux and to restart Samba to force it to immediately see the new printer.

UPLOAD THE DRIVERS

The second step is to upload the drivers. This can be done only by the printer administrator from a Windows NT 4 or Windows 2000 system. Also, you will need the CD for the Windows NT 4 Server or Windows 2000 Server. The printer drivers will be taken from this disk. Only the server disk has all the necessary drivers. The workstation versions of NT and 2000 do not have drivers for other versions of Windows. If you don't have the server disk, then you will only be able to load the drivers for Windows NT 4 or Windows 2000 systems, whichever you have.

In the Network Neighborhood/My Network Places, go to the Samba server. When you access the server, there should be a folder named *printers*. That is the print$ share. If the folder doesn't appear, then you have probably not accessed the server as the printer administrator, or you are on a Windows 9*x* system.

Open the *printers* folder. All of the installed printers should appear in the folder. In the Model field there should be a message for each printer that says, "No Driver Available for This Printer." Right-click in the folder and select Server Properties.

Go to the Drivers tab. Click on the Add button to start the Add Printer Driver Wizard. Click on Next after the welcome message opens. Choose the manufacturer and model, just as you would for a Windows workstation. After selecting, click Next and then choose the versions that you want to install on the Samba server, Windows 95 or 98, Windows NT, Windows 2000, and so on. Then click Next. The final panel shows a description of what will be installed; make sure it is correct. Then press Finish. You will be prompted to enter the CD with the drivers, and then the drivers will be installed on the Samba server. The properties for the drivers can also be set, if you need to limit access.

CONFIGURE THE PRINTERS

After the drivers have been installed on the Samba server, each printer needs to be configured with a driver. In the *printers* folder, right-click on the printer icon and select Properties. An error message will appear, indicating that the device settings cannot be displayed because there is no driver associated with the printer. The message asks if you would like to install a driver. Click on No because you won't be able to associate a driver with the printer this way. The printer Properties box will open; select the Advanced tab. In the space for a Driver, the "No Driver Available for This Printer" message will appear. From the drop-down menu, choose the appropriate driver for the printer, and then click on the Apply button.

Automatic printer services should then be completely set up and ready to go. Users should be able to access a printer in the Network Neighborhood/My Network Places and the driver will be automatically installed, if necessary.

Advanced Topics

Networking is seldom simple. Most network administrators find that either the users or their bosses are asking for more than the basic services. That's another area where Samba shines. In fact, some of Samba's advanced features aren't even available on a Windows server.

For a network that does not have a Windows domain controller, Samba can be set up as a logon server, providing many if not all of the services provided by a domain controller. This has all features that are most commonly used on a domain controller, including central user authentication, logon scripts, and user profiles.

Security is another issue that concerns both administrators and users. Samba includes support for secure connections using Secure Sockets Layer (SSL), the same technology used for secure financial transactions on the Internet. This can only be done with Samba servers; it's not an option on Windows servers.

Other advanced topics are covered in this chapter:

* Setting up virtual servers, that is, making one Samba server work and act as if it were several servers
* Internationalization of Samba to support non-English character sets
* Using the Samba server as a network time server
* Setting up fax services on a Samba server
* Accessing a Samba server across subnets on a wide-area network

Using Samba as a Logon Server

For networks with only Windows 9*x*/Me clients, Samba can service domain logons without being configured as a true domain controller. If there are Windows NT/2000 clients, then a true domain controller is necessary—either a Windows domain controller or a Samba server configured as a domain controller. For information on configuring Samba as a domain controller, see Chapter 10.

For Windows 9*x*/Me clients, Samba can be used as a logon server, including support for logon scripts and system policies as well as roaming profiles. Logon scripts, which are Windows batch files, can be used to set up network drive and printer connections. System policies, which are files listing Windows Registry modifications that define what is allowed or restricted, are applied upon login. They perform functions such as restricting access to the control panel. Roaming profiles include a user's preferences, the layout and appearance of the desktop, and the selected printers. These settings are then applied whenever a user logs in from any machine on the network.

Configure Samba for Network Logon Support

Samba must be configured to process network domain logons. Several global options have to be set on the Globals page in SWAT.

Set the security level to user:

```
security = user
```

Encrypted passwords must be enabled:

```
encrypt passwords = yes
```

Tell Samba where the encrypted passwords are kept:

```
smb passwd file = /etc/samba/smbpasswd
```

The default smbpasswd location for Red Hat Linux 7.0 and Debian GNU/Linux is */etc/samba/smbpasswd;* for Caldera OpenLinux, it is */etc/samba.d/smbpasswd*. For Red Hat 6.2 and older versions, it is */etc/smbpasswd*.

Enable domain logons to tell Samba to answer network logon broadcast requests:

```
domain logons = yes
```

Enter the domain name for the Samba server, which is entered as the workgroup name (this cannot be the same name as the computer name for the Samba server):

```
workgroup = domain_name
```

Set Samba to be the domain master browser:

```
domain master = true
preferred master = true
local master = yes
```

If you want to enable user logon scripts, enter

```
logon script = scripts\%U.bat
```

Note that this parameter uses a backslash (\) and not a forward slash. For more information on this topic, see the section on logon scripts later in this chapter.

Set the operating system level high enough that the Samba domain controller will win all browser elections:

```
os level = 64
```

Add a Netlogon Share

All Windows 9*x*/Me clients expect to see a netlogon share when they log onto a domain logon server. The netlogon share does not necessarily contain any data at all; it only has to exist so that the logon can be successful.

It is necessary to create a directory for the netlogon share. This can be done with Webmin's File Manager. If you are using an *srv* directory as the central directory for Samba file shares, create the netlogon directory there.

The Webmin File Manager is located on Webmin's Others tab. Open the File Manager and click on the New Folder button, which is to the right of the Upload button. Type in the name for the new directory, */srv/netlogon*. If you don't already have an *srv* directory, you will need to create that first, or if you are using another location for the netlogon share, then enter that. If you are going to use logon scripts, you can create a scripts directory as well, using the New Folder button and entering */srv/netlogon/scripts*. The netlogon directory must exist for this to work.

Set the permissions for the netlogon directory and the scripts directory, if you created one, so that read, write, and list are enabled for the owner, group, and others.

Then configure a netlogon share in Samba. In SWAT go to the Shares page and create a new share named *netlogon*. Set these options:

```
path = /srv/netlogon
read only = yes
guest ok = no
browseable = no
share modes = no
```

Configure a WINS Server

A network with Windows 9*x*/Me clients and a Samba logon server is usually set up with a WINS server for resolving NetBIOS network names. This is essential if the Samba server and the client machines are on different subnets.

There should be only one WINS server per subnet. The Samba logon server can also be configured as a WINS server, though it does not have to be on the same server.

To make the Samba logon server the WINS server, add the following option to the Globals configuration in SWAT:

```
wins support = yes
```

This parameter tells Samba to operate as a WINS server. There are no additional configuration files or options. Once set, the WINS server begins collecting NetBIOS names and IP addresses. For more information on WINS and NetBIOS name resolution, see Chapter 6. If you've set the Samba server to be a WINS server, do not use the WINS Server option in the Globals configuration settings on SWAT. This option is used to indicate another server that is the WINS server, and if set to point to itself on a Samba WINS server it will cause erratic behavior. Make sure the WINS server setting is blank if you've set the Samba server to be a WINS server.

After setting the Samba server to be a WINS server, make sure that all the Windows clients on the network are set to enable WINS resolution. This is set in the TCP/IP properties for each machine.

THE *LMHOSTS* ALTERNATIVE

An alternative to using WINS is to use a *lmhosts* file on each client. This is a file that contains all of the NetBIOS name resolution information needed for your network. For example, a *lmhosts* file would list the NetBIOS name for the Samba logon server followed by the IP address for the server.

Using *lmhosts* is practical only on the smallest networks. It can quickly become unwieldy because the file must be regularly updated on each machine on the network. To use a *lmhosts* file, create one using the *lmhosts.sam* file found on all Windows computers. The details for what to enter are found in the *lmhosts.sam* file. Do not use both a *lmhosts* file and WINS; doing so could result in login failures.

Add Profile Support

Windows 9*x*/Me domain logons support the use of a roaming profile server for storing user preferences information. The Windows registry uses two databases, one for the system and one for the user. The system database on Windows 9*x*/Me systems is always located in the *windows* directory. The user database is normally there as well, but in the case of roaming profiles it is downloaded from the logon server when the user logs on.

For Windows 9*x*/Me clients, the profile must be stored on the user's home share. (Windows NT/2000 clients do not have this restriction, and their profiles can be anywhere accessible by the client machine.)

The Logon Home option in the Globals section of SWAT contains the client home directory is for user profiles. The default setting is

```
logon home = \\%N\%U
```

The %N variable expands to the NetBIOS name of the Samba server, and the %U variable expands to the user's logon name. To put the user profiles in a hidden directory, use a setting like this:

```
logon home = \\%N\%U\.profile
```

This requires creating a directory named *.profile* in each user's home directory. On the Samba server, a directory with a name that begins with a dot (.) is a hidden directory. Samba translates this as a hidden directory for Windows clients.

For roaming profiles to work, user profiles must be enabled on the Windows client machines. In the Control panel, open the Passwords icon and select the User Profiles tab, as shown in Figure 5-1. Make sure to select the radio button that allows users to customize their preferences. In the User Profile Settings, check the option to include desktop icons. Optionally, you can also check Include Start Menu. Check the Start Menu option only if all the Windows clients on the network are identically configured, with exactly the same programs available on every machine.

When a Windows client is configured to enable user profiles and the machine is configured to log onto a Samba logon server, the local system automatically attempts to access the profile in the user's home directory, as set in Samba's Logon home option. It will save the current profile on the Samba home directory when the user logs out.

Add System Policies

System policies can help in administering a large network with many Windows 9*x*/Me clients. Many of the network and other settings can be set without going to each machine and opening the Control Panel and making each change individually.

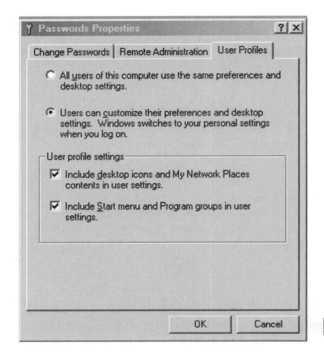

Figure 5-1   *Enabling user profiles in Windows 9x/Me.*

Before adding system policies, make sure that the Samba logon server is working properly.

The Windows policy editor, poledit, is similar to the registry editor, regedit. It is included with the Windows Resource Kit. Instructions on using the policy editor and creating system policies can be found in the "User Profiles and System Policies" chapter of the Windows Resource Kit manual. Use the version of poledit that comes with the most recent version of Windows client on your network. For example, if you have a mix of Windows 95, 98, and Me systems, use the poledit that comes with Windows Me.

The policy editor creates a file named *config.pol*. This file must be saved to the netlogon share on the Samba logon server. Also, make sure that locking is turned off for the netlogon share. In SWAT, go to Shares and select the netlogon share. In the Advanced View set the following:

```
locking = no
```

To use system policies, the Windows 9x/Me client must have user profiles enabled. In addition, each Win9x/Me machine must have the computer policy remote update enabled in its local registry. Use regedit to enable the remote update registry key.

Set *HKLM\System\CurrentControlSet\Control\Update* to a hex value of 1 for automatic remote update. A value of 0 disables the remote update.

Add Logon Scripts

To provide network logon scripts for execution by Windows 9*x*/Me clients, the logon script option must be enabled in the Samba configuration. In SWAT on the Globals page, set this option:

```
logon script = logon.bat
```

The *logon.bat* file is a file you create and place on the netlogon share. The name can be any name you choose and does not have to be *logon.bat*.

The *logon.bat* file should be created on a Windows system and saved as DOS text. If it is created on a Linux system, use a utility like mcopy, which is installed by default on Red Hat Linux, to change the line endings from the Linux default of ending each line with only a line feed to the DOS text default of a carriage return followed by a line feed. Mcopy is part of the mtools utility package. The command is

```
mcopy -t filename
```

If the file is in Linux format, it will be converted to DOS format; if the file is in DOS format, it will be converted to Linux format.

A basic logon batch file can be used to synchronize the clock in the Windows client machine with that of the Samba server and map some drive letters to shares on the Samba server. Following is a sample batch file:

```
@ECHO OFF
REM Synchronize workstation time with Samba server
net time \\SAMBA /SET /YES
REM Map the home directory to drive H:
net use h: /home
REM Map a public share that everyone uses
net use i: \\SAMBA\PUBLIC
REM Connect a printer share
net use LPT1: \\SAMBA\HP8100
```

The settings in this batch file are for a server with the NetBIOS name of the Samba. The Windows clients will run the *logon.bat* batch file immediately after logging on to the network.

Advanced Logon Scripts

On a network with more than a few users, a simple logon script may not be adequate. For a more complex logon script, Samba can be configured to execute a Linux program, such as a Practical Extraction and Reporting Language

(PERL) script, to dynamically generate the logon script. To do this, open SWAT and add the following to the netlogon share options:

```
root preexec = /srv/netlogon/logon.pl %U %G %L
root postexec =  rm /srv/netlogon/%U.bat
```

The Root Preexec and Root Postexec options are used to specify a command that executes on the Samba server whenever a user accesses the share. In this case, it is the netlogon share so that it executes whenever the user logs on. The Root Preexec and Root Postexec options must be used because the share is set to be read-only and the command must therefore be run as root in order to generate a logon script.

The Root Preexec command executes every time a user logs on and generates a logon script using the username (*%U*), the user's primary group (*%G*), and the NetBIOS name of the Samba server (*%L*). The Root Postexec command deletes the generated file after the logon process is completed.

A sample *logon.pl* PERL script for dynamically generating logons follows. If you are using a script like this, it is most useful if each user's primary group is set to a specific workgroup so that shares can be mapped by group.

```perl
#! /usr/bin/perl

# Generate a custom logon script when a user logs into the network

open LOGON, ">/srv/netlogon/$ARGV[0].bat";

# Double slashes are needed since Perl interprets a single \ as a
# control character. The first lines turn off echo and set the time
    print LOGON "\@echo off \r\n";
    print LOGON "NET TIME \\\\$ARGV[2] /SET /YES\r\n";

# Mandatory map to keep netlogon connected during the whole session
    print LOGON "NET USE Y: \\\\$ARGV[2]\\NETLOGON\r\n";

# Map common shares used by all users
    print LOGON "NET USE H: \\\\$ARGV[2]\\$ARGV[0]\r\n";
    print LOGON "NET USE I: \\\\$ARGV[2]\\Public\r\n";
    print LOGON "NET USE J: \\\\$ARGV[2]\\Applications\r\n";

# Map shares based on primary group
    if ($ARGV[1] eq "group1") {
        print LOGON "NET USE K: \\\\$ARGV[2]\\group1\r\n";
    }
    if ($ARGV[1] eq "admin") {
        print LOGON "NET USE K: \\\\$ARGV[2]\\admin\r\n";
    }

# Map printers based on primary group
if ($ARGV[1] eq "group1") {
```

```
     print LOGON "NET USE LPT1: \\\\$ARGV[2]\\HP8100\r\n";
}
if ($ARGV[1] eq "admin") {
     print LOGON "NET USE LPT1: \\\\$ARGV[2]\\HP4050\r\n";
}
```

```
close LOGON;
```

Using Samba Over SSL

Windows networking protocols do not encrypt any data passing over the network, except for passwords. That means that someone on the local network with the right tools could read files being accessed on the network server, whether it is a Windows NT/2000 server or a Samba server.

If you must have high-level security, even on local file transfers, or if you've set up your Windows network to be accessible over the Internet, this can be a major security hole. Samba includes support for secure SSL connections using the same technology employed for secure financial transactions on the Internet.

While Samba can be compiled with SSL support, this feature can't be used directly by Windows clients. Special software is necessary to enable SSL connections between a Windows client and an SSL-enabled Samba server or even an SSL-enabled Windows NT/2000 server.

There is only one Windows client software package that can be used for direct SSL connections from the Windows machine to an SSL-enabled Samba server. That is Sharity, which can be found on the Web at *http:// www.obdev.at/Products/Sharity.html*. Sharity is an expensive commercial product, but it may be worth the price for ease in setting up secure connections.

The other way to use SSL with Windows clients is to use an SSL proxy server such as stunnel, free software under the GPL license that is available on the Web at *www.stunnel.org*. With stunnel, the Windows clients connect to the proxy server in the normal, insecure way and the proxy server then passes the connection to the Samba server using a secure SSL connection. This is the most common way to use SSL with a Samba server.

The setup of SSL on Samba involves a number of steps. One or two of the steps can be skipped if you are using Red Hat Linux 7.0 and newer versions or Caldera's eServer 3.1 or newer. However, the most difficult and time-consuming steps cannot be skipped.

Red Hat Linux 7.0 and newer versions come with an SSL-enabled version of Samba 2.07 and the OpenSSL package installed by default. Caldera's OpenLinux 3.1 also has OpenSSL installed by default, but its version of Samba does not include SSL support.

On other versions of Linux, including earlier versions of Red Hat Linux and Caldera OpenLinux, the SSL package will have to be installed. For all versions of Linux, you should custom-compile Samba for SSL support using the latest version of the Samba source code available on the Samba Headquarters Web site at *www.samba.org*.

After installing OpenSSL, if necessary, and compiling Samba for SSL support, you must configure the Linux server. If you are using the SSL proxy server, then stunnel has to be installed on the Linux machine that is to act as the proxy server, and SSL certificates must be created. Then Samba's SSL options should be set. The final step is to configure the Windows machine to use the stunnel proxy server to access the Samba shares.

Install OpenSSL

Samba uses OpenSSL to provide SSL support on the server side. OpenSSL is included on the CD with most current versions of Linux. The stunnel proxy server also requires OpenSSL. Perform the installation on both the Samba server and the separate Linux server that will act as the stunnel proxy server.

Both Red Hat Linux 7.0 and later versions and Caldera OpenLinux 3.1 and later include OpenSSL. The Red Hat and Caldera RPM packages change the default location where OpenSSL is installed. If you are using Debian GNU/Linux, the Debian OpenSSL packages install to the default locations. When installing OpenSSL from either an RPM or Debian package, make sure to install both the program and the development files. These are in two separate packages.

If you are going to compile OpenSSL from the source code, download the latest release from the Web at *www.OpenSSL.org*. Follow these steps to configure, compile, and install OpenSSL from the source code. First uncompress the source code:

```
tar xvzf openssl-0.9.6.tar.gz
```

The version number may be different from what is shown in this example. Then change into the source directory:

```
cd openssl-0.9.6
```

Finally, use the following commands to compile the software and install it:

```
./config
make
make test
make install
```

Make sure that OpenSSL is installed on both the Samba server and the SSL proxy server.

Compile Samba for SSL Support

Samba must be compiled with SSL support, and the Samba packages included with most Linux distributions are not compiled with SSL support. The one exception is the Samba package included with Red Hat Linux starting with version 7.0. Even if you have a Samba package that has been compiled with SSL support, you may want to compile your own because the package included with the Linux distribution is usually an older version of Samba. To compile your own version of Samba, follow the directions for compiling Samba detailed in Chapter 2, but make sure to add this to the configuration options:

```
--with-ssl
```

Samba expects to find the OpenSSL development files in the default locations. If you've installed OpenSSL from an RPM package from Red Hat or Caldera, the locations are different. In that case, you should create a symbolic link to the default directory, or Samba will not be able to compile with SSL support. The following commands will create the necessary link for OpenSSL development files installed from either Red Hat or Caldera RPM packages:

```
mkdir /usr/local/ssl
ln -s /usr/include /usr/local/ssl/include
```

Alternatively, you can use the configure option for pointing to the OpenSSL development files. The configure option for doing it this way is

```
--with-ssl --with-sslinc=/usr/include/openssl
```

Set Up the Proxy Server

The proxy server takes the insecure traffic from the Windows clients and passes it securely to the Samba server. It can be a very basic Linux server and does not require a lot of resources. The stunnel software on the proxy server will enable the secure SSL connection.

Make sure that OpenSSL is installed on the proxy server. The installation of stunnel will fail if the program cannot find the OpenSSL libraries. There is a special patch for Samba support in stunnel that is maintained by Kai Engert. You can download the patched version on the Web from *http://www.kuix.de/ssl/*. Use the following steps, similar to the steps used for OpenSSL, to configure, compile, and install stunnel:

```
tar -xvzf stunnel-3.11-kai-gui.tar.gz
cd stunnel-3.11-kai-gui
./configure
make
make install
```

The version number may be different from what is shown in this example. At the end of the installation process, you will be prompted with a series of questions. The answers are then used to generate a certificate. The answers to the questions are publicly displayed with the certificate. The country code, state, and organization name must match the certificate on the Samba server. The common name is the fully qualified domain name, as in *host.domain.com,* and must match the host name of the machine or the client machines will complain.

Create a Certificate for the Samba Server

The Certificate Authority (CA) in SSL is a trusted third party that has authenticated the user of the signed certificate as being who he or she claims to be. If the client trusts the CA, it will trust the certificate. On the Web, SSL is used with certificates issued by a handful of CAs, such as Thawte and Verisign. Web browsers like Netscape Navigator and Internet Explorer have all the major CAs built-in.

The commercial CAs charge a yearly fee for their services. For Samba SSL you can use a commercial certificate of authority if you have one, but it is not necessary. Since this is a strictly internal transaction, you can be your own certification authority and generate your own certificates.

BECOME A CERTIFICATE AUTHORITY

You'll need a signed certificate for the Samba server. To set up a CA on the Samba server, start by creating a secure location for the certificates.

A common location is a *certificates* subdirectory in *etc.* The permissions on the directory should be set so that access is denied to all users but root. The steps involved here will be easier to do from a command prompt, which can be accessed from the Telnet Login on Webmin's Others tab. After logging in, make sure you become the root user using the su command. Then use these commands to create the directory and set its permissions:

```
mkdir /etc/certificates
chmod 0700 /etc/certificates
```

Next you'll need to edit the OpenSSL configuration file and the CA setup script named *CA.pl* to use the new *certificates* directory.

Using a text editor, edit the *openssl.cnf* file found in */usr/local/ssl.*

In *openssl.cnf,* find the entry for dir = ./demoCA and change it to read dir = /etc/certificates. Save the changed configuration file.

The setup script requires a similar change. The setup script can be found in */usr/local/ssl/misc.*

Using a text editor, open *CA.pl* and find the entry for CATOP = ./demoCA. Change it to read CATOP = /etc/certificates. Save the change.

When that is done, run the script to create a new CA certificate. From the directory with the script, enter this command:

```
./CA.pl -newca
```

After starting the script, you are prompted to press the Enter key to create a new CA certificate. The next prompt is to enter a PEM passphrase, which you will have to enter twice. Be sure to remember this passphrase. It is used to sign client certificates. (PEM means that base 64 encryption is being used, as defined in RFC 1421 for privacy-enhanced mail.)

Then a series of questions are asked, the same questions asked for creating a certificate when installing stunnel. The country code, state, and organization name must match the certificate on the stunnel server. An example entry would be

```
Country Name: US
State or Province: New York
Locality or City: New York
Organization Name: The Company
Organization Unit: Network Servers
Common Name (eg, YOUR name): Local Certificate Authority
E-Mail Address: cert-request@thecompany.hq
```

When completed, OpenSSL is configured as a CA that can be used to sign certificates.

CREATE A SERVER CERTIFICATE

The next step is to create a key and certificate for the Samba server. OpenSSL will generate a key and certificate, which then will have to be signed by a CA. In this case, you are the CA, and you will sign the certicate.

Start this step by generating the server's key and certificate request. Use the following commands to first change to the *newcerts* directory:

```
cd /etc/certificates/newcerts
```

Then generate the key and certificate request:

```
/usr/local/ssl/bin/openssl req -new -nodes -out newreq.pem
-keyout keyfile.pem
```

Make sure to use the fully qualified hostname for your Samba server for the common name, for example, *samba.thecompany.hq*. Enter the appropriate information for the Samba server:

```
Country Name: US
State or Province: New York
Locality or City: New York
```

```
Organization Name: The Company
Organization Unit: Network Servers
Common Name (eg, YOUR name): samba.thecompany.hq
E-Mail Address: help@thecompany.hq
```

Don't bother entering anything for the challenge phrase or alternate company name. They aren't needed. Just hit Return.

Now, using your newly generated CA, sign the request and create a new server certificate. Make sure that the *CA.pl* script is pointing to your CA in */etc/certificates* and not in *demoCA*.

In the */etc/certificates/newcerts* directory, run the *CA.pl* script, using the option to sign the certificate request:

```
/usr/local/ssl/misc/CA.pl -sign
```

This requires the PEM passphrase for the CA created earlier. When it is done, the signed certificate and key are now ready to be used. Copy them to the directory for certificates and rename them with a name that shows they are for the Samba server. Copying and renaming can be done in one step:

```
cp newcert.pem /etc/certificates/certs/sambacert.pem
cp keyfile.pem /etc/certificates/private/sambakey.pem
```

Using the Samba name is optional. The name can be any name you choose.

Configure Samba's SSL Options

Samba has a dozen SSL options in its global configuration. Only four need to be set. Make the following changes on the Globals page in SWAT, in the Advanced View.

SSL support must be enabled. The default is No, meaning that Samba will not use SSL. Use this setting:

```
ssl = yes
```

The next option sets the full path to the SSL server's certificate:

```
ssl server cert = /etc/certificates/certs/sambacert.pem
```

If you've used another location for certificates, then use that location here and in all the following option settings.

The next option sets the full path to the SSL server's private key:

```
ssl server key = /etc/certificates/private/sambakey.pem
```

The next option sets the full path to the directory where the certificates are stored:

```
ssl CA certdir = /etc/certificates/certs
```

After making these changes in the Samba configuration, you will need to manually start the Samba daemons from a command prompt:

```
nmbd -D
smbd -D
```

You will then be prompted to enter the PEM passphrase for the Samba server's certificate before the Samba daemons will start. If you are not prompted to enter the passphrase, then SSL has not been enabled.

Using SSL means that Samba will no longer be able to be started as daemons on bootup. You will have to manually start Samba from a command prompt whenever necessary or write a script that can respond with the passphrase.

Start the SSL Proxy Server

With the Samba server set up to support SSL, it is time to start stunnel on the SSL proxy server. Enter the following command:

```
/usr/sbin/stunnel -d 139 -r server:139 -c -n smb -D6 -f -P none
```

The *server* variable is the IP address of the Samba server. For example, the entry could be 192.168.0.4:139. The SSL proxy server is now ready to pass through requests for a secure connection to the Samba server.

Configure the Windows Machine

Accessing a share on a Samba server with SSL cannot be done in the normal way. The Network Neighborhood/My Network Places cannot be used to make the connections. Everything must be done from a command prompt using the net command. For this to work, the SSL proxy server running stunnel also must be reachable on the local network. One way to make sure the SSL proxy server can be reached by the Windows clients is to add the proxy server to the hosts file on the Windows machines.

To do this on the Windows clients, add the IP address of the stunnel machine to the hosts file in the *windows* or *winnt* directory. The entry should include the IP address and the computer name. For example:

```
192.168.0.119 proxy
```

For Windows 9*x*/Me systems, reboot before proceeding. The next step is to map a share on the Samba server to a drive letter on the Windows client machine. After rebooting, open a DOS command prompt and enter this command:

```
net use * \\stunnel_machine_name\share_on_Samba
```

This maps the next available drive letter to the share on the Samba server. Instead of *, the precise drive letter can be entered. For example, to map the R: drive to the "sales" share on the Samba server, through the SSL proxy server named proxy, enter:

```
net use R: \\proxy\sales
```

Using the secure connection on the SSL proxy server to the Samba server, all data passed between the SSL proxy server and the Samba server is encrypted. The Windows user must be logged as a user with a matching username and password on the Samba server or the connection will be refused.

Samba Virtual Servers

If you have ever had to set up a separate server for a project but didn't have a machine available, you'll like Samba's ability to run virtual servers, much like the virtual Web servers that are set up for Web hosting. A virtual server is a way to make one server appear to be multiple different servers. This is done by setting up the Samba server with more than one NetBIOS computer name.

The advantage of setting up a virtual server is that each department or project in an organization can appear to have its own server with its own file shares and printers. Everything is then maintained on one server, rather than multiple workgroup servers, which makes system administration much easier.

Samba does this with the NetBIOS Alias option. The option is set in the Globals section of the main Samba configuration file, *smb.conf*. One or more aliases can be listed. In the Network Neighborhood/My Network Places, each name listed as a NetBIOS alias will appear to be a separate server even though all the names are on the same server.

The alias is set with an option in the *smb.conf* configuration file. This can be done on the Samba server with any text editor, such as gedit, nedit, or vi. While it is also possible to edit the file on a Windows system, the different file format for text files on Windows means that every change could have to

SWAT, Webmin, and Virtual Servers

If you use virtual servers, you will not be able to use SWAT and Webmin for Samba configuration and administration. You will need to use a text editor to maintain the Samba configuration files and use other Linux tools for system administration.

go through an extra conversion process (unless you have a programmer's editor on Windows that can save in Linux text format).

For example, if you have a server named Linux and you add aliases for Server1, Server2, Server3, and Server4, add the following line to *smb.conf* in the global section:

```
netbios aliases - server1 server2 server3 server4
```

Figure 5-2 shows how these servers would appear in the Network Neighborhood/My Network Places.

Each server has its own configuration file. The configuration files use the same format at the main Samba configuration file. Samba must be told the location of the configuration files for each virtual server. This is usually done by placing the files in the same directory with the main Samba configuration file. That's in *etc/samba* on Red Hat Linux version 7.0 and higher, */etc* on older versions of Red Hat, */etc/samba.d* on Caldera OpenLinux, and */etc/samba* on Debian GNU/Linux.

The option is set using the %L variable, which expands into the NetBIOS name for the virtual server. To set the option for Red Hat Linux, enter SWAT's global configuration:

```
include = /etc/samba/smb.conf.%L
```

This will then include the configuration files for the main server and each virtual server. Using the previous example, there are now five additional configuration files that need to be created in the */etc/samba* directory: *smb.conf. linux, smb.conf.server1, smb.conf.server2, smb.conf.server3,* and *smb.conf. server4.*

Do not set any shares in the main configuration file unless you want them to appear on all the virtual servers. The shares should be defined only for each individual virtual server. These configuration files need to contain just the options specific to the virtual server. If you are using encrypted passwords, make sure that each virtual server has Encrypted Passwords enabled.

Figure 5-2

One server, Linux, set up with multiple virtual servers using NetBIOS aliases.

Here is a sample *smb.conf* configuration file for a Samba server with several virtual servers:

```
[global]
      workgroup = mygroup
      netbios name = linux
      netbios aliases = server1 server2 server3 server4
      include = /etc/samba/smb.conf.%L
      server string = Samba Server
      encrypt passwords = Yes
      username map = /etc/samba/smbusers
      log file = /var/log/samba/log.%L.%m
      max log size = 200
      socket options = TCP_NODELAY
```

The *smb.conf.linux* configuration file might look like this:

```
[global]
      logon path = \\%L\Profiles\%U
      dns proxy = No
      wins support = Yes
      printing = cups
      domain logons = yes
      domain master = yes
      preferred master = yes
      load printers = yes

[homes]
      comment = Home Directories
      path = %H
      username = %S
      valid users = %S
      read only = No
      create mask = 0750
      only user = Yes
      browseable = No

[netlogon]
      comment = Samba Network Logon Service
      path = /srv/netlogon
      guest ok = Yes
      share modes = No

[profiles]
      path = /srv/profiles
      read only = No
      guest ok = Yes
      browseable = No
```

```
[printers]
      comment = All Printers
      path = /var/spool/samba
      printable = Yes
      browseable = No
```

This file configures the main server as a logon server that also provides the homes and printers shares.

The smb.conf.server1 is then set apart for the "finance" group. Here is a sample:

```
[global]
      workgroup = finance
      hosts allow = 192.168.4.0/24
      encrypt passwords = yes

[fprinter]
      comment = Finance Printer
      path = /var/spool/samba
      valid users = @finance
      printer = finance_printer
      print ok = yes
      guest ok = no
      writable = no

[2002reports]
      path = /srv/finance/2002reports
      read only = no
```

This file creates a server with the workgroup name of *finance* that is accessible only from the finance subnet. The server also has a shared printer, and a shared folder on the server is called *2002reports*. Figure 5-3 shows

Figure 5-3   *The shares available on the virtual server Server1.*

what you would see when you open Server1 from the Network Neighborhood/My Network Places.

For another example, the smb.conf.server2 could look like this:

```
[global]
        encrypt passwords = yes

[public]
        path = /srv/Public
        write list = @users
        read only = no
        guest ok = yes
```

This code creates a server with one share, a public share, that can be accessed by everyone and written to by anyone in the "users" group.

Internationalization

Samba version 2.2 uses the ASCII character set and has only limited support for non-Roman character sets. Samba supports the international character sets for most Western and Eastern European languages as well as Russian, Greek, simplified Chinese, and Korean. It also supports the Japanese Industrial Standard Shift-JIS character set.

Samba developers are working to build Unicode support into Samba 3.0, though it may not be included with the initial release. Unicode is an ASCII superset used to represent up to 65,356 characters instead of ASCII's 256.

The Unicode character set is designed to support all known written languages around the world. Unicode uses a unique number for every character, no matter what the language. It will eventually replace ASCII as the standard character coding format for all computer systems.

Until Unicode support is available, Samba is able to use Windows code page definitions for multiple character sets. Windows code pages map the standard English characters and all other ASCII characters to other national characters. It is a limited implementation that does not support the full character sets of all languages.

There is no universal format for code pages and each code page is specific to a language. There is no consistency. Accented characters are not represented by the same ASCII values across code pages. In addition, some characters available in one code page are not available in another.

Samba can be configured to support the Windows code page being used by the client machines on the network. This setup allows filenames that use characters from the high bit set to have the matching characters in the filename on the Linux filesystem. Samba takes care of mapping the different characters and converting them from Windows to Linux and back again, when necessary.

Samba has five options for setting international character sets: Client Code Page, Code Page Directory, Character Set, Coding System, and Valid Chars. These are all found in the Advanced View on the Globals page in SWAT.

The Client Code Page Option

This option sets the Windows code page that the client machines accessing Samba are using. To find the code page the Windows client is using, go to the Windows client machine and open a DOS command prompt. At the prompt, type the command chcp. The code page number will be displayed. The default code page for the Windows operating system on computers in the United States is 437. The default for Western European releases of Windows is code page 850. If the Client Code Page setting is not changed, Samba defaults to code page 850. To change the code page, enter the new number from the client in the parameter space. Samba 2.2 includes support for the code pages shown in Table 5-1:

The Code Page Directory Option

This option sets the location of the code page files for Samba. On Red Hat Linux and Debian GNU/Linux, this is */etc/samba/codepages*. On Caldera OpenLinux, it is */etc/samba.d/codepages*.

Table 5-1	
Code Page 437	Latin US
Code Page 737	Greek
Code Page 775	Baltic Rim
Code Page 850	Latin 1 (most Western European languages)
Code Page 852	Latin 2 (Central and Eastern European languages)
Code Page 861	Icelandic
Code Page 866	Cyrillic (Russian)
Code Page 932	Japanese Shift-JIS
Code Page 936	Simplified Chinese
Code Page 949	Korean Hangul
Code Page 950	Traditional Chinese

The Character Set option

The Character Set option can be used to allow Samba to map characters used for filenames from the Windows code page set to the Linux equivalent character set. This option is available for only five character sets: Western European, Eastern European, Greek, and two Russian variants.

To map the Western European character set on the client to a Western European Linux character set on the server, for example, set the following options:

```
client code page = 850
character set = ISO8859-1
```

Samba supports converting from Windows to Linux for the character sets shown in Table 5-2:

Table 5-2	
ISO8859-1	Western European Linux character set. Use with cope page 850.
ISO8859-2	Eastern European Linux character set. Use with code page 852.
ISO8859-5	Russian Cyrillic Linux character set. Use with code page 866.
ISO8859-7	Greek Linux character set. Use with code page 737.
KOI8-R	Alternate Russian Cyrillic Linux character set. Use with code page 866.

The default setting is blank, meaning that character set mapping is disabled.

The Coding System Option

This option is used by Samba to map characters used for filenames from the Windows Shift-JIS Japanese code page set to the Linux equivalent character set. This option can be used only with clients using code page 932. The Samba code page must also be set to 932.

If you are using the coding system option, set it to one of the parameters shown in Table 5-3:

The default setting is blank, which means that the coding system is not used.

The Valid Chars Option

This option adds more characters for use in filenames, though it is not necessary. The Code Page option is the preferred choice. Valid Chars is a legacy option in Samba that may disappear in future versions.

Table 5-3	
Shift-JIS	No conversion of the incoming filename.
JIS8, J8BB, J8BH, J8@B, J8@J, J8@H	Convert to eight-bit JIS codes.
JIS7, J7BB, J7BH, J7@B, J7@J, J7@H	Convert seven-bit JIS codes.
JUNET, JUBB, JUBH, JU@B, JU@J, JU@H	Convert a Japan Unix Network (JUNET) code.
EUC	Convert to Extended Unix Code (EUC).
HEX	Convert a three-byte hexadecimal code.
CAP	Convert to the three-byte hexadecimal code used by the Columbia AppleTalk Program.

Characters can be added to Valid Chars in either integer or character form with spaces between them. Two characters listed with a colon between them are treated as a lowercase:uppercase pair.

Samba includes a utility that can be used to generate the valid characters for a code page on a client machine. The utility can be found on the Samba server in the Samba documentation directory. On Red Hat Linux that is in */usr/share/doc/*. In that directory there is a subdirectory named for the version of Samba installed on the system, such as *samba-2.2.0*. In the Samba directory, go to the *examples/validchars* directory.

The utility is called validchr.com. It can be run from a DOS command prompt on any Windows system. It generates a listing of the valid characters for the code page. To save the output to a file, enter this command:

```
validchr > validchr.txt
```

At the bottom of the file is a list of valid characters. This list can then be added to the Samba configuration in the Valid Chars option. For example, here is the Valid Chars setting for code page 850, which is used to support the Spanish character set:

```
valid chars = 73:213 213:73 73:73 33 35 36 37 38 39 40 41
45 48 49 50 51 52 53 54 55 56 57 64 97:65 98:66 99:67
100:68 101:69 102:70 103:71 104:72 105:73 106:74 107:75
108:76 109:77 110:78 111:79 112:80 113:81 114:82 115:83
116:84 117:85 118:86 119:87 120:88 121:89 122:90 94 95 96
123 125 126 127 135:128 132:142 134:143 130:144 145:146
148:153 129:154 156 155:157 158 159 164:165 166 167 168
169 170 171 172 173 174 175 176 177 178 179 180 160:181
131:182 133:183 184 185 186 187 188 189 190 191 192 193
194 195 196 197 198:199 200 201 202 203 204 205 206 207
208:209 136:210 137:211 138:212 161:214 140:215 139:216
217 218 219 220 221 141:222 223 162:224 225 147:226
```

```
149:227 228:229 230 231:232 163:233 150:234 151:235
236:237 238 239 240 241 242 243 244 245 246 247 248 249
250 251 252 253 254 255
```

If you do use this option, a client code page must be set as well, since this option is designed to add characters to an existing code page. If a code page is not set, the characters will not be added.

The Samba Time Server

Many networks make use of time servers. For some uses, the computer's time can be critical, and in most offices, even if the time setting is not critical, accurate time can be important.

The real-time clocks on personal computers are notoriously inaccurate, most gaining or losing time every day. In addition, there are two time settings, the hardware time and the system time. The system time is the time setting for the currently running system. The hardware time is the real-time clock setting on the system board. Whenever the system reboots, the system time is reset to the hardware clock time. These two time settings will drift, and unless they are regularly synchronized, they can be very different. This is a problem for both Windows and Linux systems. Samba provides a simple way to correct this difficulty and synchronize the clocks on every client machine to make them very accurate. This is a two-step process. First the Samba server is set up as a time server. Then the client machines connect and update their system time, using the Samba time service.

Set Up the Samba Server As a Time Server

To set up the Samba server as a time server, the Linux system on the Samba server needs to be configured for a high degree of time accuracy. This can be done manually or automatically using the Network Time Protocol (NTP).

Manual updates of the time on the Linux server can be handled through Webmin. In Webmin on the Hardware tab, select the link to the System Time. You can use any method to get the current time, including calling the telephone company's time service. Select the correct time for the system, and click on the Apply button. Then synchronize the hardware time to the system time.

Alternatively, if you are connected to the Internet, you can enter the name of a time server in the Time Server field and synchronize the system and hardware times to the time server. This option makes use of the public NTP time servers. These are NTP servers around the world that are synchronized to atomic clocks. Those that are connected directly to atomic clocks are referred to as primary, or stratum 1, time servers. The secondary, or stratum 2, time servers are synchronized to primary time servers.

Use one of the secondary time servers to update your Linux server. A list of secondary time servers can be found on the Web at *http://www.eecis.udel.edu/~mills/ntp/clock2.htm*. You should not use one of the primary time servers unless you are setting up your own secondary time server.

If your Linux server is connected to the Internet, it can be set up to automatically keep the system time updated to one of the secondary time servers using NTP. The NTP software is included on the Red Hat Linux distribution CD, as it is on almost every other Linux distribution. It can also be downloaded on the Web at the NTP home page at *http://www.eecis.udel.edu/~ntp/*.

The directions for installing the program from the source code can be found on the NTP Web site. The procedure is the same as it is for most software on Linux: `configure`, `make`, and `make install`.

After the software is installed, it must be configured. The configuration requires three time servers for maximum accuracy. Select three of the secondary time servers that are regionally close to your server.

The configuration file is named *ntp.conf* and is usually found in the */etc* directory. Use a text editor to modify the file. At the beginning of the configuration file, enter the names of the three secondary time servers you've chosen. Each name must be preceded by the word "server," to indicate that this is one of the time servers. A sample entry is

```
server    clock.somecompany.com
server    ntpserver.university.edu
server    time.state.gov
```

Of course, these are not actual time servers; be sure to use the names of actual time servers. It is better to use hostnames rather than IP addresses, since the IP addresses can change while hostnames change much less frequently. After the list of time servers, there should be an entry for the drift file.

One of the things the NTP software does is test the computer's clock and keep track of whether it tends to be too slow or too fast. It usually takes a day or so for the NTP software to compute a good estimate. The frequency error rate is then saved into the drift file. This information is used to get the time services quickly up to speed if the NTP software is stopped and then restarted. The frequency error rate is used to keep the system clock accurate if none of the time servers are reachable.

The entry for the drift file in the NTP configuration is

```
driftfile    /etc/ntp.drift
```

The location can vary and does not have to be in the /etc directory. If you've installed xntp from an RPM package and the location is different, there is no need to change it. Though many more options can be configured, that is all that's needed for a basic time server.

The NTP time server is ready to run. If you compiled the software from source code, it can be started manually using this command:

```
/usr/local/bin/xntpd
```

If you installed it from the RPM package from Red Hat or Caldera, the command is

```
/usr/sbin/xntpd
```

The RPM packages also install a script that will let you run the NTP server software automatically every time the system starts up. To set NTP to be run from startup this way, open Webmin's Bootup and Shutdown page on the System tab. Find NTP and set it to run on startup.

The final step to setting up the Samba server is to configure Samba. In SWAT's Globals page under Protocol Options, there is a setting called Time Server. Change this option from the default of No to Yes, and Samba will announce itself as a time server for Windows clients.

Set the Time on Windows Clients

With the Samba server set up, the time can be set on each Windows machine from a DOS prompt, using this command:

```
net time \\samba_server /set /yes
```

Use the NetBIOS computer name of the Samba server. This sets the Windows system time to match the time on the Samba server. This command can be set to run on the system's startup either through a netlogon script, if you've set up the Samba server as a logon server, or through a batch file that is run from the Windows Startup folder.

The Samba Fax Server

Samba's print sharing can be used as a fax server by setting up a printing queue that is really a fax queue. You need to set up a fax modem on the Linux machine and install fax server software like HylaFAX or mgetty+send-fax. The mgetty+sendfax package is installed with many Linux distributions.

After the fax modem and software are set up, a fax printer share is created in Samba and the Windows clients are configured to "print" to the fax printer on the Samba server.

The limitation of this setup is that the fax server software can only accept PostScript print files that are then converted into the Group 3 (G3) fax format. G3 is the compressed image format used for facsimile transmissions. This means that every document sent can only have the PostScript fonts that are installed on the Linux server. The results can be very unpredictable. In most cases it is better to set up a fax server that can accept fax files from Windows clients directly in G3 format so that none of the formatting or font information is lost.

Select the Right Modem

Before you can set up a fax server, you must have a working fax modem. Any external modem will work. Internal modems, which can be cheaper, often will not work with Linux systems.

Winmodems should not be used for a fax server. Winmodems make the CPU do the work that the modem should be doing. Plug-and-play modems can cause some problems because they may not have the same settings every time the system is started.

The best choice is an external modem that is a Class 2 or 2.0 fax modem. Class 1 modems are designed for personal use and should never be used for fax servers. The difference between Class 2/2.0 modems and Class 1 modems is that Class 2/2.0 modems do all the work, while Class 1 modems essentially pass through all the work to the computer's CPU.

Set Up the Fax Server Software

Either HylaFAX or mgetty+sendfax can be used as fax server software on a Linux system. HylaFAX can found on the Web at *http://www.hylafax.org/*; mgetty+sendfax is at *http://www.leo.org/~doering/mgetty/*.

For HylaFAX, follow the directions for installation and configuration included with the software. For mgetty+sendfax, the software may already be installed on the Linux machine. The package is included with every Linux distribution.

The configuration files for mgetty+sendfax are in the */etc/mgetty+sendfax* directory on the Linux system. Configuration requires knowledge of the Linux system and the devices installed on the computer.

The *mgetty.config* and *sendfax.config* files must be configured. In *mgetty.config,* make sure to set the `fax-id`, the `port`, `init-chat`, and `speed`.

The sendfax.config settings that must be made are the `fax-devices`, `fax-id`, and the `dial-prefix`.

In *faxrunq.config,* make sure to set `fax-devices` to the same setting as in *sendfax.config.*

The *faxheader* configuration file should be changed to include your company name and fax number.

When everything is configured, the fax server software is ready to run. Start the faxrunqd daemon, which will take care of print jobs that are sent to the */var/spool/fax* directory. This directory is created as part of the installation of mgetty+sendfax. When a print job is sent to the fax queue, it will be directed to the fax modem.

Set Up a Fax Printer in Samba

The process of handing a fax document from a Windows client to HylaFAX or mgetty+sendfax requires an intermediary that can collect the phone number and name of the fax recipient and the sender information. The Respond utility is designed to do this on a network set up with Samba and HylaFAX or mgetty+sendfax. The Respond Web page is at *http://relay.boerde.de/~horstf/.*

There are two files that must be downloaded, the *respond.zip* file—with the respond program and a configuration program—and *printfax.pl,* a script file that is used to control the fax process on the Linux server. The full instructions for using Respond are in a file named *readme.txt,* which can also be downloaded from the Respond Web site. The *printfax.pl* script must be placed in the */usr/bin* directory on the Linux server and made executable.

A fax printer must be set up in Samba that will use the *printfax.pl* program to handle incoming faxes. This can be done in SWAT on the Printers page. Create a new printer named FAX. Then configure the printer to have these options:

```
path = /var/spool/samba
postscript = yes
print command = ( /usr/bin/printfax.pl %I %s %U %m; rm %s ) &
printable = yes
```

For NT terminal servers and Windows 2000 clients, create a second fax printer with these options:

```
path = /var/spool/samba
postscript = no
print command = (echo -e '1i\n%!\n.\nw\nq'|ed %s;
/usr/bin/printfax.pl %I %s %U %m) &
printable = yes
```

Set Up the Windows Clients

For the Windows clients, you'll need the Respond program. A copy of the program must be placed on the Windows machine, and it must be included in the Windows Startup. Then use the Add Printer Wizard to add a postscript printer to the Windows machine, and set the port to the fax printer on the Samba server.

The fax printer is now ready to use. When you print to the fax printer on the Windows machine, the Respond program will pop up with a dialog box where you can enter the destination fax number, the recipient's name, and the sender's name. Clicking on OK will send the fax.

Samba, Windows, and Cross-Subnet Browsing

For existing Windows networks, adding a Samba server is like adding a Windows NT server. Nothing needs to be changed in the setup, and the Samba server should be set up so it does not compete with the existing Windows servers.

In its default configuration, the Samba server can be seen only on its own subnet.

Users on other subnets can access the Samba server either by using the Map Network Drive utility or from a DOS command prompt with the `net use` command. This requires that they know the name of the Samba server or its IP address and the name of the share.

If the clients on the network are configured to use a central WINS server, the Samba server can be configured to register with the WINS server. The Samba server will then appear whenever the clients browse the network.

The Samba server can also be set up as a WINS server, if one does not already exist. The clients must then be set to use the Samba WINS server. The Samba server will then appear when browsing the network. To configure Samba to act as a WINS server, set Samba's global options to

```
wins support = yes
```

Make sure that a WINS server has not also been set in Samba's configuration. WINS support and a WINS server cannot be set at the same time in Samba.

There should be only one WINS server for your local network. Do not configure the Samba server to be a WINS server if you already have a Windows-based WINS server.

On an existing Windows network, Samba should be set so that it does not become the master browser. Set Samba's global options to

```
os level = 20
local master = no
preferred master = no
wins server = your_wins_server
```

The existing Windows domain controller must be the master browser in the domain. The Samba server should never be set up as a master browser in a domain if there is already a Windows domain controller in the domain. If both are included, the Windows domain controller will stop functioning correctly, and clients may be unable to log onto the domain.

The OS Level of 20 means that Samba will take part in browsing, and unless there is an NT or 2000 server in the domain or workgroup, Samba will become the local master browser.

If the OS Level is left blank, Samba will never function as a local master browser.

There are three ways to enable cross-subnet browsing. One is to use a WINS server. The second way is to have a domain master browser on the network, with the clients and the Samba server registering with the domain master browser. The third way is to use Samba's Remote Announce option. This is particularly useful if you don't have a Windows domain, but you have workgroups that span multiple subnets.

The `Remote Announce` option is used to list one or more IP addresses to which the Samba server will announce itself. The Samba server will then appear when browsing the network on these machines. For example, set the option to

```
remote announce = 192.168.10.5 192.168.15.10
```

This will make the Samba server announce itself to the two IP addresses.

Configuring Windows 9x/Me/NT/2000

Connecting to a Samba server is the same as connecting to a Windows server. A Samba server usually fits seamlessly into a Windows network, appearing in the Network Neighborhood on Windows 95/98/NT4 systems and in Computers Near Me on Windows Me and Windows 2000 Professional workstations.

For this to happen, TCP/IP networking has to be working on the Windows workstations on your network. In most cases, this has already been established because TCP/IP is the networking protocol that is used by Windows NT/2000 servers.

NetBIOS and TCP/IP Networking

Windows NT/2000 networks are based on the Network Basic Input/Output System (NetBIOS) over TCP/IP, or NetBT. It is not necessary to know how Windows networking works in order to connect Windows workstations to a

Can You Skip This Chapter?

The instructions for setting up Windows 9x/NT/2000 systems connecting to a Samba server are the same instructions used for connecting to a Windows server. If you already have a Windows network, then the only part of this chapter you need to look at is the note on Samba, IPC$, and password encryption (found later in this chapter). However, if you are experiencing any problems connecting to your Samba server, you should check your setup against what you find here and make sure that everything is correctly configured.

Samba server. If you are in a hurry and just want to get down to business. skip this section and go ahead to the one called "Setting Up Windows 9x/Me.". However, knowing the nuts and bolts of Windows networking can be helpful, especially when it comes time to solve problems.

When you are at a Windows workstation and you double-click on Network Neighborhood/Computers Near Me on the desktop, what opens up is a window showing icons, each labeled with a name. The label shows the NetBIOS name for each computer represented by an icon on the network. If you use the Windows Explorer to access a mapped network drive, you'll see a drive letter, the NetBIOS name, and the name of the share.

When you double-click on a shared resource—a file share or a printer—the system looks up the NetBIOS name on a table that points to the hardware address associated with it. All network communication actually takes place using the hardware address of the network card on each computer connected to the network. The exchange protocol used on Windows networks is called the Common Internet File System (CIFS). This is the name used by Microsoft for its enhanced version of the Server Messaging Block (SMB) protocol. There is probably nothing more important on a Windows network than having NetBIOS name resolution working correctly.

NetBIOS is a programming interface that was first introduced to give networking capability to IBM DOS. It was developed for IBM in the early 1980s and was used by IBM's Lan Manager. It is also the networking protocol used by OS/2.

Initially Microsoft's NetBIOS Windows networking used a revised NetBIOS protocol called NetBIOS Extended User Interface (NetBEUI). Microsoft has been trying to move away from NetBIOS in favor of TCP/IP, but Windows networks still rely on NetBIOS. Windows NT/2000 servers use TCP/IP for networking, not NetBEUI, but they still use the NetBIOS interface for file and printer sharing. Microsoft's TCP/IP stack includes support for NetBIOS over TCP/IP. Only on a pure Windows 2000 network—all Windows 2000 servers and clients—is a Microsoft network able to use TCP/IP as the sole protocol, without NetBIOS.

There is sometimes confusion about the relationship of NetBIOS and TCP/IP. Most confusing is how the two different protocols handle name services.

Name services are used to convert a human-readable name into a computer-usable hardware address for communications. Every network interface card has a unique hardware address that is a 48-bit number, commonly written in hexadecimal format. For example, a typical hardware address on an Ethernet network card would be written as 00:04:AC:90:1C:DF. The first 24 bits (in this example 00:04:AC) indicate the manufacturer and protocol of the card; the last 24 bits are a unique number assigned by the manufacturer.

TIP — WINDOWS 9X/ME HARDWARE ADDRESSES

To get the hardware address on a Windows 9x/Me system, open an MS-DOS Prompt or a Command Prompt on Windows NT/2000 and enter the command `ipconfig /all`. The listing of the Physical Address of the Ethernet Adapter is the hardware address.

Different Naming Services: WINS and DNS

Windows networking uses NetBIOS names to find the hardware address of a shared resource on the network. To connect to a network resource, the requesting system has to know the NetBIOS name that identifies the resource on the network. For example, to connect to a server called "database," the client system broadcasts a message that essentially says "I want to connect to 'database.' If you are 'database,' please send me your hardware address." If the resource is on the network, it will send back the hardware address. Windows CIFS, or Samba, then kicks in and uses the hardware address for communication between the two machines.

Finding the hardware address through the NetBIOS broadcast works for smaller networks, but it can quickly become a bottleneck on larger networks. A more significant limitation is that this method has severely limited addressing capabilities. It uses a single-level hardware address.

TCP/IP uses a second level of addressing to define a network address. The second level address enables TCP/IP to quickly see from the address if the message request can be serviced on the local network or if it has to be routed to another network. Because NetBIOS does not use a second-level address, it has no way to distinguish between local and nonlocal messages and is therefore a nonroutable protocol.

Microsoft introduced NetBIOS over TCP/IP so that Windows networking name-request broadcasts wouldn't jam larger networks and to support routing on wide-area networks. Also, using TCP/IP gives Windows users access to standard Internet services. Before that, all Microsoft networks used the NetBEUI protocol exclusively. This legacy shows up in Windows 95, where the NetBEUI protocol is loaded by default. Windows 98, on the other hand, loads only TCP/IP.

The second-level IP addresses are 32-bit numbers. These addresses are four 8-bit numbers, for example, 192.168.1.1. Each of the four numbers is in the range of 0 to 255. IP addresses also have a human-readable form. Every IP address is assigned a domain name (don't confuse this with a Windows network domain, which is a central controller for a Windows network). The Domain Name System (DNS) converts easy-to-remember names such as *www.cnn.com* into IP addresses such as 207.25.71.24.

To get NetBIOS to work over TCP/IP, an intermediary is needed that eliminates the requirement for the general NetBIOS broadcast. Instead, Net-

BIOS sends a request to the intermediary—something like, "Hey, what's the IP address for 'database'?" The intermediary returns an IP address for the NetBIOS name. TCP/IP then handles resolving the IP address into a hardware address, and Samba or Windows CIFS takes care of the rest.

LMHOSTS and HOSTS

One intermediary to provide IP addresses is the LMHOSTS Lan Manager HOSTS (LMHOSTS) file. This is a text file that maps NetBIOS names to IP addresses. Sample HOSTS and LMHOSTS files—*hosts.sam* and *lmhosts.sam*—can be found on all Windows computers. The two files follow the format of the standard TCP/IP hosts file as it is found on all Linux systems.

LMHOSTS and HOSTS have similar but different functions. The HOSTS file on both Windows and Linux systems is used for name resolution for standard TCP/IP services such as ftp, telnet, and ping. LMHOSTS is used for NetBIOS name resolution on Windows and Samba.

There are two limitations to the LMHOSTS file. First is size. Since the file must be manually created, even if only once, and then copied onto multiple systems, it can become unwieldy on all but the smallest networks. The second limitation is that LMHOSTS can't handle dynamically assigned IP addresses. Many networks use Dynamic Host Configuration Protocol (DHCP) servers to assign IP addresses. On a network using DHCP, IP addresses can be constantly changing. To handle bigger networks and dynamic addressing, Microsoft introduced the Windows Internet Naming Service (WINS).

With WINS, a Windows system registers its current IP address and NetBIOS name with the WINS server. If the DHCP server assigns a new address, the change is registered with the WINS server. Requests to resolve NetBIOS names with IP addresses are directed to the WINS server, which can respond with the correct IP address.

Lists of Domain Names and NetBIOS Names

HOSTS and LMHOSTS are data lists. The HOSTS file is a list that maps IP addresses to hostnames. Each line has an IP address followed by either just a hostname, for local networks not connecting to wide-area networks, or the fully qualified domain name (FQDN).

An FQDN is the hostname plus the domain name, including the top-level domain. For example, *www.cnn.com* is an FQDN: *www* is the host, *cnn* is the second-level domain, and *com* is the top-level domain.

LMHOSTS lists the IP address followed by the NetBIOS name. Some additional options can be listed after the NetBIOS name, which are explained in the *LMHOSTS.SAM* file.

There are some limitations to WINS. It can operate over TCP/IP but not over NetBEUI. Also, the WINS service is tied to NetBIOS over TCP/IP and is not a standalone TCP/IP service. It cannot be used for name services for a TCP/IP network. To connect to the Internet for Web surfing, ftp, telnet, and the rest of the services found on TCP/IP networks, you need a DNS server.

Setting Up Windows 9x/Me

Windows 95, 98, and Me all include TCP/IP networking as part of the options that can be installed with the operating system. Once a network interface card has been installed, the Network Neighborhood should appear on the desktop, and the system is ready to have networking configured. TCP/IP is initially installed with the network card on Windows 98 and Me systems. On Windows 95 systems, TCP/IP will probably have to be added.

Configuring TCP/IP on Windows 95, 98, and Me is done in same way, with only small variations that are noted here. Any time you make changes on the networking configuration in either Windows 95 or 98, the system will ask for the original Microsoft operating system CD in order to make the change. Make sure you have the disk with you before you start. Windows Me is better about this, but you should probably have the disk handy anyway.

Enable Multiuser Profiles

A good place to start configuring networking on Windows 9x/Me systems is to enable multiuser profiles. This establishes User Profiles that let each user set up personalized desktop settings such as themes or colors, desktop icons, and screensavers as well as individual login names and passwords for each user of the computer. That will be important if multiple users will be using the workstation to connect to the Samba server. User Profiles are not the same as true multiuser support, which is found in Windows NT or Windows 2000. All user files and settings, including email or private documents saved on the local hard drive, will be accessible to anyone sitting at the computer, no matter what login name is used. If you need true multiuser support and security, then you'll need to upgrade to Windows NT/2000 or Linux.

To enable User Profiles, open the Control Panel. The Control Panel can be accessed either from the My Computer icon on the desktop or in Settings from the Start button.

In the Control Panel, select the Passwords icon and open it. Choose the User Profiles tab. Select the radio button for Users Can Customize Preferences and Desktop Settings, and check both options under the User Profile Settings. Press OK. (See Figure 6-1.)

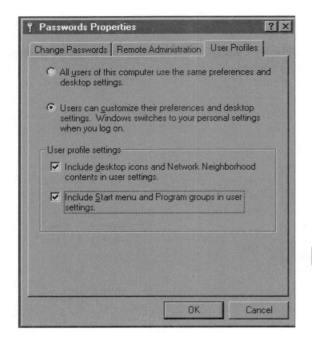

Figure 6-1

Windows 9x User Profiles enables some multiuser features, but it is not full multiuser support like that on Windows NT/2000 or Linux.

You'll have to restart the computer for the changes to take effect. The first time you log in after User Profiles have been enabled, a Windows dialog box will open asking if you would like to retain your individual settings. Answer Yes.

User Profiles are managed in User Settings, found in the Control Panel. Make sure each Windows username and password matches the username and password on the Samba server. If the two do not match, you won't be able to access Samba shares.

Configure TCP/IP Networking

After setting multiuser profiles, it does not matter which username you logon with (it does matter on Windows NT/2000 systems). To configure TCP/IP networking, return to the Control Panel and choose the Network icon. Alternatively, you can right-click on the Network Neighborhood/My Network Places icon and select Properties. In the Network control panel, you'll need to select and configure these items:

- The TCP/IP protocol
- The CIFS client (Client for Microsoft Networks)

Windows 98 and Me both install TCP/IP and the Client for Microsoft Networks by default with the network adapter. Windows 95 installs the NetBEUI protocol and the Client for NetWare Networks along with the Internet Packet Exchange/Sequenced Packet Exchange (IPX/SPX) protocol used for NetWare networks, but not TCP/IP. NetBEUI is installed for compatibility with older Windows 3.*x* networks and is rarely needed. If you are not connecting to an older Windows 3.*x* system or a NetWare server, you should remove the NetBEUI and IPX/SPX protocols and the Client for NetWare networks. Figure 6-2 shows the default networking installation on Windows 95, and Figure 6-3 shows the Windows 98/Me default.

File and print sharing can also be installed at this point. This is for the PC that is being set up and is separate from the file and printer sharing provided by the Samba server. It works with the TCP/IP protocol and does not

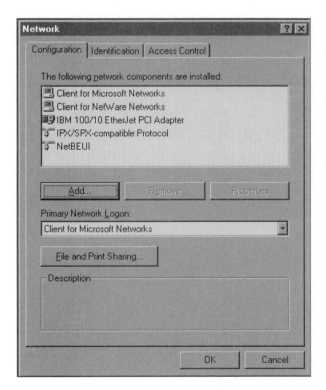

Figure 6-2 *The Windows 95 default networking installation does not include the TCP/IP protocol but does include NetBEUI and IPX/SPX, which should be removed if you are not using them.*

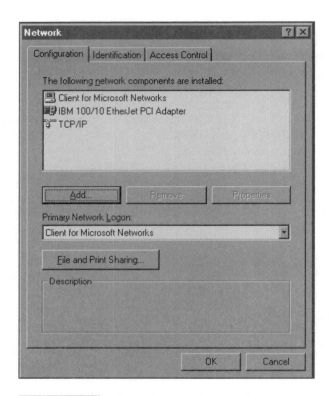

Figure 6-3 *The Windows 98/Me default network-ing installation includes everything you'll need—TCP/IP and the Client for Microsoft Networks.*

require any additional components. Click on the File and Print Sharing but-ton, and a window will open that lists the two options. Check the box beside the service you want to enable. File and Print Sharing allows others on the network to access files on your PC or to use printers attached to the PC.

If TCP/IP is not installed, click on the Add button and choose Protocol. Click Add and in the window that opens, select Microsoft in the left panel and choose TCP/IP in the right panel. Click on OK.

You are now ready to configure TCP/IP. Highlight TCP/IP in the Net-work window and click on the Properties button. This is where you'll config-ure the IP address, WINS, and LMHOSTS as well as the DNS server for this PC. Figure 6-4 shows the opening panel for TCP/IP configuration.

There are seven tabs on the TCP/IP panel, starting with the IP address. The default settings in Bindings, Advanced, and NetBIOS do not need to be changed. In the Bindings tab, the check mark by the Client for Microsoft Net-

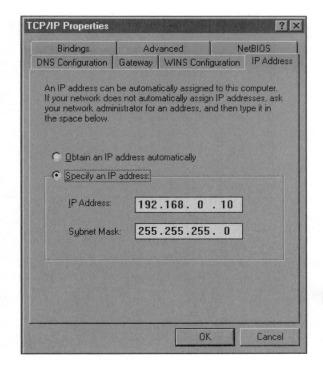

Figure 6-4

The opening panel for TCP/IP properties. The first tab is for the IP address. Other panels are for WINS and DNS server settings.

works shows that the network client will use the TCP/IP protocol. If you've enabled file and print sharing, that will also be shown with a check mark by it. The Advanced tab has nothing in it to configure. The NetBIOS tab indicates that NetBT is enabled.

IP ADDRESS AND DHCP

Setting the IP address can be handled in two ways: manually or by automatic configuration. Automatic configuration means that there is a DHCP server on your network that the computer will query for IP address information.

Note on IP-Autoconfiguration

Windows 98 and Me have IP-AutoConfiguration enabled by default. This means that if you do not manually assign an IP address to a Windows 98 system and if there is no DHCP server on the network or the DHCP server is not reachable, an IP address will automatically be assigned. A Class B address in the 169.254.x.x range is assigned. If a DHCP server is detected later, the IP address will be automatically reassigned. Details on IP-AutoConfiguration and instructions on disabling it can be found on the Windows 98 or Windows Me CD in the \tools\mtsutil\mtsutils.txt file.

Manual configuration means that a static IP address has been assigned to the computer and you will enter it manually. The example shown in Figure 6-4 shows manual configuration. The IP address is made up of four octets. The address used in the example is 192.168.0.10.

The Subnet Mask in the example is 255.255.255.0. This is a common mask on a local network. The mask indicates the portion of the IP address that doesn't change from host to host on the network.

WINS CONFIGURATION AND LMHOSTS

If the IP address is set to be obtained automatically, the WINS Configuration tab is set to Use DHCP for WINS Resolution. Make sure the radio button is checked.

If you aren't using a DHCP server, you'll either need to enable WINS or set up LMHOSTS. Using WINS is preferable. Your Samba server can be set to be a WINS server. Samba WINS servers are used on some very big networks and provide excellent performance.

If you have a WINS server—either a Samba server configured to be a WINS server or a Windows NT/2000 server as a WINS server—check the Enable WINS Resolution radio button and then enter the IP address of your primary WINS server. If you have additional WINS servers on the network add them as well. Figure 6-5 shows the WINS configuration tab with one WINS server added.

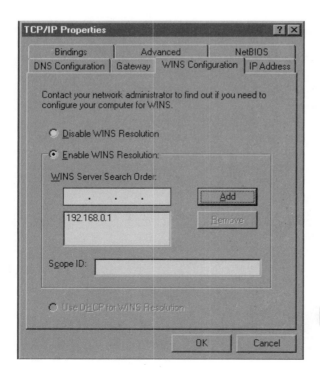

Figure 6-5   *If your network is using a WINS server, make sure Enable WINS Resolution is selected.*

CAUTION

Don't use a combination of Samba and Windows servers for your primary and secondary WINS servers. Their databases are incompatible, and name resolution will be incorrect.

If you don't have a WINS server, then you should set up and use the LMHOSTS file, using the format described earlier in the section called "Net BIOS and TCP/IP Networking," or use the *LMHOSTS.sam* file found in the *windows* directory and make the changes necessary for the local network.

One other option in the WINS configuration tab is to enter a Scope ID. Usually this is left blank. This is a security feature. A Scope ID can be assigned to a group of computers so that they can communicate only with each other and not with computers outside the group. With the Scope ID enabled, the computer can only see and be seen by other computers or servers with the same Scope ID.

Scope IDs are sometimes used to isolate a local network that's not behind a firewall so that it is invisible to the rest of the world. The Scope ID becomes essentially a site-wide password.

This is a limited security measure and does not replace overall network security. The Scope ID is easily visible and accessible to anyone on a computer on the network. It can be viewed in the WINS panel or by using the nbtstat utility. Open a DOS prompt and enter the command `nbtstat -n`. You'll see that the results include the Scope ID for the machine.

If you set up your Samba server or Windows server with a Scope ID, make sure it is configured on every computer on the network. Any computer without the Scope ID won't be able to connect to the server's resources.

All letters in your Scope ID should be capitalized. The Scope ID is case-sensitive, but on some systems the configuration information is saved all-capitalized, no matter what was entered. Therefore, if you connect to a server that saves the configuration information in mixed case, the Scope IDs will be seen as being different.

To enable the Scope ID on a Samba server, the smbd daemon has to be started with the `-i` *Scope ID* option. The Scope ID must be entered in the Globals section of SWAT in the Advanced View under Base Options as the `netbios scope`.

GATEWAY AND DNS SETTINGS

On the Gateway tab, enter the IP address of the router that is the exit point from this local network to other IP networks. If your network is not connected to other networks or does not access the Internet and you aren't using a Gateway, then you can leave this setting blank.

The DNS configuration tab is where the DNS is either disabled or enabled. On most networks, you'll want to have this enabled.

The Host should be the NetBIOS name for the machine and should match the Computer Name shown on the Identification tab of the Network configuration panel. The Domain field is for the DNS domain for the system and not the Windows workgroup domain.

Enter the IP address of the primary DNS server and click Add. You can also enter IP addresses for secondary and tertiary DNS servers. Figure 6-6 shows the DNS configuration tab.

There is no need to make any entries in the bottom section of the panel for listing the domain suffix search order.

Configure the Client for Microsoft Windows

The CIFS networking client is called the Client for Microsoft Windows. To configure the client, open the Network panel, select the Client for Microsoft Windows, and click the Properties button. This is where you set the network logon options. Figure 6-7 shows the Client configuration panel.

If this workstation is to be logged onto an NT domain controller or a Samba server acting as an NT domain controller, check the box to Log on to

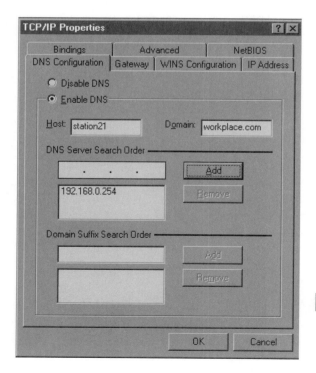

Figure 6-6 *The opening panel for TCP/IP properties. The first tab is for the IP address. Other panels are for WINS and DNS server settings.*

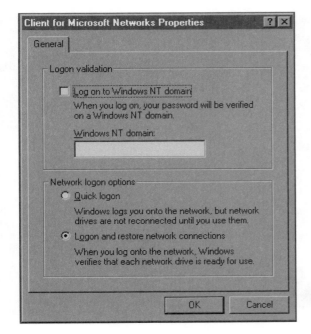

Figure 6-7

Make sure to check Logon and Restore Network Connections.

Windows NT Domain. In the Windows NT domain box, enter the Windows domain name.

On Network logon options, make sure to check the option to Logon and Restore Network Connections. This enables the reconnection of permanently mapped drives and printer ports every time the computer is started.

Choose Machine and Workgroup Names

After the TCP/IP protocol and the CIFS client have been configured, the workstation needs to be given a valid NetBIOS name. This is set in the Network control panel, accessed from the Control Panel or by right-clicking the Network Neighborhood/My Network Places. The machine name is set in the Identification tab. Figure 6-8 shows the Identification dialog box.

The space for the computer name is where the NetBIOS name for the machine is entered. This name must be unique on the network and usually matches the hostname from the fully qualified domain name of the system. This is not absolutely necessary, but it can make network management easier.

The workgroup is the group the workstation shares resources with. The workgroup name is commonly the same workgroup name defined during the Samba configuration, though again it is not necessary to use the same name. If you put the workstation in the same workgroup as the Samba server, the

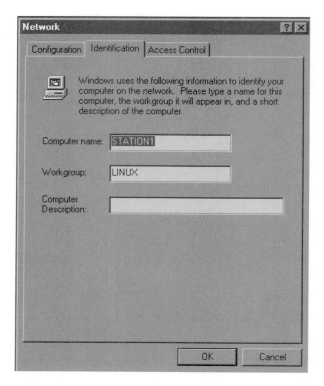

Figure 6-8 *Enter a valid NetBIOS machine name and workgroup in the Identification tab.*

Samba resources are more easily accessed with less browsing. But Windows 9.x/Me does not require that the machine belong to a specific Windows workgroup. The workstation can be in a different workgroup and still access a Samba server.

The Computer Description field in the Identification tab can contain any text or be left blank. If text is entered, it will be displayed next to the icon for the workstation in the Network Neighborhood/My Network Places.

Choose Security and Access Control Settings

The Access Control tab in the Network control panel is usually left at the default setting of share-level security. If you've enabled file or printer sharing for the workstation, this sets a security level for network access to the share.

USER-LEVEL SECURITY

User-level security requires the workstation to log onto a server. The logon name and password are checked against the server's name-and-password database. If they are authenticated, the workstation is allowed access to the server's resources. As long as the session is continued, all following requests from the workstation are allowed without requiring additional authentication. If you enabled user-level security for file and printer sharing on the workstation, you will need a logon server to authenticate the username and password. Setting up your Samba server as a logon server is described in Chapter 5.

SHARE-LEVEL SECURITY

Share-level security requires password authentication for each access to a shared file or printer. A username is never required.

Check the Connection

With networking configured, and the system restarted so that the changes are put into effect, you should be able to see the Samba server in the Network Neighborhood. If the Samba server doesn't show up there, it doesn't necessarily mean that the workstation or the Samba server is configured incorrectly.

First check the network connection and make sure that everything is working correctly. Then go through the steps for browsing and accessing in "Browsing, Accessing, and Mapping." That should take care of most of the network problems and put the Samba server in the Network Neighborhood/My Network Places. If it doesn't, look for additional steps in Chapter 7 on troubleshooting.

There are several utilities that you can use to check the network connection.

PING

The ping utility is a basic tool for seeing if the specified computer is reachable on the network. To use ping, open a DOS prompt and enter the command `ping` followed by the full domain name or IP address of the Samba server or another computer on the network:

Reboot and Reboot and ...

Every time you make a change on the Network control panel in Windows 9x, you will have to reboot the computer. On Windows Me, many but not all changes require rebooting.

```
ping samba.myserver.net
```

If ping returns a reply with connection information, your TCP/IP networking is properly configured. If ping returns with a "Request timed out" message, it can mean that there is a problem with your TCP/IP configuration or that the remote system isn't accessible (the remote system is turned off, for instance).

If you get a time-out, try pinging another computer or your default gateway. If you can't reach any other computer, it probably means that the problem is in the configuration or the hardware of the system you are working on. First check the cable and make sure it is connected. If the connection is good, then the other utilities listed here may help you find the problem.

WINIPCFG • This utility shows the IP configuration. Use it to confirm that the system is properly recognizing the configuration information you entered during TCP/IP setup. If any of the information here is incorrect, you will need to reconfigure TCP/IP in the Network control panel.

To display the IP configuration window, use Run from the Start menu. Enter the command

```
winipcfg
```

The configuration window opens. The window display shows the network adapter name and the Adapter Address, along with the IP Address, Subnet Mask, and Default Gateway. Check that the IP Address and Gateway are correct. If you are using DHCP to get the IP address, the six buttons on the bottom of the window are all enabled. These can be used to release an IP address or renew the address from the DHCP server.

The More Info button displays additional details, including host information. The host information section includes the hostname, the DNS server, the node type, and the NetBIOS Scope ID, along with other settings. If you are using a WINS server, the node type should be "hybrid." Hybrid CIFS clients resolve NetBIOS names first by using WINS and then by broadcast, if WINS fails. If you are using the LMHOSTS file for NetBIOS name resolution, the node type will be broadcast.

The Adapter Information section shows the DHCP and WINS servers.

IPCONFIG • The ipconfig utility is a DOS-based utility available on Windows 98 systems that produces the same information as winipcfg. Open a DOS window and enter the command

```
ipconfig /all
```

The IP configuration information is displayed. Check the IP information displayed and make sure it is correct. Again, if any of the information is incorrect, TCP/IP networking needs to be reconfigured.

If you are using DHCP and need to release or renew an IP address, use one of these commands:

```
ipconfig /release

ipconfig /renew
```

TRACERT • The tracert utility is used to find routing problems. If ping couldn't reach your Samba server and the server is accessed through a router, then tracert can help find where the problem is.

The original traceroute is a Unix utility. It traces a packet sent from your computer to any other computer on your intranet or on the Internet. The results display each hop the packet takes to reach the other computer.

Open a DOS window and enter the command followed by the full hostname or IP address of the remote system. For example:

```
tracert 192.168.3.64
```

Following the packet hops will let you see where there are any problems in reaching the Samba server.

NETSTAT • Netstat is a utility that displays information about the TCP connections between the computer and other systems. To use the netstat utility, run it from a DOS window. Netstat has many options. If you use the option to see all connections and ports, the results will scroll right off the screen. Instead, save the results into a text file that can then be viewed with Notepad. Enter the command

```
netstat -a > netstat.txt
```

Open the file in Notepad to see the results. Ports listed in the "Established" state are connections to servers on the network. If you have enabled file or printer sharing on this system, you should see one or more ports in the 137–139 range in the "Listening" state. These are the ports used for NetBIOS file and printer sharing.

Use the connection information to see what servers the system is connecting to. For example, if connections are shown on common ports, such as Web port 80 or pop3 port 110, then TCP/IP networking is functioning. An active connection to a Samba server should be displayed with the NetBIOS name of the server followed by a port name of nbsession. A Samba server named "Samba" would appear as an "Established" connection with the Foreign Address shown as

```
SAMBA:nbsession
```

NBSTAT • Nbtstat is similar to netstat, only it gives information for NetBIOS connections. Use it to check whether NetBIOS name resolution is working correctly. In a DOS window, enter the command

```
nbtstat -r
```

The results will show whether name resolution is properly configured and working. If the results are negative, name resolution is not working. You need to check the WINS server or the LMHOSTS file to correct name resolution.

The utility can also be used to check the status of your Samba server. If the NetBIOS name of your Samba server were "Samba," for example, you would enter the command

```
nbtstat -n -a SAMBA
```

The results show information about the status of the Samba server.

NET • The net utility has many functions, most of them described in Section 6.5 on browsing and accessing. To check connections, open a DOS window and enter the command

```
net view
```

This displays the NetBIOS servers available in the workgroup, including Samba servers and Windows NT/2000 servers as well as workstations with file or printer sharing enabled.

Setting Up Windows NT

Windows NT networking is built on the TCP/IP protocol. NT is a true multi-user system with many robust features. The user interface looks much like that found on Windows 95, but underneath the interface is a completely different operating system. The NT kernel is written in C, just like the Linux kernel and all Unix kernels. This gives NT workstations and servers greater stability and flexibility than Windows 9*x* systems.

Make sure that you have Service Pack 3 or higher. Service Pack 6, however, has a serious flaw that prevents accessing upper TCP ports. This is fixed in Service Pack 6a.

Accessing a Samba server from an NT workstation, which is explained in "Browsing, Accessing, and Mapping," is done in the same way it is done on a Windows 9*x* system. But because the operating system itself is different, configuration is handled differently.

The initial network configuration must be done as the system administrator. With the networking configured, the process of browsing, accessing, and mapping is handled by each individual user.

Windows NT does not support plug-and-play, and hardware is not automatically detected. The first step is to make sure that the driver for the network interface card is installed. In the Control Panel, double-click the Network icon and click on the Adapter tab. If the network card is not displayed, you'll need to install the driver. Each network card manufacturer has its own installation method. Be sure to follow the instructions that come with the adapter to install the driver.

Configure TCP/IP networking

TCP/IP network configuration for NT involves a few basic steps. The machine is assigned its NetBIOS name. The CIFS client and TCP/IP protocol are installed and configured. The IP address is entered, and the DNS and WINS servers are set.

ASSIGN THE NETBIOS NAME

The NT workstation must have a NetBIOS name. This is assigned in the Network setup panel, which is accessed by double-clicking the Network icon in the Control Panel. The first tab in the Network panel is for Identification. The Computer Name is the NetBIOS name for the machine. The Workgroup is the Windows network workgroup the machine belongs to, which is usually set to the workgroup name defined on the Samba server.

Click on the Change button to enter the NetBIOS name and Workgroup. The computer name should be the same as the hostname for setting up TCP/IP. Although Windows will let you enter different names for the two settings, it is much easier to maintain the system on the network when the computer is using only one name for everything.

CHECK THE CIFS CLIENT

The CIFS client is installed by default on Windows NT systems. In the Network panel, click on the Services tab. Look for Workstation service. This is the Microsoft Networking client that is needed to connect to a Samba server. If it is not installed, choose Add and install the Workstation service. You will need the Windows NT operating system CD to add the Workstation service software.

You should also check that the Workstation service is being started automatically. Look at the Services panel in the Control Panel. In the list of services, find Workstation and make sure that it is set to start automatically.

INSTALL AND SET UP TCP/IP

In the Protocol tab on the Network panel, make sure the TCP/IP protocol is installed. If it isn't listed, select Add. On the list of protocols, select TCP/IP Protocol.

The TCP/IP protocol then needs to be configured. Highlight the TCP/IP icon and click the Properties button. Make sure that the correct network adapter is selected, and then proceed.

SET THE IP ADDRESS

Start with the IP address tab. The IP address can be set by a DHCP server or configured manually. If you are using a DHCP server on your network, then make sure that radio button is selected, and move on to DNS configuration.

If the computer has been assigned a static IP address, check the radio button to specify an IP address. Enter the IP address, the Subnet Mask, and the Default Gateway. The Subnet Mask is often set to 255.255.255.0. The mask indicates the portion of the IP address that is local. The Gateway is the router used to connect to other networks.

CONFIGURE DNS • Select the DNS tab. Enter the hostname and domain name for the workstation. The hostname should match the NetBIOS name entered in the Identification tab.

To enter the DNS server information, click on Add and enter the IP address of the first DNS server. Add secondary and tertiary DNS servers, if you have either.

The DNS server is used for access to wide-area networks and the Internet. DNS servers convert human-readable names into computer-usable IP addresses.

CONFIGURE WINS • Select the WINS Address tab. Make sure the correct network adapter is selected. If you have a WINS server, enter its IP address in the space for the primary WINS server. Add the secondary WINS server, if you have one.

CAUTION

Don't use a combination of Samba and Windows servers for your primary and secondary WINS servers. Their databases are incompatible, and name resolution will be incorrect.

Generally you should use a WINS server, but if you aren't using WINS, check Enable LMHOSTS Lookup. Make sure that an LMHOSTS file is set up in the *\WINNT\system32\drivers\etc* folder. A sample file that explains the format needed by LMHOSTS can be found in that directory. The name of the file is *LMHOSTS.SAM*.

The LMHOSTS file is a text file that lists IP addresses and the corresponding NetBIOS names. The file is searched sequentially from top to bottom, so frequently used names should be listed near the top.

Check the box to enable DNS for Windows resolution. This setting means that WINS will try the DNS server if it can't find a name in its own database tables.

Finally, if you are using Scope ID to keep the workgroup private, enter the name in the space provided. Beware—if you use Scope ID, your computer won't be able to connect to any network servers that don't have the same Scope ID. If you are unsure about Scope ID, leave it blank.

Check the Connection

After networking has been configured, the Samba server should appear in the Network Neighborhood. If it doesn't show up, check the configuration and the connections to make sure that these are not the source of the problem. Next, go through the steps for browsing and accessing found in "Browsing, Accessing, and Mapping." That should clear up most network problems and put the Samba server in the Network Neighborhood. If it doesn't, look for additional steps in Chapter 7 on troubleshooting.

Checking the connection on an NT system is similar to checking it on a Windows 9*x*/Me system. To check the connection, use one of the utilities described below.

PING • Ping is used to see if other computers are accessible from your computer. Ping sends a packet to a specified computer and then waits for the reply. The result is that either the other computer is reachable or it is not. To use ping, open a Command Prompt window and enter the command `ping` followed by the full domain name or IP address of the Samba server or another computer on the network:

```
ping samba.myserver.net
```

If you get a time-out, try pinging another computer or your default gateway. If you still get a time-out, it usually means that there is either a configuration error or hardware problem on your system.

IPCONFIG • The ipconfig utility is based on the Unix ifconfig utility. To use it, open a Command Prompt window and enter the command

```
ipconfig /all
```

The IP configuration information is displayed, including the network card's hardware address. Check the IP information and make sure it is correct. If any of the information is incorrect, the TCP/IP networking needs to be reconfigured.

TRACERT • Tracert, like the Unix traceroute utility, traces a packet sent from your computer to another computer. The results can be used to see if there is a point of failure and, if there is, where the failure is occurring. To use it, open a Command Prompt window and enter the command followed by the full hostname or IP address of the remote system:

```
tracert samba.myserver.net
```

Tracert is used to find problems on large networks where various paths lead to the same point or where there are many different routers or bridges on the network.

NETSTAT • Netstat shows protocol statistics and current network connections. To use it, run it from a Command Prompt window. If you use the option to see all connections and ports, the results will scroll right off the screen. Instead, use the More option to pause each screen. Enter the command

```
netstat -a | more
```

Look at the active server connections. An active connection to a Samba server should be displayed with the NetBIOS name of the server followed by a port name of nbsession. A Samba server named "Samba" would appear as

```
SAMBA:nbsession
```

NBSTAT • Nbtstat gives information for NetBIOS connections. Use it to check whether NetBIOS name resolution is working correctly. Open a Command Prompt window and enter the command

```
nbtstat -r
```

If name resolution is working, NetBIOS name resolution and statistics will show the results. This is used to determine if the WINS server or the LMHOSTS file are working. The utility can also be used to check the status of your Samba server. To check on a server named "Samba," enter the command

```
nbtstat -n -a SAMBA
```

The results show information about the status of the Samba server.

NET • The net utility has many functions, most of them described in the section on browsing and accessing. To check connections, open a Command Prompt window and enter the command

```
net view
```

This should show the same information displayed in the Network Neighborhood.

Setting Up Windows 2000

Windows 2000 was called Windows NT 5 during its development. That's because it's built on the code for Windows NT 4. At one time Microsoft had planned to merge all of the Windows systems—the consumer Windows 9x and the business Windows NT—into Windows 2000. Instead, the company dropped the Windows 2000 Personal Edition and released the upgrade of Windows 98 called the Millennium Edition (Windows Me).

Windows 2000 Professional replaces Windows NT Workstation. In addition, there are three different server products: Windows 2000 Server, Windows 2000 Advanced Server, and Windows 2000 Datacenter Server. Windows 2000 introduces many new features, including plug-and-play capability to detect hardware on the system. More significant for administrators of Samba servers is Microsoft's move toward using TCP/IP exclusively for networking. Windows 2000 starts a move by Microsoft away from the NetBIOS protocol. This does not mean that NetBIOS is no longer supported. In fact, Windows 2000 defaults to NetBIOS compatibility mode. And the Windows 2000 TCP/IP stack includes NetBT (NetBIOS over TCP/IP) support. The Windows 2000 server also includes an enhanced WINS server even though a WINS server is not needed for a pure Windows 2000 network.

NetBIOS will continue to be the primary protocol used on a Windows network, even one with Windows 2000 servers, for a very long time to come. For one thing, it will take a long time, in some cases years, until enterprises begin incorporating the new Windows 2000 servers into existing networks. Even then, in order to eliminate NetBIOS, not only do all of the NT servers have to be replaced by 2000 servers, but all legacy Windows clients—all of those Windows 9x systems on everyone's desktops—also have to be completely replaced. That's many years away, and surely by that time the Samba development team will have made Samba servers work seamlessly on a pure Windows 2000 network.

Configure TCP/IP Networking

Windows administrators familiar with Windows NT will find that on Windows 2000, Microsoft rearranged all of the administrative tools. For example, there is a new Network and Dial-Up Connections tool for setting up TCP/IP networking. This tool combines the functions of the Windows Dial-Up Networking panel and NT 4's Network Control Panel. This section goes over the steps for configuring the Windows 2000 Professional client to connect to a Samba server. The steps include explanations of the variations from Windows NT, since that is widely known by Windows administrators. As with Windows NT, you have to be logged in as the administrator or a member of the administrator's group to configure the system.

ASSIGN THE NETBIOS NAME

The machine name and workgroup have been separated from the TCP/IP networking configuration. They are set in System Properties. In the Control Panel, select the System icon or right-click My Computer on the desktop and select Properties.

Select the Network Identification tab, shown in Figure 6-9, and click the Properties button. In the Identification Changes panel, shown in Figure 6-10, click on the More button to set the NetBIOS name for the computer. The Net-

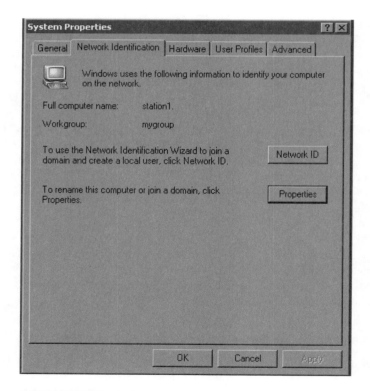

Figure 6-9   *In System Properties, the computer name and workgroup or domain are set in Network ID.*

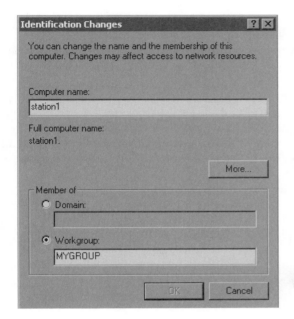

Create or update the computer's identification information.

BIOS name, identified as the Computer name in this panel, is derived from the hostname part of the fully qualified domain name for the computer. In the Network Identification panel, enter either the Windows domain or the workgroup name.

Click on the Change button to enter the NetBIOS name and Workgroup. The computer name should be the same name used as the hostname given in the Full Computer Name. Although you can enter different names for the two settings, Windows 2000 is designed to expect both names to be the same.

CONFIGURE THE CIFS CLIENT AND TCP/IP

The CIFS client is installed by default on Windows 2000 systems. To check the settings, right-click on My Network Places and select Properties. In the Network and Dial-Up Connections window, right-click on Local Area Connection and select Properties. The network interface card is listed under Connect Using in the General tab.

Under that, the Client for Microsoft Networks and Internet Protocol (TCP/IP) should both be listed as components used by this connection. If either is missing, click on Install. In the Component Type window, select Client to install the Client for Microsoft Networks or Protocol to install TCP/IP. In the next window that opens, select the component you are installing.

To configure the TCP/IP protocol, highlight the TCP/IP icon in the Local Area Connection Properties panel and click the Properties button. The Internet Protocol (TCP/IP) Properties panel opens, showing the configuration of the IP address and DNS.

SET THE IP ADDRESS • Start with the IP address. The default setting is to use a DHCP server to set the IP address. If you are using a DHCP server on your network, then leave the setting at Obtain an IP Address Automatically.

If the computer has been assigned a static IP address, check the radio button for Use the Following IP Address. Enter the IP address, the Subnet Mask, and the Default Gateway. The Subnet Mask is commonly set to 255.255.255.0. The mask indicates the portion of the IP address that is local. The Gateway is the router used to connect to other networks.

CONFIGURE DNS • On DNS, if you are using a DHCP server, leave the default setting of Obtain DNS Server Address Automatically.

Alternatively, enter the DNS server information, and select Use the Following DNS Server Addresses. Enter the IP address of the preferred DNS server. If there is an additional DNS server, add it as the alternate.

WINS AND NETBIOS COMPATIBILITY

You'll need to configure a WINS server for the Windows 2000 system. Since WINS is supposed to no longer be needed, the configuration is hidden. To configure WINS, highlight the TCP/IP icon in the Local Area Connection Properties panel and click the Properties button. The Internet Protocol (TCP/IP) Properties panel opens, showing the configuration of the IP address and DNS. Select the Internet Protocol (TCP/IP) and then click on the Advanced button. The Advanced TCP/IP Settings panel opens.

Select the WINS tab and click the Add button to add your WINS server's IP address. After adding the WINS server information, in the lower section of the panel make sure that the Enable NetBIOS Over TCP/IP radio button is checked.

Unless you have an all–Windows 2000 network, you should use a WINS server, but if you aren't using WINS, check Enable LMHOSTS Lookup. The *LMHOSTS.SAM* file that can be found on the system explains the format needed by LMHOSTS.

Check the Connection

After networking has been configured, the Samba server should appear in My Network Places. If it doesn't show up, check to make sure that TCP/IP is configured correctly and that NetBIOS compatibility is enabled. Then check the connection, following the steps below. If the configuration and connection are correct, then follow the steps for browsing and accessing found in the next section. If the Samba server still doesn't show up, look for additional steps in Chapter 7 on troubleshooting.

To check the connection, use one of the utilities described below.

PING • Ping the Samba server to see if it is reachable. To use ping, open a Command Prompt window and enter the command `ping`, followed by the full domain name or IP address of the Samba server:

```
ping samba.myserver.net
```

If you get a time-out, try pinging another computer or your default gateway. If you still get a time-out, it usually means that there is either a configuration error or hardware problem on your system.

NETDIAG • Netdiag is one of the Windows 2000 Support Tools. The support tools aren't installed as part of the Windows 2000 installation and have to be added later.

The Support Tools installation program is on the Windows 2000 CD in the *\support\tools* folder. You have to be logged in as the administrator or a member of the administrators group to install the tools. In addition to netdiag, there are 11 other tools installed. The tools can be installed on any Windows 9*x*/Me/NT/2000 computer.

Netdiag, the Network Connectivity Tester, is a command-line tool. Use it to find networking and connectivity problems. Netdiag doesn't require any parameters or switches. It is designed to initialize any parameters needed to analyze the network connection. It tests the network drivers, the protocol drivers, and the connectivity.

Open a command and enter

```
netdiag
```

NET • The net utility has many functions, most of them described in Section 6.5 on browsing and accessing. To check connections, open a Command Prompt window and enter the command

```
net view
```

This should show the same information displayed in My Network Places.

Browsing, Accessing, and Mapping

Most Windows users first access a Samba server by browsing the Network Neighborhood/My Network Places. Browsing is the common way to see what resources are available on the network. In addition to browsing, access to files on a Samba server can be established by mapping a drive to the Samba share.

Browsing and Browser Elections

The browse list is gathered from information broadcast by each machine on the network. Every Windows computer, when it starts up, announces its presence and NetBIOS name. This triggers a browser election. Browser elections are also held every 12 minutes by all the Windows machines on the network. In an election, each machine broadcasts its name, its operating system level, and a random number. The operating system level determines priority, while the random number allows machines with the same operating system level to compete with each other.

Samba's default level is 20, meaning Samba will win a local master browsing election over all Microsoft operating systems except a Windows NT 4/2000 server. This setting can be changed to match the level needed for your network. Any setting above 32 will mean that Samba should win all browser elections.

When a machine wins a browser election, it becomes the local master browser on its subnet on the network. The local master browser collates the NetBIOS names from all other machines on the subnet and advertises them. That's where the entries in Network Neighborhood/My Network Places come from.

Each subnet must have a local master browser or browsing won't work.

The operating system levels for browser elections are

Windows for Workgroups	1
Windows 9x/Me	1
Windows NT Workstation	16
Windows 2000 Professional	16
Windows NT Server	32
Windows 2000 Server	32

Samba can also become a domain master browser. This is a special machine that collects browse lists across several subnets. There can be only one domain master browser at any given time.

(continued)

In the Network Neghborhood/My Network Places, you will initially see only computers on your own subnet. A domain master browser contacts the local master browser for each subnet and gets its list of NetBIOS names and IP addresses. Then it transmits the complete list to each local master browser. That's how you can see computers not in your own subnet.

The only problem here is that because browser elections are spaced out at 12-minute intervals, some machines can show up in the Network Neighborhood/My Network Places that are no longer available, or machines that are available don't yet appear.

Browse services are something like name services. The servers that publish resources on the network are called master browsers. Master browsers differ from name servers in that there is no one server on the network that is designated the master browser server. In fact, the network can have several master browsers.

When you log onto a Windows network, your computer finds a master browser by broadcasting a request that essentially asks, "Hey, which one of you out there is the master browser?" The first master browser to get the request responds, "I'll accept all of your requests."

When a server starts up, it sends out a similar request, looking for the master browser. When a master browser replies, the server sends back a message that says, "I'm FILE_SERVER_1. I have the following resources available. Please add them to your list of servers."

The list of servers the master browser maintains is called the browse list. This is what appears in the Network Neighborhood/My Network Places. The browse list should initially display servers in your workgroup, including any Windows 9x/Me computers with file or printer sharing enabled. A Samba server should look just like a Windows NT Server on the browse list. To see the resources available on any of the servers in the browse list, double-click on the server's icon.

In addition to the master browser, there are usually backup browsers. The Samba server can be configured to be a master browser or a backup browser.

Browsing on Windows networks, however, has quirks that can make it seem that it isn't working correctly. For example, a server may appear in the browse list, but double-clicking on the icon only gets an error message, for several possible reasons. The server may not have any resources available, or the resources may not be available for the user logged in on the client workstation.

A shared resource on a Samba server can be

- browseable and accessible
- browseable and not accessible
- accessible and not browseable
- not browseable and not accessible

If the Samba server does not show up in the Network Neighborhood/ My Network Places and the network connection is known to be good, the Samba configuration should be checked. Make sure that a browseable share has been defined. See Chapter 3 on setting up file shares in Samba. The `browseable=yes` setting needs to be enabled for a Samba share to appear in the Network Neighborhood.

Another reason a Samba server could appear on a browse list but not be accessible is that it can take up to 60 minutes for a master browser to notice that a server is no longer available. That's because of the way the browse service works.

When a Samba server, or any other server, connects to the network, it announces its arrival on the initial connection and then repeats the announcement after 1 minute and again after 2, 4, 8 and 12 minutes. After that, the announcement is repeated every 12 minutes. If the server fails to make its scheduled announcement three times, the master browser removes the server from the browse list. That's 36 minutes. It can take the master browser up to 12 additional minutes to realize that the third announcement was missed. And it can take up to another 12 minutes for the master browser to remove the server from the browse list. That's potentially 60 minutes that the server has been unavailable but still on the browse list.

If the Samba server shows up on the browse list, but its resources aren't accessible, then check the server and make sure that it is up and running. Don't wait for it to disappear from the browse list before checking the status of the server.

An almost opposite problem is also possible. A share can be defined on the Samba server that is not displayed in the browse list. This can happen if you've added a new share on the Samba server or made a change in an existing one. The share isn't displayed because it wasn't available when the server first connected to the master browser. It won't appear until the master browser refreshes its list of available resources. It can take as little as a few minutes to as long as an hour for the master browser to display the newly created or changed resource on the Samba server.

If the Samba server and its shared resources don't appear in the Network Neighborhood/My Network Places and you don't want to wait up to an hour to access the share, you can use the net utility to check and access a share on the Samba server. This is run from the DOS prompt.

THE NET UTILITY • The net utility is the Swiss Army knife of network tools on your Windows workstation. Although the usual way to access a Samba server is through the Network Neighborhood/My Network Places and with Windows Explorer, the Net command-line utility has features that make it a valuable tool for troubleshooting as well as accessing Samba shares.

The Net utility can show the same browse list seen in the Network Neighborhood/My Network Places by using the Browse option. The command is

```
net view
```

To see the resources available on a server, use the Net View command followed by the NetBIOS name of the server. To see the resources on a server named "Samba," the command is

```
net view \\samba
```

This does not show resources not already displayed by the master browser's browse list and shows only what would also appear in the Network Neighborhood. But with the NetBIOS name of the server and the name of the share, you can use the Net utility to access the share. The command to map the Windows workstation's G: drive to access a file share named "public" on a server named "Samba" is

```
net use g; \\samba\public
```

Table 6.1 lists some of the Net commands and options. For a complete list use the `net help` command.

Accessing Samba File Shares

The initial access of the Samba server is usually through browsing the Network Neighborhood/My Network Places. Double-clicking the icon for the Samba server will show the shares available on the server for the username you've used to log onto the Windows machine.

The Net command can also be used to browse the Network Neighborhood. In a DOS/Command window, enter the command

```
net view
```

The same list of servers shown by double-clicking the Network Neighborhood icon is shown by Net View.

The command to see the list of shares available is

```
net view \\server-name
```

Mapping File Shares

Mapping drives is an easy way to access Samba shares, with the share appearing on the Windows computer as a drive letter. Personal home directories on the Samba server are often mapped to the H: drive.

Open Network Neighborhood/My Network Places and double-click on the Samba server icon. The available shares are displayed. The share with the same name as the login name you used to log onto the Windows computer is the home directory or home share on the Samba server. If you right-click on the share, that is, the folder with the logon name, you can select Map

| Table 6-1 | *Net Utility Commands* |

Command	Description
net config	Displays current workgroup settings
net diag	Starts Microsoft Network Diagnostics program to test connections on Windows 9x/Me
net diag /names	Starts Microsoft Network Diagnostics program with the option to give the computer a different NetBIOS name on Windows 9x/Me
net diag /status	Option to specify a computer for network diagnostics information on Windows 9x/Me
net help	Displays net commands
net help *option*	Displays details about the specified option
net print \\computer	Displays information about printer shares on the specified computer, including print job numbers
net print *job#* /delete	Using the job number, a print file can be deleted; other options include /pause and /resume
net time /set	Synchronizes your computer with a time server; requires a time server in your workgroup
net use	Connect or disconnect from a share on a server; options include:
	drive (drive letter assigned to file share) or (assign next available drive letter)
	port (assign printer port name for printer share)
	computer (NetBIOS name of server)
	directory (name of file share)
	printer (name of printer share)
net ver	Version of workgroup redirector the computer is using
net view	Displays the browse list for the workgroup

Note on IPC$ and Encrypted Passwords

If you are trying to connect to a Samba server and a dialog box opens with a request for the password for user IPC$, it means that Samba did not accept the password sent from your computer. If the client system is running Windows 9x or Me, the username and password that were used for logging onto the computer do not match the username and password on the Samba server. The two must match; you cannot have different usernames and passwords on the client computer and the server computer. Fix this problem by changing the username and password on your computer to match what is on the Samba server or by creating a username and password on the Samba server that match what you are using on the client computer.

One other possible cause of this conflict is that Samba may have been configured to use plain text passwords. The original version of Windows 95 passed plain text passwords for logging onto the server. Updated versions of Windows 95, Windows 98, Me, and 2000, as well as Windows NT with Service Pack 3 or higher, all pass encrypted passwords.

Samba's default configuration is set to accept plain text passwords. You can either change this setting to encrypted passwords and build a database of encrypted passwords on the Samba server using the smbpasswd utility, or you can edit the registry on all the Windows 98, Me, NT and 2000 systems to force them to send plain text passwords.

It is best to use encrypted passwords to maintain network security. If you want to pass plain text passwords, however, use the steps below to edit the registry. On Windows 95, 98, and Me, use regedit to open the following registry key:

```
HKEY_LOCAL_MACHINE\System\CurrentControlSet\Services\VxD\VNETSUP
```

From the menu, select Edit/New/DWORD Value. Rename New Value #1:

```
EnablePlainTextPassword
```

Press Enter; then double-click on the new entry and set the value to 1.

On a Windows NT system, use regedt32 to change the following registry key:

```
HKEY_LOCAL_MACHINE\SYSTEM\CurrentControlSet\Services\Rdr\Parameters
```

Add

```
EnablePlainTextPassword
```

of type REG_DWORD with a value of 1.

On a Windows 2000 system, use regedt32 to change this registry key:

```
HKEY_LOCAL_MACHINE\SYSTEM\CurrentControlSet\Services\LanmanWorkStation\Parameters
```

Add

```
EnablePlainTextPassword
```

of type REG_DWORD with a value of 1

For more detailed information on encrypted passwords, see *ENCRYPTION.txt* and *WinNT.txt* in the *textdocs* subdirectory of the Samba documents directory on the Samba server.

Network Drive. Choose a drive letter for the share. Figure 6-11 shows the Map Network drive dialog box from Windows 2000.

Another way to map a drive is to double-click on the My Computer icon on the desktop and click on the Map Drive button in the window that opens. A third way is to right-click the My Computer icon and select Map Network Drive.

Mapping a drive using the My Computer icon requires that you know the NetBIOS name of the Samba server and the name of the file share on Windows 9x, Me, and NT systems. Windows 2000 includes a browse option. The format used for mapping is the Uniform Naming Convention (UNC), which uses the following format:

```
\\server-name\shared-resource-name
```

Make sure to use back slashes, and not the forward slashes used in Web addresses and on Linux filesystems. For example, to access the public directory on the server "Samba," you would use

```
\\samba\public
```

UNC can also be used to identify shared printers.

In the mapping dialog box is an option to check if you want the mapping to be restored if the computer is restarted.

The net command can also be used to map network drives. In a DOS/ Command window, enter the command

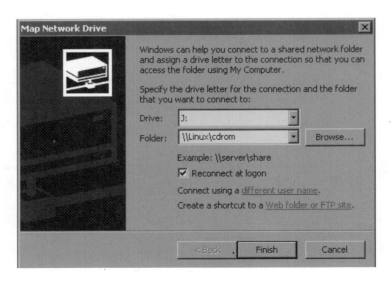

Figure 6-11   *To map a drive letter, enter the folder name or use browse.*

```
net use * \\servername\shared-resource-name
```

This command uses the * wildcard to indicate that the next available drive letter should be assigned to the mapped share. A specific drive letter can be used instead, as in this example of mapping the public share on the server named "Samba" to the P: drive:

```
net use p: \\samba\public
```

Mapping with the net command does not include the option to make the mapping reconnect on restart.

Most Windows users expect to have their shares on the Samba server automatically mapped when they log onto the computer. Setting up roaming profiles on the Samba server is a good way to make sure that the drives are mapped correctly when the user logs in. See the section on roaming profiles in Chapter 5.

Troubleshooting

Samba troubleshooting is an art. Some think it's an art like war is supposed to be an art. Well, it is less than war, but some days you wonder. If you've ever done troubleshooting on a Windows network, then you already know what's involved. Most of the time it's not difficult. The normal problems continually come up. There are only occasional problems that make you go into the trenches. For Samba, there a few common problems—all described in this chapter—that cover about 90% of the complaints.

Troubleshooting Samba works best if you are "bilingual," that is, if you understand the two different operating systems—Windows and Linux. But it is certainly not necessary to fully understand both operating systems to do troubleshooting. This chapter starts with techniques to check networking, then continues by describing a process that you can use for troubleshooting. This uses proven techniques for finding the source of the problem. Following that are descriptions of problems divided into network-related, Windows-related and Samba-related problems. The division is not always clear, so if you don't find the problem in one section, look in the others. Finally, there is a section on troubleshooting printing problems.

Problems Connecting to a New Server

More often than not, there are few problems when setting up a new Samba server. If you have just set up your Samba server and are having a problem, follow this basic two-point procedure.

Check Networking

The first step for correcting problems with a new Samba server is to check networking on the server. Make sure that the Samba server can reach other computers on the network and that you can reach it from a remote computer.

For tips on doing this, see the section on network-related problems, found later in this chapter. Use tools like ping, traceroute, and netstat to find network-related problems and then correct them.

Sometimes networking problems are caused by failing network interface cards, bad routers, or incorrect wiring. If there is a problem connecting from more than one workstation, the problem may be with the physical network.

After you've made sure that there are no problems with networking, if you still can't connect to your Samba server, then check the Samba configuration.

Check the Samba Configuration

To check the Samba configuration, open SWAT, the Web-based Samba configuration tool from a client machine on the network. If you are having trouble connecting to SWAT, see Section 7.5, which gives some tips on connecting to SWAT.

Make sure that SWAT is accessible before continuing. While it is not necessary for SWAT to be accessible to have Samba running, it is a good way to test that the Samba server is reachable on the network. It is also an easy way to also check that Samba is running and properly configured.

Once you can connect to SWAT, make sure that at least one file share is defined. That's usually the homes share, but it can be anything. If there isn't a share defined, use the procedures outlined in Chapter 3 for setting up a file share.

Next, click the Status tab on SWAT and make sure that the Samba daemons are running. If not, click the buttons to start smbd and nmbd. In Windows terms, this is the same as starting a service on an NT/2000 server. Both the smbd and nmbd daemons (services) must be running for the Samba server to work properly.

While you can force the daemons to start using the buttons on the Status tab of SWAT, you should check the Samba server and make sure that it is set up to start Samba automatically. On most Linux distributions, if you've chosen to install Linux as a server, the system will be configured to start the Samba daemons automatically. If you installed Linux as a workstation, Samba services are probably not set up to start by default.

If the server was started up after Samba was configured and Samba is not running, then you need to find why the daemons aren't starting automatically. Use Webmin, the browser-based system administration program, and check the settings for the Linux server. On the System tab in Webmin, select the link to the

Bootup and Shutdown page. Look for Samba or SMB and make sure that the Start at Boot Time option is set to Yes, as shown in Figure 7-1.

If everything appears to be set up correctly, yet Samba still does not start automatically after bootup of the system, you may need to get help from a systems engineer or service technician familiar with the Linux operating system. Once the server has been configured to start Samba automatically, you probably won't have any problems with the daemons starting again. Of course, it is also okay to start them manually, just as you might start some services manually on a Windows server. Normally you'll want the Samba services to start automatically, though.

With Samba running on the server, try to connect from a Windows workstation. Make sure that the username you've logged onto the Windows workstation with is defined in the Samba configuration as an authorized user of the file share. Also make sure that the username has been added as a Samba user.

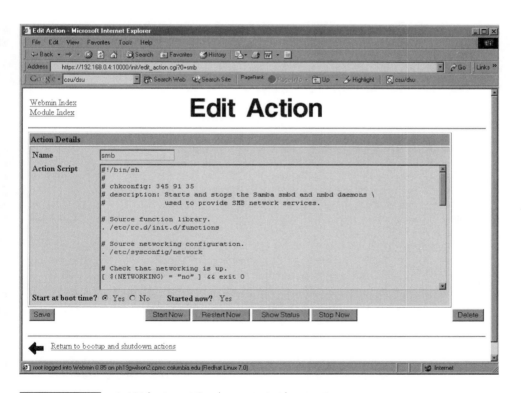

Figure 7-1   *In Webmin, set Samba to start at bootup time.*

A General Guide for Troubleshooting

Most Samba-related problems don't appear with the initial setup of the Samba server. They come when connecting a workstation to the server for the first time. Connection-related problems can be roughly divided into three areas:

- **Networking.** The Samba server isn't responding, or the Windows workstation can't reach the Samba server.
- **Windows workstation problems.** The Samba server isn't in the Network Neighborhood/Computers Near Me, or Windows is throwing up dialog boxes with error messages and refuses to connect or work correctly.
- **Samba server problems.** The Samba server won't allow the user to connect or refuses to let the user save files on the server.

Figuring out whether the problem is network-related, Windows-related, or Samba-related is the biggest part of the job of troubleshooting. A problem can seem to be Windows-related when in fact it is either a network or Samba server problem. For example, a common error message in Windows is "You don't have permission to open this file." This could be a Windows-related problem—for example, the user has logged onto the Windows workstation with a username that doesn't have read access to the file. On the other hand, it could be a Samba-related problem—for example, the user doesn't have the correct permissions on the Samba server. Then again, it could be something else. Sometimes it's necessary to check several possibilities before finding a solution.

Four Quick Things to Check

Here are four quick checks to make when having problems on a Samba network. They are listed in no particular order.

CHECK THE NETWORK WIRING

It may sound obvious, but too many times a network problem is caused by a loose connection. Check the network wiring and make sure that the connections to the network interface card and the wall jack are both good. Don't just jiggle the wires, but disconnect and reconnect them. Sometimes the contacts are bad because of humidity or dust.

RESTART THE WORKSTATION

A Windows workstation sometimes must be restarted before it will connect to a network server. If you haven't lost the network connection but you are having problems, restart the computer and then confirm that you still have the problem. Restarting the computer solves many Windows-based conflicts.

CHECK THE WINDOWS CLIENT CONFIGURATION

Check the Windows client configuration. Check especially that the client is not set up to use NetBEUI. Older Windows systems default to using NetBEUI. Samba does not support NetBEUI. The client must be set to using TCP/IP. If you are still having problems, try uninstalling the networking components, restarting the computer, and then reinstalling the networking software. This procedure can solve some particularly persistent problems. Problems with client configuration can appear on systems that have been working normally. Never assume that just because it has been working, the current configuration is correct. Find out if there were any recent software installations on the workstation. Some software installation programs automatically reconfigure the computer in ways that can produce a conflict.

CHECK THE LOGS

On a Windows server on the network, check the Event Log. Look for messages, particularly around the time the Samba server came online. The Event Log can show evidence of problems, such as domain browser conflicts. Look carefully for any unusual events. Windows servers can shut down network services based on a conflict caused by a misconfigured Samba server. You can also check the Samba logs, though they are more difficult to decipher. These logs are found in the */var/log/samba* directory on Red Hat Linux, in */var/log/samba.d* on Caldera OpenLinux, in */var/log* on Debian GNU/Linux, and in */usr/local/samba/var* on systems that use Samba's default configuration. There are two logs, one for smbd and another for nmbd. View the logs by opening them in an editor. If you are using Webmin, the Samba logs can be viewed with the Log Viewer found on the Others tab. Figure 7-2 shows the smbd log using Webmin's log viewer.

The format of the Samba logs is designed for Samba programmers. That makes them more difficult to read for nonprogrammers, though after reading through them a few times you will learn the syntax. Start reading from the bottom up because the last lines are the most recent; this is where you'll find the most recent errors listed. Look for lines that indicate failures; these can be hints as to what might be the problem.

The default debug level is 0, meaning that only Samba crashes are recorded with minimal information. This setting is good for keeping the logs small, but it does not give enough information to work with when you are trying to fix a problem. Change the Samba configuration to a debug level of 6 to get error messages that have enough information. Don't forget to change the debug level back to 0 once you've fixed the problem so that your logs don't get too big.

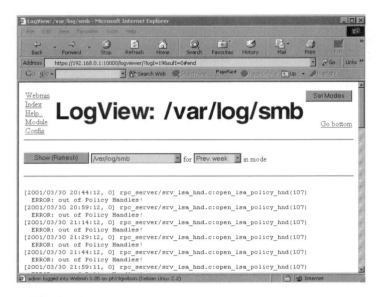

Figure 7-2   *Check Samba's logs for error messages.*

Problems With the Network Connection

Sometimes the network connection is the problem. This is the easiest kind of problem to find and solve. That's why it is a good place to start. There are many possible points of failure on a network. There can be problems with the initial configuration or with the network hardware.

There are some very good and easy-to-use tools for tracking down network-related problems. Both Windows and Linux include several network-troubleshooting tools.

Is the Network Configured Properly?

Start troubleshooting the network connection by checking the IP configuration. On Windows 9*x*/Me systems, use the winipcfg tool. On Windows NT/2000 computers, use the ipconfig tool. Either tool can be run from a DOS command prompt.

Winipcfg shows detailed information about the IP configuration for the system. It shows system information, including the Ethernet Adapter Address, IP Address, Subnet Mask, and Default Gateway, as shown in Figure 7-3. For troubleshooting, what is important here is that you can verify that the system is correctly recognizing the information that was applied during network con-

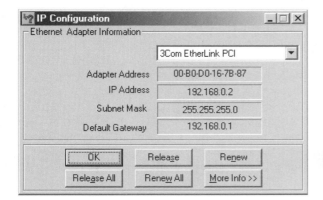

Figure 7-3

Use winipcfg on Windows 9x/Me for IP configuration information.

figuration. If any of the details here are wrong, then the network options must be reconfigured.

Ipconfig is a similar tool. Just using the `ipconfig` command will show the IP address, Subnet Mask, and Default Gateway for the system. Adding the `/all` flag will show complete network configuration information, as shown in Figure 7-4. In a DOS command window, enter this command:

```
ipconfig /all
```

```
C:\WINDOWS\System32\command.com

C:\>ipconfig /all

Windows 2000 IP Configuration

        Host Name . . . . . . . . . . . . : station1
        Primary DNS Suffix  . . . . . . . :
        Node Type . . . . . . . . . . . . : Hybrid
        IP Routing Enabled. . . . . . . . : No
        WINS Proxy Enabled. . . . . . . . : No
        DNS Suffix Search List. . . . . . : nyc.rr.com

Ethernet adapter Local Area Connection:

        Connection-specific DNS Suffix  . :
        Description . . . . . . . . . . . : IBM 10/100 EtherJet PCI Adapter
        Physical Address. . . . . . . . . : 00-04-AC-A6-81-A1
        DHCP Enabled. . . . . . . . . . . : Yes
        Autoconfiguration Enabled . . . . : Yes
        IP Address. . . . . . . . . . . . : 192.168.0.3
        Subnet Mask . . . . . . . . . . . : 255.255.255.0
        Default Gateway . . . . . . . . . : 192.168.0.1
        DHCP Server . . . . . . . . . . . : 192.168.0.1
        DNS Servers . . . . . . . . . . . : 192.168.0.1
        Primary WINS Server . . . . . . . : 192.168.0.4
        Lease Obtained. . . . . . . . . . : Saturday, March 31, 2001 6:52:03 AM
        Lease Expires . . . . . . . . . . : Tuesday, April 03, 2001 7:52:03 AM

C:\>
```

Figure 7-4

On any version of Windows, ipconfig will show the network configuration.

Can You Reach Other Computers on the Network?

Ping is one of the most important network troubleshooting tools. Ping is said to be short for "Packet INternet Groper," but that definition came after the utility was named. Ping is really named for the sound made by submarine sonar. Ping sends a packet to another computer and then waits for a reply, sort of like sonar.

The most common way to use ping is to try to reach another computer. Get the IP address of another computer on the local network and then try to reach it using ping. To ping a computer with the IP address of 192.168.0.1, open a DOS command window and enter this command:

```
ping  192.168.0.1
```

Windows will make four attempts to reach the other computer. The message that is displayed indicates whether the other computer is reachable and the number of packets sent and received. In addition, the final line of information indicates the minimum, average, and maximum round-trip times. This is an indication of how busy the route to the other computer is. Figure 7-5 shows a typical ping session.

For troubleshooting, first try to ping the IP address of the default gateway. If you don't know what the default gateway is, you can find it in the network TCP/IP properties. The default gateway is the first hop from the computer to any other computer on the network. If you can't reach the gateway, then there is a problem either with the network wiring or with the gateway.

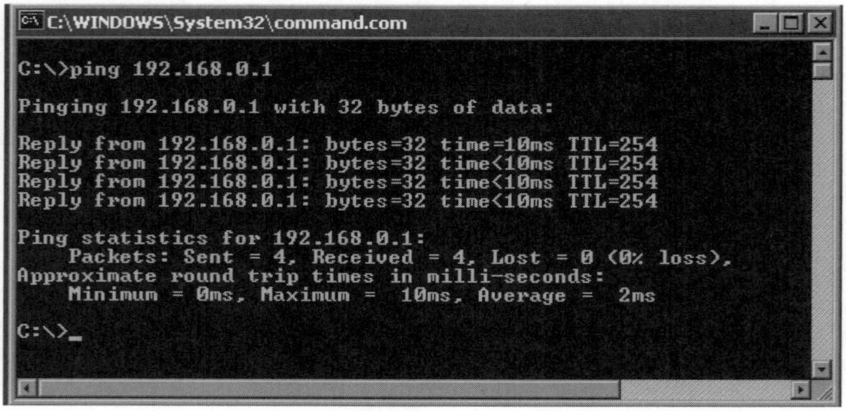

```
C:\WINDOWS\System32\command.com

C:\>ping 192.168.0.1

Pinging 192.168.0.1 with 32 bytes of data:

Reply from 192.168.0.1: bytes=32 time=10ms TTL=254
Reply from 192.168.0.1: bytes=32 time<10ms TTL=254
Reply from 192.168.0.1: bytes=32 time<10ms TTL=254
Reply from 192.168.0.1: bytes=32 time<10ms TTL=254

Ping statistics for 192.168.0.1:
    Packets: Sent = 4, Received = 4, Lost = 0 (0% loss),
Approximate round trip times in milli-seconds:
    Minimum = 0ms, Maximum =  10ms, Average =   2ms

C:\>_
```

Figure 7-5 *Use ping to see if you can reach another computer on the network.*

Once you've reached the gateway, it is best to use the traceroute tool to check the connection the rest of the way to the Samba server. Traceroute is like a super-ping utility that traces a packet from your computer to any other computer on the network, whether local or on the Internet. It shows how many hops the packet requires to reach the host and how long each hop takes.

Traceroute sends three packets for each hop. The result shows all of the intermediary hosts between your computer and the server. It also shows the round-trip time taken by each packet, which can be used to find where the longest delays are occurring. Figure 7-6 shows a traceroute session.

On a Windows computer, traceroute is run from a DOS command window and is called tracert. Traceroute is usually used the same way as ping; the command is followed by either an IP address or the full domain name of the computer you are trying to reach. Start with the IP address of the Samba server. For example:

```
tracert 192.168.0.1
```

When you use traceroute, start with the IP address of the Samba server, not the full domain name. That way you bypass the DNS server. If traceroute can reach the server directly through the IP address but can't reach the server when you traceroute the full domain name, then there is a problem with your name server.

```
C:\>tracert www.cnn.com

Tracing route to cnn.com [207.25.71.6]
over a maximum of 30 hops:

  1   <10 ms   <10 ms   <10 ms   192.168.0.1
  2    10 ms    10 ms    10 ms   10.41.0.1
  3   <10 ms    20 ms    10 ms   24.29.98.37
  4    10 ms    10 ms    10 ms   24.29.98.1
  5    10 ms    10 ms    10 ms   24.29.98.5
  6   <10 ms   <10 ms    10 ms   24.29.97.21
  7    10 ms    10 ms    10 ms   24.29.97.38
  8    10 ms    10 ms    10 ms   12.125.51.49
  9    10 ms    10 ms    10 ms   gbr2-p70.n54ny.ip.att.net [12.123.1.134]
 10    10 ms    10 ms    11 ms   gbr3-p00.n54ny.ip.att.net [12.122.5.246]
 11    10 ms    20 ms    10 ms   gbr3-p10.wswdc.ip.att.net [12.122.3.54]
 12    10 ms    21 ms    10 ms   gbr4-p60.wswdc.ip.att.net [12.122.1.130]
 13    20 ms    30 ms    30 ms   gbr4-p30.attga.ip.att.net [12.122.2.225]
 14    20 ms    30 ms    30 ms   gbr1-p60.attga.ip.att.net [12.122.5.209]
 15    30 ms    30 ms    30 ms   sar1-a360s3.attga.ip.att.net [12.123.20.93]
 16     *         *         *    Request timed out.
 17     *         *         *    Request timed out.
 18     *     12.126.31.18  reports: Destination net unreachable.

Trace complete.
```

Figure 7-6   *The* tracert *command is like a super-ping utility.*

Are the WINS and DNS Name Services Working?

Unless you have an all–Windows 2000 network, it is strongly recommended that you use a WINS server on your network in addition to a DNS server. However, if either one is not working correctly, then you will have trouble connecting to your Samba server.

If you try to ping or traceroute to another computer on the network using the full domain name—not the IP address—and you get an error message like "Unknown host," then there is a problem with the DNS server.

Check the TCP/IP Properties panel of the Network Control Panel and make sure that the DNS server is entered correctly. Try to ping the IP address of the DNS server and make sure that it is reachable and running. If not, then you need to get the DNS server working before you can proceed.

To check the WINS server, first look at the WINS configuration using either the winipcfg or ipconfig tool. With winipcfg, click on the More Info button to see the primary secondary WINS server. With ipconfig, use the /all option. Make sure that the WINS server is listed correctly.

Then ping or tracert to the WINS server. This will verify if the server is available.

Windows Reports a Problem

Troubleshooting often begins when you get an error message in Windows: either you can't connect to a file share on a Samba server, or the server doesn't show up in the Network Neighborhood/Computers Near Me. Too often Windows error messages don't tell you enough about the problem, so you don't know where to begin to fix it. In this section several of the common Windows error messages are shown, along with suggestions on solving each problem.

Why Isn't the Samba Server in the Network Neighborhood/Computers Near Me?

When you open the Network Neighborhood or Computers Near Me icon on the desktop, an icon for the Samba server should be there. If it's not there, check the possible problems and solutions described below.

YOU HAVEN'T WAITED LONG ENOUGH

When the Samba server has started, and after each and every change made on the server, it can take a minute or more before the server or the changes can be seen on the network.

NO SHARES ARE AVAILABLE

Before you can see the Samba server in the Network Neighborhood/My Network Places, there has to be at least one file share available on the server, and it has to be browseable by the user that is logged onto the Windows workstation.

THE WORKSTATION AND THE SAMBA SERVER ARE IN DIFFERENT WORKGROUPS

If you are using workgroups and not a domain, check the Workgroup setting in the Network control panel on the workstation in the Identification tab. Make sure that it matches the workgroup setting for the Samba server. That is found in the Global settings tab on SWAT. The first setting is for the workgroup.

If the workstation is not supposed to be in the same workgroup as the Samba server, then make sure that the workstation is using the same WINS server as the Samba server. The Samba server can be the WINS server.

THE WINS SERVER IS NOT REACHABLE

The Windows workstation needs to contact the WINS server to resolve names into IP addresses. Check that the WINS server is properly configured, that the server is reachable on the network, and that nmbd is running if the Samba server is your WINS server.

THERE IS NO GUEST ACCOUNT ON THE SAMBA SERVER

Initially when you browse the Network Neighborhood/My Network Places from Window NT/2000, you are browsing the network as Guest. If there is no guest account defined on the Samba server and if guest access hasn't been defined in the Samba configuration, then you won't be able to see the Samba server. You might get an error message asking for your username and password. The default configuration for Samba defines the guest account as being the "nobody" user on the Samba server. This is a default username found on all Linux servers that is used for administrative tasks. Make sure that the Samba configuration hasn't been changed to make "Guest" a user that doesn't exist on the server. Because anyone on the network is automatically a guest user, the guest user usually has limited rights on the server. Normally you wouldn't want to change this.

SAMBA ISN'T RUNNING

Open SWAT, and on the Status tab, check to make sure that both the smbd and nmbd daemons are running.

THE WORKSTATION OR THE SAMBA SERVER ISN'T CONNECTED TO THE NETWORK

Make sure that the Samba server is connected to the network. And go through the steps outlined previously in "Problems with the Network Connection" to make sure that your computer is properly connected to the network.

THERE IS NO MASTER BROWSER ON YOUR NETWORK

The Windows network requires a master browser, and by default your Samba server is set not to be the master browser. If there are other Windows servers on the network, setting the Samba server to be the master browser could open up browser wars. If there are no Windows servers on the network, make the Samba server a master browser. Look in SWAT at the global settings. In the section for Browse Options, the OS Level should be 20 or higher to make the Samba server the master browser. You can try raising this setting to 33 or higher, which would give the Samba server precedence as the master browser. To let a Windows server on the network become the master browser, set the OS Level to 0. Change the setting for preferred master from Auto to True to force the Samba server to become the master browser. If you make any changes, the nmbd daemon must be restarted before the changes go into effect.

MORE THAN ONE COMPUTER IS SET TO BE THE MASTER BROWSER

A variation on the master browser problem can be seen when the Samba server appears and then disappears in the Network Neighborhood/My Network Places. Or sometimes you get an error message that the workstation is unable to browse the network and sometimes you don't get the error message. This problem can be caused by two or more computers on the network fighting to become the master browser. Setting more than one computer on the network to be the preferred master browser on the network—Samba, Windows 9x/Me, or Windows NT/2000—precipitates a browser war, with each continuously sending out packets that flood the network in an attempt to become the master browser.

Make sure that none of the Windows 9x/Me machines is configured to be the master browser. Check this setting in the Network control panel. In the Configuration tab, highlight the option for File and Printer Sharing for Microsoft Networks, and click on Properties. In the Advanced tab, Browse Master should be set to Disabled. If it is set to Auto or Enabled, change it to Disabled. Make sure that only one computer on the local network is set to become the preferred master browser.

The same thing can be done by editing the Windows 9x/Me workstation's Registry. Set the value of `HKLM\System\CurrentControlSet\Services\VxD\VnetSetup\MaintainServerList` to 0.

On Windows NT/2000, prevent the workstation from becoming a master browser by setting the value of `HKLM\System\CurrentControlSet\Services\Browser\Parameters\MaintainServerList` to No.

If that clears up the problem, then you know that it was a browser war that was causing the problem.

If the Samba server is not supposed to be the master browser, set Samba to an OS Level of 0, and set the Local Master, the Preferred Master Browser, and the Domain Master all to No.

THE SAMBA SERVER IS ON A DIFFERENT SUBNET

In the global settings for Samba, open the Advanced View. In the Miscellaneous options, set either the Remote Announce options or Remote Browse Sync options. These settings tell the Samba server to announce the workgroup availability to other master browsers or specified IP addresses. You can also set the Samba server to be the Domain Master Browser. In SWAT on the Globals tab in the Browse options, set Domain Master Browser to True. Note that if you have a Windows NT/2000 server, that is set to be the Domain Controller, setting Samba to be the Domain Master Browser could cause conflicts.

THE SAMBA SERVER BLOCKS BROWSING AND SAYS "INVALID PASSWORD" OR "NOT AUTHORIZED"

The original Windows network used plain text passwords between the workstation and the server. This is an obvious security problem, and starting with Windows 95 Patch 3, Windows began using encrypted passwords. Samba, which changed to encrypted passwords when Windows changed, has full backward compatibility with systems that use only plain text passwords. If the Global setting in the Samba Security options is set to No for encrypted passwords, then you will get an "Invalid password" error message if you try to connect from Windows 9*x*/Me and NT or a patched version of Windows 95. From Windows 2000 Professional, you'll get a message saying "The account is not authorized," as shown in Figure 7-7. You should update the Samba server to use encrypted passwords. If you absolutely cannot do this for some reason, then a file named *ENCRYPTION.txt* in the Samba documents directory on the Samba server gives the steps you have to take to change your workstations to plain text passwords. The documents directory for Samba 2.2 on Red Hat Linux is */usr/share/doc/samba-2.2.0/docs/textdocs*. For other versions of Samba, look in the directory named with that version number.

THERE IS MORE THAN ONE DOMAIN CONTROLLER ON THE NETWORK

If you have a Windows domain controller and there are no users shown in the User Manager for Domains after you add a Samba server to the network, check the Event Log. Look for domain controller errors such as "Could not

Figure 7-7   *If Samba is not set to use encrypted passwords, a connection from a Windows 2000 workstation will be "not authorized."*

find domain controller for this network." This probably means that the Samba server has been configured as the domain controller for a domain that already has a domain controller. The conflict cancels out both controllers.

Why Are There Problems Accessing Files or Folders on the Samba Server?

Difficulties accessing files or folders on a Samba server seem to be the second most common problem, after networking problems. Some of the most common problems, with possible solutions, are described here.

THE DRIVE LETTER HAS DISAPPEARED

This problem is mostly reported by users who are not familiar with Windows drive mapping. Check the drive mapping, and if you aren't using roaming profiles, make sure that the box is checked to reconnect at logon. It is usually worthwhile to give users short tutorials on network drive mappings.

THE SHARE NAME WAS NOT FOUND

When you try to map a share, you get an error message saying, "The share name was not found." Often this is because the share name was not typed in correctly. Check the spelling and retype the share name.

THE NETWORK PATH WAS NOT FOUND

The error message "The network path could not be found," as shown in Figure 7-8, can mean that you are trying to map to a share that has not been defined on the Samba server. Check the Samba configuration and make sure that the share has been set up correctly. Also, make sure that you are mapping to the correct path information for the Samba server and the share. You will also get this error message if you are logged onto the workstation with a username that does not have access rights to the share. Also, check to make sure that the workstation has not been blocked in Hosts Deny in the Security options of the Global settings for Samba.

Windows

The network path \\samba\admin could not be found.

OK

Figure 7-8 *Mapping to a share that hasn't been set up produces an error message.*

YOU MUST SUPPLY A PASSWORD TO MAKE THIS CONNECTION

This error message, as shown in Figure 7-9, often comes up because you've logged onto the Windows workstation with a password that is different from the password set on the Samba server. Windows 9*x*/Me machines cannot have a Samba password that is different from the machine's logon password. With a Windows NT or Windows 2000 workstation, the Samba password does not have to match the logon password. If you get this error on a Windows NT/2000 connection, try typing in the user's password for the Samba server. It is usually simpler to set the password on the Samba server be the same as the password used to log onto the Windows workstation.

This same error message also comes up if the Samba server is not set to accept encrypted passwords.

THE PASSWORD IS INVALID

This is similar to the previous error. On Windows 9*x*/Me systems, make sure that the password used to log onto the Windows workstation is the same as the password set for the user on the Samba server. Also if you have defined valid users or a list of invalid users in the Global settings, make sure that the

Enter Network Password

You must supply a password to make this connection: OK

Cancel

Resource: \\LINUX\PUBLIC

Password:

☑ Save this password in your password list

Figure 7-9   *Check how you are logged in if you get an error message saying that you must supply a password.*

username used to log onto the Windows workstation is also a permitted user. Check the Samba configuration settings for Hosts Allow, Host Deny, Valid Users, and Invalid Users. A wrong setting for any of those four configuration options could generate this error message. One way to see if one of these Samba options is causing the problem is to temporarily remove any settings in those four options and then test the connection.

THE NETWORK IS BUSY

This error message is usually caused by a setting on the Samba server that denies the Windows workstation access to the server. Check to see if the workstation has been blocked by a setting in the Hosts Deny section of the Globals configuration in SWAT. One fix is to add the workstation's IP address to the Hosts Allow section of the Globals configuration in SWAT.

ACCESS IS DENIED

Perhaps you have tried to access a file or folder or have tried to save a file into a folder, but you get an "Access is denied" error message, as shown in Figure 7-10. Usually this error is caused by permission problems on the Samba server. The share may be set as read-only, which means you can't save to it. This is the default setting in all new shares that you define. Change the Read Only setting to No in the Security options for the share. This error can also be caused if the user does not have the correct access permissions in Linux. Check the permissions and ownership on the file or folder in Linux.

CONNECTION REFUSED

If you get a "Connection refused" or "Not accessible" message, as shown in Figure 7-11, then the Samba service may not be running. Use SWAT to check the status of the smbd daemon, and start it if it is stopped.

SESSION REQUEST FAILED

A "Session request failed" message means the Samba server refused the connection. Check the Hosts Deny and Hosts Allow settings in the SWAT Globals settings as well as Hosts Deny and Hosts Allow settings for the share. This

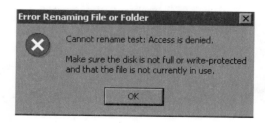

Figure 7-10   *If access is denied, check the permissions on the folder or file.*

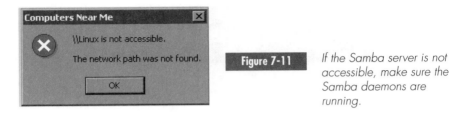

Figure 7-11 *If the Samba server is not accessible, make sure the Samba daemons are running.*

error could also be caused if the network connection to the Samba server is not working. Check to make sure the Samba server is running and reachable on the network.

Why Are There Logon Problems?

If you've set up the Samba server to be a domain logon server, you may have some problems. Some common logon problems and their solutions are described here.

THE LOGON SCRIPT DOES NOT RUN

You've set up a netlogon script that doesn't run when users log on. First make sure that the script does indeed exist and that it is in the *netlogon* directory. Then make sure that users have access rights to the *netlogon* directory. Make sure that neither the Hosts Allow nor the Hosts Deny settings are preventing users from accessing the netlogon share. Also check the permissions for the logon script. Finally, check to make sure that the script does not have any bad commands that are causing it to not run. The netlogon script must be saved in DOS format, not Linux format (that is, there is a carriage return and line feed at the end of each command, not the Linux format of just a line feed). Also make sure you can run the script on the Windows workstation in a DOS command window.

NO DOMAIN SERVER IS AVAILABLE TO VALIDATE YOUR PASSWORD

The "No domain server is available to validate your password" message means that there is no netlogon service available. First make sure that the nmbd daemon is running on the Samba server. Then, if the Samba domain controller is on a different subnet than the Windows workstation, check that the workstation is set up to use the same WINS server used by the Samba domain controller. This is usually set to be the Samba server itself.

Finally, make sure that the Samba domain controller is also the Domain Master Browser for the domain. To find the master browser for the domain,

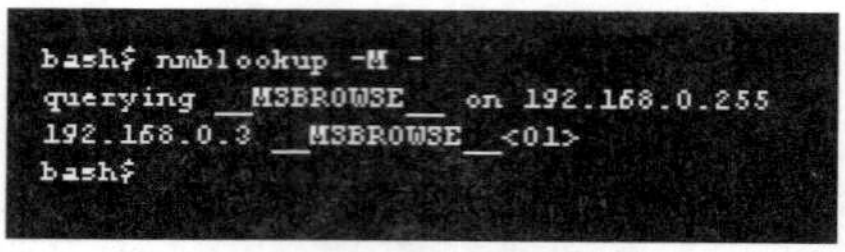

```
bash$ nmblookup -M -
querying __MSBROWSE__ on 192.168.0.255
192.168.0.3 __MSBROWSE__ <01>
bash$
```

Figure 7-12   *Use Samba's nmblookup to find the master browser.*

Samba includes the nmblookup tool. Nmblookup is used on the Samba server to look up NetBIOS name information.

To find the master browser on a subnet, open a terminal window on the Samba server and enter this command:

```
nmblookup -M -
```

Figure 7-12 shows the output of nmblookup.

If the Samba server is not the master browser, then you should make sure that the Samba server is configured to be the master browser and that the OS Level is set high enough to win any browser elections. After making any changes, restart the Samba daemons on the SWAT Status tab.

THE PASSWORD YOU SUPPLIED WAS INCORRECT

The error message "The domain password you supplied was incorrect" could mean just that. Log onto the Windows workstation again. Check the user-name and retype the password. On shared workstations, users often forget to change the username from the previous user to their own logon name. Also check that neither the Hosts Allow nor the Hosts Deny settings in Samba's global settings are blocking access to the workstation.

Samba-Related Problems

The Samba-related problems usually fall into two areas. One, Samba isn't run-ning. Two, SWAT can't be opened.

Samba is not running

If you can't reach the server from a workstation and you can't connect to the SWAT Web page to see the status of your server, how can you find out if Samba is running? In Webmin, open the Running Processes icon on the Sys-tem tab. Select the Search display. On the search page, select the Matching radio button, and then enter mbd and click on the Search button.

This produces a list of running processes that have "mbd" in the name of the process, as shown in Figure 7-13. If smbd and nmbd don't show up in the results list when you run this search, then the daemon isn't running.

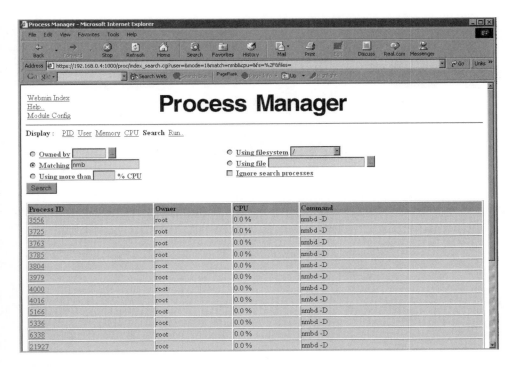

Figure 7-13   *Use Samba's nmblookup to find the master browser.*

The following are things to check when the daemon isn't running.

THE SAMBA SERVICES DID NOT START

If the Samba services aren't started, make sure that the Samba server is set up to start Samba during system startup. If you are using Webmin to administer your Samba server, check the Bootup and Shutdown settings on the System tab, as shown at the beginning of this chapter. Find Samba and make sure that it is set to run on startup.

SAMBA HAS NOT BEEN CONFIGURED

The Samba daemons won't start if Samba hasn't been configured. Open Webmin and go to the Servers tab. Select Samba. If Samba has not been configured, you'll get an error message like the one shown in Figure 7-14.

On the Samba server, look in the directory for the configuration file. On Red Hat 7.0 and later systems, as well as Debian systems, that's in the */etc/samba* directory. On Caldera systems, it's in */etc/samba.d*. On Red Hat

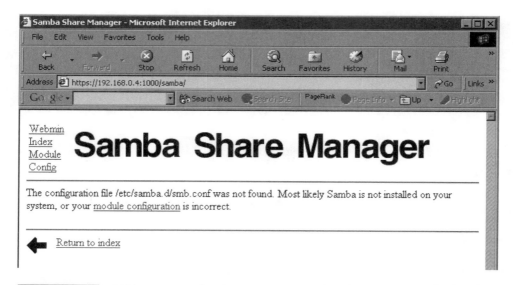

Figure 7-14
Webmin reports that the minimum required configuration cannot be found.

6.2 and older systems, look in */etc*. The configuration file is named *smb.conf.* If the file is not there, a sample *smb.conf.default* file should be there. If the sample file is there, make a copy named *smb.conf.* You can start with the sample and build from there.

If you installed Samba from an RPM or DEB package, try searching the Samba server for the default file. The command is

```
find / -iname smb.conf.default
```

If this does not turn up a copy of the default configuration file on your system, then you can get it in the Samba source package, which can be downloaded from the Samba Web site at *www.samba.org*.

WHAT DO THE LOGS SAY?

One way to find the reason Samba won't start is to read the logs, which is like reading the Event Viewer on a Windows server. There are separate logs for the smbd and nmbd daemons. The logs are text files found in */var/log/ samba* on Red Hat Linux, in */var/log/samba.d* on Caldera OpenLinux, and in */var/log* on Debian GNU/Linux.

One of the errors you might find in the logs is an "Unknown host" error. Both smbd and nmbd look up the hostname of the Samba server on which they are running and try to translate the name into an IP address.

Make sure that the Samba server is correctly configured to find a DNS server, or put the information in the */etc/hosts* file.

If you find a message in the logs that says "Bind has failed on port 139 socket_addr=0.0.0.0 (Address already in use)," this usually means that Samba has been configured to automatically start on system startup and to also start up as a manual service through inetd. Inetd, the Internet services daemon, is an alternative way to run services on a Linux server. The default setting for Debian GNU/Linux is to start the Samba service through inetd, though no other Linux distribution uses this default. This is almost like using a Windows service in manual mode, with a daemon not starting until it is requested and then shutting down after answering the request. This setup can be a big drain on system resources. It is strongly recommended that you do not run Samba this way. The response can be so slow that Samba will suffer from frequent failures. The best solution is to remove Samba from inetd and let Samba be run as an automatic service at startup.

Another error that you might find in the logs is the message that there are no local interfaces. This means that the Ethernet card is not responding or is not configured.

SWAT Can't Be Opened

SWAT is installed and available as part of the standard Samba installation. You should not have to take any special steps to open SWAT from the Samba server. However, you'll have to make changes to the defaults if you want to access SWAT from a remote system.

SWAT is not usually run as a service from startup, but rather is run on demand using inetd, the Internet services daemon. Make sure that inetd is configured to properly run the service and that the Linux system is configured to allow access from other computers on the network.

On Red Hat Linux 7 and higher versions, check xinetd, a program that combines inetd and TCP wrappers. For Red Hat Linux 6.2 and earlier versions and most other Linux distributions, check inetd and its related configuration files.

For xinetd in Red Hat 7.0, there is a configuration file in the */etc/xinetd.d* directory for SWAT. Check the file named *swat* and make sure that has the correct settings. The original Red Hat 7.0 shipped with it misconfigured. The correct settings are as follows:

```
service swat
{
    port = 901
    socket_type = stream
    wait = no
    only_from = localhost
    user = root
```

```
       server = /usr/sbin/swat
       log_on_failure += USERID
       disable = no
}
```

The `only_from` setting was incorrect on the original Red Hat 7.0. Also, add the subnet IP for your local network if you want to access it from other computers on the network. To do that on a local network that is on subnet 192.168.0., the `only_from` setting should be changed to read

```
only_from = localhost 192.168.0.1/24
```

For Red Hat 6.2 and earlier as well as most other Linux systems that use inetd and TCP wrappers to prevent unauthorized access to SWAT, first make sure that the workstation you are using has been given access rights in the *hosts.allow* file in */etc* directory on the Samba server. You need the IP address of the workstation. For example, enter this line for a workstation with the IP address of 192.168.0.166:

```
swat: 192.168.0.166
```

You might want to also add it as an exception in the *hosts.deny* file. In *hosts.deny* there may be a line that starts with swat and looks like this:

```
swat: ALL EXCEPT 127.0.0.1
```

After 127.0.0.1 put a space and then the IP address of the workstation that you want to have access to SWAT, for example, 192.168.0.166. Then make sure that SWAT is listed in the services. Look in the */etc/services* file on the Samba server. There should be a line for SWAT; if not, add it. The line should read

```
swat   901/tcp
```

Finally, check that SWAT is listed in the */etc/inetd.conf* files. The line should read

```
swat   stream   tcp   nowait.400   root   /usr/sbin/tcpd   swat
```

If you've made any changes to the services or the *inetd.conf* files, then you need to restart inetd. To do this, enter the command

```
/etc/rc.d/init.d/inet stop
```

and then the command

```
/etc/rc.d/init.d/inet start
```

If you aren't using TCP wrappers, then just check that SWAT is listed in the services and that there is a line in the *inetd.conf* file for SWAT, but without the TCP wrappers daemon tcpd. It should look like this:

```
swat  stream  tcp  nowait.400  root  /usr/sbin/swat  swat
```

Also, on systems using PAM for secure logins, check to make sure that when you login on SWAT, your username and password can be authenticated. Check the PAM configuration file for the Samba service. There should be a file named *samba* in the */etc/pam.d* directory. The contents of the file should read

```
auth     required  /lib/security/pam_pwdg.so shadow nullok
account  required  /lib/security/pam_pwdb.so
```

Printer Problems

Samba treats printer shares much like file shares, and you can usually solve printer problems in the same way you solve file share problems. Many times not having access to a printer can be solved in the same way that not having access to a file or folder is solved. Check the Samba printer share configuration and permissions settings.

The Samba print server can handle print jobs for printers connected to the server and for other printers on the network that either have their own Ethernet connection or are connected to another computer. Each kind of printer connection has its own setup options in the printer configuration. Check all of the configuration options. Also, make sure that you can print to the printer without going through the Samba server.

You need to check the Linux printer setup. One problem may be the permissions and ownership settings on the Samba spool directory. The spool directory needs to be accessible to anyone, but the permissions have to be set so that only the individual user can remove a file from the queue. This means enabling the Sticky Bit. (For more information on the Sticky Bit and Linux file permission, settings, see Chapter 3.)

Make sure that the Samba spool directory has the correct permissions set. Open the Webmin File Manger and select the Samba spool directory, either */var/spool/samba* for Red Hat Linux and Debian GNU/Linux or */var/spool/samba.d* for Caldera OpenLinux. Click on the Info button and make sure that Read, Write, and List permissions are enabled for User and

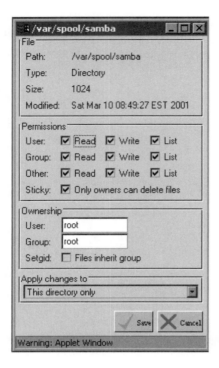

Figure 7-15 *The correct settings for the Samba spool directory.*

Group and that the box is checked to enable the Sticky Bit, as shown in Figure 7-15.

This can also be done from a command prompt on the Linux server with this command:

```
chmod 1777 /var/spool/samba
```

Also check the permissions for */dev/null* on the Samba server. Anyone should be able to write to */dev/null*. This can be done in the Webmin File Manager. Open the *dev* folder and select Null in the right panel. Click the Info button and make sure that write access is enabled for User, Group, and Other, as shown in Figure 7-16.

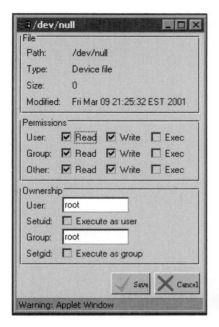

Figure 7-16   *The permission settings for the /dev/null directory.*

Samba's printing services use */dev/null* to discard the output of print commands and must be able to write to it to do this.

Sometimes printing fails because the Linux print tools are not correctly entered in the Samba configuration. Chapter 4 has the details for proper configuration of Samba printing.

Linux System Administration Essentials

Linux is the most popular operating system for Samba servers. While Samba can run on almost any UNIX platform in addition to Linux, it was initially built on Linux servers. Linux has many features in its favor, in addition to its low initial cost—less than $100 for a CD, an operating manual, installation support, and unlimited user licenses. The Linux operating system is rock-stable and rarely crashes. In addition, it can give server-level performance on inexpensive, low-end Intel-compatible machines. Linux is the second most popular server platform after Microsoft Windows servers.

There are some myths about Linux, as well as some realities. Linux is a lot easier to install and use than is often believed by those new to the system. If it were too difficult, there wouldn't already be millions of servers in operation. Installing Linux is no more difficult than installing Windows NT. As you'll see in this chapter, administering Linux can mostly be done using your favorite Web browser. Using the Webmin program, Linux system administration is a matter of point and click.

The reality of Linux is that it's not Windows. There are some fundamental differences in the way things work and the way that you have to approach the system. Linux and Windows are both operating systems that work on the same hardware and have to do many of the same tasks. If you know how to do something in Windows, you'll find that there is usually a Linux equivalent. This chapter will get you started on the fundamental Linux system administration tasks. Many of the steps include pointers to Windows similarities.

Understanding Linux Distributions

Linux is available in more than a dozen different distributions. The best known is Red Hat Linux. Having so many different distributions is often confusing to new users. The first thing to know about all the distributions is they have more similarities than differences. All use the same Linux kernel. There is no difference on that.

The differences are in the packaging. It's less like the differences between Coke and Pepsi and more like the differences between Coke, Cherry Coke, and Diet Coke, which all use the basic Coca-Cola formula for their base. Each distribution includes a set of Linux utilities and applications that have all been configured and tested to work together. Each distribution includes a slightly different mix of utilities and applications, often referred to as packages. The location of the installed software packages varies somewhat from distribution to distribution. For developers, the mix of compilers, editors, programming languages, libraries, and so on is also slightly different for each distribution.

Three leading distributions are Red Hat Linux, Caldera OpenLinux, and Debian GNU/Linux. The Debian distribution is one of the most difficult to install, but it is also the most popular with system administrators who are already familiar with UNIX systems. If you use Webmin for managing your Linux server, it won't matter much which distribution it is. Webmin is aware of the differences; all you have to do it tell it what you want to do, and Webmin will do it in the right way for the specific distribution.

Samba doesn't care which Linux distribution you use. Samba requires only the Linux operating system and TCP/IP networking. The examples used in this chapter use Red Hat Linux.

You can purchase a computer with Linux installed and ready to go, like you would a Windows server. IBM, Dell, Compaq, VA Linux, and many other manufacturers sell servers with Linux already installed. If you've chosen to install Linux yourself, follow the instructions that come with the Linux distribution. If there is a server option, choose that. The files needed for a server shouldn't take up more than about 250 Mb.

Xwindows and Terminals

On a Windows system, the graphical interface is part of the operating system. On Linux, the operating system does not include a graphical interface. In fact, Linux without any kind of graphical interface looks a lot like a DOS system. The look is similar, but there are differences, of course. One difference is that it is easy to add a graphical interface to the basic Linux operating system.

This is usually done with Xwindows, though there are other windowing systems available. Xwindows was developed in the 1980s as a UNIX graphical interface so that UNIX users could have the kind of easy-to-use interface found on Windows and Macintosh machines.

Linux has a modular structure, so the graphical interface couldn't just be included as part of the operating system. Instead, Xwindows is added as a separate server, like a Samba server, a Web server, or an FTP server, all running on the same Linux system; but this is a server that offers users a graphical interface.

An Xwindows server lets users connecting to the server have access to a graphical terminal on the Linux machine. Xwindows uses the X networking protocol so that the graphical interface can be displayed both on a monitor connected to the Linux machine and on other monitors on systems connecting over the network.

For the Xwindows server to be accessed, a user client must connect to the server. So the graphical display on the Linux system is actually divided into two parts. One part is the Xwindows server. The second part is the X client that connects to the X server. The X client is what you actually see.

There are a wide variety of X clients, including KDE and GNOME, Enlightenment, twm, and fvwm. The X client defines the graphical look and feel; some clients imitate the look of Windows or Macintosh, but most have their own unique design. Some are minimal interfaces, while others include a wide variety of tools.

Each X client is at minimum a window manager; that is, it is an application that can manage and display lots of windows running other applications, from WordPerfect to FTP.

This is a very flexible system. Once you have the X server set up on Linux, any of a variety of X clients can be used to connect to the X server. The setup of the X server is usually handled during Linux installation. The standard X server on Linux is XFree86, an open source project.

KDE and GNOME

The most popular X clients on Linux are KDE and GNOME. Each has its own strengths, and there are strong advocates for both systems.

Red Hat Linux is the primary developer of GNOME, but you can choose either client when you install Red Hat Linux. KDE has been in development longer than GNOME. KDE released version 2.0 in October 2000; GNOME announced version 1.4 in April 2001.

Reasons Not to Use Xwindows

Xwindows is not really necessary for a server. Some system administrators prefer not to use it, and that certainly is an option. One reason not to use it is that Xwindows takes up system resources. KDE or GNOME will use a minimum of 32 Mb of system memory, in addition to as much video memory as you can afford. Xwindows applications also use memory, sometimes a lot of memory. Some versions of Netscape, for example, will use 64 Mb of system memory when running in Xwindows.

If system memory on the server is limited, then there is no reason to use Xwindows. It is not only not necessary, but it will make no difference in your ability to administer the system if you are using Webmin. That's because administration can handled through a Web browser run from a client machine on the network, like your Windows desktop system using Microsoft's Internet Explorer.

Don't abandon Xwindows unless you must. Xwindows can make everything you do when you are sitting in front of the server and working directly on it much easier and more efficient. See "Security Tips" for help with working on a nongraphical terminal.

TIP — LINUX FILESYSTEM FUNDAMENTALS

Even if you are using KDE or GNOME, you should look through the section called "Security Tips" for info on using the nongraphical terminal. Many fundamentals of the Linux filesystem are described in this section. The filesystem fundamentals don't change if you are using a window manager like KDE or GNOME.

Using Webmin

Webmin is a software package that includes a number of modules that are tools for system administration. It is the most advanced administration system available for Linux. Many Linux distributions include the Webmin package, and Red Hat recommends that you use it if you are doing remote management of the system. If you don't have Webmin on your Linux server, or if you have it but want to get the latest version, Webmin can be downloaded from *www.webmin.com*. It is available under the BSD open license, which means it can be freely distributed for commercial or noncommercial use.

Webmin can be accessed using any Web browser from any workstation—Windows or Linux or whatever. Use it to manage users and groups, configure network settings on the Linux system, and administer printers. Webmin includes a module for administering Samba that adds features not available with SWAT, the standard Web-based tool for Samba administration and configuration.

Webmin itself includes a mini–Web server so that you don't need to run Apache or any other Web server on your system in order to be able to use Webmin. This feature adds to Webmin's security. Webmin and its modules are all written in the PERL programming language. The modules run as Common Gateway Interface (CGI) programs that directly update the Linux system files.

If you need to install Webmin on your system, first make sure that PERL version 5.0 or higher is installed. Every Linux distribution includes PERL. If its not installed, install it from the Linux CD or get it from the PERL Web site at *www.perl.com.*

To check to see if PERL is installed—and if it is, what version is installed—open a terminal window on the Linux machine and enter the command `perl -v`. If there is no response or you get an error message, then PERL is not installed or is not correctly installed. You should get a response showing what version of PERL is installed.

The Webmin package is downloaded from the Web in Red Hat Package Manager (RPM) format or as source files to be compiled and installed. Download the RPM version and install it either from a package manager like the GNOME RPM package manager or Kpackage, or from the command line with this command:

```
rpm -i webmin-version.number.rpm
```

If you want to install the source file rather than the RPM version, download the file with the *.tar.gz* extension.

Put the file into the */usr/local* directory. This can be done with the Move command. For example, if the file was downloaded into the */tmp* directory, the Move command would be

```
mv /tmp/webmin-0.86.tar.gz /usr/local
```

The name may vary depending on which version you've downloaded. The file can be unzipped and untarred in one step. To do this with Webmin version 0.86, for example, use the following command:

```
tar xvzf /usr/local/webmin-0.86.tar.gz
```

This puts everything into a directory named *webmin-0.86*. The setup script can then be started using this command:

```
/usr/local/webmin-0.86/setup.sh
```

The setup requires that you know what Linux distribution and version you are using. Make sure that you read all the messages on the screen during setup. The first time you install Webmin, it will tell you which port to use when accessing Webmin as well as the default username. You'll supply the password. The default port is usually 10000 and the default username is usually "admin." Some Webmin installations use port 1000, and sometimes the default username is "root."

Once Webmin is installed, you can access it from the Linux machine using a Web browser and opening *http://localhost:10000/.* (Of course, if you are using a different port, then use that port number instead.) From a workstation on the network, you can access Webmin by entering either the IP address or the full domain name of the Linux server. For example, you could open *http://192.168.0.4:10000/* or *http://samba.linux.penguin:10000/*.

If Webmin doesn't open, make sure that the Webmin server is started. To start it manually, enter the command

```
/etc/rc.d/init.d/Webmin start
```

When you connect to Webmin, you will be prompted to enter the username and password.

Securing Webmin with SSL

If you want secure connections with Webmin, you can use SSL, the same security system used for commence on the Web. OpenSSL is an open source software package that makes full security possible. It can be found on the Web at *www.openssl.org.*

The OpenSSL libraries are available as an RPM binary package and can be found on the CD on many Linux distributions. They can also be downloaded from the OpenSSL Web site.

Install OpenSSL as you would any other software package. The RPM version puts OpenSSL in a different location than the defaults, which means that the PERL SSLeay module won't be able to find OpenSSL without some modifications, either to the system or to the installation procedure.. The easiest way to set up OpenSSL so that the PERL SSLeay module can find the necessary libraries is to install OpenSSL from the source code, not the RPM package. To do this, download the OpenSSL source code from *www.openssl.org*. Then in the download directory, enter these commands to uncompress the OpenSSL package and compile it:

```
tar xvzf openssl-version.number.tar.gz
cd openssl-version.number
./configure
  make
  make install
```

Then install the SSLeay modules for PERL. If Webmin is already installed, go to the Others tab and select the link to PERL Modules. Select From CPAN and type in Net::SSLeay (yes, that's two colons). This will automatically install the SSLeay modules.

That's it. Now, configure Webmin to use SSL by going to the Webmin page and opening the Webmin Configuration link. An icon link to SSL Encryption should be on the page. If it's not, then there was an error in the installation. If it is there, click on the link, select the Enable SSL radio button, and click on Save.

If you had an error, there is a more detailed document on enabling OpenSSL for Webmin at *www.webmin.com.*

Remember, after you've enabled SSL encryption Webmin will be accessible only by using the secure URL https. For example, if your connection to Webmin without SSL encryption was *http://192.168.0.4:10000*, then after enabling SSL it will be *https://192.168.0.4: 10000.* Don't forget the *s*, or you won't be able to connect to Webmin.

Managing Bootup Options

The Linux bootup procedure has some resemblance to the Windows NT 4 bootup procedure. Sometimes the first screen is a list of possible systems to boot into, such as Windows if the system has been set up for dual booting into multiple operating systems.

Linux starts by first loading the kernel and then any device drivers needed for the system (these are called modules). After loading the kernel and modules, the system is started, then the daemons (called services on Windows systems) are initiated, and then Xwindows starts up (if you are using a windowing environment like KDE or GNOME).

Webmin has a Bootup and Shutdown module so that you can configure what daemons are run on startup. It also has two buttons on the bottom of the page to either shut down the system or to reboot the system.

Select the System tab on Webmin and click on the Bootup and Shutdown link. The Bootup and Shutdown module will open. Figure 8-1 shows the Bootup and Shutdown module.

The first column on the Bootup and Shutdown page is labeled "Action." This column lists the daemons, or services, that are installed on the system. If a daemon isn't listed, that usually means the application hasn't been installed.

As with Windows services, the daemons can be set to be started manually or automatically on bootup. The second field of the table shows whether the daemon is set to start at bootup.

The third field is for a short description of the daemon. If you are unsure what a daemon does and the short description is not enough, consult a good Linux manual for an in-depth description. You can also read the manual pages for the daemon. At a terminal window, enter the command man followed by the name of the daemon. Every daemon listed should have a manual help file installed with it.

Check for the Samba daemon. It should be configured to start at bootup.

Each daemon listed is really a startup script, which is similar to a script file in Windows or a batch file in DOS. Click on the name of the daemon,

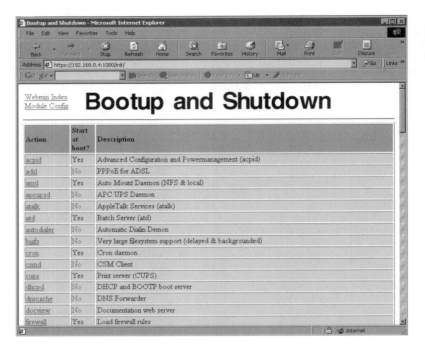

| Figure 8-1 | *Configure startup in Webmin's Bootup and Shutdown module.* |

and a page opens that shows the full startup script as well as radio buttons letting you choose whether to start the daemon on bootup. There is also a pair of buttons to let you manually start or stop a daemon. If you change the startup option, you must click on the Save button for the change to take effect.

The Delete button will let you delete a daemon, but this should almost never be done unless you are a Linux expert and know what you are doing.

Managing Users and Groups

One of the biggest jobs in system administration is managing users and groups. If you aren't using Winbind and users and groups are being handled by a Windows domain controller, then you can use Webmin for managing users and groups. On the System tab, click on the link to Users and Groups. The page that opens in shown in Figure 8-2.

Before adding users, check your configuration of the Webmin Samba modules. Webmin can be configured to synchronize your Linux users list with the Samba users list. Samba must have the Encrypt Passwords option set to Yes before you can enable this feature.

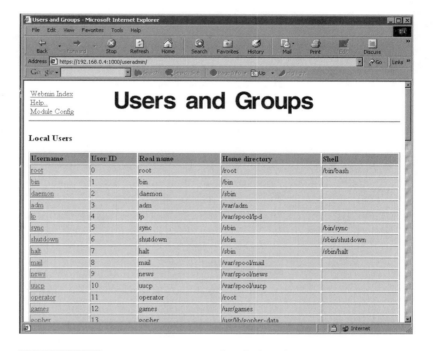

Figure 8-2   *User management is handled on the Users and Groups page.*

To add a new user to the Linux server (and at the same time add the user as a Samba user if you've enabled synchronization), click on the option to Create a New User in Users and Groups, which appears after the table listing all current users.

The following options can be set for each user. Clicking on the option name on the Webmin page will open a help window with a description of the option.

Username   The login name assigned to the user.

Real name   The user's real name. This setting is optional and is not used by Samba. It is helpful for the system administrator, though, because it can make it easier to identify users since usernames are often cryptic.

Shell   The login shell for users who connect to the server using a console or telnet. Samba users never need a shell connection. Normally for Samba-only users, the shell should be set to /bin/false or any other setting that does nothing. This makes the account more secure since it prevents unauthorized shell access to the server.

User ID   A unique ID number assigned to each user. Normally Webmin inserts the next logical number in the user ID sequence on the server. This does not need to be changed.

Home directory   The directory where each user usually saves files. This is the most heavily used directory on most Samba servers. On Linux systems, the home directory is a subdirectory in */home*. The subdirectory should be the user's login name. Type in the name of the home directory in the space provided. For example, for user Janet Henry with a username of "jhenry," enter */home/jhenry*. Webmin will create this directory.

Password   A password should be assigned to each new user. The default setting is No Login Allowed. That means that the user will be denied all access to the server and won't be able to access Samba. To allow access, click the Normal Password radio button and then type in the assigned password. If you already have the encrypted form of the password, select Pre-encrypted instead and enter the encrypted password. If no password required is selected, the user account will be insecure and accessible to anyone on the network.

Password changed   Shows the most recent date when the user's password was changed.

Minimum days   The minimum number of days a user must keep a new password before it can be changed again. This setting is meant to prevent a user from changing a password and then changing it back again to the old value. The default setting is blank, which means that it is disabled.

Warning days   Sets the number of days before the password expires, if it is set to do so, when the user will start getting warnings to change the password.

Expiry date   The date the user account expires. If set, the user will no longer be able to access the server after that date.

Maximum days   The maximum number of days a password is valid before the user has to change the password. Leaving this blank, the default, disables this setting.

Inactive days   The number of days after the password expires until the account will be automatically disabled if the password hasn't changed.

Primary group   The user's primary group. Some Linux systems assign every user to the group "Users." Don't use this approach. Other systems, including OpenLinux, use the login name to create a new group that has only the new user as a member. This second approach is the only secure way to set up group membership.

Secondary group   There is no limit on the number of groups to which a user can belong. Assign as many additional groups as needed.

Create home directory?   Normally set to Yes so that Webmin will automatically create the directory and assign the correct user rights for the directory.

Copy files to home directory?   On a Samba server, where users never need shell access to the server, set this option to No. The files that are copied are configuration files for shell users.

SECURITY TIP

Watch out for group membership on your Samba server. Samba gives users the same rights they would have if they were connecting to the Linux server. Linux access rights are handled in a different way than they are handled on Windows systems. On Linux, group membership is used to give rights to access directories and files that are not owned by the user. If you are a member of a group, you have access rights to any files or folders that are "owned" by the group. If all the users are all members of the same group, every user can access anyone else's home directory. That's because the directories are all "owned" by the same group ID. Some Linux versions default to making every user a member of the "Users" group. This creates a situation that is not expected by anyone experienced with Windows systems. Most assume that home directories are completely private for each individual user. The only way to keep home directories private is to assign each user a unique group ID and limit shared group IDs to directories that are to be shared by multiple users.

Samba Configuration

The Webmin Samba modules, found by clicking the Servers tab, can be used in much the same way SWAT is used. The general settings are divided between several configuration modules: UNIX Networking, Windows Networking, Authentication, Windows to UNIX Printing, Miscellaneous Options, File Share Defaults, and Printer Share Defaults.

UNIX Networking   Here you can configure the networking options for Samba, such as Idle Time Before Disconnect. These settings are not usually changed.

Windows Networking   As the name indicates, these settings are required by the Windows network. They include the Workgroup name and WINS server information.

Authentication   This module has all of the Samba configuration settings concerning passwords, including enabling the use of encrypted passwords.

Windows to UNIX Printing   This module opens the Printing Options page.

Miscellaneous Options   These options are rarely changed.

File Share Defaults and **Printer Share Defaults**   The primary default settings are made in these modules. For more information on the setting options, see Chapters 3 and 4.

The Webmin modules do not have all the help features found in SWAT. But if you know what all the settings are, the configuration can all be done here.

The links to create a new file or printer share have two steps. First, to create a new file share, click on the Create a New File Share link and name the share. The new share is then listed in the table of share names. Click on the name of the new share; the window that opens has configuration modules for the share, including security and access control, file permissions, file naming, and miscellaneous options. Creating a new printer share is done in the same manner by clicking on the Create a New Printer Share link.

The Create a New Copy link lets you create a copy of an existing share and give it a new name. This is used when you need to create multiple shares that are similar.

The View All Connections link opens a page that shows all the Samba connections to the Linux server, along with their process IDs.

At the bottom of Webmin's main Samba page are links for user management. The Edit Samba Users and Passwords link opens a page where every Samba user is listed. Click on a username to make changes or delete the user.

The Convert UNIX Users to Samba Users link is used to convert existing UNIX users to Samba users.

The Configure Automatic UNIX and Samba User Synchronization link opens a page that lets you add options to synchronize UNIX and Samba users. You should enable this option so that every user you create through Webmin's Users and Groups is also added as a Samba user.

Printer Administration

Use Webmin to manage any printers connected to the Samba server, as well as to create printer definitions for other printers on the network that are accessed through a Samba share.

First make sure that Webmin is correctly configured. On Webmin's Hardware tab, select Printer Administration. In the upper left corner of the Printer Administration page, click on the Module Config link.

Make sure that the settings are correct for your Linux distribution. For Printer Configuration Style, choose LPRng for Red Hat version 7.0 and higher. For earlier versions of Red Hat, the Linux radio button should be selected to indicate that you are using the regular Linux BSD printing service. This is also the setting used for Debian GNU/Linux. Caldera OpenLinux 3.1 and higher versions use CUPS, while earlier versions used LPRng.

TIP — MULTIPLE PRINTERS

If your Samba server will be handling more than one printer — either multiple printers connected to the server or spooling jobs to be delivered to other printers on the network — make sure that either LPRng or CUPS is installed on the Linux server. Both of these printer daemons are designed to be used on networks and to handle the wide variety of configuration possibilities used for network printing.

After selecting the configuration style, make sure that the correct printer driver style is selected. If your Linux distribution isn't shown, then choose Webmin. The other settings should be left at their defaults. Click on the Save button to keep any changes.

To add a new printer, click on the Add a New Printer link.

In the Printer Configuration section, enter a name for the printer, one that describes the printer. One common way to name printers is by their location, such as Room123. After the printer has been given a name, the description field is optional. The Print banner field refers to the option of printing an info page before the print job to indicate the print job's owner. Make sure that Accepting Requests and Printing Enabled are set to Yes. The first setting indicates that the printer is available and opens a print queue to accept print spools. The second is needed to release jobs from the print queue and deliver them to the printer. Max Print Job Size shouldn't be changed in most cases. Print jobs can be much bigger than you might expect.

In the Print Destination and Print Drivers sections, there are several options:

- If you are adding access to a printer on the network that has an HP JetDirect connection, select Direct TCP Connection. Enter the full hostname or IP address of the JetDirect connection. In the Port field, enter 9100. The Printer Driver should be set to None, the setting for a remote printer. Click the Create button on the bottom of the page to save the configuration.
- If you are adding a network printer that does not have an HP JetDirect connection but is connected to another Samba server, select the Remote UNIX Server radio button and enter the full hostname or IP address of the server. In the Printer field, enter the printer's name on the Samba server. The Printer Driver should be set to None. Click the Create button on the bottom of the page to save the configuration.

- For a Windows printer, that is, a shared printer connected to a Windows computer on the network, choose Remote Windows Server. Enter the full hostname or IP address of the Windows server. The printer name is the name of the share. Also enter a valid username and password for accessing the printer as well as the workgroup name. The Printer Driver should be set to None. Click the Create button on the bottom of the page to save the configuration.
- To set up a local printer, that is, a printer connected directly to the Samba server, select Local Device in Print Destination. The Printer Driver should be set to the appropriate driver for your printer, or one that is close in make and model if an exact match is not possible. Set the correct paper size (note that Webmin defaults to A3). Click the Create button to save the configuration.

Any printer created through the Webmin Printer Administration module will automatically be added as a shared printer for anyone connecting to the Samba server.

Software Management

The Software Management module, located on Webmin's System tab, is a complete system to handle software on the Linux server. The initial screen shows a collection of folders divided into categories. Clicking on any folder will open up the category and show a list of any related software installed on the server.

Each software package filename is also a link to a page that gives a short description of the software. A button on the left side of the screen can be clicked to list all of the files that are installed as part of the package. A button on the right side of the screen can be clicked to uninstall the software.

Below the package folders is a form for searching the package database. Use this to find any installed package.

The form below the Package Search button is used to install a new package. The new software that is to be installed must be located either on the workstation you are using to connect to the Linux server (From Uploaded File option) or on the server itself (From Local File option). Alternatively, if the package is available from an FTP or Web server, enter the full URL to access it. In the latter case, Webmin first downloads the package from the FTP/HTTP server and then installs it.

Other Webmin Modules

Webmin includes modules for taking care of the most common administrative tasks on a Linux server. Following are short descriptions of the other Webmin modules and their functions.

Webmin Configuration Configures how Webmin can be accessed, who has access rights, which port to use for accessing Webmin, and other settings related to Webmin's operations.

Webmin Help Searches Webmin's help files.

Webmin Servers Index Locates and lists all Webmin servers on the network.

Webmin Users Assign access rights to Webmin users. Each Webmin user is assigned access to one or more modules. This module can be used for purposes such as allowing someone limited access for managing the user database.

Disk Quotas Quotas are used to control how much space a user or group can use. Most Linux distributions do not have quota support enabled by default. One exception is OpenLinux eServer, which comes with quotas installed as part of the filesystem. If Webmin reports that no local filesystems support quotas, make sure that quotas have been enabled. To do so, go to the Webmin Disk and Network Filesystems. Select the mount that should have quotas enabled. On the lower right part of the screen, find the Use Quotas option. Choose the level of quotas: User Only, Group Only, or User and Group. Then click the Save button, followed by the Apply to Permanent List button. Then remount the filesystem so that the change can take effect. Then each user and group can be limited in the amount of space that party can use on the server.

Disk and Network Filesystems Lists all of the disk drives; shows the partitions and how each partition is mounted. Mounting options can be modified by clicking on the mount name.

NFS Exports Network File System (NFS) is the UNIX file-sharing protocol. It is like Samba for Linux. It lets UNIX systems share files by allowing a system to mount a partition across the network. This module is used to add, delete, and edit NFS directory shares.

Running Processes A complete list of all the processes running on the system. Click on the process ID to get more information or to kill a process that has stopped responding or is out of control.

Scheduled Cron Jobs Cron is the Linux system scheduler. There are various system tasks that have to be run on a regular schedule, such as rotating the logs. The cron schedule can be adjusted and new jobs added.

SysV Init Configuration Configures which processes are started at bootup and during normal operation.

System Logs A complete list of system logs; configures options for what to log.

Apache Webserver Configures the Apache Web server; normally not used on a Samba server.

BIND DNS Server   Configures a server that acts as a DNS server.

DHCP Server   Configures a server that is also a DHCP server. Use this module to set up subnets and shared network for DHCP.

FTP Server   Configures FTP service if you have enabled FTP access to your Samba server. Red Hat Linux, like most other Linux distributions, uses the WU-FTP daemon for FTP service. FTP service is not necessary on a Samba server and is usually not enabled.

Internet Services and Protocols   Configures dozens of Internet services. Click on a service name to see configuration information, including which port the service uses and its protocol.

Majordomo   Configures the Majordomo List Manager; not normally enabled on a Samba server.

MySQL Database Server   Configures MySQL, a simple database server for Linux systems; not normally enabled on a Samba server.

PPP Accounts   Configures Linux dial-in and dial-out services.

Postfix Configuration   A mail agent; an alternative to sendmail. Only one mail agent should be enabled on the server.

PostgreSQL Database Server   Another simple database server for Linux systems; not normally used on Samba servers.

Sendmail Configuration   Manages the sendmail configuration file.

Squid Proxy Server   Configures the Squid proxy/caching server; not normally used on a Samba server.

Linux Bootup Configuration   Configures bootup options.

Linux RAID   If Linux Redundant Array of Inexpensive Drives (RAID) software is installed, configures RAID options.

Network Configuration Controls   Network card and network configuration, including IP address, gateway, and DNS servers.

Partitions on Local Disks   Configures disk partitions. You can add, modify, and delete partitions. Drive settings can be configured and the speed of the drive can be tested.

System Time   Synchronizes system time with network time servers.

Custom Commands   Adds commonly used commands to Webmin.

File Manager   A Java-based file manager that works something like Windows Explorer. Use this for creating directories on the Linux server for Samba shares and other file management tasks. The File Manager can also be used to create an initial file share for Samba, using the Sharing button on the menu bar.

Telnet Login   A Java-based telnet applet. Lets you open a nongraphical terminal window on the Samba server.

Using the Nongraphical Terminal

The Linux terminal looks a lot like DOS, and if you know DOS, getting around on a Linux nongraphical terminal will seem familiar. For one thing, DOS borrowed its file structure from UNIX, and many of the commands are the same or similar.

When you are using a Linux terminal, what you see in front of you is called a shell. A shell is the program that acts as a nongraphical interface between the user and the operating system. It's a single-window interface.

The standard Linux shell is named Bash, the Bourne Again Shell. It is an enhanced version of the Bourne shell commonly used on UNIX computers. Steve Bourne at Bell Labs wrote the original UNIX shell, which now carries his name.

When you log onto a Linux terminal, the prompt indicates whether you've logged on as a regular user or as the administrative user, that is, as root. For a regular user, the prompt is the $ symbol; when you log on as root, the prompt is the # symbol.

There is only one administrative user. That is root. Administrative rights cannot be assigned to other users.

Mostly you should log on as a regular user. It's not a good idea to regularly log on as root, where it is too easy to make a mistake that can't be undone. In fact, for most administrative tasks done at a terminal, you don't have to log on as root. When you are logged in as a regular user, you can temporarily switch to become the root user and take care of any administrative business necessary. This is a safer approach.

To switch to the root user while logged in as a regular user, use the su command. Follow the command with a space and then a minus sign (–). This lets the system change all of the environment variables, such as the path information, to those of the root user. They get reset back to the regular user's settings whenever you exit from the su session. The command is

```
su  -
```

You will be prompted for the root password. After entering the password, you will have full administrator rights and can do whatever tasks are needed.

The Bash shell has startup files that are similar to the *autoexec.bat* file in DOS. There can be several different configuration files for Bash. The primary configuration file is named *profile,* and it can be found in the */etc* directory. This is the default configuration for all users on the system.

Each individual user also has configuration files that are found in the user's home directory, typically found in the directory named *home* in a subdirectory named with the user's username. For example, the home directory for Janet Henry, whose username is "jhenry," is */home/jhenry*. The home directory for root, however, is */root*. That's the only exception, for security reasons.

In addition, there are a number of other Bash configuration files for each individual user. Personal configuration changes are usually saved in the *.bashrc file*.

To see the current Bash settings on any Linux system, type the command `set` at the prompt.

Two useful features of Bash are command history and command completion. On DOS systems and in the DOS command window on Windows systems, the DOSkey utility can be used to get a command history. Each command that is entered is saved into a history file. To retrieve a command from the history file, use the Up Arrow key on the keyboard.

The default size for command history is 500; that is, the last 500 commands should be available by scrolling through them with the Up or Down Arrows. In practice, there are some limitations that often prevent so many commands from being available. Once the command is displayed on the command line, it can be edited using the Left Arrow or Right Arrow to move along the line and executed using the Enter key.

Command completion is a popular shortcut. Start entering a command, and after partial entry press the Tab key. If the rest of the command includes a filename or a directory, the name will be filled out. For example, to change to */home/jhenry* using command completion, enter this command:

```
cd /home/j<Tab Key>
```

The display will then change to

```
cd /home/jhenry
```

If there is another directory that starts with the letter "j," then you'll have to add more letters until the part to be completed is unique to the filename or directory name.

CAUTION!

A common mistake made by Windows users working on Linux is to use the backslash where the forward slash should be used. The backslash is a common character in Windows used for UNC designations of directories and servers such as *\\ntserver\sales\2001*. In Linux, the forward slash is used for the same function. Think of the Internet and Web pages where forward slashes are also used because the Internet was originally built on UNIX systems. Use the regular forward slash for working on Linux. The backslash is a special character in Linux that you may use infrequently, if at all.

Bash and DOS share some similarities in the use of wildcards. The ? and * can be used in the same way they are used on a DOS system. The ? wildcard is used to match a single character in a filename. The * wildcard is used to match multiple characters. For example, to get a directory listing of all the files that start with the word "memo," you can enter this command:

```
dir memo*
```

Some Linux systems don't have the `dir` command. The more widely used command on Linux is `ls`. Use it just like you'd use `dir`. For example:

```
ls memo*
```

To match a single character, use the ? wildcard. Use the command this way:

```
dir memo-draft2?
```

This would show a list of all files such as *memo-draft21, memo-draft22,* and *memo-draft23* but not *memo-draft21a.*

THE FILE SYSTEM

Linux treats files differently than the way you think of files on DOS, Windows, or Macintosh systems. Everything on Linux is a file, whether it is hardware or software, whether it is a directory or a word-processed document.

Linux uses a tree structure, where everything branches off the root level, which is represented by a single slash (/).

NOTE ON ROOT

There are two uses of the word "root" in Linux systems. Root is the base level of the filesystem, and everything else branches off it. Root is also the username for the administrator account. Watch out, particularly in written instructions, to make sure that you aren't confusing the user "root" (the administrator) with the filesystem's root level.

Each branch off the root level of the filesystem is called a directory. Each directory can have subdirectories. DOS also calls these directories, while Windows labels directories as folders. This mix of terminology is continued by KDE and GNOME on Linux, which also label directories as folders.

On DOS, Windows, and Macintosh systems, files are either executable programs or data. On Linux, data and executable programs are files, but so are all of the hardware components of the computer. The hard drive, monitor, keyboard, mouse, network card, CD-ROM, and any other device on the computer is seen as a file on Linux. When you use a device, Linux reads from or writes to one of the device files.

As with Windows, the layout of the Linux filesystem can be customized to anything the user wants. On Windows the operating system doesn't absolutely have to be in *\winnt* or the *\windows* directory; the applications don't have to be installed in *Program Files*. But if you decide to customize and install everything somewhere other than the standard default, you could run into problems.

The layout of the filesystem on most Linux distributions follows the File System Hierarchy (FSH) as defined by the Linux Standard Base organization (*www.linuxbase.org*). The FSH specifies which directories are needed and what should be in them. Here's a brief look at some of the key directories in the Linux filesystem.

/   The root level. This directory usually contains only subdirectories. On most Linux systems no files are saved on the root level.

/bin   Programs for startup. This directory has basic Linux command files for system startup as well as the most commonly used commands. These are commands that can be executed by all users.

/etc   System configuration files. Almost everything in Linux is configured with a file found in the */etc* directory. This includes the list of users (the password file), the networking information, startup and shutdown scripts, email sending and receiving configuration, and so on.

/home   User home directories. When a user is logged in, the Linux system automatically puts users in their home directory. Unless the user's rights have been changed by the administrator, each user will have permission to create and change files only in the home directory.

/lib   Shared libraries that are needed for system startup. These are like the Dynamic Link Libraries (DLLs) in Windows. These are the libraries of code that are shared by many programs.

/opt   Additional software applications. This directory is used for installation of larger programs, usually commercial software, such as Corel WordPerfect or StarOffice.

/proc   Process information. This is not a real directory. Each file in this directory and its subdirectories represents system information. Since these are not really files, they don't take up any space on the hard drive. Viewing any of the files in */proc* will show system information. Some of the files can be changed in order to change system settings. Any changes made this way disappear when the system is shut off or restarted because these are only temporary files that aren't saved anywhere.

/sbin   System programs used for startup and system administration; like */bin,* but these can be executed only by the system administrator.

/tmp   Temporary file space. Like the *temp* directory on a Windows system, users or programs can use this for saving temporary files. One difference is that any time the system is restarted, all the files in the */tmp* directory are deleted.

/usr Primary collection of program files. This is where most of the program files on Linux are located, much like the program files folder on a Windows system. One difference is that the subdirectories aren't divided by application but rather by function.

/usr/bin The primary directory for executable programs.

/usr/sbin Subdirectory for executable programs used only by the system administrator.

/usr/lib Subdirectory for shared libraries (the Linux version of DLLs). These are the libraries used by the executable programs in */usr/bin* and */usr/sbin* as well as the libraries used for compiling programs.

/usr/X11R6 Location where the Xwindows system files are installed. The name indicates that it is Release 6 of the Xwindows system.

/usr/local Traditionally, the subdirectory for installation of additional software. The */opt* directory was added later to deal with very large software programs. This is the default directory where Samba is installed. Most Linux distributions modify the default so that the Samba daemons are run from */usr/sbin* and the Samba tools run from */usr/bin*.

/usr/doc The location for Linux documentation. Every application installed on Linux should have its full documentation installed in this directory. Some packages are installed without the documentation in order to save space, and the documentation has to be installed separately. This documentation is often treated in the same way as the instruction booklet that comes with a new radio; it gets ignored. However, the documentation often has important information that is needed to make an application work properly.

TEXT EDITORS

All configuration files on Linux are in a plain text format. Changes in configuration are typically made using a text editor. If you are using KDE or GNOME, you can use a text editor like nedit or gedit. These editors are easy to learn and use.

For nongraphical terminals, there are no really easy-to-learn text editors. The vi (pronounced "vee-eye") text editor is the most universally available text editor on Linux. It is found not only on every Linux distribution but also on all UNIX systems. The name "vi" comes out of UNIX history. It was the first visual editor for UNIX, meaning that it could display a whole page of text rather than displaying text one line at a time. Vi may be appear to be difficult to use, but it is actually not too hard to learn. To start a basic text editing session, enter the command

```
vi filename
```

This starts the editor and opens the file, if it exists, or creates the file if it is new. There are three modes of operation in vi: command, command line, and insert. When a file is opened, vi is in command mode.

Command mode Every action is driven by a command. Commands are invoked by single keystrokes or combinations of keystrokes. For example, pressing the <x> key does not insert the letter "x" into the document; it invokes the Delete command and removes the character under the cursor.

Command-line mode More complex commands are handled with command-line mode. Press the colon key <:> to switch to the command line. Letter and <alt ctrl> or Shift key combinations are used to enter commands such as Save and Exit.

Insert mode Change from command mode to insert mode by pressing the <i> key. You have to be in insert mode to enter text. To exit insert mode, press the <Esc> key.

To get a list of commands and help information while you are working in vi, go into command-line mode (press the <:> key) and type the word "help" followed by the Enter key.

Entering Text in vi

To enter text in vi, change to the insert mode. Move the cursor to the point where you want to enter text and press the <i> key (Insert) or the <a> (Append) key. To exit from insert mode, press the <Esc> key.

Undo in vi

If you are in command mode and make a mistake while deleting a character, word, or line, press the <u> key immediately after the deletion. That will restore the deleted text.

Searching in vi

Searches are done in command mode. To start a forward search, use the forward slash key </>. To start a backward search, use the question mark <?>. For example, entering ?samba would begin a backward search for the word "samba." To repeat a search, press </> or <?>, depending on whether you want to search forward or backward.

Saving and Quitting in vi

To save a file, go to command-line mode. If you are in text insert mode, first press the <Esc> key and then press the colon key <:>. At the command line the letter "w" saves—or writes—the file. To save with a different name, put a space after the "w"and type in a new filename. To save and quit, use the command :wq. To quit and ignore any changes made to the document, use the command :q!.

BASIC FUNCTIONS ON A NONGRAPHICAL TERMINAL

When you've logged onto a Linux terminal, there is nothing more than a $ prompt in front of you (or a # prompt is you are logged in as root). How do you move around to different directories, get a list of files in a directories, see what is in a file, and do all the rest of what needs to be done? Following are the basic commands for working at a Linux terminal.

MOVING AROUND • To move around from the command prompt, first you should know where you are starting from. The command to find out is `pwd`. It is short for Print Working Directory. Enter it at the prompt, and the full path name to your current location will be displayed.

To move from one directory to another, use the Change Directory command: `cd`. It works much like the `cd` command in DOS (DOS "borrowed" the command from UNIX). To move up one level, use the command

```
cd ..
```

Note that there must be a space before the two dots, unlike DOS, which lets you enter the command with or without the space.

Another shortcut is to use the tilde symbol, which is used to indicate you home directory. At any point you can change to your home directory with this command:

```
cd ~
```

The tilde symbol can also be used in other commands as shorthand for your home directory.

THE DIR COMMAND • The `dir` command lists all the files in a directory. It is really the `ls` command. You can use either one, though most regular Linux users generally stick to the two-character `ls` command.

When you get a directory listing, the list can scroll right off the screen, and it's not easy to see whether something is a file or a folder, which files are data and which are applications that can be run.

In DOS there are a vast number of options that can be added to the `dir` command. The same is true in Linux.

The options for `dir` and `ls` are the same. The examples used here all refer to `dir`, since that's easy enough for Windows users to remember. But `ls` could be used instead in every case.

To any `dir` command, add the −color option. With that, any directories are listed in blue and executable files are listed in green.

You can use wildcards such as

```
dir *.txt
```

The `dir` command lists just filenames. Add the `-l` option to list files in the long format, with details on the file size and the time and date the file was saved. Use the `-h` option to show file sizes in "human-readable" format (288K instead of 288451, for example). All of the options can be combined. For example, to get a long listing showing file sizes in human-readable format, use

```
dir -lh
```

Use the More command to pause between screens of text. This works the same way on Linux as it does on DOS. It requires the use of the pipe key <|>. A sample is

```
dir -lh | more
```

To see all files, including hidden files, use the `-a` option. Hidden files in Linux are files with names that begin with a dot, such as *.profile*.

VIEWING FILE CONTENTS • To see what's in a file, you can use either the `cat` or the `more` command.

VIEWING A FILE WITH CAT • The simplest way to view a file is to use the `cat` command. This command is short for "concatenate." The `cat` command is designed to concatenate (join together) multiple files. The command can also be used to display a short file on the terminal.

Typing `cat` followed by a filename displays the contents of the file on the monitor. The limitation is that if it is a large file, the contents will scroll past faster than you can possibly read them. In that case, use the `more` command to view the file.

VIEWING A FILE WITH MORE • The `more` command will display the contents of a file one page at a time. Simply enter the command `more` followed by the name of the file you want to view.

The display is paused until you press the space bar. The next page of data is then displayed. To change the display line by line, use the Enter key rather than the space bar. Press <q> at any time to quit the display.

COPYING FILES

The `cp` command is similar to the DOS Copy command. One difference is that the `cp` command does not warn you if it is overwriting a file of the same name. For example, this command would make a backup copy of the *reply.txt* file:

```
cp /home/pmadvig/letters/reply.txt /home/pmadvig/backup
```

To be warned about overwriting a file, add the `-i` flag:

```
cp -i /home/pmadvig/letters/reply.txt /home/pmadvig/backup
```

To copy files including the directory structure, much like `xcopy` in DOS, use the `-r` option.

RENAMING AND MOVING FILES • Linux does not have a Rename command. The Move command is used both to move files to another location and to rename a file in the same location. Just like the Copy command, the Move command does not warn you about overwriting a file. Use the `-i` option to be asked for confirmation before overwriting a file.

The Move command is `mv`. For example, to rename the *reply.txt* file, enter the command

```
mv reply.txt reply.old
```

This command would move the file with confirmation before overwriting:

```
mv -i /home/pmadvig/letters/reply.txt /home/pmadvig/backup
```

DELETING FILES • Use the `rm` command to delete files. *Be careful: there is no Undelete command in Linux.* To delete a file and be asked for confirmation before deleting, use the `-i` option.

CREATING DIRECTORIES • The `mkdir` command creates directories, just as it does in DOS. However, there is no shorter version (`md`) as there is in DOS, one of the few cases where Linux does not have a shorter command name.

Directory names can contain letters, numbers, the period, the hyphen, and underscore characters. Unlike the case in Windows, directory names cannot have spaces or any other characters—only letters, numbers, the period, the hyphen, and the underscore characters.

REMOVING DIRECTORIES • The command to remove a directory is `rmdir`, followed by the name of the directory you want to delete. Directories can be deleted only if they are empty. If you get an error message saying that a directory is not empty, check to make sure there aren't hidden files still in the directory. The command `dir -a` will display all files, including hidden files.

OTHER LINUX COMMANDS FOR DOS USERS • Many commonly used DOS commands are matched by Linux commands that provide a similar function. Don't forget that DOS borrowed its file structure from UNIX so there are often similarities. If there isn't a similar command, there is often a command that can be used to get similar information.

Check Disk

The `chkdsk` command in DOS does not have any direct equivalent. But the `du` command can be used to show disk usage. Use the `-h` option to put sizes in human-readable format. The `df` command will display the size of the disk drives, the amount of space used, and the amount of free space left. Be sure to use the −h option with this command as well.

Time and Date

The Date command in Linux is a little different from that in DOS. In Linux it can be used to display the current time and date as well as change it by entering the change information after the Date command before pressing the Enter key. The Time command in Linux is completely different. It is used as a timer to measure time.

Disk Format

In Linux, the mke2fs is the format command. It is used to format a disk. Use it with caution. Only someone logged in as root can format a disk.

Memory Usage

Though not an exact equivalent of the DOS mem command, the Linux free command will display how much memory is being used, both RAM and virtual memory (swap). It also shows how much free memory is still available to use.

Log Viewer

There is no event viewer in Linux to display system logs. The general system log is the *messages* file in the */var/log* subdirectory. To view the log, enter this command:

```
more /var/log/messages
```

To search the log for specific lines, use the grep command, which will find characters inside the file:

```
more /var/log/messages | grep samba
```

That will display every line in the log with the word "samba" in it.

To see only the most recent system log messages, use the Tail command:

```
tail /var/log/messages
```

That will show the last ten lines of the log file.

Finding Files

The Locate command will find files. The command to find the file *reply.txt* is

```
locate reply.txt
```

This search uses a database that is typically updated once a day, usually in the early hours. To force an update of the database, you have to be logged in as root and then run the command `updatedb`. You might do this is you are searching for a file that you know was recently created and isn't in the Locate database.

Security Tips

Successful security of a Linux server starts with the basics. Make sure that the computer is in a secure location. The easiest way to break into a system is to have physical access to the computer itself.

With the system secure, the next step is to address user security. Security is ultimately in the hands of the users. All the best security measures in the world won't do any good if carelessness by an individual user compromises the system.

Users are mostly uneducated in security issues. They need to know your security policies and procedures. Teach users to be aware of the importance of security, and show users what they can do to protect themselves and the network.

PASSWORD PROTECTION • The most important level of security is password protection. Typically, users choose passwords that are easy to remember, which means they are also easy to break.

To protect the system, passwords should never be guessable. One way to enhance security is to assign passwords. The biggest mistake made in assigning passwords is to make them complex. If the password is difficult to remember, the user will write it down in a convenient place, such as on a sticky note next to the terminal.

Assign passwords that are easy to remember while being impossible to guess or to break using a dictionary. A six-to-eight-character "word" that is pronounceable but is not a real word has proved to be an effective form of secure password. Two sample passwords of this type are "hodrut" and "plannity."

A password generator that will create eight-character passwords of this type is an open source java applet written by Tom Van Vleck. This applet generates a list of ten "pronounceable" passwords. The applet can be run from Van Vleck's web site at *http://www.multicians.org/thvv/gpw.html,* or you can download the source from the same site.

FILE PERMISSIONS • The next level of security is to apply what is known as the *principle of least privilege.* That is, never give a user more access rights than necessary. Determine what each user needs and the minimum set of rights required to meet those needs. Then give the user exactly that level of access, but no more.

This usually involves setting file and directory access rights. Every file on a Linux system has nine switches that set who can read, write, or execute a file. Make sure that access rights for files and directories are set so that even legitimate users on the system can't go prying into other users' files. See Chapter 3 for more information on Linux file permissions.

Each file has three separate sets of permissions: one for the owner of the file, another for the group assigned to the file, and one for everyone else. Each of the three can be assigned read, write, and/or execute permissions. You must have read permission to view the contents of a file, write permission to make changes to a file or save a new file, and execute permission to start a program.

To see file permissions, use the `dir -l` command. The first column of information shows the file permissions in the format of *-rwxrwxrwx.* The first character in this block is a hyphen for a regular file; a "d" indicates that the file is a directory. The next nine characters show permissions. The first three indicate permissions for the owner of the file, the second three indicate group permissions, and the last three are permissions for everyone else. A hyphen in any of the permissions indicates that the permission is denied. The three permissions are "r" for read rights, "w" for write rights, and "x" for the right to execute, or run, a program file.

Only the owner of a file or the administrator can change file permissions. To change permissions, use the `chmod` command. This command works with a formula. The command is followed with options that define the rights. The options are "u" for the user, or owner, of the file; "g" for the group assigned to the file; "o" for other users, that is, everyone else; and "a" for all possible users, a combination of "u," "g," and "o." After this there is either a + or - sign to indicate if permission is being added or subtracted, followed by the permission being granted or denied: "r" for read, "w" for write, and "x" for execute. For example, to make a file readable by everyone in the group, use this command:

```
chmod g+r report.doc
```

To make it readable by anyone:

```
chmod a+r report.doc
```

There are also special `chmod` settings called the Sticky Bit, suid ("set user ID") and sgid ("set group ID").

Turning on the Sticky Bit for a directory means that no one except the owner of a file the directory can move or delete the file, no matter what other permissions exist. That means that a file can be readable and changeable by anyone with the proper permissions, but only the user that created the file can remove it from the directory. This is particularly useful for shared directories and is a setting that you will make use of on a Samba server.

The suid option controls what happens when a file is executed. If suid is enabled, the user ID of the process that is started is that of the owner of the file rather than the user that executed the file. This option is used to give certain programs additional permissions. For example, the `passwd` command is used to change your password. It requires root privileges to modify the password, but any regular user can execute the command. That's because suid permission has been enabled, and when the `passwd` command is run, it is run as the program file's owner, which is root.

The sgid option is like suid. A file executed with sgid enabled is run as the group assigned to the program.

The Sticky Bit, suid, and sgid are enabled or disabled with the `t` and `s` options:

```
chmod u+s filename (enable suid)
chmod u-s filename (disable suid)
chmod g+s filename (enable sgid)
chmod g-s filename (disable sgid)
chmod o+t directory (enable Sticky Bit)
chmod o-t directory (disable Sticky Bit)
```

CHANGING PERMISSIONS USING OCTAL NUMBERS • An alternative method for `chmod` uses octal numbers. Either method produces the same results, though the octal numbers are more cryptic and more difficult for new users to understand. The numbers are the form of permissions used for Samba settings.

The numeric method uses either three or four digits. A four-digit number includes the Sticky Bit, suid, or sgid; a three-digit number does not.

The optional first digit is a 1 to enable the Sticky Bit, a 2 to enable sgid permission, or a 4 to enable suid permission. The numbers can be combined to combine permissions. For example, a 3 would indicate that the Sticky Bit is to be enabled as well as sgid permission. Sometimes a 0 (zero) is used to indicate that no special permissions are being enabled.

The three following digits set permissions for the user, for the group, and finally for everyone else. The digit itself is determined by adding up the permissions. No permission is 0. Execute permission is 1. Write permission is 2. Read permission is 4.

To use octal numbers to give read, write, and execute permission, for example, you would add 1 plus 2 plus 4 for a total of 7. For only read and write permission, the total is 6. For read-only, the total is 4. So the number to give the user all permissions, the group read and write permissions, and everyone else read-only permission is 764. A program file that is to be executed only by members of the group might have its permission set as 750, giving the owner of the file full permission and the group read and execute permission (the two permissions necessary to run the program); everyone else is denied access to the file.

MONITORING THE SYSTEM • Another component of security is monitoring your system. The logs can show when the system's security has been compromised. There are many logs on a Linux system. All are found in the */var/log* directory. The Secure log is a record of all access and password-related activity. Check it regularly to see who accessed your system and when. This does not stop someone from breaking into the system, but it helps you trace what happened if someone has broken into the server.

Two commands can also help. The `last` and `lastb` commands will display the last person to log on and the last unsuccessful logon attempt. The file */var/log/btmp* is required for `lastb` to work. If it isn't there, create it using the Touch command:

```
touch /var/log/btmp
```

FIREWALLS AND SECURE CONNECTIONS • There are several additional steps that can be taken to secure a Linux server. One is to make sure it is running behind a firewall. Firewalls put a barrier between the Internet, or other external systems, and your internal network.

If users on the network need to access the server using telnet or FTP, use the OpenSSH secure shell software that allows logins where the entire connection is encrypted. This requires secure shell software on both the server and the workstation connecting to the server. It is installed by default on most of the current Linux distributions, though it was not included with older distributions.

Another way to secure a remote connection is to use a one-time password system. Each time a user logs on, a unique password is required. Special software is used to calculate a new password for each connection. Even if the password is discovered by an unauthorized user, it cannot be used to create a new connection.

S/Key is a free, software based one-time password system. You can find the latest version on the Web at *http://www.ibiblio.org/pub/linux/system/security/*. The file is called *skey-2.2.tar.gz*.

A commercial one-time password system, SecureID, is available from RSA Security. It can be found on the Web at *http://www.rsasecurity.com/*.

Handling Emergencies

What about emergencies? If you are new to Linux systems, dealing with an emergency can be daunting. Here are some steps to take so that you can be prepared for any emergencies.

BACK UP REGULARLY • The first step is to make sure that you have a regular backup schedule. Data security and recovery are key to meeting any emergency. Tape backups are the most reliable and long-lasting of all the systems available.

Also consider some of the alternative systems as secondary backups. ATA hard disk drives are inexpensive. It is easy to set up a backup drive that will have all the data copied to it daily or even more frequently. There are many replication programs that can be used to do this on a regular schedule. One is rsync, which was developed by Andrew Tridgell, the same developer who created the initial Samba program. The program and documentation are available at *http://rsync.samba.org*. It is widely used to create mirror Web sites as well as for system backup. Appendix C covers Linux backup procedures, including the use of rsync.

KEEP RECORDS • One of the most frustrating tasks when you are dealing with an emergency is having to reconstruct a complete record of the system's hardware and software configuration.

To make this task easier, use a notebook to record a summary of the system's configuration. Any time there is a change to the operating system or new hardware is added, update the notebook. Some key files should be copied regularly. If you have copies, it is easy to restore the system if something happens. The configuration files on a Linux system are all found in the */etc* directory. The key files to keep current copies of are

- smb.conf (the Samba configuration file)
- smbpasswd (Samba users and their passwords)
- fstab (the disk partition table)
- passwd (Linux users)
- shadow (passwords for Linux users)

If you want the maximum ability to restore configurations, copy the entire */etc* directory and all of its subdirectories.

Some system administrators also keep an online set of notes in a file named *README* in the */etc* directory. These notes should include any software configuration information, especially anything that varies from the standard defaults. Make sure to update the notes any time a change is made, and include the time and date of each new entry.

CREATE A RESCUE BOOT DISK • Unlike the Windows NTFS filesystem, the Linux filesystem can be installed onto a floppy disk and run in an emergency to rescue a failed system.

Most Linux distributions include the creation of an emergency floppy disk as part of the initial installation. If you didn't create the disk, you can create an emergency disk using one of the Linux microdistributions. These are Linux systems designed to fit everything on one floppy disk.

The most popular of these is the one created by Tom Oehser. It's called Tomsrtbt, which stands for "Tom's floppy which has a root filesystem and is also bootable." It is available on the Web at *http://www.toms.net/rb/*. The disk can be created from either a Windows system or a Linux computer. Read the FAQ on the Web site for more information.

Commonly referred to as Tom's rescue disk, this single disk has everything on it that you would need for rescue and recovery operations in an emergency. In fact, it is so useful that you might want to get it and create a Tom's rescue disk even if you already have a rescue disk created with your Linux distribution.

Use of Tom's rescue disk requires that you have a good working knowledge of Linux and its commonly used tools. It boots to a basic nongraphical terminal. The editor included on the disk is vi. It also includes about two dozen of the most-needed Linux tools for system recovery.

Optimizing Performance

Samba's performance out of the box without any performance tuning is certainly acceptable. Benchmark tests suggest that a small-to medium-sized network with a Samba server running on a single-processor Intel-based PC with the Linux operating system can outperform a Windows NT 4 server on the same Intel-based PC. The same tests show that on multiprocessor Linux systems, Windows usually outperforms Samba. That's not because of Samba, but because of a limitation in Linux. The Linux 2.2 kernel was the first to support multiprocessor systems, and it had all the problems that are usually associated with the first version of any software. The 2.4 kernel has multiprocessor support that equals Windows multiprocessor performance.

Linux, Windows 2000, Solaris for Intel computers, and FreeBSD were compared by *SysAdmin* magazine (July 2001) in a report titled "Which OS is Fastest for High Performance Network Applications?" All the operating systems were tested on the same hardware. The conclusion was: "We found Linux to be the best performing operating system based on our metrics, performing 35% better than Solaris, which came in second, followed by Windows, and finally, FreeBSD." To get the best performance from their Linux server they increased the file handle limits, a tuning technique described later in this chapter.

The performance of any Samba server can be improved by fine-tuning the system. Some measures can significantly improve performance. Others will make a small improvement that may be noticeable only on a heavily used system.

Maximizing performance is almost always a compromise between the possibilities and the budget. Many optimization recommendations involve nothing more than throwing more hardware into the mix. That's one solution, but it's not always the most efficient or cost-effective way to solve your network problems.

Performance is mostly affected by three factors—the server, the network, and the application. These are the areas of system performance tuning that are covered in this chapter.

The hardware section includes information on how to calculate your minimum hardware needs as well as making recommendations for the best hardware choices available. If possible, check these recommendations before you get your Samba server. For many, however, your first Samba server is not a new system; rather, it's built on an older machine that was replaced by a new, high-performance system. In that case, you should check that the older system meets the minimum hardware requirements. If not, upgrade it.

Samba servers running on older Pentium 200 Mhz-based systems can give excellent performance. The amount of memory and the speed of the hard drives are more important to the performance of a Samba server than the speed of the processor. Benchmark tests run by the Samba team and included with the Samba documentation shows that a standard SCSI hard drive can transfer data at about 560 Kbps, while a 133-MHz Pentium processor can handle a load of 5,600 Kbps. The hard drive is clearly the bottleneck in terms of server hardware.

There is also a section on optimizing the Linux operating system, including tips on how to adjust the system defaults. Most Linux distributions use the default configuration, which is more appropriate for a workstation than a file server.

Finally, the Samba configuration can be fine-tuned. Samba has several settings affecting performance that you should check.

Performance Issues

The first sign that you have a performance problem is usually complaints from users. Some performance problems are easy to figure out. For example, you might get an out-of-memory error message. The obvious solution is to add memory to the system. There are other problems that are not as apparent. The source of the problem may not be easily identified, or there may not be a clear solution. In those cases, you need to start tracking down the source of the problem. Part of that process is monitoring system performance. Monitoring can help you determine if the problem is in the server, the network, or the application. The next section in this chapter goes over some tools you can use to monitor a Linux server. Most UNIX servers have similar tools.

The Biggest Bottleneck

The performance of the hard drive controller is the biggest hardware bottleneck on any server. If users of your network are complaining about sluggish performance, start monitoring your hard drive's performance. If this is the bottleneck, check the section on hard drives to see the choices available for upgrading. In particular, consider the RAID controllers. RAID controllers can give the best performance of all the various choices available.

First, you can narrow down the area you need to monitor. Look for these common symptoms: slow system response, slow network connections, and excessive activity by the disks on the server. Also look in the Event Viewer and system logs for signs of trouble. All these procedures can help you to more quickly find where you have a performance problem.

SLUGGISH SYSTEM RESPONSE • If the response from the Samba server seems to be slow, and reading or writing to a file takes a long time, the problem could be either an inadequate hard drive system or not enough memory on the server. Make sure you have a hard drive and drive controller that will meet the needs of your server. See the section on hard drives for details on what to look for in hard drives. For inadequate memory problems, see the section on monitoring performance for tips on checking memory use on your server. This will help you determine whether your system needs more memory. Also, the hardware section includes details on how to calculate the minimum amount of memory your server needs.

SLOW NETWORK CONNECTIONS • If connections to the Samba server are being dropped, or drive mappings are being lost, there may be a problem in the network. You can use the traceroute tool to check network connections. Make sure that there are no problems in connecting to the server from the workstation. Also look in the hardware section of this chapter for tips on optimizing networking hardware.

EXCESSIVE DISK ACTIVITY • A high level of activity by the hard drives may indicate that the server is engaging in frequent page swapping. Users will probably be complaining about slow response from the server. This could indicate that there isn't enough memory on the server for the workload. See the section on monitoring performance for the information on how to monitor page swapping on the server. If it looks like you need more memory for the system, the hardware section has information on the minimum memory needs for Samba.

SYSTEM ERROR MESSAGES • Check the Event Viewer on your Windows servers and the error logs on your Samba server. Look for messages that indicate system problems. See if any of them are related to the Samba application. Correcting problems that show up in the logs, even if they don't appear to be related to Samba, can often fix performance problems.

MONITORING PERFORMANCE

To monitor performance on a Linux system, start with the uptime utility. If you are using Webmin for system administration, there is no uptime module. However, you can open the Running Processes link on the System page and select Run. Type in the command as shown below and the result will be displayed. You can also do this directly in a terminal window on the Samba server or by opening a telnet session from your workstation. At the prompt, enter the command

uptime

Figure 9-1 shows a sample uptime report.

Uptime tells you the current time, how long the system has been running, the number of users, and three load averages. The figures show the load average over the last minute, the last 5 minutes, and the last 15 minutes. The load average is based on the average number of jobs waiting to run within the given period of time. Note whether the load average is going up or decreasing. If system performance is slow but the load average is declining, then system performance will probably improve by itself.

Regular monitoring of uptime will give you an indicator of the typical load average for your system. On a day when the system seems slow, check uptime and see if the system load is higher than normal. If it is, the sluggishness may only be temporary and will take care of itself after the heavy processing is done.

A high load average means that the CPU is being subjected to heavy usage. Systems with lots of memory can sometimes tolerate heavy CPU usage, but in general it's not a good idea to overload the CPU.

A load average that is less than 3 indicates that demand is low. Most active servers will show a load average of 3 to 6. If your load average is over 6, your CPU is overloaded. You should take steps to distribute the load to other servers, add a faster CPU, or add more CPUs if you have a multiprocessor system.

The vmstat utility can be used to learn more details about CPU usage. Run this the same way you run uptime. The vmstat utility uses this syntax:

vmstat *interval count*

The interval is the number of seconds between reports, and the count is the total number of reports to give. If you leave off the count, vmstat will run continuously until you stop it with Ctrl+C. At the prompt, enter the command

vmstat 5 4

Figure 9-2 shows a sample of vmstat output.

The first line reports the average for each statistic since boot time. This is not useful for determining bottlenecks and should be ignored for any analysis of system performance. Each additional line reports the current status.

```
6:40pm  up 6 days,  2:14,  6 users,  load average: 0.18, 0.15, 0.23
```

Figure 9-1   *The Uptime command shows the load average on the server.*

```
   procs                         memory      swap         io      system        cpu
 r  b  w    swpd    free   buff  cache  si  so    bi      bo   in    cs  us  sy  id
 0  0  0   21164   20388 319184  75972   0   0    19       1    4    61  20   3  77
```

Figure 9-2   *CPU usage is shown with the vmstat utility.*

The first three fields report on the three possible states of running processes. The first, *r*, is the number of processes waiting to be run. The second, *b*, is the number of sleeping processes. The third, *w*, is the number of processes swapped out. The number of processes waiting to be run should generally be low. A number higher than 10 indicates that the system is overloaded.

The CPU information will tell you more. Look at the last three fields: *us*, *sy*, and *id*. The *us* statistic is the percentage of CPU cycles used for user tasks. The *sy* statistic is the percentage of CPU cycles used for system tasks, including disk reads and writes. The *id* statistic is the percentage of CPU cycles that were not used, that is, the amount of idle time.

Check these statistics regularly over a period of time during peak usage. The CPU usage should be roughly equally divided between user tasks and system tasks. A high CPU usage percentage with no idle time over a protracted period can be an indicator that the CPU is being overloaded. However, don't rush to this conclusion. It takes monitoring the system over a long period of time to determine this, since any number of events will cause a high level of CPU usage that is actually only short-lived. If the percentages remain high over a long period of time, however, then the CPU is probably overloaded.

After checking CPU usage, you can use vmstat to check memory paging and disk reading and writing.

Using the same vmstat command, look at the memory and swap statistics. In the memory section the swpd figure is the amount of virtual memory being used. The free statistic is the amount of idle memory. The buff listing is the amount of memory used as buffers. And cache is the amount of memory left in the cache.

In the swap section, *si* is the amount of memory swapped in from disk. The *so* figure is the amount of memory swapped out to disk.

If the memory free figure is regularly below 5,000, that's a good indicator that your system does not have enough RAM. Adding memory to such a system should mean a significant boost in performance.

Also look at the swap-out (*so*) figure. This indicates the amount of memory being swapped out to the disk and should be very close to zero. If it isn't, processes are contending for available memory and the system is paging. You will notice frequent disk writing on such a system. A high swap-out figure can indicate that the system is performing desperation swapping. Desperation swapping means that the system has severe memory shortages. This is an acute problem that can significantly slow down performance. The only solution is to add more memory.

The *io* section of vmstat indicates disk reading and writing performance. The *bi* figure is the number of blocks written to the block device; on most systems, that's the hard drive. The *bo* figure is the number of blocks read from the hard drive. The *cs* figure is the number of context switches per second.

On a busy Samba server, the *io* figures can be from a hundred to even several thousand. However, if the *bi* and *bo* figures are consistently high, it is an indication that your hard drive is working under a heavy load. Adding more disk drives with their own controllers could improve your server's performance.

Another method for identifying problems is to monitor the running processes. This can be done in Webmin by going to the System tab and selecting the Running Processes module. Webmin's Process Manager is a browser-based version of the Linux ps tool. Initially the display is sorted by process ID (PID). You can also sort the display by username, memory usage, and CPU time consumed.

If you click on CPU, the processes are listed in order of decreasing CPU usage. You can use this to see which processes are using the most CPU time. This should be monitored over a long period of time before taking any action. The results that are shown on the Running Processes page are just a snapshot of the moment you requested the report.

If a process is using a large amount of CPU time over a long period, it may be in an infinite loop. If you double-click on the PID, the Process Information Web page opens. If you need to terminate a looping process, you can choose the Kill command next to the Send Signal button. When Kill is showing in the selection box, click the Send Signal button. This will stop the process.

Maximizing Your Hardware

Probably nothing affects performance more than hardware. There are four hardware areas that can be maximized for best overall performance. They are the network hardware, the hard drives, server memory, and the server CPU.

Network Infrastructure

Optimizing the network infrastructure can be difficult. Every change you make on one machine affects the performance of the overall network as well as each individual workstation on the network. For example, replacing a cable on a network can change network performance because cable length affects the rate at which data moves on the cable. Adding a higher-performance network card to a workstation can interfere with the performance of other computers on the network that have lower-performance network cards.

The infrastructure of the network determines certain physical characteristics that you can't alter with any ease. You can't use optimization techniques on a 10-Mbps Ethernet network to make it give you 100-Mbps bandwidth.

Another physical limitation is the age of your network. Cables get older, as do connectors and the electronics that support the network. The Registered Jack (RJ) plugs on the cables have springs that ensure a tight connection. These springs are subject to metal fatigue and eventually lose their flex so that you don't get the same level of connectivity. A bad connection between the cable and the network card can result in corrupted packets. The connector doesn't fail; it just doesn't perform as well as it once did. Also, older cables get brittle and are subject to hidden breaks.

After making sure that your old hardware isn't causing the network to slow down, the primary way to improve network performance is to increase the bandwidth of the network itself. This usually involves upgrading or replacing the network wiring, the network cards in the workstations and servers, and using the latest high-speed switches.

Most Ethernet networks are using the original 10-Mbps hardware. For more bandwidth you can upgrade the network to 100 Mbps or Gigabit Ethernet. The higher speeds require wiring, network cards, and switches that all match. Don't try to mix 10 Mbps with 100 Mbps or 100 Mbps with Gigabit Ethernet, or you'll take a real hit in performance.

ATA, SCSI, and RAID

The speed of accessing the hard drive can be the biggest factor in the performance of a busy file server. Hard drives are mechanical devices with moving parts that must retrieve and store data for multiple users in real time. Every disk read or write is a temporary pause in the flow of data.

Hard drives are packed with a great number of mechanical components, from the platters with the magnetic coating that actually holds the data, to the spindles that spin the platters, to the read/write heads that store and retrieve the data while moving rapidly back and forth across the platters.

The access time for a hard drive takes eons compared to the access time for computer memory. The access time for Static RAM (SRAM) is 10 nanoseconds (billionths of a second). The slowest Dynamic RAM (DRAM) chips have an access time of 50 to 150 nanoseconds.

Disk access time includes seek time, that is, the time it takes for a read/write head to locate a sector on the platter. Fast disk drives typically have an access time of 9 to 15 milliseconds (thousandths of a second), making disk accesses 200 times slower than DRAM.

While you want to get the fastest hard drive you can afford, consider buying multiple disks instead of one big drive. Two 9-Gb hard drives will perform better than one 20-Gb drive because the workload is distributed over multiple disks, decreasing the amount of time needed to access data on the disks. You can get even better performance with RAID disk drive systems.

Most servers should have Small Computer Systems Interface (SCSI) disk drives. While SCSI is the gold standard for servers, Linux servers are often set up with AT Attachment (ATA) drives, often called Integrated Drive Electronics (IDE), Enhanced Integrated Drive Electronics (EIDE), or Ultra Direct Memory Access (UDMA) drives. ATA drives are standard on Intel-based machines. Some manufacturers sell Intel-based systems with ATA drives as server machines.

Most hard drive manufacturers make both ATA and SCSI disk drives. The drives themselves are identical and their rated speeds will look similar. A disk's speed is usually given in revolutions per minute (rpm). Of course, faster is always better. A standard ATA or SCSI drive is usually rated at 5,400 rpm. There are higher-speed drives rated at 7,500, and SCSI drives rated at 10,000 rpm.

What's not the same for these drives is the controller. The differences between ATA and SCSI may not appear to be that great. Each controller type has its strengths and weaknesses. What you want for a server, however, is not the same as what you would want on a workstation.

ATA DISK DRIVES

ATA drives are often referred to generically as IDE drives. But there are other kinds of IDE drives that are not intended for use on Intel-based PCs, such as Macintosh IDE drives. ATA refers to the AT Attachment standard, a standard for connecting disk drives to AT-type computer systems. AT was the IBM designation for the PC model introduced after the XT and has become an industry-standard term for any current PC.

There have been several revisions of the ATA standard, mostly to support faster modes of data transfer. The current revision is ATA-3. The Ultra ATA or UDMA terms used by drive manufacturers are not formally established standards. These drives use a faster DMA transfer mode than the one defined in the ATA-3 standard.

ATA drives do not have a separate controller card as SCSI drives do. The controller is on the drive itself. However, there can be only one controller per channel, so the drives are set to be either primary or secondary. The secondary drive has the controller disabled either through jumpers on the drive or through the system BIOS.

Another characteristic of all ATA drives is that they connect to the computer system board with the same cable, the original cable used for the first ATA drives that had a throughput of 5 Mbps.

Controllers on ATA drives do not have processing capabilities and rely on the computer's CPU to handle all processing. This means that there could be a noticeable slowdown on the system any time a big file is being read from or written to the disk. The process ties up the CPU until the drive work is done.

ATA-3 adds Direct Memory Access DMA capability to the standard. This has meant a significant improvement in overall performance. That's because DMA allows the ATA drive controller to read and write from system memory directly, thus bypassing the need to use the CPU. This process is also referred to as bus mastering.

There are other factors as well that affect ATA drive performance; they probably don't matter on a workstation but do matter for a server. By design, ATA drives cannot multitask. That is, they are single-threaded; commands do not overlap. When a drive is carrying out a command such as a seek, read, or write, the next command can't be issued until the first process has completed.

In addition, a computer system can support only two ATA channels, and only one ATA device on a channel can be active at a time. That means that if you do use an ATA drive on a server, you should avoid adding a second drive to a channel. This can become a significant bottleneck because the controller on the primary drive has to handle the whole workload and the controller is really only designed for the single drive it is attached to.

The only exception to this is ATA RAID controllers, which are designed to overcome these limitations. These are controller cards that are installed separately from the ATA drives. All of the ATA drives have their built-in controllers disabled; that is, they are set to run as secondary drives. ATA RAID controllers can closely match the performance of SCSI controllers.

The advantage of ATA drives is price. Even the most expensive superfast UDMA drives are cheaper than SCSI drives. And the performance of these drives is certainly respectable. For a small office, UDMA drives may be the most cost-effective choice.

Tuning ATA Drives

Red Hat Linux 7.1 automatically optimizes ATA drives for optimum performance. All earlier versions of Red Hat Linux and other Linux distributions default to slower settings that do not take advantage of DMA transfers. On these non-optimized systems, the hdparm utility is a Linux tool that can be used to bet the best possible performance from ATA drives.

The hdparm utility can be used to enable 32-bit transfers, rather than the default 16-bit I/O rate, and also enable multisector access, rather than the default single-sector access.

Just a warning. The hdparm utility can cause total data loss if something goes wrong. Make sure you have a complete and reliable backup before setting it up on your system.

Start by getting a detailed report on the drive that will be reconfigured. Use the command

```
hdparm -v /dev/hda
```

Of course, for a drive other than the first ATA drive, replace */dev/hda* with any other device name to be checked.

The result shows whether the drive is operating in 16-bit or 32-bit mode (I/O support) and multisector access (`multcount`). A more detailed report can be gotten by using the `-I` parameter.

Before making any changes, test the system. Enter the command

```
hdparm -t /dev/hda
```

This tests buffered disk reads. Save the results and then run the test again after making adjustments so you can make sure that performance has been improved.

To enable 32-bit transfers, enter the command

```
hdparm -c 3 /dev/hda
```

The `-c 3` parameter is the standard choice for 32-bit support. To disable it, use the `-c 0` parameter. The `-c 1` parameter also enables 32-bit support, with less overhead, but it is not supported by most drives.

Multisector transfer mode, sometimes called block mode, is enabled with this command:

```
hdparm -m 16 /dev/hda
```

The `-m 16` parameter enables 16-sector transfers. The optimum setting for most drives is 16 or 32, except for Western Digital drives. Western Digital drives use small 32-Kb buffers and actually slow down with a setting over 8. A setting of 4 is probably optimal for Western Digital drives. The `-m 0` parameter disables multisector access.

Multisector access reduces the load on the CPU by 30 to 50 percent. It can increase data transfer rates by up to 50%.

The parameters can be combined, once you've determined the best settings for your system. Add the command to the */etc/rc.d/rc.local* file (on Debian GNU/Linux, add a script to */etc/init.d*) so that the settings will be enabled whenever the system is rebooted. For example, add a line that says

```
hdparm -c 1 -m 32 /dev/hda
```

SCSI DISK DRIVES

SCSI drives are found on all the top-performing servers. SCSI drives, by design, are much faster than the fastest ATA-UDMA drives. A SCSI controller can process multiple commands, allowing commands from multiple devices to overlap during processing.

The labeling used for SCSI controllers can be confusing, however. Manufacturers use the term "SCSI" for both standard SCSI controllers and devices and their nonstandard controllers and devices.

The SCSI-2 standard includes Fast SCSI, which means bus transfers at 10 Mbs, and Wide SCSI, which means 16-bit rather than 8-bit throughput. SCSI-2 supports up to 16 devices in a chain attached to the controller. Most SCSI drives and controllers are designed to meet this standard.

The SCSI-3 standard is not yet formalized. It includes Ultra SCSI, which is a 40-Mbps bus transfer rate. When a manufacturer lists a controller as Ultra Wide SCSI, it means it is capable of 16-bit throughput at a 40-Mbps transfer rate, the top speed for most SCSI drives. Fast-Wide SCSI means a 20-Mbps transfer rate with 16-bit throughput.

SCSI-3 also covers Serial SCSI, marketed as FireWire. Serial SCSI has a 400-Mbps bus rate, as well as many technological improvements. A fiber-channel SCSI is used for hard drives on IBM and Sun servers. It supports 100-Mbps transfer rates.

RAID DISK DRIVE CONTROLLERS

The basic idea of a Redundant Array of Inexpensive Drives (RAID) is to combine multiple small, inexpensive disk drives into a series of disk drives that can give the same performance level as a single drive on a mainframe computer.

RAID drives appear to be a single drive. RAID performance can be enhanced by the use of striping, where data blocks are spread across two or more drives. Striping uses parallel processing: disk reads and writes take place simultaneously on parallel data paths. Striping speeds up disk reads and writes over the speed of reading and writing on the same drives without striping.

A 1987 study at the University of California at Berkeley, co-sponsored by IBM, developed RAID and defined different levels of RAID. There are six levels of RAID. Of those, Linux supports three, levels 0, 1, and 5.

Level 0 is data striping, the fastest and most efficient form of RAID. Data is split across more than one drive, which allows higher data throughput. However, striping alone is risky. There is no data mirroring, so the failure of any one of the disks in the array will result in total data loss on the whole array.

Level 1 is full disk mirroring, the most secure but slowest form of RAID. A copy of every bit of data written to the primary disk is also written to a secondary disk. Level 1 RAID is generally slower on writes compared to a single drive, but it can be faster on reads. If either one of the drives fails, no data is lost. This is the most expensive level of RAID because every drive must be duplicated. It is the best choice if data security is primary.

Level 5 might be called a combination of levels 0 and 1. It requires three or more disk drives in the array. Level 5 uses disk striping and a parity checksum. The capacity is the total of all the drives in the array, less one drive. If any disk in the array is lost, the data can be rebuilt using the parity checksum. The performance is very good for reads. Writes are slower because the parity data must be updated each time. This is the most popular RAID configuration. It provides both speed and security. If a disk fails, the array continues to operate in a degraded mode until the failed drive is replaced.

RAID systems are primarily built on SCSI controllers, though there are some ATA RAID controllers. Most RAID systems also include fault tolerance, that is, the ability to continue to function even if a piece of the hardware fails. Many RAID controllers support hot swapping; that is, they have connectors that allow the removal and replacement of a defective drive without having to power down the computer.

SCSI RAID controllers are the most sophisticated, powerful, and expensive SCSI controllers available. An Intel-based server with a SCSI RAID controller will produce the best performance levels possible today. Of course, the price of such a system reflects this fact.

FILESYSTEM

The server's filesystem also affects performance, particularly that of the disk drive. The Linux standard is the Extended 2 (ext2) filesystem. Ext2 is a high-performance system that is fragmentation-resistant.

What most standard Linux distributions don't include is a journaling filesystem. Most UNIX servers have a journaling system that keeps a log of file modifications. Journaling systems are designed to facilitate a fast recovery from a server crash. On a nonjournaling filesystem, if there is a server crash, the amount of time it can take to check and recover the hard disk can be hours or even days, depending on the size of the disk drives and the data stored on them.

On a journaling system, the same kind of check is not necessary because there is a log of all file transactions. The system can be back up in a matter of minutes. This can be important for a critical Samba server holding essential files that everyone on the network needs to access. Downtime is virtually eliminated.

There are several open source journaling systems being developed for Linux, and most Linux distributions with the 2.4 kernel have the option of formatting the disk drives with the ReiserFS journaling system. ReiserFS includes many performance-improving features, such as a balanced tree algorithm that enhances overall response times for large directories. More information on ReiserFS can be found on its Web page at *www.namesys.com.*

Another open source journaling system for Linux is being developed by IBM. JFS for Linux from IBM is based on the journaling filesystem developed for IBM's OS/2 and is similar to IBM's JFS for AIX. The Web site for JFS for Linux is *http://oss.software.ibm.com/developer/opensource/jfs.*

XFS is a journaling filesystem being developed by SGI. It is based on XFS for IRIX (SGI's version of UNIX). For information see *http://oss.sgi.com/projects/xfs/.*

Finally, ext3, the next generation of Linux's ext2 filesystem, is under development and includes journaling. Its development is behind the others, though. There isn't an informational Web site for ext3, only an FTP site where alpha versions of the software can be downloaded. That's at *ftp://ftp.linux.org.uk/pub/linux/sct/fs/jfs/.*

A journaling system would be good for any Samba server. As these journaling systems move out of beta and into operational systems, look at the features of each one and see which one best meets your needs.

Memory Requirements

For optimum performance, install the maximum amount of memory the server's system board will support. Relative to the other costs of the server, memory is inexpensive. That doesn't mean it's always in the budget to max out the memory on the server. If cost is a problem, you should first monitor your system to determine whether memory is a bottleneck. The section on monitoring performance outlines one way to monitor memory performance on a Linux server. Monitoring memory can show you whether adding memory will affect the server performance.

Memory is much faster than hard disks, and the more memory you have, the less time the server will have to spend accessing the hard drive, particularly reading and writing to the disk for virtual memory (called swap space on a Linux server).

If you can't put in the maximum possible amount of memory, use the following figures to get an idea of the minimum you'll require for a Linux server running Samba. When you calculate the minimum amount of memory needed, don't forget that the operating system needs memory. On a Linux server this is the amount of memory required for loading the kernel and the device modules. If you aren't sure how much memory is required for the operating system on the server, check the amount of memory used after starting the server and before launching any additional programs. That will give you a starting point. A typical Linux server will require a minimum of 32 Mb of memory or 64 Mb if you are using a graphical interface like KDE or GNOME.

If the Linux server is being used for anything besides Samba file and printer sharing, such as email services or as a Web server, then the memory requirements for those processes have to be added in as well.

To calculate the memory requirements for Samba, start with the daemons (services) smbd and nmbd. The smbd daemon takes about 2 Mb for the program and shared libraries. The nmbd daemon and its auxiliary process take about 1 Mb. Also, a new smbd daemon is started for each connected user, taking about 512 Kb for each user. SWAT and Webmin add about 512 Kb each as well.

Using these figures, for example, a 50-user server would require a minimum of 29 Mb in memory, plus the operating system's memory requirement. Actually that figure is for supporting 50 simultaneous connections. On most networks, not all users are connected all the time to the server, so that's probably enough memory to support more than 50 users.

There is one other consideration for maximizing memory on a Linux server. In order to make the best use of the Linux system's file-caching capabilities, the server should have twice the memory calculated for the minimum. That will minimize the necessity to swap data to disk. The result, for example, is that on a Linux server requiring 32 Mb for the operating system and 29 Mb for Samba, you should add 61 Mb for file caching. That's a total of about 120 Mb of memory. Using that as a base and working with the 32 Mb minimum increments for most server system boards, a system with 128 Mb would be the amount of memory required for a Linux server handling 50 Samba users. You should plug in your own figures to see what your memory needs are.

If you already have a Linux server, you can use these figures to get an idea of how your system compares. These memory figures are really just guides, and you should make sure to include as many of the variables as possible when calculating your memory needs.

CPUs and SMP

CPUs are rarely a bottleneck. If you are dealing with complaints that the Samba server is responding poorly, the CPU is usually not the problem. Make sure you monitor CPU performance. If the processor is idle much of the time, the system probably won't benefit from adding processing power. If the a system shows a heavy load, with many simultaneously executing processes, and CPU utilization is high, then adding a more powerful processor or multiple processors can increase system performance.

The uptime utility shows the CPU's load average. Check it to see if the CPU load is high. Also look at the CPU usage information, shown by vmstat as outlined in "Performance Issues" on monitoring performance. If the CPU shows idle time, it still has cycles to spare and the CPU is not a bottleneck. Adding another CPU will have no affect on performance, and upgrading to a faster CPU will show little or no improvement.

If do have a CPU bottleneck and are considering an upgrade, or if you are getting a new system, get a multiprocessor system. Symmetrical multiprocessing (SMP) is a special architecture that allows multiple processor chips to be installed on the system board. Each separate CPU chip can execute processes at the same time, producing remarkable performance on a single system. The SMP support in the Linux 2.4 kernel was developed by SGI and HP and is generally considered to be industrial-strength.

Samba scales very well on multiprocessor systems. Benchmark tests on four-processor UNIX systems running under a heavy user load show that Samba outperforms Windows servers on four-processor systems. Samba will scale well on multiprocessor systems running the Linux 2.4 kernel as well.

Optimizing the Linux Server

The default configuration of any operating system is designed to meet a wide variety of possible uses. It is the best configuration for general use, but not necessarily the best configuration for a specific use.

The performance of Windows file servers, for example, can be improved by changing the default configuration. A Microsoft-funded study by Mindcraft that compares Windows servers and Linux servers includes excellent information on how to tune a Windows NT 4 server in order to improve performance. If you want some tuning tips for a Windows NT 4 server, look at the report, published on the Web at *http://www.mindcraft.com/whitepapers/ openbench1-ph12.pdf*. See the section on Windows file server configuration. The study's Linux tuning is not so good and should be ignored. According to Linus Torvalds, Mindcraft refused to allow Linux technicians access to enough information to properly tune the Linux system, even refusing to answer their follow-up questions.

The conclusion of the Mindcraft study, which is that Windows outperforms Linux, is skewed both by the poor tuning of the Linux server and by using a default configuration known to favor Microsoft's strengths. Since Microsoft paid for the study, it is a good idea to be skeptical of the results. Mindcraft did similar studies, also paid for by Microsoft, that concluded that Windows outperforms Sun servers and Novell Netware.

Like Windows servers, Linux servers can benefit from tuning the system specifically to the needs of a file server. Most Linux distributions default to workstation settings.

The Linux filesystem can be managed through the */proc* directory. This is really a virtual filesystem that separates the running Linux kernel into directories. In the directory, each file represents either a process or a device. The contents of the file are either a variable or a value. Think of the */proc* filesystem as the "registry" for Linux. Making changes to it is similar to using regedit on a Windows system. The parallels aren't exact, but this gives you an idea of what's involved when making changes in */proc*.

Be cautious in making any changes in */proc*. Some settings will make system performance worse; some will make the system unstable. The changes are not permanent, and the system returns to the defaults any time the server is rebooted. Add any changes to the */etc/rc.d/rc.local* file (on Debian GNU/Linux, add a script to */etc/init.d*) to make sure that they are enabled every time the system restarts.

All adjustments to the */proc* filesystem take place immediately and don't require any further steps. The adjustments are made by "echoing" a new value to the file for the setting. To make any changes, open a terminal window and make sure that you are logged in as root.

There are several settings in */proc* that can be improved for Samba servers. These settings are the same for Linux kernels 2.2 and 2.4.

NOTE

The virtual memory subsystem of the Linux kernel has many parameters that can be configured to improve performance. This section suggests possible changes to two of the default settings, bdflush and buffermem. For details on these and all the other kernel parameters related to virtual memory, see the *vm.txt* file that is usually found in the */usr/src/linux/ Documentation/sysctl/* directory on a Linux system.

DISK WRITE CACHING • The bdflush value determines how long data stays in cache before being "flushed," that is, written to the disk. It also determines how much data to write at a time.

To see the current setting, use the `cat` command and enter the name of the bdflush setting file:

```
cat /proc/sys/vm/bdflush
```

The default values for Red Hat 7.1 are

```
30 64 64 256 500 3000 60 0 0
```

Of the nine values, only six are actually used by the Linux system. The fifth parameter and the last two are dummy settings.

The first parameter sets the maximum percentage of dirty buffers in the buffer cache. "Dirty" means that the contents have not been written to disk. Making the percentage higher means that disk writes can be delayed for a long time. The default is 30. This value can be increased to 80 percent.

The second parameter sets the maximum number of blocks to write to the disk each time bdflush is activated. The default is 64. This can be increased to 5000.

The third parameter sets the number of clean buffers that bdflush will load onto to the list of free buffers when `refill_freelist()` is called. The default is 64. A good value for this is 640.

The fourth parameter sets the number of dirty buffers found during a `refill_freelist()` operation that will cause bdflush to be activated. The default is 256. Try setting this value to 512.

The fifth parameter is not used by the kernel and is a dummy setting. It can be left at the default of 500.

The sixth parameter is the maximum time the kernel waits before writing a dirty data block to disk. The time is given in jiffies, also called clockticks. There are 100 jiffies per second. The default is 3000. This can be increased to 30000.

The seventh parameter is the maximum time the kernel waits before writing nondata buffers to disk. The default is 60. This can be set to 5000.

The last two settings are not used and don't need to be changed from the defaults of 0 and 0.

Although three of the values are not used, all the parameters must be included when making any changes, even the unused values. To change the values of bdflush to file server–optimized settings, use the following command:

```
echo "80 5000 640 512 500 30000 50000 0 0" > /proc/sys/vm/bdflush
```

To make the change take effect any time the system is started, for Red Hat Linux 6.2 and higher, edit the */etc/sysctl.conf* file and add these lines:

```
# Disk write caching for Samba server
vm.bdflush = 80 5000 640 512 500 30000 50000 0 0
```

For earlier versions of Red Hat Linux and Caldera OpenLinux, add this line to */etc/rc.d/rc.local* (on Debian GNU/Linux, add a script to */etc/init.d*):

```
echo "80 5000 640 512 500 30000 50000 0 0" >
/proc/sys/vm/bdflush
```

DISK CACHE SIZE • The buffermem value controls how much memory should be used in memory. The value is a percentage of the total system memory.

To see the current setting, use the `cat` command and enter the name of the buffermem setting file:

```
cat /proc/sys/vm/buffermem
```

The default values are

```
2 10 60
```

The first parameter sets the minimum percentage of memory for the buffer cache. The default is 2. Change this to 60 for better cache performance. The other two values are not used, and changing them would not change anything.

To change the values of buffermem, use the following command:

```
echo "60 10 60" > /proc/sys/vm/buffermem
```

To make the change take effect any time the system is started, for Red Hat Linux 6.2 and higher, edit the */etc/sysctl.conf* file and add these lines:

```
# Disk cache size for Samba server
vm.buffermem = 60 10 60
```

For earlier versions of Red Hat Linux and Caldera OpenLinux, add this line to */etc/rc.d/rc.local* (on Debian GNU/Linux add a script to */etc/init.d*):

```
echo "60 10 60" > /proc/sys/vm/buffermem
```

FILE HANDLE LIMITS • The default value for `file-max`, which sets the number of file handles, is good for a workstation but not necessarily for a server. A busy Samba server can easily run out of file handles. The 2.4 kernel defaults to 8192. At minimum, there should be 512 file handles for every 4 Mb of memory. That would mean that a server with 256 Mb of memory should be set to 32768. This amount could easily be doubled. A busy Samba server can require a large number of file handles.

To see the current setting, use the `cat` command and enter the name of the `file-max` setting file:

```
cat /proc/sys/fs/file-max
```

The default value for 2.2 kernels is 4096. The default for 2.4 kernels is 8192.

To change the value of `file-max`, use the following command:

```
echo "32768" > /proc/sys/fs/file-max
```

To make the change take effect any time the system is started, for Red Hat Linux 6.2 and higher, edit the */etc/sysctl.conf* file and add these lines:

```
# File handle limits for Samba server
fs.file-max = 32768
```

For earlier versions of Red Hat Linux and Caldera OpenLinux, add this line to */etc/rc.d/rc.local* (on Debian GNU/Linux, add a script to */etc/init.d*):

```
echo "32768" > /proc/sys/fs/file-max
```

INODE LIMITS • On all versions of Red Hat before 7.1, the number of inode handlers set in `inode-max` meets the needs of a workstation. The `inode-max` value should be three to four times the `file-max` value. This is because every open file requires multiple inodes. On a system with a `file-max` setting of 32768, multiplying by four means that the `inode-max` setting should be 131072. This can also be doubled for a busy system.

To see the current setting, use the `cat` command and enter the name of the `inode-max` setting file:

```
cat /proc/sys/fs/inode-max
```

The default value is 16376.

To change the value of `file-max`, use the following command:

```
echo "131072" > /proc/sys/fs/inode-max
```

To make the change take effect any time the system is started, for Red Hat Linux 6.2 and higher, edit the */etc/sysctl.conf* file and add these lines:

```
# Inode handler limits for Samba server
fs.inode-max = 131072
```

For earlier versions of Red Hat Linux and Caldera OpenLinux, add this line to */etc/rc.d/rc.local* (on Debian GNU/Linux, add a script to */etc/init.d*):

```
echo "131072" > /proc/sys/fs/inode-max
```

TCP/IP TIMEOUT SETTINGS • The default TCP/IP values in Red Hat Linux 7.1 keep connections open long after they are no longer active. The kernel defaults can be adjusted to decrease the amount of time it takes to close a connection and the amount of time it takes to close an inactive connection. The same changes should be applied to other versions of Linux.

There are five settings to adjust. The default value for `tcp_fin_timeout` is 60. This can be reduced to 30. The `tcp_keepalive_time` is 7200. This can be reduced to 1800. The `tcp_window_scaling`, `tcp_sack`, and `tcp_timestamps` settings all default to 1. All three can be set to 0, which disables them.

To change the settings use the following commands:

```
echo "30" > /proc/sys/net/ipv4/tcp_fin_timeout
echo "1800" > /proc/sys/net/ipv4/tcp_keepalive_time
echo "0" > /proc/sys/net/ipv4/tcp_window_scaling
echo "0" > /proc/sys/net/ipv4/tcp_sack
echo "0" > /proc/sys/net/ipv4/tcp_timestamps
```

To make the change take effect any time the system is started, for Red Hat Linux 6.2 and higher, edit the */etc/sysctl.conf* file and add these lines:

```
# TCP/IP timeout settings for Samba server
net.ipv4.tcp_fin_timeout = 30
net.ipv4.tcp_keepalive_time = 1800
net.ipv4.tcp_window_scaling = 0
net.ipv4.tcp_sack = 0
net.ipv4.tcp_timestamps = 0
```

For earlier versions of Red Hat Linux and Caldera OpenLinux, add this line to */etc/rc.d/rc.local* (on Debian GNU/Linux, add a script to */etc/init.d*):

```
echo "30" > /proc/sys/net/ipv4/tcp_fin_timeout
echo "1800" > /proc/sys/net/ipv4/tcp_keepalive_time
echo "0" > /proc/sys/net/ipv4/tcp_window_scaling
echo "0" > /proc/sys/net/ipv4/tcp_sack
echo "0" > /proc/sys/net/ipv4/tcp_timestamps
```

TCP PORTS • Servers support a large number of concurrent sessions. The number of available open ports is set by `ip_local_port_range`. This file has two parameters. The first is the first local port allowed for TCP and User Datagram Protocol (UDP) traffic. The second is the last local port allowed.

To see the current setting, use the `cat` command and enter the name of the `ip_local_port_range` setting file:

```
cat /proc/sys/net/ipv4/ip_local_port_range
```

The default value for Red Hat 7.1 is 32768 61000.

To open the maximum possible number of ports, use the following command:

```
echo "1024 65535" > /proc/sys/net/ipv4/ip_local_port_range
```

To make the change take effect any time the system is started, for Red Hat Linux 6.2 and higher, edit the */etc/sysctl.conf* file and add these lines:

```
# TCP port range for Samba server
net.ipv4.ip_local_port_range = 1024 65535
```

For earlier versions of Red Hat Linux and Caldera OpenLinux, add this line to */etc/rc.d/rc.local* (on Debian GNU/Linux add a script to */etc/init.d*):

```
echo "1024 65535" > /proc/sys/net/ipv4/ip_local_port_range
```

FILE ATTRIBUTES • The records the Linux filesystem keeps for every file include the times the file was created, last modified, and last accessed. For Samba shares, the last accessed time is not needed and only adds additional write time for each file, as the information must be updated regularly. There is an option, when you mount the drive, to turn off the recording of access time. Turning this off does not change any other attributes, and the time the file is written will continue to be updated.

If you turn off this option, the Samba shares should be on their own partition, since making this change will eliminate recording of access time for all files on the partition.

The Noatime parameter stops Linux from updating the access time every time a file is simply being read. Setting a partition to Noatime involves editing the *fstab* file in the */etc* directory. The *fstab* file lists all of the partitions that will be mounted when Linux starts up.

Use a test editor and open the *fstab* file in the */etc* directory. Find the line for the partition or partitions that will be loaded with access time writing turned off. Add the Noatime parameter after the Defaults option. Here's an example of what would appear in *fstab* for the */dev/hda8* partition that is mounted as */samba:*

```
/dev/hda8   /samba ext2   defaults,noatime   1 2
```

Any changes to *fstab* do not take effect until the system is restarted.

GIGABIT ETHERNET • For servers with Gigabit Ethernet network adaptors, the socket buffer settings (SO_RCVBUF and SO_SNDBUF) should be changed from the standard default in the Linux 2.2 and 2.4 kernels of 64 Kb. Changing these settings to 256 Kb will significantly improve performance.

To see the current setting, use the cat command and enter the name of the socket buffer setting file:

```
cat /proc/sys/net/core/rmem_max
```

The default value should show 65535, or 64 Kb.

This is the optimum setting for 10 Mbps or 100 Mbps Ethernet. To optimize this setting for Gigabit Ethernet, the following command will set the value to 256 Kb:

```
echo 262144 > /proc/sys/net/core/rmem_max
echo 262144 > /proc/sys/net/core/wmem_max
```

To make the change take effect any time the system is started, for Red Hat Linux 6.2 and higher, edit the */etc/sysctl.conf* file and add these lines:

```
# TCP port range for Samba server
net.core.rmem_max = 262144
net.core.wmem_max = 262144
```

For earlier versions of Red Hat Linux and Caldera OpenLinux, add these lines to */etc/rc.d/rc.local* (on Debian GNU/Linux, add a script to */etc/init.d*):

```
echo 262144 > /proc/sys/net/core/rmem_max
echo 262144 > /proc/sys/net/core/wmem_max
```

Fine-Tuning the Samba Configuration

Many of Samba's configuration settings can affect performance. Getting them all just right for maximum performance can take time, as you adjust the many different settings. Ideally you'll be able to test the various possible combinations before you put the server online. More likely you'll find that you'll be making adjustments on a running server.

Most of the adjustments you make in the Samba configuration don't require that you restart the server. Be careful, however, whenever you make these kinds of adjustments. Just as some changes can improve performance on one server, the same changes on another server could have a negative impact. That's because there are a number of variable factors that change from one network to another. That's why these are all options, with various possible settings. Add changes to the configuration one at a time and monitor performance over a period of time, at least 24 hours, so that you can get a true idea of the impact of each change on performance. Some changes can have a negative impact; some can actually halt the server. When you've fully tested one change, then you're ready to add the next, and so on, until you're done.

The following changes are listed in their order of appearance in the Globals section of SWAT. This is not an order of importance. Probably the most important section to configure for performance is the Tuning Options settings, particularly the socket options. After getting the Tuning Options set, go on to the other sections, in any order that you choose.

Note, however, that not all of the Tuning Options need to be set. In fact, some should definitely not be changed from the default. They are all described here because they are all listed as tuning options.

Fine-Tuning Logging Options

Keeping records of activity on the server can be useful for debugging problems, but every log entry takes system resources. A high level of logging detail can degrade system performance.

Log Level

This sets how detailed the log entries should be. Every increase in log level increases the amount of information Samba must write to the log files. Sometimes, when you are trying to figure out the source of a problem, you might set a higher log level. This will slow down performance. For everyday use, keep the log level low. The default setting of 0 will give the best performance. A setting of 1 will log more details, for those who want more information. Settings of 3 and higher, the maximum is 10, should be used for debugging purposes only since they will slow down system performance.

Fine-Tuning Protocol Options

The speed of reads and writes on the Samba server can be improved using the Read Raw and Write Raw settings.

The Read Raw Setting

A raw read lets Samba use 64K buffers, which improves performance with larger files. Most files, including word-processing files, are typically bigger than 64K. However, if your system primarily uses very small files—smaller than 64K—you may actually find a performance increase by turning this option off. For example, if your server is supporting users who primarily compose one-page letters, then you should test setting this option to No. For most systems the best choice is to enable raw reads. The default setting is Yes, and the Samba team makes a strong recommendation that you don't change the default. If you do change it, make sure that the Write Raw setting matches the Read Raw setting.

The Write Raw Setting

This is the other side of Read Raw. This lets Samba use 64K buffers for faster writes. The setting you use should match the one set for Read Raw.

The `max xmit` Setting

This is the maximum packet size Samba will attempt to use. The default setting is 64K. Like Read Raw and Write Raw, this setting shouldn't be changed for most operations. However, if you have users who are working predominantly with very small files, then you can try adjusting this downward to see if you get improved performance. Never go below 2K. And keep the setting in 1K increments.

Fine-Tuning Tuning Options

Samba's tuning options are where most of the adjustments are made for improving Samba's performance. Although these changes are Samba-specific, most of the settings have to do with improving network performance and not the performance of Samba itself.

Change Notify Timeout

This is the Samba implementation of the Windows NT change notification. If there is a change on a file share on the server, the client is updated. The setting is the number of seconds between checks for changes on a share. Frequent checks will bog down the server. The default setting is 60 seconds. You can make this less frequent, such as 300 seconds, or longer, such as 15 minutes. This is probably adequate for all but the busiest networks, where frequent updates may increase performance. That's because frequent manual requests for change updates—refreshing the file list, for example—can slow down the system.

Dead Time

The Dead Time setting is the number of minutes a session can be inactive before it is terminated. Inactivity means that no files are open. Windows Explorer, for example, will keep a connection open even if Explorer is closed. Excessive open sessions by inactive connections can drain system resources. The default setting is 0, which means that no sessions will be disconnected because of inactivity. Windows clients have an auto-reconnect feature, so that auto-closing a session is transparent to users. The reconnection of a closed session will be slow, however. Try a setting of 15 minutes to reduce the drag of excess open sessions.

The getwd cache Setting

This setting enables a cache of the current directory, thus avoiding going through the whole directory structure each time to find the directory. The default setting is Yes. This usually results in an improved response times.

Keepalive

Keepalive sets the number of seconds between checks to see if a client is still there. If the client doesn't respond, the connection can be closed. The default setting is 0, or Off. That's because the SO_KEEPALIVE parameter in Samba's socket options (see below) is the preferred method. If you aren't using the socket option, then enable this with a setting of 14400, for four-hour intervals.

The lpq Cache Time

This option sets the number of seconds Samba will keep printer status information. At the designated time, Samba will update the status information by issuing an lpq command. The new information is then held in the queue for display in any queries on printer status. By keeping the information in queue, the lpq command doesn't have to be restarted too frequently. This improves performance by lowering the number of processes running on the Samba server. The default setting is 10 seconds, which is often more frequent than usually needed. Try setting to 30 seconds.

The max disk size Setting

This setting gives the maximum size of disks on the Samba server as they appear to the user and to applications requesting disk size. This setting has no effect whatever on actual disk size. This deception is necessary for some older software that will refuse to run if the disk size exceeds 1 Gb. The default setting is 0, which means that the true disk size is reported. Change this only if you have software that won't run without it. To set the reported size to 1 Gb, enter the value of 1000.

The Max Open Files Setting

This option puts an upper limit on the number of file processes that a client connection can have open at one time. The default setting is 10000 and is rarely changed. The underlying operating system on the Samba server, such as Linux, usually sets the limits for the number of open files.

Read Size

This option sets the number of bytes Samba will read ahead so that it doesn't get behind in writes or transmissions across the network. This can be the number of incoming bytes read before writing to the disk on the Samba server, or the number of bytes read ahead from the disk before starting to send over the network. The default setting is 16384. The factors at play in this setting are the speed of the network versus the speed of the hard drive. If there is a disparity between the two, making this value smaller might make a small performance improvement. If it is made too small, there will be a noticeable network slowdown. The lowest possible value is 1024, but you should probably never set it below 2048.

Optimizing Socket Options

Optimizing the TCP socket options can make significant improvements in performance. These settings control how your server handles TCP connections. The socket options are defined by the operating system. The options listed here are the TCP socket options for Linux. Each option should be separated by a space, if you add any. Some options have parameters that are added with an = sign. Many options have no parameters.

TCP_NODELAY

This is the most important socket option to include. It is the only one included by default in the Samba configuration. This setting forces TCP packets to be sent immediately without any delay between sends. This can double a Samba server's read performance.

ITOS_LOWDELAY

This setting enables IP packet delivery through router connections with a low delay. If you are using TCP_NODELAY, then you should add this setting as well.

IPTOS_THROUGHPUT

This setting optimizes IP packet delivery through wide-area network (WAN) connections. If your Samba server is part of a WAN, then you should add this option.

SO_KEEPALIVE

This option sends a probe every four hours to check that a connection is still active. If the connection does not respond, it is closed. This setting does not improve performance, but it is used to conserve system resources. If you enable this option here, then you don't need to use the separate Keepalive option.

SO_SNDBUF

The speed of file saving, copying, and moving are determined by network speed and by the SMB block size. Windows servers generally use 4K blocks. Increasing the block size can improve the performance overall. The maximum value this can be set at is 64K.

On Samba servers, the block size is often set to 4K (4096) buffers to match the default setting for Windows. The exact value that works best depends on your specific configuration, but 14K (14,596) is a value that has been shown to work well in a fairly standard Ethernet environment. It is what Microsoft recommends as the best value for NT servers handling Windows clients. See the Microsoft Knowledge Base document Q177266. It also works well for Samba servers handling those same Windows clients. To set the value to 14K, enter this:

```
SO_SNDBUF=14596
```

SO_RCVBUF

This option sets the size of the receive buffer. This is the other side of the send buffer. If you change the send buffer from the default, then the receive buffer should be set to the same value. For example, for 14K blocks, enter

```
SO_RCVBUF=14596
```

Stat Cache Size

This option sets the number of entries allowed in the statistics (stat) cache. The stat cache stores the results of recent stat() system calls, which gather information about specified files. The default size is 50 and should never need to be changed.

Fine-Tuning Filename Handling

Synchronizing filename handling between Windows and Linux is not always necessary. If you choose to have strict mapping of some of the attributes such as hidden files, the performance of the server may be degraded.

Hide Files

This is a setting that can have a negative impact on Samba's performance. Hide Files is used to add the Hidden attribute to a directory or a set of files. Use this only if you absolutely must hide some files or directories. Hiding files will slow down Samba because it forces a check of every file and directory every time one is accessed or even browsed to make sure it doesn't match any of the files or directories to be hidden. For maximum performance, make sure that this setting is left blank.

Veto Files

This option lists files and directories that should not be visible or accessible. Listing anything in this option will degrade performance because Samba is forced to check all files and directories for a match on every read, write, and directory listing command.

Veto Oplock Files

This option lists opportunistic lock (oplock) files that should not be locally cached by clients Databases that are accessed by multiple clients with both read and write rights are significantly slowed down by oplocks. Use this setting to disable oplocks for certain files or file types. Databases and files that need to be immediately visible should be included in the list. Items in the list are separated by a slash. To disable oplocks on all Microsoft Access database files, enter /*.mdb/*.MDB/.

Fine-Tuning Locking Options

File locking can significantly improve read and write performance for clients. However, if the locking options are not set correctly performance can be degraded rather than enhanced.

OPLOCKS

Opportunistic locks (oplocks) let a user open a file with an exclusive lock on the file, allowing changes to be cached locally. This can significantly improve performance. Oplocks will usually improve read/write performance by more than 25%. Here's how oplocks work: as long as a client workstation has exclusive access to a file, all other access is locked out. Reading, modifying, and saving are cached on the local workstation for later writing to the server. Without oplocks, when you have a file open and you make a change, the changes are directly transmitted from the workstation to the server. This takes both transport time across the network and the time for the disk write on the server.

Oplocks will work only if there is a single user of the file. If there are multiple users, the advantage is lost. When a second workstation client requests access to the file, the server breaks the oplock and forces a write from the workstation that has the file locked. This is a relatively slow process and can noticeably slow down performance.

Normally oplocks are set to be on. For shares such as databases that require concurrent mutiuser access, oplocks are turned off for the share. If you have a share that has mixed use, meaning that some files are multiuser and others are primarily single-user, you can use the Veto Oplock Files setting to disable oplocks for individual files or file types by using a wildcard and extension, such as *.mdb.

One caution on oplocks. If your network is in any way unstable or there is a regular risk of losing network connections, you may want to turn off oplocks. Because oplocks allows local caching of a file, if the network connection is lost or if the workstation crashes the file may be corrupted.

LEVEL 2 OPLOCKS

Level 2 oplocks are used only by Windows NT and 2000 workstation clients. Level 2 oplocks are designed for shares that are accessed in read-only mode, primarily applications.

Level 2 oplocks will work only if oplocks are also enabled. What happens with a share that has Level 2 oplocks enabled is that the first client to open a file gets read/write access to the file. If a second client accesses the file, rather than breaking the oplock, the oplock is downgraded to Level 2. This is a read-only local cache. Multiple users can access the file and cache the reads. If a client workstation writes to the file, an Oplock Break command is sent to every workstation with the file open, writes are forced from every client workstation, and the regular oplock level is reinstated. Obviously, Level 2 oplocks are effective only on file shares that are read from but not written to.

If you are running an office suite from a Samba share, you would use Level 2 oplocks for the share. This would let NT clients cache the executable files. Level 2 oplocks should not be turned on in the global section. They should be enabled for individual shares that can take advantage of the setting.

STRICT LOCKING

Normally, strict locking is not necessary. Most software will properly check to find out whether another user has a lock on a file. This is necessary to prevent corruption of the file. Some older programs, including all DOS-based programs, do not perform proper file lock checks. If you are using such a program, put it on its own share and enable strict locking for that share alone. Otherwise, strict locking can significantly slow down operations. With strict locking enabled, the Samba server will check locking for every file access. The default setting is No; that is, it is turned off. If your server is performing slowly, check to make sure that strict locking is not enabled.

WRITE CACHE SIZE

This option sets the size of a cache used by Samba while writing oplocked files. The default size is 0, which disables the setting. On servers with a RAID disk array, you can significantly improve file-writing performance with this option. It is will also improve write performance on servers with lots of memory but slow disks.

This setting lets Samba use bigger byte sizes for writing oplocked files. The setting indicates byte size of the write cache that Samba will create for an oplocked file. Set this parameter to the stripe size of a RAID volume for maximum performance. For example, if your stripe size is 64K, enter a write cache size value of 65536. Up to 10 write caches can be active simultaneously, so make sure you have enough free memory. The warning for oplock files applies to this setting. If the network connection is lost or if the workstation crashes, any cached files may be corrupted.

Fine-Tuning Miscellaneous Options

There is only one miscellaneous option that can affect performance, the Wide Links option. This option is enabled by default, which is also the best choice for optimum performance.

WIDE LINKS

By default, this setting is on, which means that a client workstation can access files or subdirectories on a share even if they are really only links. A link on the Samba server is similar to a shortcut on a Windows system. Turning off Wide Links can have a negative impact on performance. If the Wide Links setting is turned off, then Samba will check every access to a file or directory to make sure that it is not a link. This seriously slows down all accesses.

Replacing Windows with Samba

By design, a Samba server fits seamlessly into a bigger Windows network. Even multiple Samba servers can be easily plugged into a Windows network. It is this trouble-free interaction between Samba and Windows that is behind Samba's success. Many Windows networks have been expanded by the addition of Samba servers. In fact, because Samba servers perform so well on Windows networks, many system administrators decide to convert their entire network to Samba for file and print services.

The process of setting up a new Samba server and adding it to a Windows network is covered in the previous chapters. This chapter is about the process of replacing an existing Windows server with a Samba server.

Why would you replace a Windows server with a Samba server? If you've already started adding Samba servers to your network, it certainly might make sense.

There may be no reason to continue to support the Windows server, if all you are using are file services and printer sharing. For budget-savvy administrators, replacing Windows servers with Samba can mean a savings of thousands of dollars or more. In fact, choosing Samba is such a no-brainer, many computer industry professionals are predicting that that Linux servers running Samba will eventually replace Windows for file and print services on most networks, big or small. That's because Samba/Linux servers eliminate the need to spend money on client licenses.

The hardware costs for a Linux server are also lower. To get similar performance, the Linux operating system does not require as much memory or hard drive space as a Windows server. And other hardware needs, such as video RAM, are also lower for Linux.

The setup and configuration of Samba is not difficult. But if your office is Windows-only and there is no Linux- or UNIX-experienced staff, then you'll need to factor in the cost of training for a new operating system or hiring someone with Linux experience. The costs of training in Linux are no more than the costs of training for Windows servers.

Eliminating Windows servers altogether isn't for everyone. A Samba server does not have all of the features found on a Windows 2000 server. Among other differences, the current version of Samba can be used as a domain controller only on a network structured for a single domain controller. This works for a small or medium-sized network but does not scale well in large organizations. Logins can be slow, and file sharing can get bogged down. Most enterprise-level networks involving hundreds or thousands of computers use multiple domain controllers. On networks like this, a Samba domain controller can't be used and therefore can't replace a Windows domain controller.

There are other limitations on an all-Samba network. Samba/Linux servers won't give you an Exchange Server or a Microsoft SQL Server. While there are Linux alternatives for mail and database services, it is not a simple process to change from one to the other.

A Samba network just gives you rock-solid file and printer sharing.

If that's what you want, then you can probably go ahead and replace your Windows servers with Samba. On a small or medium-sized network, you can also replace a Windows domain controller with a Samba domain controller. Of course, there could be other reasons you want to replace Windows with Samba. Whatever the reason, here are the steps to take to make such a changeover.

Replacing a Windows File Server

The main part of the job of replacing a Windows server with a Samba server is account translation. That is the process of converting information from Windows domains or Active Directory domains into Linux accounts, passwords, and groups. Much of the information used by the two systems is similar: a logon name and password, the user's real name, a user ID (UID) and primary group ID (GID), and a home directory on the server.

There are some differences, however. On a Windows server, but not on a Linux server, a security ID (SID) maps each user to a specific domain controller or machine. The Windows access control list (ACL) cannot be transferred to a Samba server, even one that has Linux ACL support. The permissions will have to be built from scratch after accounts are moved to the Samba server, and they may not be able to exactly match previous settings. There's a limitation on how accurately you can translate Windows permissions into Linux permissions.

Also, while both Windows and Linux systems encrypt passwords, each uses different security algorithms. The differences in permissions and password encryption do not mean that Linux is more or less secure or more or less flexible, just that the way these are handled is different.

Most of the work of moving from a Windows server to a Samba server involves account translation, making a Windows user look the same on the Samba server so that users don't even notice the change in servers. Most of the time you can find a way to emulate the Windows model on a Samba server, but sometimes you'll find you just have to do it the Linux way.

This section describes a five-step process for replacing a Windows server with a standalone Samba server. The process begins on the Windows server. You'll need to get the user and group information from the Windows server, as well as the file and printer sharing information on the server. Then you'll create the equivalent user accounts, groups, and shares on the Samba server. The Samba server is then tested. When that's done, the files from the Windows server can be moved to the Samba server.

Step 1: Get the User, Group, File, and Printer Sharing Information

Start by getting a complete list of users and groups on the Windows network. This information can be obtained from the User Manager on Windows NT 4 running as standalone, nondomain controller systems or from the User Manager for Domains on Windows NT 4 domain controllers. On Windows 2000 servers, user information for standalone systems is in the Computer Management tool, and for any accounts on a domain controller, the information can be found in the Active Directory Users and Computers tool.

A more efficient way to get the information is to run the net utility from a command window. The net utility can be used to display names and at the same time create a file of usernames that can be used to simplify the process of creating a matching users list on the Samba server. First, look at what the net utility shows. In a command window on the Windows server (on Windows 2000 systems, select Run from the Start button and enter command.com as the program to run), enter this command:

```
net user /domain
```

The *domain* option means that the domain controller is used to get the user information. If you don't have a domain controller on your network, then leave off the *domain* option.

To get a list of groups, enter the command

```
net group /domain
```

Adding the name of a user or group to the command will show additional information. For example, to find out the complete account information for a user named "jhenry," enter this command:

```
net user jhenry /domain
```

In the next section, the output of the net utility is used to create a file that can be used to add all the users at once on the Samba server.

One way to see a list of file shares on the Windows server is to open the Network Neighborhood/My Computer Places and double-click on the server. This may not show you all the available shares on the server, however. It only shows the shares available to the user you are logged on as. A complete list of shares can be made by working directly on the Windows server, using the Windows Explorer and checking the properties for share information on each drive and folder. This is an inefficient method, however, and some shares could be missed.

The net utility is again the best method for getting complete share information. Log in as the administrator on the Windows server, and in a command window, enter this command:

```
net share
```

That will display a complete list of shares. The format shows the share name, the resource (which is the full path to the share), and any remarks attached to the share. Using the resource information, you can get the file and directory permissions for each shared directory on the Windows server.

Use Windows Explorer to locate the shared directory, right-click on the directory name, and select Sharing. On the Sharing tab, click on the Permissions button. This will show the access permissions for the share.

The permissions for a directory or file are found by right-clicking in Windows Explorer on the file or directory icon and selecting properties. Click the Security tab and then press the Permissions button.

Step 2: Create User and Group Accounts on the Samba Server

Whether you get the user and group information from the User Manager or from the net utility, writing down all this information can be a time-consuming process. One alternative is to create a text file with the user information and then edit the file so that it contains all of the user information. Then you can use the Webmin administration program on the Samba server to create all the users at once. This method has the advantage of creating both the user accounts and the encrypted Samba password file at the same time, if you need it.

Of course, you can use the regular method to create an account for each new user on the Samba server. See Chapter 8 on the essentials of Linux administration for the steps to add users one by one.

ADDING USERS WITH THE WEBMIN UTILITY

To add all the users at once through Webmin using a text file with user information, you first need to create the file. You can create a file that has all the usernames already entered by using the net tool. Open a command window and change to a directory where the file will be saved. You might want to create a separate directory just for this file. Once you've changed to the directory where the file will be saved, enter this command:

```
net user /domain > users.txt
```

This creates a text file with all the usernames in it. The header information at the top and the concluding line at the bottom should be removed. This file can be edited to add the additional user information. Open the file in a text editor. Each username should be on its own line, and each line must follow this format:

```
username:passwd:uid:gid:realname:homedir:shell:min:max:war
n:inactive:expire
```

The only essential fields are username, passwd, GID, homedir, and shell.

The group ID (GID) must already exist. The easiest way to handle this is to put everyone in the "Users" group. Use Webmin's Users and Groups module to see the GID for Users. If you want to have a unique group for each new user, you will have to create all of the groups for all users before you add the users. Webmin can be used to create all of the groups you need.

The standard home directory on a Linux server is */home/username,* where *"username"* is the login name of the user. Webmin will automatically create this directory as part of the process. The standard default shell for Linux servers is */bin/bash,* but if the users will be accessing the server only through Samba, make the shell */bin/false,* which will prevent shell access to the server.

If the User ID (UID) field is left empty, Webmin will assign an ID number automatically. All the other fields, which define password expiration, can be left empty. This leaves the default setting, which is that the password never has to be changed. The Min field defines the minimum number of days required until the password is changed. Setting this to 0 means the password never has to be changed. The Max field is the maximum number of days allowed until the password is changed. A setting of -1 disables the maximum limit.

The Warn field is the number of days before the password expires to start giving a warning. The Inactive setting is the number of days the account can be inactive before the account is disabled. The Expire setting is the date on which the password expires. This is a number based on the number of days since January 1, 1970. An entry of -1 disables the setting.

Every : delimiter must be included, even where the field is blank. For example, to create an entry for user Janet Henry, with the username of "jhenry," and the *users* group ID (GID) is 100, the minimum necessary entry would be

```
jhenry:tioncele::100::/home/jhenry:/bin/false:::::
```

The password is entered in plain text. When the account is created on the server, the password is then encrypted.

When the *users.txt* file is completed with all the user account information, it can then be read into Webmin.

If you have a Samba server that is a logon server for the network and handles user authentication, then you can move on to the next step, adding the new users through Webmin. If your Samba server is acting as a standalone server and you haven't disabled encrypted passwords, then you'll need to create the *smbpasswd* file. This file holds the encrypted passwords for access to file and print shares on the Samba server. Normally this would involve using the smbpasswd utility and entering each username and password individually, a long and time-consuming process. Fortunately, Webmin will automatically do this for you.

In Webmin on the Servers tab, choose the Samba Windows File Sharing module. Scroll down. Near the bottom of the page is a line that says, "Configure automatic Unix and Samba user synchronisation." Click on the link, and then every user you create through Webmin's Users and Groups will also be added to the Samba encrypted password file.

With that enabled, go to the System tab in Webmin and open the Users and Groups module. Scroll down to below the list of users. Click on the Create Multiple Users link. Select the file. If you are connecting to the Samba server from another computer on the network, click on Browse on the line for Uploaded New Users File. Find and select the *users.txt* file. Or you can type in the file location information. If you are on the Samba server, click on "…" button on the line that says, "Local new users file." Find and select the *users.txt* file. Alternatively, you can type in the full path information. Make sure that the radio button says Yes for "Create home directories?"

Then click the Create Users button. All the new users will be added. Watch for error messages and correct any errors indicated. The most common error is to leave out one of the : delimiters for a field that is blank.

After creating the user accounts, use the Webmin Users and Groups module to create the groups needed. Every group on the Windows server needs to be recreated on the Samba server, except for the default groups like Replicator, if you aren't using them.

Scroll to the bottom of the Users and Groups page and click on Create a New Group. Enter the group name. A GID number is automatically inserted. Make sure that No Password Required is selected. Clicking on the button with three dots in it to the right of the Members frame will show a list of all the users on the system. Click on the usernames to add them to the group.

Group names should be short and kept under 11 characters. Spaces are not valid characters in a group name. The Domain Users group on the Windows server is similar to the default users group on a Linux server. There is no exact equivalent to the Windows Domain Admins group on a Linux server, so you should create a group called Admins. You'll probably also want a group called Guests.

After adding all of the groups, you are ready to move on to configuring the Samba server.

ADDING USERS WITHOUT THE WEBMIN UTILITY

If you don't have Webmin, the useradd utility can add each user one by one. Then use smbpasswd to add the Samba password. The command to add a user named Janet Henry is

```
useradd -c 'Janet Henry' -d /home/jhenry -g users -s
/bin/false -n jhenry
```

The −c parameter is the user's full name. The −d parameter is the location of the home directory that will be the user's primary file share. The −g parameter is the default group for the user.

The −s parameter is for the login shell on the Linux server. The default setting on most Linux systems is /bin/bash. However, by making this setting /bin/false it means that the user cannot log on directly to the Linux server. This makes the server more secure, and it does not in any way inhibit the user's ability to access the files on the computer through Samba.

The −n parameter is the user's logon name.

Creating individual accounts this way can be time-consuming. After the user accounts are created, the Samba password file has to be created. This is done with the smbpasswd utility. The command to add the user named Janet Henry to the Samba password file is

```
smbpasswd -a jhenry
```

You will then be prompted to enter the password twice.

This process can be shortened a little, but only a little, by using the pwdump utility. This utility, originally created by one of Samba's lead developers, Jeremy Allison, can extract the contents of a Windows server's ACL.

An enhanced version of the original pwdump was created by Tod Sabin of Bindview and is called pwdump2. This version works with both Windows NT and Windows 2000 servers. You can get this utility at *http://razor.bindview.com/tools/* Use the utility on the Windows server. In a command window, enter

```
pwdump2 > smbpasswd
```

The program extracts the user information from the Windows ACL, including the password in encrypted format. The file is in the format used by the Samba password file.

You'll need to clean up the file in a text editor on the Samba server (or if you do it on a Windows text editor, you'll have to convert the files because Windows files have a different end-of-line character than Linux files). The UID numbers will also need to be updated so that the UID matches the ID for the user on the Samba server.

The file is then ready to be placed in the appropriate location (the */etc* directory, for example, on a Red Hat Linux server), and all of the users' passwords from the Windows server will be retained.

CAUTION!

The pwdump and pwdump2 utilities are designed to extract user information from a Windows server for use on a Samba server. However, don't use this utility if your network will continue to use Windows domain controllers. The extracted information is designed to be used on a Samba-only network, but it is incomplete for a network that includes both Samba and Windows servers. Use pwdump only to move to an all-Samba network.

After creating the user accounts, add the group accounts. There are two ways of adding new groups. The first is with the groupadd tool; the second way it to edit the */etc/group* file with a text editor. Either way, you will need to use a text editor to add users to each group.

When creating a new group, remember that each one must have a GID. You should have a list of existing GIDs, since each group needs a unique number. Of course, the groupadd tool won't let you use a GID that already exists. To create a group called "financial" with a GID of 501, enter the command

```
groupadd -g 501 financial
```

This creates the following entry in the */etc/group* file:

```
financial::501:
```

Each line in group starts with the group name, followed by a colon. Next is the password. If there is no password, nothing is entered, except for the colon delimiter. The third field is the GID, also followed by a colon. After the last colon comes a list of usernames that belong to the group. A comma separates usernames.

To add users (and as an alternative way to add groups), open the file in a text editor and type in the usernames. If you add groups this way, just follow the format of the other groups already in the file. Make sure each group has a unique GID. Any typographical errors, such as a missing colon, will make the group unusable.

Step 3: Configure the Samba Server

Before files can be moved from the Windows server to the Samba server, the directories for the files must be created and Samba should be configured.

When the users were added to the Samba server, a default home directory was created for each user. This corresponds to the user's private home folder on a Windows server. When files are moved into the directory, however, they won't have the correct user and group permissions to make them accessible. Fixing that will come after the files have been moved. First all the necessary directories should be created.

Group directories will have to be added manually. Every group from the Windows server also has a shared directory. You can put the shared directories almost anywhere on the Samba server, but most commonly they are either put in the */home* directory, a */home/group* directory, or a */srv* directory. Putting the groups all together in a separate */srv* directory probably simplifies group and share management.

When you create the directory for the group, you also have to apply the permissions that will make the directory accessible to everyone in the group. Members of the group will be given read, write, and execute permissions for the directory. The administrator—root—is given user ownership of the directory.

To create the directories, open Webmin and go to the Others tab. Select the File Manager. Create a directory named *srv,* if you don't already have one. To create the new directory, click on the folder icon labeled "New" on the Webmin File Manager's menu bar. In the popup window that opens, type in /srv and then click on the Save button.

When the *srv* directory is created, on the left panel click the *srv* folder. Its contents are displayed in the right panel. Create a new directory for a group share by clicking on the folder icon labeled "New" (for new folder) on the Webmin File Manager's menu bar. Create a new directory for each group. After you create all of your directories, then permissions have to be set for each directory. Select a group directory on the right panel and click on the Info button on the menu bar.

In the permissions panel, Read, Write, and List should all be checked for both User and Group. Nothing should be checked in Others. In the Ownership panel, the User should be root and the group ownership should be the name of the group. Also, check the "Setgid" box, which will force all files saved in the directory to be given ownership by the group.

Then click the Save button. Follow the same procedure for all the other group directories.

ADDING GROUP DIRECTORIES WITHOUT WEBMIN

To add group directories without Webmin, open a terminal window on the Linux server make sure that you are the root user, using the su command. Create the *srv* directory and change into the directory. Finally, create a directory for each group and set the permissions.

To create the *srv* directory, enter this command:

```
mkdir /srv
```

Then you are ready to add the group directories. For example, to add a directory for the "finances" group to the group directory, enter these commands:

```
cd /srv
mkdir finances
chown root.finances finances
chmod 2770 finances
```

This creates the directory; assigns read, write, and list permissions to the owner and group; and adds the Set GID bit to the directory.

CONFIGURING SHARES ON SAMBA

With the users, groups, and directories set up on the Samba server, the next step is to configure sharing. This is where you'll have to translate Windows account permissions into Linux permissions.

From your Web browser, open the SWAT page from the Samba server. For setting the global parameters, use the steps outlined in Chapter 2.

THE HOMES SHARE • Open the Shares window on SWAT and start with the homes share. Open it from the Choose Share drop-down list. This is a default share that is usually included in any Samba configuration.

Use the Advanced View. The path to the home directory doesn't need to be included because Samba will take the information from the user's account information.

Read Only should be set to No. Make sure that Guest Account is blank. User Only should be set to No. Browseable is No.

For the Create Mask, enter 0700. And the Directory Mask should also be 0700.

As a security measure to limit access, enter a range of IP addresses for the local network for the computers that will be accessing the Samba server.

Click the Commit Changes button to save these settings.

Setting the Create Mask and Directory Mask options to 0700 means that user will have read, write, list, and execute permissions for every file and directory, and access is blocked for everyone else. This is similar to setting the permissions on a Windows share to Change for the user and No Access for Everyone or Domain Users.

THE GROUP SHARES • The group shares have more permissions to be set. Group members are given read, write, and execute permission, meaning that any user in the group can read, modify, or delete a file or directory in the share. Administrators will be given the same permissions.

Create a share for each group. You'll need the Advanced View to make all of the settings. In the comment field, enter the group name or something descriptive about the group. The path should show the location of the shared directory. For example, the path for the "finances" group might be */srv/ finances.*

Read Only should be set to No. Browseable is Yes.

The Valid Users will include all the users in the group. This is indicated by adding the @ symbol to the group name. For example, @finances in the Valid Users field would give access to all members of the "finances" group. This setting limits access to members of the group or groups listed.

If you've got an administrators group, include that as well. Add the Admin group to the Admin Users field as @admin. This is also a way to give Windows change-level access to administrators. The equivalent of Windows full-control access requires direct access to the Samba server, bypassing Samba. This can be done through the Webmin system administration tools.

Add the group name to the Force Group field in SWAT. You need to do this because on Linux systems, any new file or directory is automatically assigned to the user that created it and to that user's primary group. Forcing all files saved to belong to the group is part of making sure that all group members have complete change rights.

The Create Mask and Directory Mask should both be set to 0770. This gives both users and the group read, write and list permissions.

For security, be sure to set the Hosts Allow field to the IP addresses or range of addresses for the members of the group.

Don't forget to click the Commit Changes button to save the new settings.

OTHER SHARES AND PRINTERS • The last set of shares to create is for other uses. Typically this might be a share that holds an application run by users on the network. Or it might be a public directory that holds files accessed by all the users on the network. Printers are added in the same way printers are added to any Samba server, as detailed in Chapter 4.

Step 4: Test the Samba Server

Testing the Samba server is done by using it. Log onto a Windows workstation on the network and then access the Samba server. Check the Network Neighborhood/My Computer Places and see if the server is there. Open the server icon and see if the shares are there.

Then map a drive to the Samba home directory.

Next make sure that you can copy files to the new Samba drive on the Windows workstation. Then open the file, edit it, and save the changes. This checks the read and write permissions. On a Samba server, write permission includes the right to modify a file.

The group shares should also be tested. Log onto a Windows workstation as a user authorized to access a group share. Test reading, writing, and modifying files in the group directory.

Also test any directories that have read but not write permissions. Try to save a file to the directory. You should get an "Access is denied" error message.

Printers can be tested. A printer icon should show up in the Network Neighborhood/My Computer Places when you open the Samba server's icon. You can double-click each printer available on the server, and Windows will start the configuration process. Once the printer has been added, print a test page to make sure it is working correctly.

Step 5: Move Files to the Samba Server

There's no simple shortcut to moving files. There's really only one way to do it—have users move files from the Windows server to the Samba server. Any other method runs into complications involving file ownership and permissions.

There have been several attempts at working out a method to get around this problem and automate the moving of files from one server to the other, but none of them is foolproof. Most require additional steps after the files have been moved. And some make the moving process even more complicated, increasing the chance of error and lost files.

The direct approach is best. You can either instruct users on how to connect to both the Windows server and the Samba server and move their files from one to the other, or you can arrange to do it yourself while logged on as each user.

When you are doing this, use the Windows Explorer and drag the files from one server to the other. It is a simple and quick way to move the files, and the permissions and ownership rights are preserved. Also, any configuration problems are quickly revealed this way.

Setting Up a Samba Domain Controller

Samba version 2.2 can function as a domain controller on your network. It has many but not all of the features of a Windows NT 4 domain controller. Samba version 3.0 is expected to have a full implementation of domain controller capabilities.

If you are planning to replace Windows with Samba, you should replace your Windows domain controller with a Samba domain controller. Do not attempt to have both a Windows domain controller and a Samba domain controller on the same local network.

With a few exceptions, Samba 2.2 can act like a Windows NT 4 Primary Domain Controller (PDC) for Windows 9*x*/Me/NT/2000 clients. Windows 2000 clients will have to connect in the same way they would connect with a Windows NT 4 server, not a Windows 2000 server. This means that for the machines that have joined the domain controlled by a Samba PDC, users can

- be authenticated to the domain to access resources
- execute login scripts
- have roaming profiles

There are some Windows NT capabilities that are not yet implemented:

- Samba cannot become a Backup Domain Controller or work with one.
- Samba cannot participate in any trust relationships with either Samba or NT servers.
- Samba cannot display a list of domain users in the User Manager for Domains.

CONFIGURE SAMBA

There are several global options to be set and a netlogon share to be added to the Samba configuration for Samba to be an NT PDC. All of the options are set on the Globals page in SWAT.

Encrypted passwords must be enabled:

```
encrypt passwords = yes
```

Tell Samba where the encrypted passwords are kept:

```
smb passwd file = /etc/smbpasswd
```

The default location for Red Hat Linux and Debian GNU/Linux is */etc/samba/ smbpasswd;* for Caldera OpenLinux and older versions of Red Hat before 7.0 it is */etc/samba.d/smbpasswd.*

The security level must be set to User:

```
security = user
```

Enable domain logons to tell the clients that Samba is the PDC:

```
domain logons = yes
```

Enter the domain name, which is entered as the workgroup name (this cannot be the same name as the machine name for the Samba server):

```
workgroup = domain_name
```

Set Samba to be the domain master browser:

```
domain master = true
preferred master = true
local master = yes
```

Set the operating system level high enough that the Samba domain controller will win all browser elections:

```
os level = 64
```

SET UP NETLOGON

Windows clients expect to see a netlogon share when they log onto a domain controller. The directories can be created in Webmin's File Manager. If you are using a *srv* directory, create the netlogon directories there.

Create a directory named *netlogon,* and in that directory create another directory named *scripts* where logon scripts will be stored. Set the permissions for both directories so that read, write, and list are enabled for the owner, group, and others.

In SWAT go to the Shares page and create a new share named netlogon. Set these options:

```
path = /srv/netlogon
read only = no
guest ok = no
guest only = no
browseable = no
share modes = no
```

CREATE MACHINE ACCOUNTS

For Windows NT/2000 workstations, machine trust accounts must be created. This is not necessary for Windows 9*x*/Me machines. Adding machine accounts is a manual job in Samba 2.2. In version 3.0, the User Manager for Domains can be used.

ADDING MACHINE ACCOUNTS • Adding a machine to a Samba 2.2 domain controller is different from adding a machine to a Windows NT server. One limitation is the Linux 11-character maximum for usernames. Make sure to use NetBIOS machine names that are 10 characters or less, with no spaces, periods, or underscore characters.

On the Linux server, create a group for the domain member machines; you can call the group "Machines." Use the Webmin Users and Groups tool to create the group. Then for each machine, create a workstation trust account using these three steps:

1. Add a user to the Samba server in the usual way, with some exceptions. The username is the machine name with a $ added at the end of

the name. Set the shell to /bin/false and the home directory to /dev/null. This is a user account that will never need to have shell access to the server. Set the primary group to Machines and make sure that the Webmin options to create a home directory and to copy files to the home directory are both set to No.

2. Tell Samba that this is a machine account. This can only be done either at the server itself or through a telnet terminal connection to the server. In Webmin, on the Others tab select the Telnet Login. Make sure to become the root user, using the su command. Enter the command to add a machine to Samba:

```
smbpasswd -a -m machine_name
```

Be sure to leave off the $ character. This adds the machine as a Samba user and gives the machine a unique security identifier.

3. On the Windows machine, set the Identification of the workstation to Domain and enter the name of the domain for the Samba controller.

For Windows 9x/Me clients, logging onto an NT domain is set by accessing the Network icon in the Control Panel. In the properties for the Client for Microsoft Network, select Logon to Windows NT Domain and enter the name for the domain (the workgroup setting in Samba). The machine will have to be rebooted in order to log onto the domain.

For Windows NT, in the Control Panel select the Network Properties icon. Click the Change button, and in the Member Of section select the Domain option and enter the name of the domain (the workgroup setting in Samba). Do not click on Create Account in the Domain option. When you click on OK, you should get a confirmation message.

For Windows 2000 Professional, in the Control Panel select the System Properties icon. On the Network Identification tab, select the Properties button. In the Member Of section select the Domain option, then enter the name of the domain (the workgroup setting in Samba). When you click on OK, you will be prompted to enter a valid username and password to join the domain.

ADDING DOMAIN ADMINISTRATORS • Samba domain administrators are designated by setting the option for Domain Admin Group. This can be set to the Linux group adm. Make sure that all domain administrators are then included in the group.

The setting for this is in the Globals page of SWAT under Domain options. Set the option to

```
domain admin group = @adm
```

The group does not have to be adm and can be any other group of your choosing. Domain administrators have full administrator rights, including the right to change permissions on files and add users.

OTHER OPTIONS • In the Globals section of SWAT, there are several logon options that are useful for domain logons. In addition, user profiles, policies, and logon scripts can be used. See the procedures for enabling profiles, policies, and scripts in Chapter 5 on advanced networking.

The domain-related logon options in Globals are Logon Drive, Logon Home, Logon Path, and Logon Script.

Logon Drive

This option sets the drive letter to which the user's home directory will be mapped during the logon process.

Logon Home

This option sets the path to the user's home directory. The default setting is \\%L\%U. The %L variable expands to the NetBIOS name of the Samba server, and the %U variable expands to the name of the user. This is the user's home directory. This option is used for roaming profiles for Windows 9x/Me clients

Logon Path

This option sets the path to user profiles. The default setting is \\%L\Profiles\%U, which expands to the user's profile directory on the Samba server. This option is used for roaming profiles for Windows NT/2000 clients. It requires that the profiles share has been created for storing all roaming profiles in a central directory on the Samba server. The profiles share is optional, and the logon path can be set to be the same as the user's home directory, as with the Logon Home option for Windows 9x/Me clients, though there are reported to be occasional problems with saving NT/2000 user profiles in the user's home directory.

Logon Script

This option sets the name of the Windows batch file (*.bat*) or command file (*.cmd*) to be run on logon.

An example setting for logon options would be

```
logon drive = H:
logon home = \\%L\%U
logon path = \\%L\Profiles\%U
logon script = smblogon.bat
```

Samba Command and Configuration Option Reference

Samba is a suite of programs with a great many configuration options. This appendix lists the Samba programs and the configuration options. The options are listed in the order they appear in SWAT, the Samba Web Administration Tool.

The Samba Suite

The Samba suite is a collection of daemons and utilities.

Daemons

The Samba suite includes three daemons, the basic programs that provide networking services.

SMBD

The SMB/CIFS daemon is the file-sharing server. It responds to all requests for file or printer access. It also handles user authentication and resource locking.

The smbd daemon is controlled by the *smb.conf* configuration file. The configuration file is automatically checked every minute, and if there are changes, the new options take effect immediately, with only a few exceptions.

The startup options include the following:

-D Run in daemon mode. This is the usual way to run smbd. The default setting.

-a Append a message to the log file for each new connection. The default setting.

−o Overwrite the log file for each new connection. Not the default setting.

−P Run in passive mode; that is, smbd does not send any network traffic. Used only by the Samba developers.

−h Display help information.

−v Display the version number for smbd.

−d *debug level* Set the debug level. The debug level is indicated by an integer from 0 to 10. Normally set to 0 or 1 for production use. Higher values produce very large log files and are used only when debugging a problem.

−l Specify an alternative log filename, different from the one that was set when the program was compiled.

−O *socket option* An alternative way to set socket options. Normally socket options are set in the tuning settings in the global configuration settings.

−p *port number* Set the UDP port to which smbd listens. Normally this is 139, the default value.

−s *configuration file* Specify an alternative configuration file. The default configuration file is *smb.conf* in a directory set when the program was compiled.

NMBD

The NetBIOS name server daemon provides WINS and NetBIOS name service over IP. It also provides browse lists for the Network Neighborhood/My Network Places. The startup options include the following:

−D Run in daemon mode. This is the usual way to run nmbd. The default setting.

−a Append a message to the log file for each new connection. The default setting.

−o Overwrite the log file for each new connection. Not the default setting.

−h Display help information.

−H *filename* Specify an alternative filename for the NetBIOS lmhosts file.

−v Display the version number for nmbd.

−d *debug level* Set the debug level. The debug level is indicated by an integer from 0 to 10. Normally set to 0 or 1 for production use. Higher values produce very large log files and are used only when debugging a problem.

-l Specify an alternative log filename, different from the one that was set when the program was compiled.

-n primary NetBIOS name Specify the computer's NetBIOS name. This setting overrides the NetBIOS name option in the global configuration options.

-p port number Set the UDP port to which nmbd listens. Normally this is 137, the default value.

-s configuration file Specify an alternative configuration file. The default configuration file is *smb.conf* in a directory set when the program was compiled.

WINBINDD

Winbind is a "service switch" daemon for resolving user and group information names from Windows domain controllers. A name service switch controls how a system gets network information. The Winbind name service switch make it possible for the Samba server to use a Windows domain controller for name service. The Winbind daemon has two options:

-d debug level Set the debug level. The debug level is indicated by an integer from 0 to 100. Normally set to 0 or 1 for production use. Higher values produce very large log files and are used only when debugging a problem.

-i Interactive debugging mode. This option is only used by developers when debugging is required.

Client Tools

Samba's client tools are run from a command prompt.

Rpcclient

A utility for remote access of a Windows NT/2000 system from a Linux workstation. It was originally written by Samba developers to test Remote Procedure Call (RPC) functionality in Samba. An RPC is used by Windows NT/2000 for network communication. Many Windows services such as remote administration, printing, and user authentication are implemented using RPC.

The rpcclient utility can be used to make remote procedure calls to Windows NT/2000 systems. The utility has several command options. Entering rpcclient -h at a command prompt will produce a list of all the options.

Smbtar

A utility for backing up Windows-based systems to a disk file or tape on a Linux system. Similar to the Linux tar utility.

Smbclient

An FTP-like utility that can be used to transfer files between a Linux workstation and Windows or Samba server.

Smbmnt

A Helper utility for smbmount. It should not be run from the command line by users.

Smbmount

A utility used to mount Windows file systems on Linux machines. It can be enabled only at compile time. Options are similar to the mount utility on Linux systems.

Smbspool

A print spooling utility for sending a print file from a Linux system to a Windows print share. Used by the smbprint program.

Smbprint

A utility to print from a Linux system to a shared printer on a Windows system. This utility is included with the packaged versions of Samba that come with most Linux distributions. If you have compiled Samba from source, the smbprint utility must be copied from the source archive in the *examples/printing* directory into */usr/bin* or */usr/local/bin*.

Smbumount

A utility used to unmount Windows file systems. Used in conjunction with the smbmount program.

Diagnostic Utilities

The diagnostic utilities are command-line programs for checking Samba's status and configuration and for checking the network.

Smbstatus

A utility to get information on the status of current Samba connections. Used to get information about who is accessing the Samba server and what shares they are using.

Testparm

A utility for checking the Samba configuration file *smb.conf*. Used for troubleshooting Samba configuration problems.

Testprns

A utility for checking the Samba printer configuration. Used for troubleshooting Samba printer problems.

Nmblookup

A utility used to look up NetBIOS computer names. Used to troubleshoot browsing and name resolution problems.

Configuration Options

SWAT divides Samba's configuration options into three areas: Globals, Shares, and Printers. The following list presents the options in the order in which they are listed in SWAT.

The following share names in Samba are predefined and cannot be changed:

[Global]

The global section of the Samba configuration is not a share, but is the section of the configuration file reserved for global configuration options. Some options can be set only in the global section.

[Homes]

The default share for users' home directories.

[Printers]

The default configuration options for Samba printer shares.

[Print$]

A special share required for Windows NT–like automatic printer services on a Samba server.

[Netlogon]

Windows clients look for a netlogon share when they log onto a domain controller. If present, the client will run any batch file set by the Logon Script option.

[Profiles]

A share for users' roaming profiles.

Globals

Following are the options listed on the Globals page of SWAT in the Advanced View.

BASE OPTIONS

The global base options set the basic networking operations for the Samba server including the NetBIOS name for the Samba server and the workgroup or domain.

Coding System

Used to map characters used for file or directory names from the Japanese Industrial Standard Shift-JIS code page set to the Linux equivalent character set. This option can be used only with clients using code page 932. The Samba code page must also be set to 932.

The default setting is blank, meaning no coding system is used. The other possible parameters are listed here:

SJIS No conversion of the incoming filename.

JIS8, J8BB, J8BH, J8@B, J8@J, J8@H Convert to eight-bit JIS codes.

JIS7, J7BB, J7BH, J7@B, J7@J, J7@H Convert seven-bit JIS codes.

JUNET, JUBB, JUBH, JU@B, JU@J, JU@H Convert a JUNET code.

EUC Convert to EUC code.

HEX Convert a three-byte hexadecimal code.

CAP Convert to the three-byte hexadecimal code used by the Columbia AppleTalk Program.

Client Code Page

Sets the Windows code page that the client machines accessing Samba are using. The default code page for the Windows operating system on computers in the United States is 437. The default for Western European releases of Windows is code page 850. Samba defaults to code page 850. See Table A-1 for code pages supported by Samba 2.2.

Code Page Directory

Defines the location of Samba's client code page files.

Workgroup

The workgroup for the Samba server. If Samba is set up to be the domain controller or a logon server, the workgroup parameter defines the name of the domain. There is no default setting.

Netbios Name

The NetBIOS computer name for the Samba server. This is the name seen in the Network Neighborhood/My Network Places. The default name is the same as the first part of the host's DNS name.

Netbios Aliases

This is a list of one or more NetBIOS computer names that are aliases used for the Samba server on the network. The alias names will not be used for WINS services or logon services. Only the primary name of the Samba server will be used for those options.

Table A-1	Code Pages Supported by Samba 2.2
Code Page 437	Latin US
Code Page 737	Greek
Code Page 775	Baltic Rim
Code Page 850	Latin 1 (most Western European languages)
Code Page 852	Latin 2 (Central and Eastern European languages)
Code Page 861	Icelandic
Code Page 866	Cyrillic (Russian)
Code Page 932	Japanese Shift-JIS
Code Page 936	Simplified Chinese
Code Page 949	Korean Hangul
Code Page 950	Traditional Chinese

Netbios Scope

The Scope ID for the Samba server. If you are using Scope ID to isolate a Windows network, enter the ID here. If anything is entered in the netbios scope option, the Samba server will be accessible only to other machines with the same Scope ID. The default setting is blank, meaning there is no Scope ID and the server can be seen by any machine on the local network.

Server String

A short description of the server, displayed in the comments field in network browsing.

Interfaces

An option that lets you override the default network interface card that Samba will use. Normally Samba uses the default set by the Linux system.

Bind Interfaces Only

An option to limit which network interface cards on the Linux machine Samba will use. If set to Yes, Samba will allow access only on the interfaces specified by the Interfaces option. If Bind Interfaces Only is set, the network address 127.0.0.1 must be added to the Interfaces option or smbpasswd and SWAT may not work as expected.

SECURITY OPTIONS

The global security options include the four levels of user authentication, enabling use of encrypted passwords, the guest account settings, and a number of options that control permissions for files and directories on shares. The hosts allow and hosts deny options are frequently used to limit access to the server.

Security

The Security parameter sets the authentication process used by the Samba server. The default is setting is User. There are four options for the security parameter: Share, User, Server, and Domain.

Share security is used by for Windows 95 file or printer sharing. This means that every time a connection is requested to a share, Samba checks the username and password from the user database, and if a match is found, the connection is accepted.

User security employs a logon process for each client. If the user logon is authenticated, the connection is accepted. As long as the session is maintained, any additional connection requests by the client do not require that the authentication process be repeated.

Server security is similar to user security, except that the initial logon authentication is passed to a password server. The Password Server option must be set to identify the authentication server.

Domain security is used when the Samba server is a member of a Windows domain.

Encrypt Passwords

All versions of Windows, except the initial release of Windows 95 and Windows NT before Service Pack 3, use encrypted passwords. The default value for this option is No. In most cases, it should be set to Yes. If it is set to Yes, the Samba server must have an smbpasswd file with Samba users and passwords in encrypted format, or the server must be authenticating users from a domain controller or a logon server, or it must be using Winbind for user authentication.

Update Encrypted

For systems moving from unencrypted passwords to encrypted passwords, this option can be used to update user passwords in the smbpasswd file from plain text to encrypted. This option will work only if the Encrypt Passwords option is set to No. If it is set to Yes, once all the passwords have been encrypted, this option should be set to No and the Encrypt Passwords option set to Yes. The default value is No.

Allow Trusted Domains

This option allows access to users who are authenticated by a domain controller or a logon server. It is only recognized on Samba servers with the security option set to Server or Domain. If set to Yes, Samba will accept logons from domains or workgroups trusted by the domain controller. If set to No, Samba will refuse the connections even if the domain or workgroup is trusted by the domain controller. The default value is Yes.

Alternate Permissions

This is an obsolete option that has been disabled. It was used in Samba versions prior to 2.0.

Hosts Equiv

Sets the name of a file that has a list of machine names that are allowed access without using passwords. The default setting is None, meaning that no machines are allowed access without using passwords.

Min Passwd Length

Sets the minimum number of characters for plain text passwords.

Map to Guest

Sets access for logins that don't match a valid user. The possible values are Never, Bad User, and Bad Password. If set to Never, access will be denied no matter how other options are set. If set to Bad User, any login attempt with an invalid username is granted access as a guest user. If set to Bad Password, any login attempt with a valid username but a bad password is granted access as a guest user.

The default setting is Never.

Null Passwords

If set to Yes, allows access to users with no (null) password. The default value is No.

Obey PAM restrictions

If Encrypt Passwords is set to no and Samba was compiled to enable Pluggable Authentication Module (PAM) support, this option can be used to enable PAM authentication of users. If set to yes, Samba will use the options set in /etc/pam.d/samba for user authentication. This option is ignored if Encrypt Passwords is set to yes because PAM modules cannot authenticate Samba's encrypted passwords. The default setting is no.

Password Server

The NetBIOS computer name of the password server. Used with the security options of Server or Domain. If you have a domain controller, enter the name of the domain controller. The default value is None, meaning that there is no domain controller or password server on the local network.

Smb Passwd File

The name of the file that has the Samba server's usernames and encrypted passwords. The default is set when the Samba is compiled.

Root Directory

An option to change the root directory used by Samba. Uses the Linux `chroot` command, which makes it possible for any directory to appear to be the root directory. Used for extra security because it denies access to the real root file system on the server. Requires that a `chroot` environment be set up on the Samba server that mirrors all necessary files to the `chroot` directories. Changing the root directory is not necessary for secure operations. The default value is to leave the root directory unchanged from the Linux default.

PAM Password Change

If PAM support is enabled in Samba, and this option is set to yes, PAM authentication is used for requests to change user passwords. If this is enabled, the Password Chat option must be changed to work with PAM. The default setting is no.

Passwd Program

The name of the program used by the Linux system to set user passwords. The default setting is */bin/passwd*.

Passwd Chat

The command Samba should run to change user passwords. The default value is set when Samba is compiled.

Passwd Chat Debug

For debugging only. If set to Yes, the entire password chat, including passwords, is written to the log using debug level 100.

Username Map

The name of the file that maps Windows usernames to Linux usernames.

Password Level

If plain text passwords are being used, sets the number of upper- and lowercase combinations of a password Samba will try before rejecting it. Some older Windows clients, particularly Windows for Workgroups, play havoc with case combinations on passwords. The default value is 0, meaning that the password is tried as it is sent and as all lowercase.

Username Level

Sets the number of upper- and lowercase combinations of a user login name Samba will try before rejecting it. The default value is 0, meaning that the username is tried as it is sent.

Unix Password Sync

If set to Yes, Samba will attempt to change the user's Linux password whenever the user changes his or her Windows password.

Restrict Anonymous

If set to Yes, all anonymous access is denied. This should never be set to Yes if the Samba server is acting as a domain controller or a logon server. Anonymous access is required whenever a client is revalidating its machine account when a new user logs on. Also Windows NT and 2000 sometimes use anonymous access when browsing the network. The default value is No.

Lanman Auth

If set to No, restricts Samba to using only Windows NT/2000–style passwords. This would mean that Windows 9x/Me machines could not be authenticated. The default value is Yes, allowing all variants of the Windows password hash.

Use Rhosts

If set to Yes, Samba allows access from hosts listed in the users' *.rhosts* file without checking for password authentication. The default is No.

Username

If a client does not provide a username, Samba will try to use any username set with this option. This option is needed only for compatibility with Windows for Workgroups clients. When usernames are listed this way, Samba can end up timing out all user validations as it attempts to repeatedly validate all usernames listed in this option. The default setting is None.

Guest Account

The Linux username for guest access to the Samba server. Guest access is used for printing and for any shares with Guest Okay set to Yes. The default, which is set when Samba is compiled, is usually the "nobody" user.

Invalid Users

List of usernames and/or groups not allowed to have access.

Valid Users

List of usernames and/or groups allowed access.

Admin Users

List of usernames and/or groups given administrator (root) access.

Read List

List of usernames and/or groups given read-only access.

Write List

List of usernames and/or groups given write access even if a share is set to be read-only.

Printer Admin

List of usernames and/or groups given administrator (root) access to printer shares using Windows printer administration tools.

Create Mask

Sets the maximum allowable permissions for new files. Possible values are octal values from 0 to 0777. The default setting is 0744.

Force Create Mode

Permission settings that Samba forces when creating files. Possible values are octal values from 0 to 0777. The default setting is 0, meaning that Samba does not force any permission settings.

Security Mask

Sets the permissions that Samba allows users to change from Windows NT/2000 clients. Possible values are octal values from 0 to 0777. If not set explicitly, the value is set to the Create Mask value.

Force Security Mode

Permission settings that Samba forces when a user changes permissions from Windows NT/2000 clients. Possible values are octal values from 0 to 0777. If not set explicitly, the value is set to the Force Create Mode value.

Directory Mask

Maximum permissions allowed for new directories created in a share. Possible values are octal values from 0 to 0777. The default setting is 0755.

Force Directory Mode

Permission settings that Samba forces when creating directories. Possible values are octal values from 0 to 0777. The default setting is 0, meaning that Samba does not force any permission settings.

Directory Security Mask

Sets the permissions on directories that Samba allows users to change from Windows NT/2000 clients. Possible values are octal values from 0 to 0777. If not set explicitly, the value set to the Directory Mask value.

Force Directory Security Mode

Permission settings that Samba forces when a user changes directory permissions from Windows NT/2000 clients. Possible values are octal values from 0 to 0777. If not set explicitly, the value is set to the Force directory Mode value.

Hosts Allow

List of hosts by name or IP address that can access shares on the Samba server. If left blank, any machine is allowed access.

Hosts Deny

List of hosts by name or IP address that are denied access to the Samba server. If left blank, no machine is denied access.

LOGGING OPTIONS

The global logging options are used to increase or decrease the amount of information stored in Samba's logs. These values only need to be changed when trying to debug a problem with the server.

Log Level

Sets the level of detail saved into Samba's logs. Possible values are from 0 to 10. Any value over 3 can seriously slow down the Samba server. The default value is 0.

Syslog

Sets the debug level for messages sent to the system log. The default value is 1.

Syslog Only

If set to Yes, Samba's log messages are sent only to the system logs and not to the standard Samba log files. The default value is No.

Log File

The name and location of the Samba log file. The default value is set when the Samba program is compiled.

Max Log Size

The maximum size for the log file. The size is set in kilobytes. The default value is 5000.

Timestamp Logs

If set to Yes, Samba adds a timestamp to each log entry. The default value is Yes.

Debug Hires Timestamp

If set to Yes, Samba adds timestamps to each log entry with microsecond accuracy. Used for performance tuning. The default value is No.

Debug pid

If set to Yes, the process ID (PID) of the Samba server is added to log entries. The default value is No.

Debug uid

If set to Yes, the user ID (UID) and group ID (GID) of the user are added to log entries. Default value is No.

Status

If set to Yes, Samba logs connections to a file that smbstatus can access. The default value is Yes.

PROTOCOL OPTIONS

The global protocol options set the values for the SMB protocol including the compatibility level and the version number the Samba server uses when announcing itself as an available server. Normally none of these values should be changed from the default settings.

Protocol

Sets the SMB protocol level Samba will use. The default is NT1, also known as the Common Internet File System (CIFS). This is the maximum value and is necessary for compatibility with Windows NT/2000 systems. It should not be changed. Samba will automatically negotiate the proper protocol if left to the default setting.

Max Protocol

Sets the top SMB protocol level Samba will use. The default level is NT1, which is Windows NT's CIFS. The options include the original Core (CORE) protocol, Core Plus (COREPLUS), LAN Manager 1.0 (LANMAN1), LAN Manager 2.0 (LANMAN2), and CIFS 1.0 (NT1). This value should never be changed.

Min Protocol

Sets the minimum SMB protocol level Samba will use. The default level is CORE, which is the earliest version of the SMB protocol. The options start with the original Core (CORE) protocol, and include Core Plus (COREPLUS), LAN Manager 1.0 (LANMAN1), LAN Manager 2.0 (LAN-MAN2), and CIFS 1.0 (NT1). This value should never be changed.

Read bmpx

This is an obsolete option.

Read Raw

Allows fast reads over TCP/IP using 64Kb buffers. The default value is Yes.

Write Raw

Allows fast writes over TCP/IP using 64Kb buffers. The default value is Yes.

Nt smb Support

If set to Yes, allows use of NT SMB/CIFS features. The default value is Yes.

Nt Pipe Support

A developer debugging option used to set whether Windows NT clients can connect to IPC$ pipes. The default setting is Yes and should be left alone.

Nt acl Support

If set to Yes, Samba will attempt to map Linux permissions and owner-ships into Windows access control lists (ACLs). The default value is Yes.

Announce Version

Sets the SMB server version Samba announces. The default is 4.2. Do not change this unless there is a special need to downgrade the Samba server.

Announce As

Sets the Windows version that Samba announces itself to be. The default is NT Server, which can also be written as NT. The other options are NT Workstation, Win95, and WfW. Changing this setting can disable some features on the Samba server and even make the server unusable.

Max mux

Sets the maximum number of simultaneous operations Samba accepts from Windows clients. The default is 50 and should not be changed.

Max xmit

Sets the maximum packet size accepted by the Samba server. The default is 65535.

Name Resolve Order

Sets the order used to look up IP address for NetBIOS computer names. The default is `lmhosts host wins bcast`.

Max Packet

Obsolete option that was replaced by `max xmit`.

Max ttl

Sets the time to keep NetBIOS names in cache while performing a lookup. The value is set in seconds. The default is 259300 (3 days).

Max Wins ttl

If Samba is set to be a WINS server, sets the time to keep NetBIOS names and associated IP address in the WINS cache. The value is set in seconds. The default is 518400 (6 days).

Min Wins ttl

If Samba is set to be a WINS server, sets the minimum time to keep Net-BIOS names and associated IP address in the WINS cache. The value is set in seconds. The default is 21600 (6 hours).

Time Server

If set to Yes, Samba will provide time service to Windows clients. The default value is No.

TUNING OPTIONS

The global tuning options set values that affect the way the Samba server performs reads and writes between the client and the server.

Change Notify Timeout

Sets the number of seconds between checks for changes to a directory. The default value is 60.

Deadtime

Sets the number of minutes of inactivity before a connection is considered to be "dead" and is disconnected. Since Windows clients have an auto-reconnect feature, this disconnect is transparent to the user. On most servers this should be set to 5 minutes in order to prevent resources from being tied up by inactive connections. The default value is 0, meaning there is no time limit.

Getwd Cache

If set to Yes, Samba caches the name of the current working directory. The default value is Yes.

Keepalive

The number of seconds between checks to see if a client is still present and responding. The default value is 300.

Lpq Cache Time

Sets how long in seconds Samba caches the print queue status. The default value is 10.

Max smbd Processes

Sets the maximum number of concurrent smbd processes that can be running. The default value is 0, meaning there is no limit.

Max Disk Size

Sets the maximum disk size in megabytes that Samba reports to clients. This option makes no change in the actual size of the disk or the actual available space on the disk. It is used for software that won't work with disk sizes larger than 1 or 2 gigabytes. The default value is 0, which means that there is no limit on the disk size reported.

Max Open Files

Sets the maximum number of open files a Windows client can have on a Samba server at one time. This setting should not be changed. The default value is 10000.

Read Size

Sets the number of bytes Samba will receive before writing to disk or transmitting over the network. The default value is 16384.

Socket Options

Sets networking socket options. The socket options are specific to the operating system. The default is TCP_NODELAY.

Stat Cache Size

The number of client names cached. The default value is 50 and should never need to be changed.

PRINTING OPTIONS

The global printing options set overall values for Samba's printing operations. Individual printer options are set in the printer configuration section.

Total Print Jobs

Sets the maximum number of jobs accepted by a printer share. The default value is 0, meaning there is no limit.

Load Printers

Loads all printers set up on the Linux system. The default value is Yes.

Printcap Name

Sets the name for the printer configuration file. The default value is */etc/printcap* for BSD and LPRng printing systems and *lpstat* for the CUPS printing system.

Printing

Sets the server's printing system. On most Linux systems, the possible values are BSD, LPRng, and CUPS.

Print Command

Sets the command used to send a file to the printer. The default value is determined by the printing system used. For BSD and LPRng, the command is `lpr -r -P%p %s`. For CUPS, the command is `lp -d %p -o raw %s; rm -f %s`.

Lpq Command

Sets the command used to get the printer queue status. The default setting for BSD and LPRng is `lpq -P%p`. If the printing system is set to CUPS, this value does not need to be entered.

Lprm Command

Sets the command used to delete a print job. The default setting for BSD and LPRng is `lprm -P%p %j`. If the printing system is set to CUPS, this value does not need to be entered.

Lppause Command

Sets the command used to pause a print job.

Lpresume Command

Sets the command used to resume printing a paused print job.

Queuepause Command

Sets the command used to pause a print queue.

Queueresume Command

Sets the command used to resume a paused print queue.

Enumports Command

Windows associates every printer with a port. Linux does not define printer connections as ports. On Linux systems, printers are accessed as devices, and there is no way to directly map Windows ports to local devices on a Linux server. By default, Samba has only one port defined: `Samba Printer Port`. This is what is displayed by Windows clients using a Samba printer share. This is displayed so that a port will be shown in Windows. It is not necessary to display the actual device information in order for the printer to work. The printer connection information is handled separately. If you want a list of ports to be displayed, you can create a script that will generate the information in a list, with one per line. Enter the command line to run the script as the `enumports command`.

Addprinter Command

Beginning with Samba 2.2, Samba supports the Windows NT/2000 Add Printer Wizard. The Add Printer Wizard can be used to also add a printer to the Samba server only if you create an addprinter script that generates all the necessary steps to add a printer to your Linux server. Normally printers are added through the Linux system and not through the Windows NT/2000 Add Printer Wizard.

Deleteprinter Command

Beginning with Samba 2.2, Samba supports the Windows NT/2000 printing services. This means that it is possible to delete a printer on the Samba server from a Windows NT/2000 client. This requires that you create a `deleteprinter` script that generates all the necessary steps to delete a printer from your Linux server.

Show Add Printer Wizard

Beginning with Samba 2.2, Samba supports the Windows NT/2000 printing services. When Windows NT/2000 clients browse the network, a *Printers* folder will appear on the Samba server. If this option is set to Yes, the Windows Add Printer Wizard will appear in the *Printers* folder. The default value is Yes.

Os2 Driver Map

Sets the name of the file that maps Windows printer driver names to OS/2 printer drivers names. The default is blank.

Printer Driver Location

This is an obsolete option and should be left blank.

FILENAME HANDLING

The global filename handling options set values for maintaining compatibility between Windows filename handling and Linux filename handling.

Strip Dot

If set to Yes, Samba strips the trailing dots from filenames. Some CD-ROMs use filenames that have a dot at the end. The default value is No.

Character Set

The Linux character set to which Windows filenames are translated. The default value is None.

Mangled Stack

Sets the cache size for mangled filenames. Mangled filenames affects only DOS files or files created by programs that work in DOS mode. Mangling involves converting long filenames into the DOS 8.3 name limit. The stack is the list of recently mangled names. The default value is 50.

Case Sensitive

Sets whether filenames are case-sensitive. The default setting is No, which is how Windows and DOS work.

Preserve Case

Sets whether new filenames are created with the case sent by the user. The default setting is Yes.

Short Preserve Case

Sets whether new files that conform to the DOS 8.3 filename syntax are saved in the case sent by the user. The default setting is Yes.

Mangle Case

Sets whether to change filenames that are both upper- and lowercase to the case set by the default case option. The default setting is No.

Mangling Char

Sets the unique character used when mangling filenames. The default setting is ~.

Hide Dot Files

Sets whether Linux's hidden files (files with names that start with a dot) are given the Hidden attribute when viewed from a Windows client. The default setting is Yes.

Delete Veto Files

Veto files are a list of files to be hidden. If set to Yes, when you delete a directory that contains veto files, the hidden veto files will also be deleted. If set to No and the veto files are not deleted, the directory can't be deleted. The default setting is No.

Veto Files

A list of files and directories that are not visible or accessible. These are files that will not show up even if Windows is set to show hidden files. Listing veto files can significantly slow down Samba, as every file and directory request must be checked against the list. The default value is blank.

Hide Files

A list of files that are hidden. These are files that will appear only if Windows is set to show hidden files. Listing hidden files can significantly slow down Samba, as every file and directory request must be checked against the list. The default value is blank.

Veto Oplock Files

A list of files that Samba will not oplock.

Map System

If set to Yes, Samba maps the Linux Group execute permission to any file that is set with the Windows System attribute. The default value is No.

Map Hidden

If set to Yes, Samba maps any file set with the Windows Hidden attribute to the Linux Others execute permission. The default value is No.

Map Archive

If set to Yes, Samba maps any file set with the Windows Archive attribute to the Linux User execute permission. The default value is Yes.

Mangled Names

If set to Yes, when a DOS system or software running in DOS mode writes a file or directory, Samba will create a DOS 8.3–compliant name if necessary because the name is too long or has unsupported characters. The default value is yes.

Mangled Map

A table of names to remap, such as *.html* to *.htm*.

Stat Cache

If set to Yes, Samba will cache case-insensitive mappings. The default is Yes.

DOMAIN OPTIONS

All the domain options, which were introduced in Samba 2.2, are experimental. Some may be removed or changed. Some may not work as intended.

Domain Admin Group

A list of usernames and/or groups that are granted administrator rights as a member of the "Domain Admins" group on a Samba PDC.

Domain Guest Group

A list of usernames and/or groups that are granted access as "Domain Guests" on a Samba PDC.

Machine Password Timeout

If a Samba server is a member of a Windows domain, sets how often the machine password changes. Default is 604,800 seconds (1 week).

LOGON OPTIONS

The global logon options are used when the Samba server is acting as a logon server.

Add User Script

Specifies a program or script that will be run to add a user to the Linux system. If Samba is set to be a domain controller, this option is also used to add a machine.

Delete User Script

If `security=domain` is set, this option specifies a program or script to run to remove a user if the domain controller reports that the user no longer exists.

Logon Script

The batch file or NT command file in the `[netlogon]` share to be run when a user successfully logs in.

Logon Path

The path to where the Windows roaming profile files, such as *USER.DAT* or *NTuser.dat,* are kept. The default setting is `\\%N\%U\profile`. This option is used only if Samba is set up as a logon server.

Logon Drive

Specifies the local path to the home directory. Used only by NT workstations, and only if Samba is set up as a logon server. The default setting is the Z: drive.

Logon Home

Set the user's home directory if Samba is acting as a domain controller or a logon server. The default setting is `\\%N\%U`.

Domain Logons

If set to Yes, Samba accepts domain logons for the workgroup it is in. The default value is No.

BROWSE OPTIONS

The global browse options set how the Samba server will be seen in browser elections on the local network.

Os Level

Sets the operating system level used in local or domain master browser elections. Samba must be a higher OS level than competing operating systems on the local network in order to win. The default OS level is 20, which is higher than Windows 9x/Me and NT/2000 workstations, but lower than NT/2000 servers.

Lm Announce

If set to Yes, produces SMB broadcasts necessary for OS/2 networks. The default setting is Auto, which means that Samba will respond if it gets an announcement from an OS/2 client.

Lm Interval

Sets the interval, in seconds, between OS/2 SMB broadcast announcements. The default is 60.

Preferred Master

If set to Yes, Samba will force a browser election when the server comes online and will attempt to become the master browser for its workgroup. The default value is Auto.

Local Master

If set to Yes, the Samba server will stand for election as the local master browser. The default value is Yes.

Domain Master

If set to Yes, Samba will attempt to become the domain master browser. The default value is No.

Browse List

If set to Yes, Samba will return a list of available shares to clients that request the browse list. The default value is Yes, and it should not be changed.

Enhanced Browsing

A new option that was not available in the initial release of Samba 2.2, but will be added to an intermediate release. The option is expected to be fully functional in version 3.0. If set to yes, cross-subnet browsing enhancements are enabled that make browsing across network segments more reliable. The default value is yes.

WINS OPTIONS

The global WINS options are used to set the Samba server as a WINS server or to point to the WINS server on the local network.

Dns Proxy

If set to Yes, and if `wins support` is set to Yes, Samba will look up host names in DNS when they are not found using WINS. The default value is Yes.

Wins Proxy

If set to Yes, Samba will respond to WINS requests on behalf of some older clients that require it where the WINS server is located on another subnet. The default value is No.

Wins Server

Sets the IP address or fully qualified domain name of the WINS server.

Wins Support

If set to Yes, Samba will act as a WINS server. The default value is No. If set to Yes, the `wins server` option must be blank.

Wins Hook

Specifies an optional command to run whenever Samba updates its WINS database when it is acting as a WINS server.

LOCKING OPTIONS

The global locking options set the file locking parameters for the Samba server, including opportunistic locking (oplocks), which can improve performance for Windows client systems.

Blocking Locks

If set to Yes and a request from a client for a write lock cannot be met, Samba will queue the request and periodically retry to complete the request until the time period expires. If set to No, Samba will fail the request immediately if the write-lock request cannot be met immediately. The default value is Yes.

Kernel Oplocks

If the operating system has kernel-based oplocks support, this option allows them to be enabled or disabled. Only IRIX and Linux 2.4 have kernel oplocks. The default value is Yes.

Locking

If set to Yes, Samba performs file locking. If set to No, Samba will appear to accept lock requests but no locking will occur. The default value is Yes.

Oplocks

If set to Yes, Samba will support client oplocks (opportunistic locks). The default value is Yes.

Level2 Oplocks

If set to Yes, Samba will support client level2 (read-only) oplocks. The default value is Yes.

Oplock Break Wait Time

The delay time, in milliseconds, Samba waits before responding to an oplock break request. The default value is 0. This value should never be changed.

Oplock Contention Limit

The number of oplocks Samba will grant for each file share. The default value is 2. This value should not be changed.

Posix Locking

If set to Yes, Samba's file locks will be consistent with file locks used by the Portable Operating System Interface for Unix (POSIX) standard for applications that access the files not through Samba. The default value is Yes.

Strict Locking

If set to Yes, Samba checks each read or write access for file locks. If set to No, Samba checks for file locks only when the client requests a check. The default value is No.

Share Modes

If set to Yes, Samba will support Windows-style exclusive read or write locks.

SSL OPTIONS

The global SSL options are available—and will appear in SWAT—only if Samba was compiled with SSL enabled.

Ssl

If set to Yes, Samba will accept SSL secure connections. The default value is No.

Ssl ca Certdir

Specifies a directory that contains SSL CA certificates.

Ssl ca Certfile

Specifies a file that contains information on trusted CAs.

Ssl Ciphers

Specifies ciphers that should be offered during SSL negotiation.

Ssl Client Cert

SSL client certificate used by smbclient.

Ssl Client Key

SSL client key used by smbclient.

Ssl Compatibility

Specifies whether SSLeay should be configured for bug compatibility with other SSL implementations. The default value is No.

Ssl Hosts

A list of hosts that can connect to the Samba server only through SSL connections.

Ssl Hosts Resign

A list of hosts that can connect to the Samba server without SSL.

Ssl Require Clientcert

If set to Yes, Samba will reject connections from clients that don't have a valid certificate.

Ssl Require Servercert

If set to Yes, the smbclient will request a certificate from the server.

Ssl Server Cert

Specifies the file with the SSL server certificate used by Samba.

Ssl Server Key

Specifies the file with the SSL private server key used by Samba.

Ssl Version

Specifies the SSL version used by Samba. The options are SSL version 2 (`ssl2`), SSL version 3 (`ssl3`), or `ssl2or3`, which enables a dynamic negotiation between both versions. The new Transport Security Layer version 1 option can be designated with `tls1`. The default value is `ssl2or3`.

MISCELLANEOUS OPTIONS

The miscellaneous global options include any parameters that don't fit into the other categories.

Add Share Command

Starting with Samba 2.2, shares can be added to a Samba server using the Windows NT 4.0 Server Manager. The Add Share Command is an external program or a script that runs all the steps necessary to add a share. The Add Share Command will run only if you are connected to the Samba server as an admin user. The command has four parameters: configFile is the location of the smb.conf file; shareName is the name of the new share; pathName is the location of the directory used for the share; comment is a comment string attached to the new share. The directory indicated in the pathName parameter must be created before creating the share with the Server Manager. The default value is none.

Change Share Command

Starting with Samba 2.2, shares can be added to a Samba server using the Windows NT 4.0 Server Manager. The Change Share Command is an external program or a script that runs all the steps necessary to change an existing share. You must be connected to the Samba server as an admin user to modify a share with the Server Manager. The command has four parameters: configFile is the location of the smb.conf file; shareName is the name of the share; pathName is the location of the directory used for the share; comment is a comment string attached to the share. The default value is none.

Delete Share Command

Starting with Samba 2.2, shares can be added to a Samba server using the Windows NT 4.0 Server Manager. The Delete Share Command is an external program or a scrip that runs all the steps necessary to remove a share from a Samba server. You must be connected to the Samba server as an admin user to remove a share with the Server Manager. The command has two parameters: configFile is the location of the smb.conf file; shareName is the name of the share. The default value is none.

Preload

Specifies a list of shares that will always appear in browse lists.

Lock Dir

Specifies the directory for lock files.

Default Service

The default share (service) used if the client does not specify one.

Message Command

Sets the command to run when a WinPopup message is received by a Samba server.

Dfree Command

Specifies a script or program that can be run to calculate the total disk space and amount available. Normally this is handled with internal routines and no external command should be necessary.

Valid Chars

Specifies additional characters that should be considered valid by Samba in filenames.

Remote Announce

A list of remote addresses where the Samba server will announce itself to the master browser. Specified as IP address/workgroup, for example, `192.168.4.255/STAFF`.

Remote Browse Sync

Enables browse list synchronization with other Samba local master browsers.

Socket Address

Sets a specific IP address on which to listen for connections. The default value is blank, meaning that Samba will listen to connections from all IP addresses.

Homedir Map

For the Sun Network Information System (NIS) naming system, Samba will use the `nis homedir` setting to locate the user's home directory.

Time Offset

Specifies the number of minutes to add to the system time for clients, to fix some clients that incorrectly handle daylight savings time. The default value is 0.

NIS Homedir

If set to Yes, the NIS `homedir map` will be used to look up a user's home directory. The default value is No.

Source Environment

Specifies a file that has Linux system environment variables for Samba to read on startup. The default value is blank.

Wide Links

If set to Yes, Samba will follow links (like Windows shortcuts) out of the current file share. The default value is Yes.

Follow Symlinks

If set to Yes, Samba will follow symbolic links (like Windows shortcuts). The default value is Yes.

Delete Readonly

If set to Yes, Samba will allow users to delete read-only files. The default value is No.

Dos Filemode

If set to Yes, any user with write permission for a file can change the file's permissions. This is the way Windows works, but not Linux, where only the owner of the file can change permissions. The default value is No, meaning that Linux-style permissions are used.

Dos Filetimes

If set to Yes, the file timestamp will be updated any time a file is modified. This is the way Windows works, but not Linux, where only modifications by the file's owner will change the file timestamp. The default value is No, meaning that Linux-style file timestamps are used.

Dos Filetime Resolution

If set to Yes, Samba will round up the file creation time to the next even second. This is the way Windows works, but not Linux. The default value is No. It should be set to Yes for some Windows software development tools, such as Visual C++.

Fake Directory Create Times

If set to Yes, Samba sets all directory creation times to midnight on January 1, 1980. Required for some Windows software development tools, such as Visual C++, that will not work properly with Linux's directory creation times. The default value is No.

Panic Action

Specifies a command to run if Samba crashes. This option is for Samba developers.

Hide Local Users

If set to Yes, local Linux users such as root are hidden from remote clients. The default value is No.

VFS OPTIONS

There is only one virtual file system (VFS) option. It is used to enabled the Windows distributed file system on the Samba server.

Host msdfs

If set to Yes, Samba will act as a distributed filesystem (DFS) server. The default value is No.

WINBIND OPTIONS

The global Winbind options set the values used for unified logons between a Samba server and a Windows domain controller.

Winbind uid

Specifies the range of user IDs available to Winbind. The range of numbers must not include any ID numbers already assigned.

Winbind gid

Specifies the range of group IDs available to Winbind. The range of numbers must not include any ID numbers already assigned.

Template Homedir

Specifies the home directory for Windows NT/2000 clients. The default value is */home/%D/%U*.

Template Shell

Specifies the default Linux login shell for Windows NT/2000 clients. The default value is */bin/false*.

Winbind Separator

Specifies the character used when listing a username in the form of *DOMAIN \user*. The default value is \.

Winbind Cache Time

Specifies the number of seconds Winbind will cache user and group information before launching a new query. The default value is 15.

Shares

Following are the options listed on the Shares page of SWAT in the Advanced View.

BASE OPTIONS

There are two share base options, one is a comment and the other is the path to the directory for the share.

Comment

Sets the comment that appears with a share in the browse list.

Path

The directory to be shared.

SECURITY OPTIONS

The share security options are used to limit access on each share and to control access permissions for the share.

Username

A comma-separated list of usernames that are tried when Samba is set to share-level security. For use with Windows for Workgroups clients.

Guest Account

A Linux username for guest access to the share. Do not change it here unless the share is to have a different guest account than the account set in the global section. The default is usually the "nobody" user.

Invalid Users

List of usernames and/or groups not allowed to have access to this share.

Valid Users

List of usernames and/or groups allowed access to this share.

Admin Users

List of usernames and/or groups given administrator (root) access for this share.

Read List

List of usernames and/or groups given read-only access for this share.

Write List

List of usernames and/or groups given write access even if the share is set to be read-only.

Force User

Specifies a username Samba will assign for all accesses to the share.

Force Group

Specifies a group name Samba will assign for all accesses to the share.

Read Only

If set to Yes, Samba will treat the share as read-only. The default value is Yes.

Create Mask

Set the maximum allowable permissions for new files on the share. Possible values are octal values from 0 to 0777. The default setting is 0744.

Force Create Mode

Permission settings that Samba forces when creating files on the share. Possible values are octal values from 0 to 0777. The default setting is 0, meaning that Samba does not force any permission settings.

Security Mask

Sets the permissions that Samba allows users to change on files on the share from Windows NT/2000 clients. Possible values are octal values from 0 to 0777. If not set explicitly, the value set to the Create Mask value.

Force Security Mode

Permission settings that Samba forces when a user changes permissions on files on the share from Windows NT/2000 clients. Possible values are octal values from 0 to 0777. If not set explicitly, the value is set to the Force Create Mode value.

Directory Mask

Maximum permissions allowed for new directories created in the share. Possible values are octal values from 0 to 0777. The default setting is 0755.

Force Directory Mode

Permission settings that Samba forces when creating directories in the share. Possible values are octal values from 0 to 0777. The default setting is 0, meaning that Samba does not force any permission settings.

Directory Security Mask

Sets the permissions on directories in the share that Samba allows users to change from Windows NT/2000 clients. Possible values are octal values from 0 to 0777. If not set explicitly, the value is set to the Directory Mask value.

Force Directory Security Mode

Permission settings that Samba forces in the share when a user changes directory permissions from Windows NT/2000 clients. Possible values are octal values from 0 to 0777. If not set explicitly, the value is set to the Force Directory Mode value.

Inherit Permissions

If set to Yes, permissions on new files and directories are based on those of the owner of the parent directory. The default value is No.

Guest Only

If set to Yes, only guest access to the share will be accepted. The default value is No.

Guest Ok

If set to Yes, any access will be accepted (no password authentication is performed).

Only User

If set to Yes, only users in the username list will be accepted. The default value is No.

Hosts Allow

List of hosts by name or IP address that can access this share. If left blank, any machine is allowed access.

Hosts Deny

List of hosts by name or IP address that are denied access to this share. If left blank, no machine is denied access.

LOGGING OPTIONS

There is only one logging option for shares. It is used to enable logging of connections to the share.

Status

If set to Yes, Samba logs connections to the share that smbstatus can access. The default value is Yes.

TUNING OPTIONS

The share tuning options include setting the maximum number of connections to the share. The synchronization options, if enabled, can slow system performance.

Max Connections

Sets the maximum number of connections allowed to the share. The default value is 0, meaning there is no limit.

Strict sync

If set to Yes, Samba synchronizes to disk whenever a Windows client sends a request for a synchronization. The default value is No.

Sync Always

If set to Yes, Samba forces a disk synchronization with every write. The default value is No.

Write Cache Size

If set, Samba will create a cache in memory for each oplocked file. Used for optimizing writes to RAID disks. The default value is blank.

FILENAME HANDLING

The share filename handling options are used to maintain compatibility between Windows filename handling and Linux filename handling.

Default Case

Sets the case used for saving new filenames from DOS-based clients or DOS programs. The default value is lower.

Case Sensitive

If set to Yes, Samba uses the exact case DOS-based clients supply. The default value is No.

Preserve Case

If set to Yes, Samba will preserve the case of filenames clients supply. The default value is Yes.

Short Preserve Case

If set to Yes, Samba will preserve the case of DOS-based filenames.

Mangle Case

If set to Yes, filenames that have characters that are in the default case will be mangled to conform. The default value is No.

Mangling Char

Sets the unique character used when mangling filenames. The default setting is ~.

Hide Dot Files

Sets whether any Linux hidden files (files with names that start with a dot) on the share are given the Hidden attribute when viewed from a Windows client. The default setting is Yes.

Delete Veto Files

If set to Yes, if you delete a directory on the share that contains veto files, the hidden veto files will also be deleted. If set to No and the veto files are not deleted, the directory can't be deleted. The default setting is No.

Veto Files

A list of files and directories on the share that are not visible or accessible. These are files that will not show up even if Windows is set to show hidden files. The default value is blank.

Hide Files

A list of files on the share that are hidden. These are files that will appear only if Windows is set to show hidden files.

Veto Oplock Files

A list of files on this share that Samba will not oplock.

Map System

If set to Yes, Samba maps the Linux Group execute permission on any file on the share that is set with the Windows System attribute. The default value is No.

Map Hidden

If set to Yes, Samba maps any file on the share set with the Windows Hidden attribute to the Linux Others execute permission. The default value is No.

Map Archive

If set to Yes, Samba maps any file on the share with the Windows Archive attribute to the Linux User execute permission. The default value is Yes.

Mangled Names

If set to Yes, when a DOS system or software running in DOS mode writes a file or directory on the share, Samba will create a DOS 8.3–compliant name if necessary.

Mangled Map

A table of names to remap, such as *.html* to *.htm*.

BROWSE OPTIONS

There is one share browse option. It is used to enable the share to appear in Windows network browse lists.

Browseable

Specifies if the share is to appear in browse lists. The default value is Yes.

LOCKING OPTIONS

The share locking options set file locking parameters for the share. These options are for the individual share and will override the global settings.

Blocking Locks

If set to Yes and a request from a client for a write lock on a file on the share cannot be met, Samba will queue the request and periodically retry to complete the request until the time period expires. The default value is Yes.

Fake Oplocks

If set to Yes, Samba will respond positively to client requests for oplocks, but won't create them. For use only on read-only shares. The default value is No.

Locking

If set to Yes, Samba performs file locking on the share. If set to No, Samba will appear to accept lock requests but no locking will occur. The default value is Yes.

Oplocks

If set to Yes, Samba will support client oplocks on the share. The default value is Yes.

Level2 Oplocks

If set to Yes, Samba will support client level2 (read-only) oplocks on the share. The default value is Yes.

Oplock Contention Limit

The number of oplocks Samba will grant for the share. The default value is 2.

Posix Locking

If set to Yes, Samba's file locks for the share will be consistent with file locks used by POSIX-compliant applications accessing the files not through Samba. The default value is Yes.

Strict Locking

If set to Yes, Samba checks each read or write access on the share for file locks. The default value is No.

Share Modes

If set to Yes, Samba will support Windows-style exclusive read or write locks on the share.

MISCELLANEOUS OPTIONS

The miscellaneous options for the share include parameters to enable the execution of Linux-based programs on the Samba server. Other options include several for DOS compatibility.

Exec

Sets a command to run before connecting to the share.

Preexec Close

If set to Yes, an error by the command set in `exec` will cause Samba to close the connection.

Postexec

Sets a command to be run when closing a connection to a share.

Root Preexec

Sets a command to be run as root before connecting to the share.

Root Preexec Close

If set to Yes, an error by the command set in `root preexec` will cause Samba to close the connection.

Root Postexec

Sets a command to be run as root when closing a connection to a share.

Available

If set to Yes, the share is available. If set to No, all access to the share is denied. The default value is Yes.

Volume

Sets a volume label for the share. Use with CD-ROMs that require a particular volume label to run.

Fstype

The file system type Samba reports to client requests. The default value is NTFS, the Windows NT filesystem. Other possible values include FAT (the DOS file allocation table) or Samba.

Set Directory

Allows Digital Pathworks clients to use the `setdir` command. The default is No.

Wide Links

If set to Yes, Samba will follow links out of the share. The default value is Yes.

Follow Symlinks

If set to Yes, Samba will follow symbolic links on the share. The default value is Yes.

Dont Descend

A list of subdirectories on a share that are to be made inaccessible.

Magic Script

A Linux script file that, when opened, is executed as a command on the Linux system whenever it is closed by the client. This allows clients to run scripts on the Samba server.

Magic Output

If a Magic Script develops output, it is saved into the file specified by Magic Output.

Delete Readonly

If set to Yes, Samba will allow users to delete read-only files on the share. The default value is No.

Dos Filemode

If set to Yes, any user with write permission for a file on the share can change the file's permissions. This is the way Windows works, but not Linux, where only the owner of the file can change permissions. The default value is No, meaning that Linux-style permissions are used.

Dos Filetimes

If set to Yes, the time will be updated whenever a file on the share is modified. This is the way Windows works, but not Linux, where only modifications by the file's owner will change the file timestamp. The default value is No, meaning that Linux-style file timestamps are used.

Dos Filetime Resolution

If set to Yes, Samba will round up the file creation time of files on the share to the next even second. This is the way Windows works, but not Linux. The default value is No.

Fake Directory Create Times

If set to Yes, Samba sets all directory creation times on the share to midnight on January 1, 1980. Required for some Windows software development tools, such as Visual C++, that will not work properly with Linux's directory creation times. The default value is No.

VFS OPTIONS

The VFS options are used to enable virtual file systems or the Windows distributed file system for the share.

VFS object

Virtual file systems by default use normal disk access routines. If the VFS requires a different disk access operation, then the shared object file for the VFS access operations is set here.

VFS options

Sets options for the VFS that are initialized by Samba on startup.

Msdfs Root

If set to Yes, Samba treats the share as a DFS root. The default value is No.

Printers

Following are the options listed on the Printers page of SWAT in the Advanced View.

BASE OPTIONS

There are two base options for printers; one is a comment and the other is the path to the printer spool directory.

Comment

Sets the comment that appears with a share in the browse list.

Path

The printer spool directory where print jobs are queued.

SECURITY OPTIONS

The printer security options can be used to limit access to each shared printer.

Guest Account

A Linux username for guest access to the printer. Do not change it here unless the printer is to have a different guest account than the account set in the global section. The default is usually the "nobody" user.

Printer Admin

List of usernames and/or groups given printer administrator access.

Guest Ok

If set to Yes, any access will be accepted (no password authentication is performed). All printer shares should allow guest access.

Hosts Allow

List of hosts by name or IP address that can access this printer. If left blank, any machine is allowed access.

Hosts Deny

List of hosts by name or IP address that are denied access to this printer. If left blank, no machine is denied access.

LOGGING OPTIONS

The printer logging option is used to enable log entries for each connection to the printer.

Status

If set to Yes, Samba logs connections to the printer that smbstatus can access. The default value is Yes.

TUNING OPTIONS

The printer tuning option can be used prevent the printer queue from taking up all available disk space.

Min Print Space

Sets the minimum amount of free disk space that must be available if Samba is to accept jobs from the users for this printer. The default value is 0, meaning there is no limit.

PRINTING OPTIONS

The printing options will override the global printer settings. Normally most of these options are not changed on an individual printer share, but are set in the global options.

Max Print Jobs

Sets a limit to the number of jobs that can be in the queue for this printer. The printer will give an error message if the limit is exceeded. The default value is 1000.

Printable

If set to Yes, clients will be able to submit print jobs to this printer. The default value is No.

Postscript

If set to Yes, Samba will add %! to the beginning of all print jobs. The default value is No.

Printing

Sets the printing system. On most Linux systems, the possible values are BSD, LPRng, and CUPS.

Print Command

Sets the command used to send a file to the printer. The default value is determined by the printing system used. For BSD and LPRng, the command is `lpr -r -P%p %s`. For CUPS, the command is `lp -d %p -o raw %s; rm -f %s`.

Lpq Command

Sets the command used to get the printer queue status. The default setting for BSD and LPRng is `lpq -P%p`. If the printing system is set to CUPS, this value does not need to be entered.

Lprm Command

Sets the command used to delete a print job. The default setting for BSD and LPRng is `lprm -P%p %j`. If the printing system is set to CUPS, this value does not need to be entered.

Lppause Command

Sets the command used to pause a print job.

Lpresume Command

Sets the command used to resume printing a paused print job.

Queuepause Command

Sets the command used to pause a print queue.

Queueresume Command

Sets the command used to resume a paused print queue.

Printer Name

The name of the printer.

Printer Driver

This option is obsolete.

Printer Driver File

This option is obsolete.

Printer Driver Location

This option is obsolete.

BROWSE OPTIONS

The printer browse option is used to enable the printer to appear in Windows network browse lists.

Browseable

Specifies whether the printer is to appear in browse lists. The default value is Yes.

MISCELLANEOUS OPTIONS

The miscellaneous options for printers include parameters to enable the execution of Linux-based programs on the Samba server.

Exec

Sets a command to run before putting a print job in the print queue.

Postexec

Sets a command to be run when closing a print job.

Root Preexec

Sets a command to be run as root (administrator) before putting a print job in the print queue.

Root Postexec

Sets a command to be run as root (administrator) when closing a print job.

Available

If set to Yes, the printer is available. If set to No, all access to the printer is denied. The default value is Yes.

Finding Help

There are many sources of help and additional information about Samba as well as Linux. There are extensive help files on the Samba server as well as on the World Wide Web. In addition, there are several companies that have Samba support services, including most companies that provide Linux support.

Samba's Complete Documentation

The complete Samba documentation can be accessed from SWAT's initial home page. On the SWAT documentation page there are links to help files for the following:

- Samba daemons: smbd, nmbd, and winbindd
- Samba configuration files: smb.conf, lmhosts, and smbpasswd
- Samba administrative utilities: smbpasswd, smbrun, smbcontrol, and other utilities
- Samba client tools: rpcclient, smbclient, and other tools
- Samba diagnostic utilities: smbstatus, testparm, testprns, and nmblookup
- The HTML version of the *Using Samba* book
- The Samba "How-To" Collection

In addition, every configuration option shown in SWAT has a link to the Samba manual page for the option.

Help on the Web

There are many sources of Samba help on the Web. There are even more sources of Web help for Linux, and many of the Linux sources also have Samba help. The rapid rise in popularly of both Samba and Linux means that new sites are constantly opening on the Web. Here is a list of sites to get you started. You can also use a good Web search engine like Google or Yahoo to find the latest Web-based information sites.

Samba Help

There are several sources for Samba-specific information on the Web.

THE SAMBA HEADQUARTERS

The main Samba Web page at *www.samba.org* displays a list of mirror sites around the world where the complete Samba Web pages can be accessed, including the latest version of the Samba source code. This is not where you should get the latest version to work with a specific Linux distribution; for that, go to the Web site of the specific Linux distribution.

SAMBA LISTS

For the latest information on Samba and to get answers to many Samba-related questions, the best source is often the Samba discussion lists. There are several Samba-related lists, and most of them are very active. All the Samba-hosted lists can be found on the Web at *lists.samba.org*.

The discussion lists include the following:

- **samba** General discussion about Samba-related issues
- **samba-announce** Announcements from the Samba team
- **samba-technical** Developer discussions about Samba's development

Of all the lists, the samba list is the best one for general information and discussion. If you are unsure which list to join, choose samba. With any question you ask, please be specific and include as much information as you can, including the version of Samba and the Linux version. Remember that everyone answering questions on the lists is a volunteer; it can sometimes take a while for answers to come. Many of the Samba team members are in Australia, and if someone in the United States or Europe asks a question, it can take a day or more for an answer to come back. While many of the questions asked on the Samba lists are answered by members of the Samba team, other people also volunteer answers. The Samba discussion lists are an excellent source for reliable, expert-level Samba information.

The archives of the lists can also be found at *lists.samba.org,* and a searchable archive of the Samba discussion lists can be found at *marc. theaimsgroup.com.*

SAMBA NEWSGROUP

There is also a Samba-related Usenet newsgroup named *comp.protocols.smb.* This Usenet newsgroup can be accessed like any other newsgroup or on the Web at *groups.google.com.* The Google archive of *comp.protocols.smb* is also searchable.

FREE SOFTWARE FOUNDATION

Samba is distributed under the GNU General Public License. For more information on the Samba license and on free software, go to the Free Software Foundation Web site at *www.fsf.org.*

Webmin

Webmin, found on the Internet at *www.webmin.com/webmin,* is a Web-based interface for system administration for Linux. Webmin requires a browser that supports tables and forms (and Java to use the Webmin File Manager). Webmin includes a simple Web server and a number of CGI programs that directly update Linux system files. It includes extensive support for Samba. It is the most developed and easy-to-use system administration tool available for Linux.

Red Hat Linux

The Red Hat Web site has a great deal of Red Hat–specific information, including information on using Samba on Red Hat Linux. Use the search function to find Samba-related information. The main Red Hat Web site is at *www.redhat.com.* Software updates, including the latest RPM version of Samba, can be accessed by FTP at *updates.redhat.com.* Red Hat also has user discussion lists where you can get help with any Red Hat–specific problems.

Caldera OpenLinux

Caldera has a Web site at *www.caldera.com* that includes a great deal of OpenLinux-specific information as well as general Linux information. It includes a searchable knowledge base at *support.caldera.com* that has many Samba-related documents, including several Samba-specific technical guides. Caldera offers a great deal of Samba support, including a Samba solution guide. The Caldera users discussion group is a good source for technical information and includes a number of Linux experts as regular contributors.

Subscription information can be found at *www.caldera.com/support/forums.* It is one of the best Linux discussion groups on the Internet.

Debian GNU/Linux

The Debian Web site at *www.debian.org* includes links to the latest versions of the Debian software and documentation. There are also links to subscribing to the discussion list and the discussion list archives. There is a great deal of Debian-specific information on this site, probably everything you'll need to answer any questions about Debian.

Progeny is a Debian distribution that offers commercial support. Progeny was founded by Ian Murdock; he was also the founder of Debian GNU/Linux. Progeny is offering a number of commercial products along with its customized distribution of Debian, including commercial support services. Progeny can be found on the Web at *www.progeny.com.*

Other Linux Sites

The following list includes sites that have information about Linux in general or specific components of Linux.

www.linuxdoc.org   The Linux Documentation Project is the most complete collection available of Linux guides, how-to documents, FAQs, manual pages, and other information about Linux. This is probably the single most comprehensive site for Linux-related documents on the Web.

www.freshmeat.net   Freshmeat is the primary index of open source software available on the Internet. The listings are updated daily. If you are looking for Linux software, this is the place to start.

linuxkb.cheek.com   The Linux Knowledge Base is a searchable collection of Linux-related documents, the "technical Linux info site for technical Linux people."

www.linux.org   Linux Online is a clearinghouse for everything related to Linux. Linux Online includes links to software, FAQs, the Linux Documentation Project, and much more.

howto.tucows.com   The Tucows Linux help center includes most of what is available from the Linux Documentation Project plus reviews of selections of Linux software.

www.linuxnewbie.org   Many Linux-related documents on the Linux Newbie site have been rewritten to make them easier for new Linux users to understand.

sourceforge.net   SourceForge is a site for open source software developers.

www.li.org   Linux International is a nonprofit association of groups, corporations, and others organizations that promote Linux.

www.linuxhq.com   The Linux Headquarters site has complete information about the Linux kernel development, including a searchable archive of the Linux kernel discussion list.

www.firstlinux.com   First Linux is a site for beginners.

www.linuxnow.com   Linux Now is another site with Linux documents and links. It calls itself the most complete Linux reference on the Internet.

www.kde.org   KDE is the home page for the K Desktop Environment, a powerful graphical desktop environment for Linux.

www.gnome.org   GNOME is the home page for the Gnome Project, a graphical desktop environment for Linux.

www.xfree86.org   The XFree86 Project produces the free X Window System run on most Linux systems. This is the software that runs behind desktop environments like KDE and GNOME and makes the graphical desktop possible on Linux systems.

www.openssl.org   This is the Web site for the open source Secure Sockets Layer (OpenSSL) project. SSL is required for secure use of Webmin.

www.openssh.org   OpenSSH is a free version of the SSH protocol suite of network connectivity tools. It replaces telnet, rlogin, FTP, and other such programs that transmit data across the Internet in an insecure, unencrypted format, with a secure, encrypted connection.

www.toms.net/rb/   The emergency backup disk, tomsrtbt, stands for "Tom's floppy which has a root filesystem and is also bootable." This is the best emergency backup disk for Linux systems. Requires expert knowledge of Linux to use.

www.usenix.org/sage   The System Administrators' Guild (SAGE) is an organization that provides resources for system administrators.

Commercial Support

There are a number of commercial sources of support for Samba, and new ones are opening all the time. In addition to those listed here, many companies that provide support for Linux systems also include Samba support as part of their services.

www.valinux.com   VA Linux Systems, a complete provider of Linux systems and support, has several Samba developers on its staff, including Andrew Tridgell, the original developer of Samba and the lead developer of Samba 3.0, and Jeremy Allison, the lead developer for Samba 2.2.

www.linuxcare.com Linuxcare is a commercial provider of Linux technical support.

www.questionexchange.com Question Exchange is an online help desk where Linux users can ask questions and get answers, for a fee. Past questions, with answers, can be found through a search of the site.

Publications

There are many Linux-related publications on the Web. Following are a few of them.

www.linuxjournal.com The first Linux magazine, *Linux Journal* is available on the Web as well as in a printed version. The magazine has an emphasis on technical articles.

www.linuxworld.com A Web-only publication that is regularly updated, *LinuxWorld* is also the sponsor of the LinuxWorld Expo.

www.linux-mag.com Available in print and on the Web, *Linux Magazine* includes both general and technical articles.

www.linuxfocus.org *Linux Focus* is the only multilingual magazine on Linux. It is Web-based and available in English, French, German, Spanish, Dutch, Russian, and Turkish. A completely volunteer-based publication with irregular publication dates, it averages about six issues a year.

www.linuxgzaette.com *Linux Gazette* is a Web-only publication published by the publishers of the *Linux Journal*.

www.lwn.com *Linux Weekly News* is a weekly Webzine.

www.linuxtoday.com *Linux Today* offers daily news about Linux.

www.debianplanet.org *Debian Planet* is a Webzine for Debian GNU/Linux users.

www.linuxorbit.com *Linux Orbit* is another Linux-oriented Webzine.

Linux Backup Procedures

Backups are essential for all network servers. Backing up a Samba server is in many ways similar to backing up a Windows server. In fact, if you already have a backup system in place, it should be a simple matter to add the Samba server to your central system backup.

There are a few steps to take before that can be done, however. Neither Samba nor Linux has a Backup Operators group like the one found on Windows servers. Something similar can be created that will allow a backup of the Samba server from a Windows system by creating a backup operators group that has administrator access to a specific share.

There are some limitations to this approach. The Windows backup software may not properly save the user and group ownership and permission rights because of the differences between the ways Linux and Windows systems handle these rights. Before you make the final decision to back up the Samba server from a Windows system, make sure to fully test the backup, including restoration of files from the Windows-based backup. Make sure that a reliable and usable backup is being made. If all the files are being backed up, but the user information and access rights are lost, then the backup is not really usable. Such a backup would require you to manually go through and reset user and group permissions for every file and directory, which can involve an unacceptable amount of time and may not be totally accurate.

In that case, a Linux-based backup is necessary.

What to Back Up

Whether you use a Windows-based backup or a Linux-based backup, the first step is to decide what must be backed up.

The primary purpose of a backup is to make a copy of any files that can't be easily restored from another source. The most important files to back up on a Samba server are usually the files found in the users' home directories as well as in the shared directories. These are data files that are frequently changed and which are not easily replaced if lost.

This is data from the system administrator's perspective. It can include anything that has been saved to a share on the Samba server, including applications.

Also essential to back up on a Samba server are the Samba configuration files, including the main configuration file, *smb.conf*, as well as the Samba user file, *smbpasswd*.

Additionally, the Linux configuration files should be backed up.

Other files that might be included with a backup are any additional, nonstandard applications that are installed on the Samba server, the Linux logs (which might be useful if you are trying to troubleshoot a failed server), and the installed package information files for the Linux server.

There is no need to create a backup copy of system files; these can be restored from the Linux distribution CD-ROM. As for a full backup of the system, that might be done once, but it is usually unnecessary. Full backups take a long time and require greater resources, such as multiple tapes on a tape backup system, for something that is of limited use at most. Some contend a full backup is of no use at all since operating systems are hardware specific and usually must be installed (not recovered from a tape) on any failed system.

These directories should be backed up on a Linux-based Samba server:

```
/home
/srv
/etc
/usr/local
/var/log
/var/lib
```

This recommendation assumes that user home directories are in */home* and that the Samba shares are all set up in */srv*. If you've used different directories, such as */exports,* which is often found on UNIX systems instead of */srv,* then those should be backed up.

For Red Hat, Caldera, and Debian, the Samba configuration files are in */etc,* as are all of the Linux configuration files. On systems that use Samba in its default configuration, the files are in */usr/local/samba/lib*. The entire */usr/local* directory is where added software is normally installed. The */var/log* directory is where system logs are kept, and the */var/lib* is where the record of the installed packages is kept, along with other information about the state of various software packages installed on the system.

On Debian systems, the */var/backups* and */var/cache/apt* directories should also be backed up.

All the other directories on the Linux server do not need to be part of regular backups.

Backing Up from a Windows System

To back up the Samba server from a Windows-based backup system, start by creating a backup group on the Samba server and add all the users who will handle backups. Each entry must include the username used to access the Samba server from the Windows backup system.

For backups that are part of individual shares on the Samba server, the backup group can be added as Admin users in the share definition.

Add Backup Operators to a Share

When you want to add backup operators to a share—for example, if you have a file share named "finances" on the Samba server—open the share in SWAT. In the Advanced View, go to Admin Users in the Security options section and add the backups group, which for this example is named "backups":

```
admin users = @backups
```

The group name can be any group name you've chosen. There is nothing special about the group name "backups" on a Samba server or a Linux system.

The Admin users are given full administrator access to the share, which will also allow you to do a full backup of the share from a Windows system.

This approach can be used for backing up user data files, but it will not give you access to Linux files that should also be backed up. For that, you can either use a Linux backup solution or use one of two methods that will let you also back up the Linux files:

- Create special backup shares for each of the Linux directories that will be backed up from the Windows backup system.
- Use a combined Linux-Windows solution to create a special backup directory that is updated by tools on the Linux system and then backed up on the Windows backup system.

Create Separate Backup Shares

For each of the directories that are to be backed up, a special limited-access share can be created. This share can then be backed up by the Windows backup system.

If you don't already have one, create a group for backup operators. To set up a backup share for */homes,* for example, that can be used to back up all users' home directories on the Samba server, open SWAT and create a new share called HomesBAK or any other name that you prefer. Then secure the share and restrict access to the Backup Operators group using the following settings. In the Hosts Allow section, enter the IP address of the Windows system that is used for running backups:

```
path = /home
read only = no
valid users = @backups
admin users = @backups
hosts allow = 192.168.0.55
browseable = no
dos filetimes = yes
```

This creates a share that gives full administrative access to a restricted set of users—the backups group—from only one workstation, that being the Windows system being used for backups.

Shares are needed for each directory, in addition to */home: /srv, /etc, /usr/local, /var/log,* and */var/lib.* Then each share can be backed up by the Windows backup system.

A Linux-Windows Solution

A second approach is to create a combined Linux-Windows solution. This is the most flexible and secure approach.

Create a separate directory for storing backups, preferably on a separate hard drive on the Linux server. There is more on using a separate hard drive—a snapshot partition—for backups in the following section on Linux-based backups.

All of the files that are to be backed up on a daily basis can be copied to the snapshot partition. This can be done using Linux backup tools like rsync, as outlined in the section on Linux-based backups.

A Samba share can then be created for the snapshot partition. This single share can then be backed up from the Windows-based backup system. This share is set up in a way that is similar to creating separate backup shares, described earlier. For a snapshot partition that is mounted as */backups,* for example, open SWAT and create a new share called "backups" or any other name that you prefer. Then secure the share, restricting access to the Backup Operators group and the IP address of the Windows system that is used for running backups:

```
path = /backups
read only = no
valid users = @backups
admin users = @backups
hosts allow = 192.168.0.55
browseable = no
dos filetimes = yes
```

This share can then be backed up regular by the Windows backup system.

Backing Up from a Linux System

A Linux-based backup will be just as good as a Windows-based backup and even has some advantages. One advantage is that there is never any problem with maintaining file locations as well as user and group ownership and access permissions on a properly created Linux backup of a Linux system. That's because there's no Linux-to-Windows-and-back-again translation going on.

Several tools included with every Linux distribution can be used to create backups: tar, rsync, cpio, and dump. There are others as well, but those are the most commonly used. There are also commercial backup programs, such as BRU from Enhanced Software Technologies at *http://www.estinc.com,* that offer point-and-click simplicity to Linux backups.

Tar

Although tar (the Tape ARchive utility) isn't the fanciest backup software, it has been around a long time and is quite reliable. It creates a backup archive that can be accessed not just from the system it was created on, but from any Linux system, any UNIX system, or even any Windows system. It is almost impossible to lose any data saved with tar. The only feature tar lacks is a searchable index or log of its contents.

Rsync

The remote synchronization (rsync) tool is designed as a remote copy, or synchronization, program. It was developed by Andrew Tridgell, the same developer who started Samba. Rsync can be used to efficiently replicate files from on system to another or from one directory to another. It is not a true backup system, but it can be an effective backup tool. Rsync is very fast and efficient, automatically implementing incremental updates.

Cpio

Though the copy-in, copy-out (cpio) utility is similar to tar, it is more complex to use. There is little difference between the features of the GNU cpio and the GNU tar that ship with all Linux distributions.

Dump

The dump tool backs up file systems, not specific files. Because it accesses the internal structure of the file system, a specific version of dump is required for each file system. The dump utility is very efficient, but has some limitations. Separate backups must be kept for each partition, and the backup archive that is created may not be accessible from another system.

To back up the systems I set up, I use rsync and tar. I use rsync to replicate the directories that must be backed up onto a separate snapshot partition. These backup files are then easy to access for any quick file recovery that may be necessary. I use tar for weekly backups of the snapshot partition onto tapes as well as for monthly, quarterly, and yearly backups.

Snapshot Partitions

ATA hard disk drives are inexpensive, especially when compared to the cost of other backup systems. ATA drives can hold up to 80 gigabytes, more than any but the most expensive tape backup systems.

A separate ATA hard drive can be installed on any system and used for daily snapshots of essential files, all the files that should be backed up. Although this type of snapshot partition is not a true filesystem snapshot, such as the snapshot created on a tape by the dump program, it is more flexible and convenient.

Tape drives are slow and inflexible. Restoring files from tape can be a lengthy and involved process, with long lags while the tape advances to find the requested files. A snapshot partition gives you instant access, providing a copy of any file that is at most one day old.

Rsync, with its efficient incremental updating capabilities, can be used for daily updates of the snapshot partition. The program is included with most Linux distributions. It can also be downloaded from the Internet at *http://rsync.samba.org.*

An example of using rsync to create the snapshot follows. If the backup disk drive to be used as the snapshot partition is mounted as */backups,* this command would create a snapshot of the */home* directory onto the backup partition:

```
rsync -a --delete /home /backups/
```

The -a option creates an archive; the --delete option tells rsync to delete any files in the archive that no longer exist in the originating directory. The command can be put into a script that is run daily by Linux's cron scheduler. Use a script something like this that is saved in the */etc/cron.daily* directory on the Samba server:

```
#!/bin/sh
#
# back up main files daily
#
PATH=/usr/local/bin:/usr/bin:/bin export PATH
```

```
rsync -a --delete /home /backups/
rsync -a --delete /srv /backups/
rsync -a --delete /etc /backups/
rsync -a --delete /usr/local /backups/
rsync -a --delete /var/log /backups/
rsync -a --delete /var/lib /backups/
```

Make sure that the script is executable. This can be done with this command:

```
chmod 755 /etc/cron.daily/backup.daily
```

A variation on this, if you have the extra disk space, is to create separate snapshots for each day of the week. This script will do that:

```
#!/bin/sh
#
# back up main files daily
#
PATH=/usr/local/bin:/usr/bin:/bin
DAY='date +%A_
export PATH DAY

rsync -a --delete /home /backups/$DAY
rsync -a --delete /srv /backups/$DAY
rsync -a --delete /etc /backups/$DAY
rsync -a --delete /usr/local /backups/$DAY
rsync -a --delete /var/log /backups/$DAY
rsync -a --delete /var/lib /backups/$DAY
```

When recovering a file from the backup, you can use the Linux Copy command, but make sure to use the -a parameter, which preserves user ownership and permissions. For example, use this command to restore the file *letter.txt* from backup:

```
cp -a /backups/home/jhenry/letter.txt /home/jhenry/letter.txt
```

Back Up to Tape with Tar

The tar backup program stores files in an archive on a tape. The tar utility combines a group of files into a single file. The resulting file has a *.tar* extension.

The GNU tar utility that is included with Linux can compress files as well as archive them. These files have an extension of *tar.gz* and are comparable to files that have been compressed with WinZip. Most Windows compression utilities, including WinZip, can open (untar) a tar file.

While tar can compress files, it is not generally a good idea to compress essential backups because any compression errors can make the whole tar file unusable.

The tar utility was designed to put archives onto tape, but it can also be used to create archive files that are saved to disk or to another backup medium such as writable CDs.

The backup plan described here is only one of many possibilities, although it is a thorough backup plan with more flexibility than most. For other backup plans, consult a good book on Linux system administration.

Creating a Tape Backup

To create a tape archive of the snapshot partition, use these commands:

```
mt -f /dev/st0 rewind
tar cpf /dev/nst0 --label="backup created on 'date +%Y-%m-%d'" /backups
```

The mt command refers to the magnetic tape utility on Linux. The command tells Linux to rewind the tape. The device name */dev/st0* is the standard rewinding mode for a SCSI tape drive. The nonrewinding device name is */dev/nst0.*

The c option specifies that an archive is being created. The p option preserves permissions. The f option indicates that the next parameter is the name of the device being written or the name of the archive file.

Here is a script that will create a weekly tape backup:

```
#!/bin/sh
#
# back up main files daily
#
PATH=/usr/bin:/bin
export PATH

mt -f /dev/nst0 rewind
tar cpf /dev/st0 --label="backup created on 'date +%Y-%m-%d'" /backups

mt -f /dev/st0 rewoffl
```

The last line rewinds and then ejects the tape. Put the script in */etc/cron. weekly* and make it executable. If the script is named *backup.weekly,* use this command to make it executable:

```
chmod 755 /etc/cron.weekly/backup.weekly
```

A monthly and quarterly tape backup should also be made. It can be done using the same procedures for creating a weekly tape backup. At minimum, with weekly, monthly, and quarterly tapes, your backups should go back one year.

Restoring from a Tape Backup

As important as making regular backups is the ability to recover files from the backups. The snapshot partition makes daily recovery a simple task, but going back more than a week requires recovery from a tape.

The xp parameters will extract a tar archive and preserve permissions.

To restore files from tape, make sure you are logged in as root, the administrator account on Linux. The restoration will overwrite any existing files. To restore all the files from the tar archive to the snapshot partition mounted as *backups,* use the following commands:

```
cd /
tar xpf /dev/st0
```

This restores the files from the tape in exactly the same location as when they were saved onto the tape. All existing files will be overwritten without any warning. If you don't want to overwrite existing files, you can restore specific files by adding the name of the file you want to extract.

To restore a specific file from an archive on tape, for example, user jhenry's *letter.txt* file, use the following commands:

```
cd /
tar xpf /dev/st0 /backups/home/jhenry/letter.txt
```

If you just want to see what files are on the tape, use this command:

```
tar tf /dev/st0
```

The GNU General Public License

Following is a complete copy of the GNU General Public License that covers both Samba and Linux.

Text of the License

Version 2, June 1991

Copyright © 1989, 1991 Free Software Foundation, Inc., 59 Temple Place, Suite 330, Boston, MA 02111-1307 USA
Everyone is permitted to copy and distribute verbatim copies of this license document, but changing it is not allowed.

Preamble

The licenses for most software are designed to take away your freedom to share and change it. By contrast, the GNU General Public License is intended to guarantee your freedom to share and change free software—to make sure the software is free for all its users. This General Public License applies to most of the Free Software Foundation's software and to any other program whose authors commit to using it. (Some other Free Software Foundation software is covered by the GNU Library General Public License instead.) You can apply it to your programs, too.

When we speak of free software, we are referring to freedom, not price. Our General Public Licenses are designed to make sure that you have the freedom to distribute copies of free software (and charge for this service if you wish), that you receive source code or can get it if you want it, that you can change the software or use pieces of it in new free programs; and that you know you can do these things.

To protect your rights, we need to make restrictions that forbid anyone to deny you these rights or to ask you to surrender the rights. These restrictions translate to certain responsibilities for you if you distribute copies of the software, or if you modify it.

For example, if you distribute copies of such a program, whether gratis or for a fee, you must give the recipients all the rights that you have. You must make sure that they, too, receive or can get the source code. And you must show them these terms so they know their rights.

We protect your rights with two steps: (1) copyright the software, and (2) offer you this license which gives you legal permission to copy, distribute, and/or modify the software.

Also, for each author's protection and ours, we want to make certain that everyone understands that there is no warranty for this free software. If the software is modified by someone else and passed on, we want its recipients to know that what they have is not the original, so that any problems introduced by others will not reflect on the original authors' reputations.

Finally, any free program is threatened constantly by software patents. We wish to avoid the danger that redistributors of a free program will individually obtain patent licenses, in effect making the program proprietary. To prevent this, we have made it clear that any patent must be licensed for everyone's free use or not licensed at all.

The precise terms and conditions for copying, distribution, and modification follow.

GNU GENERAL PUBLIC LICENSE TERMS AND CONDITIONS FOR COPYING, DISTRIBUTION AND MODIFICATION

0. This License applies to any program or other work that contains a notice placed by the copyright holder saying it may be distributed under the terms of this General Public License. The "Program", below, refers to any such program or work, and a "work based on the Program" means either the Program or any derivative work under copyright law: that is to say, a work containing the Program or a portion of it, either verbatim or with modifications and/or translated into another language. (Hereinafter, translation is included without limitation in the term "modification.") Each licensee is addressed as "you."

   Activities other than copying, distribution, and modification are not covered by this License; they are outside its scope. The act of running the Program is not restricted, and the output from the Program is covered only if its contents constitute a work based on the Program (independent of having been made by running the Program). Whether that is true depends on what the Program does.

1. You may copy and distribute verbatim copies of the Program's source code as you receive it, in any medium, provided that you conspicuously and appropriately publish on each copy an appropriate copyright notice and disclaimer of warranty; keep intact all the notices that refer to this License and to the absence of any warranty; and give any other recipients of the Program a copy of this License along with the Program.

   You may charge a fee for the physical act of transferring a copy, and you may at your option offer warranty protection in exchange for a fee.

2. You may modify your copy or copies of the Program or any portion of it, thus forming a work based on the Program, and copy and distribute such modifica-

tions or work under the terms of Section 1 above, provided that you also meet all of these conditions:

a. You must cause the modified files to carry prominent notices stating that you changed the files and the date of any change.

b. You must cause any work that you distribute or publish, that in whole or in part contains or is derived from the Program or any part thereof, to be licensed as a whole at no charge to all third parties under the terms of this License.

c. If the modified program normally reads commands interactively when run, you must cause it, when started running for such interactive use in the most ordinary way, to print or display an announcement including an appropriate copyright notice and a notice that there is no warranty (or else, saying that you provide a warranty) and that users may redistribute the program under these conditions, and telling the user how to view a copy of this License. (Exception: if the Program itself is interactive but does not normally print such an announcement, your work based on the Program is not required to print an announcement.)

These requirements apply to the modified work as a whole. If identifiable sections of that work are not derived from the Program, and can be reasonably considered independent and separate works in themselves, then this License, and its terms, do not apply to those sections when you distribute them as separate works. But when you distribute the same sections as part of a whole which is a work based on the Program, the distribution of the whole must be on the terms of this License, whose permissions for other licensees extend to the entire whole, and thus to each and every part regardless of who wrote it.

Thus, it is not the intent of this section to claim rights or contest your rights to work written entirely by you; rather, the intent is to exercise the right to control the distribution of derivative or collective works based on the Program.

In addition, mere aggregation of another work not based on the Program with the Program (or with a work based on the Program) on a volume of a storage or distribution medium does not bring the other work under the scope of this License.

3. You may copy and distribute the Program (or a work based on it, under Section 2) in object code or executable form under the terms of Sections 1 and 2 above provided that you also do one of the following:

a. Accompany it with the complete corresponding machine-readable source code, which must be distributed under the terms of Sections 1 and 2 above on a medium customarily used for software interchange; or,

b. Accompany it with a written offer, valid for at least three years, to give any third party, for a charge no more than your cost of physically performing source distribution, a complete machine-readable copy of the corresponding source code, to be distributed under the terms of Sections 1 and 2 above on a medium customarily used for software interchange; or,

c. Accompany it with the information you received as to the offer to distribute corresponding source code. (This alternative is allowed only for noncommercial distribution and only if you received the program in object code or executable form with such an offer, in accord with Subsection b above.)

The source code for a work means the preferred form of the work for making modifications to it. For an executable work, complete source code means all the source code for all modules it contains, plus any associated interface definition files, plus the scripts used to control compilation and installation of the executable. However, as a special exception, the source code distributed need not include anything that is normally distributed (in either source or binary form) with the major components (compiler, kernel, and so on) of the operating system on which the executable runs, unless that component itself accompanies the executable.

If distribution of executable or object code is made by offering access to copy from a designated place, then offering equivalent access to copy the source code from the same place counts as distribution of the source code, even though third parties are not compelled to copy the source along with the object code.

4. You may not copy, modify, sublicense, or distribute the Program except as expressly provided under this License. Any attempt otherwise to copy, modify, sublicense or distribute the Program is void, and will automatically terminate your rights under this License. However, parties who have received copies, or rights, from you under this License will not have their licenses terminated so long as such parties remain in full compliance.

5. You are not required to accept this License, since you have not signed it. However, nothing else grants you permission to modify or distribute the Program or its derivative works. These actions are prohibited by law if you do not accept this License. Therefore, by modifying or distributing the Program (or any work based on the Program), you indicate your acceptance of this License to do so, and all its terms and conditions for copying, distributing or modifying the Program or works based on it.

6. Each time you redistribute the Program (or any work based on the Program), the recipient automatically receives a license from the original licensor to copy, distribute or modify the Program subject to these terms and conditions. You may not impose any further restrictions on the recipients' exercise of the rights granted herein. You are not responsible for enforcing compliance by third parties to this License.

7. If, as a consequence of a court judgment or allegation of patent infringement or for any other reason (not limited to patent issues), conditions are imposed on you (whether by court order, agreement or otherwise) that contradict the conditions of this License, they do not excuse you from the conditions of this License. If you cannot distribute so as to satisfy simultaneously your obligations under this License and any other pertinent obligations, then as a consequence you may not distribute the Program at all. For example, if a patent license would not permit royalty-free redistribution of the Program by all those who receive copies directly or indirectly through you, then the only way you could satisfy both it and this License would be to refrain entirely from distribution of the Program.

If any portion of this section is held invalid or unenforceable under any particular circumstance, the balance of the section is intended to apply and the section as a whole is intended to apply in other circumstances.

It is not the purpose of this section to induce you to infringe any patents or other property right claims or to contest validity of any such claims; this section has the sole purpose of protecting the integrity of the free software distribution system, which is implemented by public license practices. Many people have made generous contributions to the wide range of software distributed through that system in reliance on consistent application of that system; it is up to the author/donor to decide if he or she is willing to distribute software through any other system and a licensee cannot impose that choice.

This section is intended to make thoroughly clear what is believed to be a consequence of the rest of this License.

8. If the distribution and/or use of the Program is restricted in certain countries either by patents or by copyrighted interfaces, the original copyright holder who places the Program under this License may add an explicit geographical distribution limitation excluding those countries, so that distribution is permitted only in or among countries not thus excluded. In such case, this License incorporates the limitation as if written in the body of this License.

9. The Free Software Foundation may publish revised and/or new versions of the General Public License from time to time. Such new versions will be similar in spirit to the present version, but may differ in detail to address new problems or concerns.

    Each version is given a distinguishing version number. If the Program specifies a version number of this License which applies to it and "any later version," you have the option of following the terms and conditions either of that version or of any later version published by the Free Software Foundation. If the Program does not specify a version number of this License, you may choose any version ever published by the Free Software Foundation.

10. If you wish to incorporate parts of the Program into other free programs whose distribution conditions are different, write to the author to ask for permission. For software that is copyrighted by the Free Software Foundation, write to the Free Software Foundation; we sometimes make exceptions for this. Our decision will be guided by the two goals of preserving the free status of all derivatives of our free software and of promoting the sharing and reuse of software generally.

    No warranty

11. BECAUSE THE PROGRAM IS LICENSED FREE OF CHARGE, THERE IS NO WARRANTY FOR THE PROGRAM, TO THE EXTENT PERMITTED BY APPLICABLE LAW. EXCEPT WHEN OTHERWISE STATED IN WRITING THE COPYRIGHT HOLDERS AND/OR OTHER PARTIES PROVIDE THE PROGRAM "AS IS" WITHOUT WARRANTY OF ANY KIND, EITHER EXPRESSED OR IMPLIED, INCLUDING, BUT NOT LIMITED TO, THE IMPLIED WARRANTIES OF MERCHANTABILITY AND FITNESS FOR A PARTICULAR PURPOSE. THE ENTIRE RISK AS TO THE QUALITY AND PERFOR-

MANCE OF THE PROGRAM IS WITH YOU. SHOULD THE PROGRAM PROVE DEFECTIVE, YOU ASSUME THE COST OF ALL NECESSARY SERVICING, REPAIR, OR CORRECTION.

12. IN NO EVENT UNLESS REQUIRED BY APPLICABLE LAW OR AGREED TO IN WRITING WILL ANY COPYRIGHT HOLDER, OR ANY OTHER PARTY WHO MAY MODIFY AND/OR REDISTRIBUTE THE PROGRAM AS PERMITTED ABOVE, BE LIABLE TO YOU FOR DAMAGES, INCLUDING ANY GENERAL, SPECIAL, INCIDENTAL, OR CONSEQUENTIAL DAMAGES ARISING OUT OF THE USE OR INABILITY TO USE THE PROGRAM (INCLUDING BUT NOT LIMITED TO LOSS OF DATA OR DATA BEING RENDERED INACCURATE OR LOSSES SUSTAINED BY YOU OR THIRD PARTIES OR A FAILURE OF THE PROGRAM TO OPERATE WITH ANY OTHER PROGRAMS), EVEN IF SUCH HOLDER OR OTHER PARTY HAS BEEN ADVISED OF THE POSSIBILITY OF SUCH DAMAGES.

End of Terms and Conditions

APPLYING THESE TERMS TO YOUR NEW PROGRAMS

If you develop a new program, and you want it to be of the greatest possible use to the public, the best way to achieve this is to make it free software which everyone can redistribute and change under these terms.

To do so, attach the following notices to the program. It is safest to attach them to the start of each source file to most effectively convey the exclusion of warranty; and each file should have at least the "copyright" line and a pointer to where the full notice is found.

```
one line to give the program's name and a brief idea of what it does.
Copyright (C) year name of author
```

This program is free software; you can redistribute it and/or modify it under the terms of the GNU General Public License as published by the Free Software Foundation; either version 2 of the License, or (at your option) any later version.

This program is distributed in the hope that it will be useful, but WITHOUT ANY WARRANTY; without even the implied warranty of MERCHANTABILITY or FITNESS FOR A PARTICULAR PURPOSE. See the GNU General Public License for more details.

You should have received a copy of the GNU General Public License along with this program; if not, write to the Free Software Foundation, Inc., 59 Temple Place, Suite 330, Boston, MA 02111-1307 USA

Also add information on how to contact you by electronic and paper mail.

If the program is interactive, make it output a short notice like this when it starts in an interactive mode:

```
Gnomovision version 69, Copyright (C) year name of author
Gnomovision comes with ABSOLUTELY NO WARRANTY; for details, type "show
w". This is free software, and you are welcome to redistribute it under
certain conditions; type "show c" for details.
```

The hypothetical commands "show w" and "show c" should show the appropriate parts of the General Public License. Of course, the commands you use may be called something other than "show w" and "show c"; they could even be mouse clicks or menu items—whatever suits your program.

You should also get your employer (if you work as a programmer) or your school, if any, to sign a copyright disclaimer for the program, if necessary. Here is a sample; alter the names.

Yoyodyne, Inc., hereby disclaims all copyright interest in the program "Gnomovision" (which makes passes at compilers) written by James Hacker.

```
signature of Ty Coon, 1 April 1989 Ty Coon, President of Vice
```

This General Public License does not permit incorporating your program into proprietary programs. If your program is a subroutine library, you may consider it more useful to permit linking proprietary applications with the library. If this is what you want to do, use the GNU Library General Public License instead of this License.

A

Access, 160–67
  Samba print shares, from Windows, 96–97
  Samba server, using net utility, 162–63
  Samba shares, using the Net command, 163
  SWAT, 34
Addprinter Command, 292
Add Printer Wizard, 96–97, 130–31
Add Share Command, 301
Add User Script, 296
Admin Users option, 69–70, 284
Allison, Jeremy, 325
Allow Trusted Domains option, 281
Alternate Permissions option, 281
Announce As setting, 288
Announce Version setting, 288
Apache Webserver module, Webmin, 209
Application sharing, 84
ASCII character set, 122
AT Attachment (ATA) drives, 233–35
Authentication module, 205
Automatic printer services, 98–102
  configuring Samba for, 98–100
    adding a printer administrator, 98
    creating a printers directory, 98–99
    creating a prints share, 99
    setting permissions, 99–100
    installing printers/drivers, 100–102
Available option, 313, 319
  homes share, 56

B

Backing up, 225
Backslash, in Windows, 212
Backup procedures, Linux, 327–35
Bash, 211–12
  command completion, 212
  command history, 212
  compared to DOS, 212–13
Basic group share, 68–69
  short version, 75–76

Basic public directory, 78
Binaries, for Samba, 21
BIND DNS Server module, Webmin, 210
Bind Interfaces Only option, 280
Blocking Locks option, 73, 299, 312
Block mode, 235
Bootup module, defined Shutdown module, 201
Bootup options, Linux, managing, 201–2
Browseable option, 73, 311, 318
  homes share, 56
  Printers configuration, 94
Browse list, 161
Browse List option, 297
Browse options, 297–98, 311, 318–19
  Browseable, 311, 318
  Browse List option, 297
  Domain Master option, 297
  Enhanced Browsing option, 297
  Lm Announce option, 297
  Lm Interval option, 297
  Local Master option, 297
  Os Level option, 297
  Preferred Master option, 297
Browser elections, 160
Browsing, 160–67
  options, 73
BSD, 93
Bus mastering, 235

C

Case Sensitive option, 293, 310
Case sensitivity, Linux, 11
cat command, 218
cd command, 217
CD-ROMs, sharing in Samba, 80–82
Certificate Authority (CA) in SSL, 114
Change Notify Timeout option, 249, 289
Change Share Command, 301–2
Character Set option, 124, 293
chkdsk command, 219–20
CIFS/9000, 5
CIFS (Common Internet File System), 3

Client Code Page option, 123, 279
Client tools, 275–76
  rpcclient utility, 275
  smbclient utility, 276
  smbmnt utility, 276
  smbmount utility, 276
  smbprint utility, 276
  smbspool utility, 276
  smbtar utility, 276
  smbumount utility, 276
Clockticks, 243
Code Page Directory option, 123, 279
Coding System option, 124, 278
Command completion, Bash, 212
Command history, Bash, 212
Comment setting, Shares, 306
Comments option, homes share, 54
Common Internet File System (CIFS), 134
Compiling Samba, 23–26
Configuration files, 29
  lmhosts, 29
  smb.conf, 29
  smbpasswd, 29
  smbusers, 29
Configuration module, Webmin, 209
Configuration options, 277–315
  Globals page of SWAT in Advanced View, 277–80
  base options, 278–80
  browse options, 297–98
  domain options, 295–96
  filename handling options, 293–95
  locking options, 299–300
  logging options, 286–87
  logon options, 296–97
  miscellaneous options, 301–4
  printing options, 291–93
  protocol options, 287–89
  security options, 280–86
  SSL options, 300–301
  tuning options, 289–91
  VFS options, 304–5
  Winbind options, 305
  WINS options, 298
  Printers page of SWAT in Advanced View, 316–19
  base options, 315–16

Configuration options
  Printers page of SWAT in Advanced View (*continued*)
    browse options, 318
    logging options, 316
    miscellaneous options, 319
    printing options, 317–18
    security options, 316
    tuning options, 316–17
  Shares page of SWAT in Advanced View, 305–15
    base options, 305–6
    browse options, 311
    filename handling options, 309–11
    locking options, 312–13
    logging options, 309
    miscellaneous options, 313–15
    security options, 306–9
    tuning options, 309
    VFS options, 315–16
Configure Automatic UNIX and Samba User Synchronization link, 206
Connection-checking utilities, 147–50
  ipconfig utility, 148–49
  nbstat utility, 150
  netstat utility, 149
  net utility, 150
  ping utility, 147–48
  tracert utility, 149
  winipcfg utility, 148
Convert UNIX Users to Samba Users link, 206
Copy files to home directory? option, 205
cpio utility, 331
Create home directory? option, 205
Create Mask option, 71, 285
Create a New Copy link, 206
Create a New File Share link, 206
Create a New Printer Share link, 206
Cross-subnet browsing, 131–32
CUPS, 93
Custom Commands module, Webmin, 210
Customizing individual printers, 94–95

▼ D

Daemons, 273–75
  Linux, 13–14
  NMBD daemon, 274
  SMB/CIFS daemon, 273–74
  WINBINDD daemon, 275
Date command, 220
Dead Time option, 43, 249–50, 289–90

Debian GNU/Linux, 21–22, 87, 93, 123, 173, 243–47
  help, 324
Debug Hires Timestamp setting, 287
Debug pid setting, 287
Debug uid setting, 287
Default Case setting, 310
Default Service, 302
Defragmenting drives, 15
Deleteprinter Command, 292–93
Delete Readonly option, 75, 304, 314
Delete Share Command, 302
Delete User Script, 296
Delete Veto Files option, 294, 310
Dfree Command, 302
DHCP Server module, Webmin, 210
Diagnostic utilities, 276–77
  nmblookup, 277
  smbstatus, 277
  testparm, 277
  testprns, 277
Digital Equipment Corporation (DEC), 4
dir -a command, 219
dir command, 217–18
Directories:
  defined Shutdown module, Webmin, 201
  Linux:
    creating, 219
    removing, 219
    setting up for sharing, 58–68
Directory Mask option, 71, 285
Directory Security Mask option, 285
Directory structure, Linux, 12–13
dir -l command, 222
Disk cache size, 243–44
Disk and Network Filesystems module, Webmin, 209
Disk Quotas module, Webmin, 209
Disk write caching, 242–43
Distributions, Linux, 196
DNS (Domain Name System), 135
Dns Proxy option, 298
Domain, joining, 44–45
Domain administrators, 271
Domain logon options, 272
Domain Logons, 297
Domain Master option, 297
Domain options, 295–96
  Domain Admin Group option, 295
  Domain Guest Group option, 295
  Machine Password Timeout option, 295
Dont Descend option, 75, 314
Dos Filemode option, 304, 314
Dos Filetime Resolution option, 75, 304, 315
DOS Filetimes option, 75, 304, 314–15

Drive letters, and Linux, 12–13
Dump utility, 331–32
Dynamic Host Configuration Protocol (DHCP) servers, 136

▼ E

Email help lists, 51
Emergencies, handling, in Linux, 225–26
Encrypt Passwords option, 42, 281
Engert, Kai, 113
Enhanced Browsing option, 297
Enhanced Integrated Drive Electronics (EIDE), 234
Enumports Command, 292
eServer 3.1 (Caldera), 111
Exec setting, 313, 319
Execute permission, 59–60

▼ F

Fake Directory Create Times option, 75, 304, 315
Fake Oplocks option, 312
Fax printer, setting up, 130
Fax server software, setting up, 129–30
File attributes, 246–47
File handle limits, 244
File locking options, 73–74
  Blocking Locks option, 73
  Level 2 Oplocks, 74
  Locking option, 73–74
  Oplocks option, 74
  Share Modes option, 74
  Strick Locking option, 74
File Manager module, Webmin, 210
Filename handling options, 72–73, 293–95, 309–11
  Case Sensitive option, 293, 310
  Character Set option, 293
  Default Case setting, 310
  Delete Veto Files option, 294, 310
  hidden attribute on dot files, 72
  Hide Dot Files option, 294, 310
  Hide Files option, 72, 294, 311
  Mangle Case option, 294, 310
  Mangled Map option, 295, 311
  Mangled Names option, 295, 311
  Mangled Stack option, 293
  Mangling Char option, 294, 310
  Map Archive option, 72–73, 295, 311
  Map Hidden option, 295, 311
  Map System option, 295, 311
  Preserve Case option, 293, 310
  Short Preserve Case option, 294, 310

Stat Cache option, 295
Strip Dot option, 293
Veto Files option, 72, 294, 310
Veto Oplock Files option, 294, 311
File permissions, 222-23
  Linux, 58-60
    execute permission, 59-60
    read permission, 58-59
    write permission, 59
File Share Defaults module, 206
File shares, mapping, 163-67
File system, 238-39
File system, Linux, 213-15
  key directories, 214-15
Firewalls, 224
Follow Symlinks option, 74-75, 303,
  314
Force Create Mode, 71, 285
Force Directory Mode, 71, 285
Force Directory Security Mode, 286
Force Group, 70
Force Security Mode, 285
Force User, 70
format commnad, 220
FreeBSD, 227
free command, 220
Free high-quality software, secret to,
  2-3
Free Software Foundation, 323
  GNU software license, 2-3
fstab file, 246
Fstype setting, 314
FTP Server module, Webmin, 210
Fully qualified domain name
  (FQDN), 136

▾ **G**

Getwd Cache setting, 250, 290
Gigabit Ethernet, 247
Globals, SWAT, and printer support, 92
Globals page of SWAT in Advanced
  View, 277-80
  base options, 278-80
  browse options, 297-98
  domain options, 295-96
  filename handling options, 293-95
  locking options, 299-300
  logging options, 286-87
  logon options, 296-97
  miscellaneous options, 301-4
  printing options, 291-93
  protocol options, 287-89
  security options, 280-86
  SSL options, 300-301
  tuning options, 289-91
  VFS options, 304-5
  Winbind options, 305
  WINS options, 298

GNOME, 197, 201
Gnome RPM package manager, 22
GNU General Public License, 2-3,
  323, 337-43
grep command, 220
Group share, 68-69
Guest access, adding, 79-80
Guest Account option, 284, 306, 316
  homes share, 55
Guest accounts, 42-43, 79-80
Guest Ok option, 308, 316
  homes share, 55

▾ **H**

Hardware maximization, 232-41
  AT Attachment (ATA) drives,
    233-35
  CPUs and SMP, 240-41
  file system, 238-39
  memory requirements, 239-40
  network infrastructure, 232-33
  RAID disk drive controllers,
    233-34, 237-38
  SCSI disk drives, 233-34, 236-37
Help, 321-26
  commercial sources of support,
    325-26
  complete Samba documentation,
    321
  Debian GNU/Linux, 324
  Free Software Foundation, 323
  Linux sites, 324-25
  main Samba Web page, 322
  OpenLinux (Caldera), 323-24
  publications, 326
  Red Hat Linux, 323
  Samba lists, 322-23
  Samba newsgroup, 323
  on the Web, 322-26
  Webmin, 323
Help module, Webmin, 209
Hewlett-Packard, and Samba, 5, 51
Hide Dot Files option, 294, 310
Hide Files option, 72, 294, 311
Hide Local Users option, 304
Homedir Map option, 303
Homes share, 54-58
  adding features to, 76
  Available option, 56
  Browseable option, 56
  Comments option, 54
  Guest account option, 55
  Guest OK option, 55
  Hosts Allow option, 55
  Hosts Deny option, 55
  Path option, 55
  Read Only option, 55
  securing, 56-58

Create Mask option, 58
%H Path option, 57
Valid Users option, 57-58
Host msdfs option, 305
HOSTS, 136-37
Hosts Allow option, 71-72, 286, 308,
  316
  homes share, 55
  Printers configuration, 94
Hosts Deny option, 71-72, 286, 309,
  316
  homes share, 55
  Printers configuration, 94
Hosts Equiv option, 281
*How Microsoft Ensures Virus-Free
  Software*, 7
HylaFAX, 129

▾ **I**

IBM:
  and Samba/Linux, 5
  and Samba support, 51
IDE drives, 234
Inode limits, 244-45
Integrated Drive Electronics (IDE),
  234
Interfaces option, 280
internationalization, 30, 122-26
  Character Set option, 124, 293
  Client Code Page option, 123, 279
  Code Page Directory option, 123,
    279
  Coding System option, 124, 278
  Valid Chars option, 124-26, 302
Internet, and open source develop-
  ment model, 2
Internet Services and Protocols mod-
  ule, Webmin, 210
Invalid Users option, 69, 284
ipconfig utility:
  and Windows 9x/Me configura-
    tion, 148-49
  and Windows NT configuration,
    153-54
IPCS, and encrypted passwords, 164
IPTOS_THROUGHPUT, 253
ITOS_LOWDELAY, 252

▾ **J**

Jiffies, 243

▾ **K**

KDE, 197, 201
Keepalive setting, 250, 290
Kernel Oplocks option, 299

▼ **L**

Lanman Auth option, 284
last and lastb commands, 224
Level 2 Oplocks, 74, 254, 312
Limited public directory, 78
Linux, 2–4, 227
  administrator access, 13
  backing up, 225
  backup procedures, 327–35
  bootup options, managing, 201–2
  case sensitivity of, 11
  cat command, 218
  cd command, 217
  chkdsk command, 219–20
  common device names in, 13
  common Linux questions, 13–16
  converting Microsoft text files to
      Linux text format, 49–50
  Copy files to home directory? op-
      tion, 205
  Create home directory? option,
      205
  daemons, 13–14
  Date command, 220
  defragmenting drives, 15
  dir -a command, 219
  dir command, 217–18
  directories:
    creating, 219
    removing, 219
    setting up for sharing, 58–68
  directory structure, 12–13
  distributions, understanding, 196
  and drive letters, 12–13
  emergencies, handling, 225–26
  event viewer, lack of, 15
  file contents, viewing, 218
  and file deletion, 12
  and file extensions, 12
  file permissions, 58–60
    execute permission, 59–60
    read permission, 58–59
    write permission, 59
  files:
    copying, 218–19
    deleting, 219
    renaming, 219
  file system, 213–15
    key directories, 214–15
  format commnad, 220
  and forward slash, 11
  free command, 220
  GNOME, 197
  grep command, 220
  groups, managing, 202–5
  hidden files in, 16
  and IBM, 5
  KDE, 197

links, 15
locate command, 221
ls command, 217–18
mkdir command, 219
modules, 201
more command, 218, 220
move command, 219
moving around, 217
and open source applications, 3
OpenSSL, 31
passwords, 259
primary group option, 204
recordkeeping, 225
rename command, 219
rescue boot disk, creating, 226
rm command, 219
secondary group option, 205
security tips, 221–24
  changing permissions using
      octal numbers, 223–24
  file permissions, 222–23
  firewalls/secure connections,
      224
  monitoring the system, 224
  password protection, 221–22
server, hardware requirements, 6
shared directories:
  settings for a group of users, 65
  settings for a public share, 65
  settings for a single users, 63
shortcuts, creating in, 15
stability of, 8
startup files, 14
system administration essentials,
    195–226
system registry, lack of, 14–15
tail command, 220
task manager, lack of, 14
text editors, 215–17
Time command, 220
tools, 14
updating, 21–23
  using Webmin, 22–23
user manager, lack of, 14
users, managing, 202–5
Webmin management of
      users/groups, 198–201
  expiry date option, 204
  home directory option, 204
  inactive days option, 204
  maximum days option, 204
  minimum days option, 204
  password changed option, 204
  password option, 204
  real name option, 203
  shell option, 203
  user ID option, 204
  username option, 203
  warning days option, 204

and Windows, 11–16
Xwindows:
  reasons not to use, 197–98
  and terminals, 196–97
Linux backup procedures, 327–35
  backing up from a Linux system,
      331–34
    cpio utility, 331
    dump utility, 331–32
    rsync utility, 331–32
    tar utility, 331, 334
  backing up from a Windows sys-
      tem, 329–31
    adding Backup Operators to a
        share, 329
    creating separate backup
        shares, 329–30
    Linux-Windows solution,
        330–31
  snapshot partitions, 332–33
  tape backup:
    creating, 334
    restoring, 335
    with tar utility, 333–34
  what to back up, 327–29
Linux Bootup Configuration module,
    Webmin, 210
Linux RAID module, Webmin, 210
Linux server hardware costs, 257
Linux server optimization, 241–47
  disk cache size, 243–44
  disk write caching, 242–43
  file attributes, 246–47
  file handle limits, 244
  Gigabit Ethernet, 247
  inode limits, 244–45
  TCP/IP timeout settings, 245
  TCP ports, 246
Linux sites, 324–25
Linux terminal, 211–21
  administrative rights, 211
  Bash, 211–12
    command completion, 212
    command history, 212
    compared to DOS, 212–13
    basic functions on, 217–18
    root password, 211
    root user, 211
    user's home directory, 211–12
Linux vendors, and Samba support,
    51
lists.samba.org, 51, 322
Lm Announce option, 297
lmhosts, 29, 106, 136–37
LMHOSTS Lan Manager HOSTS
      (LMHOSTS) file, 136
Lm Interval option, 297
Load Printers option, 92, 291
Local Master option, 297

`locate` command, 221
Lock Dir option, 302
Locking options, 253-55
    Blocking Locks, 299, 312
    Fake Oplocks option, 312
    Kernel Oplocks, 299
    Level 2 Oplocks, 254, 312
    Locking setting, 299, 312
    Oplock Break Wait Time setting,
        299
    Oplock Contention Limit setting,
        299, 312
    Oplocks, 253-54, 312
    Posix Locking option, 299-300,
        312
    Share Modes option, 74, 300, 313
    Strict Locking option, 74, 254-55,
        300, 313
    Write Cache Size setting, 255
Locking setting, 73-74, 299, 312
Log File option, 286
Logging options, 309, 316
Log Level option, 286
Logon Drive option, 272, 296
Logon Home option, 272, 296-97
Logon options, 296-97
    Add User Script, 296
    Delete User Script, 296
    Domain Logons, 297
    Logon Drive, 296
    Logon Home, 296-97
    Logon Path, 296
    Logon Script, 296
Logon Path option, 272, 296
Logon Script option, 272, 296
Logon scripts:
    adding, 109
    advanced, 109-11
Lppause Command, 292, 318
Lpq Cache Time, 250, 290
Lpq Command, 93, 291, 317
Lpresume Command, 292, 318
Lprm Command, 93-94, 291, 318
LPRng, 93
lpstat, 93
`ls` command, 217-18

M

McAfee Anti-Virus, 77
Machine accounts:
    adding, 270-71
    creating, 270-72
    domain administrators, 271
Machine Password Timeout option,
    295
Magic Output option, 314
Magic Script option, 314
Majordomo module, Webmin, 210

Mangle Case option, 294, 310
Mangled Map option, 295, 311
Mangled Names option, 295, 311
Mangled Stack option, 293
Mangling Char option, 294, 310
Map Archive option, 72-73, 295, 311
Map to Guest option, 282
Map Hidden option, 295, 311
Map Network Drive utility, 131
Mapping, 160-67
Map System option, 295, 311
Max Connections setting, 309
Max Disk Size setting, 250, 290
Max Log Size setting, 286-87
Max mux setting, 288
Max Open Files setting, 251, 290
Max Packet setting, 289
Max Print Jobs setting, 317
Max Protocol setting, 287
Max smbd Processes setting, 290
Max ttl setting, 289
Max Wins ttl setting, 289
Max xmit setting, 249, 289
Memory requirements, 239-40
Message Command, 302
mgetty+sendfax, 129
Microsoft Access database, sharing,
    82-83
Min Passwd Length option, 282
Min Print Space option, 317
Min Protocol setting, 288
Min Wins ttl setting, 289
Miscellaneous options, 301-4, 319
    Add Share Command, 301
    Available setting, 313, 319
    Change Share Command, 301-2
    Default Service, 302
    Delete Readonly option, 75, 304,
        314
    Delete Share Command, 302
    Dfree Command, 302
    Dont Descend option, 75, 314
    Dos Filemode option, 304, 314
    Dos Filetime Resolution option,
        304, 315
    Dos Filetimes option, 75, 304,
        314-15
    Exec setting, 313, 319
    Fake Directory Create Times op-
        tion, 75, 304, 315
    Follow Symlinks option, 74-75,
        303, 314
    Fstype setting, 314
    Hide Local Users option, 304
    Homedir Map option, 303
    Lock Dir option, 302
    Magic Output option, 314
    Magic Script option, 314
    Message Command, 302

NIS Homedir option, 303
Panic Action option, 304
Postexec setting, 313, 319
Preexec Close setting, 313
Preload option, 302
Remote Announce option, 303
Remote Browse Sync option, 303
Root Postexec setting, 313, 319
Root Preexec Close setting, 313
Root Preexec setting, 313, 319
Set Directory setting, 314
Socket Address option, 303
Source Environment option, 303
Time Offset option, 303
Valid Chars setting, 302
Volume setting, 313
Wide Links option, 255, 303, 314
Miscellaneous Options module, 206
`mkdir` command, 219
Modem, selecting, 129
Monitoring the system, 224
`more` command, 218, 220
`move` command, 219
`mt` command, 334
MySQL Database Server module,
    Webmin, 210

N

Name Resolve Order setting, 289
Name Service Switch (NSS) module,
    33
Naming services, 135-36
nbstat utility:
    and Windows 9x/Me configura-
        tion, 150
    and Windows NT configuration,
        154
NetBIOS, and TCP/IP networking,
    133-36
Netbios Aliases option, 279
NetBIOS Extended User Interface
    (NetBEUI), 134-35, 173
Netbios Name option, 279
Netbios Scope, 280
netdiag utility, Windows 2000 config-
    uration, 159
Netlogon share, adding, 105
netstat utility:
    and Windows 9x/Me configura-
        tion, 149
    and Windows NT configuration,
        154
net utility:
    accessing a Samba server using,
        162-63
    commands, 164
    and Windows 9x/Me configura-
        tion, 150

net utility (*continued*)
  and Windows 2000 configuration, 159
  and Windows NT configuration, 154
Network Attached Storage (NAS) systems, 53
Network Basic Input/Output System (NetBIOS) over TCP/IP (NetBT), 133–35
Network Configuration Controls module, Webmin, 210
Network connection problems, 174–78
  checking the configuration, 174–75
  checking WINS and DNS name services, 178
  reaching other computers on the network, 176–77
Network infrastructure, 232–33
Networking, 103
Network logon support, configuring Samba for, 104–5
Network Neighborhood/My Network Places, installing printers from, 97
Network security, 7
Network Time Protocol (NTP), 126–27
New server connection problems, 169–71
  check networking, 170
  check Samba configuration, 170–71
NFS Exports module, Webmin, 209
NIS Homedir option, 303
nmbd, 27–28
NMBD daemon, 274
nmblookup utility, 30, 277
Nt acl Support setting, 288
Nt Pipe Support setting, 288
Nt smb Support setting, 288
Null Passwords option, 282

O

Obey PAM restrictions option, 282
Octal numbers, changing permissions using, 223–24
Oehser, Tom, 226
OpenLDAP project, 9
OpenLinux (Caldera), 22, 43, 87, 111–12, 123, 173, 196, 243–47
  help, 323–24
OpenLinux Webmin package (Caldera), 31, 33
Open source development model, 2

Open source licensing, 6
Open source software, 21
  integrity and stability of, 2
OpenSSH secure shell software, 224
OpenSSL, 31, 111–18
  downloading, 112
  installing, 112
Oplock Break Wait Time setting, 299
Oplock Contention Limit setting, 299, 312
Oplocks, 253–54, 312
Oplocks option, 74
Os2 Driver Map, 293
Os Level option, 297

P

PAM password change option, 283
Panic Action option, 304
Partitions on Local Disks module, Webmin, 210
Passwd Chat Debug option, 283
Passwd Chat option, 283
Passwd Program option, 283
Password Level option, 283
Password protection, 221–22
Passwords:
  assigning, 221
  changing, 48
Password Server option, 282
Path option, 94
  homes share, 55
  Printers configuration, 94
Path setting, Shares, 306
Pathworks protocol, 4
Performance, 227–55
  biggest hardware bottleneck, 228
  hardware, maximizing, 232–41
  issues, 228–32
    excessive disk activity, 229
    slow network connections, 229
    sluggish system response, 229
    system error messaes, 229
  Linux server, optimizing, 241–47
  monitoring, 229–32
  Samba configuration, optimizing, 247–55
ping utility:
  and Windows 9x/Me configuration, 147–48
  Windows 2000 configuration, 159
  and Windows NT configuration, 153
Pluggable Authentication Module (PAM), 33
Posix Locking option, 299–300, 312
Postexec setting, 313, 319

Postfix Configuration module, Webmin, 210
PostgreSQL Database Server module, Webmin, 210
Postscript setting, 317
PPP Accounts module, Webmin, 210
Preexec Close setting, 313
Preferred Master option, 297
Preload option, 302
Preserve Case option, 293, 310
Printable option, 94, 317
Print Admin option, 318
Printcap Name setting, 92–93, 291
Print Command, 93, 291, 317
Printer administration, Webmin, 206–8
Printer administrator, adding, 98
Printer Admin option, 92, 285
Printer Driver File option, 318
Printer Driver Location option, 293, 318
Printer Driver option, 318
Printer Name setting, 318
Printer problems, 191–93
Printers configuration:
  Browseable option, 94
  Hosts Allow option, 94
  Hosts Deny option, 94
  Path option, 94
  Printable option, 94
Printers directory, creating, 98–99
Printers/drivers, installing, 100–102
Printer Share Defaults module, 206
Printer sharing:
  choosing a connection, 91
  configuring, 88–94
  creating a spool directory, 91–92
  naming the printer share, 90–91
  WebMin Printer Administration tool, 88–90
Printers page of SWAT in Advanced View, 316–19
  base options, 315–16
  browse options, 318
  logging options, 316
  miscellaneous options, 319
  printing options, 317–18
  security options, 316
  tuning options, 316–17
Printer support configuration, 92–94
  Load Printers option, 92
  lpq command, 93
  lprm command, 93–94
  Printcap Name, 92–93
  Print Command, 93
  Printer Admin, 92
  Printing option, 93
Printing options, 291–93
  Addprinter Command, 292

Deleteprinter Command, 292–93
Enumports Command, 292
Load Printers setting, 291
Lppause Command, 292, 318
Lpq Command, 291, 317
Lpresume Command, 292, 318
Lprm Command, 291, 318
Max Print Jobs setting, 317
Os2 Driver Map, 293
Postscript setting, 317
Printable setting, 317
Printcap Name setting, 291
Print Command, 291, 317
Printer Driver File option, 318
Printer Driver Location, 293
Printer Driver Location option,
    318
Printer Driver option, 318
Printer Name setting, 318
Printing setting, 91, 317
Queuepause Command, 292, 318
Queueresume Command, 292, 318
Show Add Printer Wizard, 293
Total Print Jobs setting, 291
Printing setting, 93, 291, 317
Print sharing, how it works, 86–87
Prints share, creating, 99
Profile support, adding, 106–7
Protocol options, 248–49, 287–89
Announce As setting, 288
Announce Version setting, 288
Max mux setting, 288
Max Packet setting, 289
Max Protocol setting, 287
Max ttl setting, 289
Max Wins ttl setting, 289
max xmit setting, 249, 289
Min Protocol setting, 288
Min Wins ttl setting, 289
Name Resolve Order setting, 289
Nt acl Support setting, 288
Nt Pipe Support setting, 288
Nt smb Support setting, 288
Protocol setting, 287
Read Raw setting, 248–49, 288
Time Server setting, 289
Write Raw setting, 249, 288
Public directory, 77–79
basic, 78
limited, 78
secured, 78–79
pwdump2, 263–64
pwdump, 263

▼ **Q**

Queuepause Command, 292, 318
Queueresume Command, 292, 318

▼ **R**

RAID disk drive controllers, 233–34,
    237–38
Read List, 70
Read List option, 284
Read Only option, 71
homes share, 55
Read permission, 58–59
Read Raw setting, 248–49, 288
Read Size setting, 251
Recordkeeping, 225
Red Carpet software management
    software (Ximian), 22
Red Hat Linux, 22, 31, 87, 93, 123,
    173, 196, 243–47
help, 323
and SSL, 111–12
Remote Announce option, 303
Remote Browse Sync option, 303
Removable drive share, 82
rename command, 219
Rescue boot disk, creating, 226
Restrict Anonymous option, 284
rm command, 219
Root Directory option, 282–83
Root password, Linux terminal, 211
Root Postexec setting, 313, 319
Root Preexec Close setting, 313
Root Preexec setting, 313, 319
Root user, Linux terminal, 211
rpcclient utility, 275
rsync utility, 331–32
Running Processes module, Webmin,
    209

▼ **S**

Samba:
base settings, 40
compared to Windows, 5–11
compiling, 23–26
compiling for SSL support, 113
complete documentation, 321
configuration:
    updating, 44–45
    variables, 40–43
configuration files, 29
    lmhosts, 29
    smb.conf, 29
    smbpasswd, 29
    smbusers, 29
configuration optimization,
    247–55
configuring, 17–51, 257
    matching Red Hat's configura-
        tion, 26–27
cross-subnet browsing, 131–32

customization, 21
Dead Time option, 43
defined, 1
domain, joining, 44–45
email lists, 20
fax server, 128–31
file server, 3, 53–84
and free software, 3
help services, 50–52
    commercial support, 51
    configuration pages, 51
    email help lists, 51
    online manual, 50–51
    on SWAT's home page, 50
and Hewlett-Packard, 5
history of, 4–5
initial configuration, 39–43
installation, 17–51
    checking, 17–18
    looking at what's installed,
        27–30
installed version, when to use,
    18–20
internationalization, 30, 122–26
    Character Set option, 124
    Client Code Page option, 123
    Code Page Directory option,
        123
    Coding System option, 124
    Valid Chars option, 124–26
and lower software/hardware
    costs, 6
NetBIOS name, 40
and network security, 7
and open source licensing, 6
permissions, setting from Win-
    dows, 61
printer server, 85–102
print server, 3
proxy server, setting up, 113–14
Samba 1.0, 18
Samba 2.0, 19
Samba 2.2, 19
Samba 3.0, 20
security settings, 41–43
    Encrypt Passwords option, 42
    guest accounts, 42–43
    Security parameter, 41–42
server programs, 27–29
    nmbd, 27–28
    smbd, 27
    winbindd, 29
server string, 40
services, starting, 43–44
setting up SSL on, 111
setup of, 257–58
Socket options, 43
software, where to look for, 20–21

Samba (*continued*)
source of name, 3–4
SSL options, configuring, 116–17
SSL proxy server:
configuring the Windows machine, 117–18
starting, 117
strengths, 5–8
SWAT, 34–39
time server, 126–28
troubleshooting, 169–93
tuning settings, 43
updates, where to find, 21
user management, 46–50
matching Windows and Linux usernames, 48–49
using as a logon server, 104–11
using over SSL, 111–18
utility programs, 29–30
nmblookup, 30
smbpasswd, 29–30
smbstatus, 30
SWAT, 29
testparm, 29
and vendor independence, 7
virtual servers, 118–22
and Web-based administration, 7–8
Webmin, 30–34
configuration page tabs, 31–32
setting up for Samba administration, 31–34
and user account management, 32
Webmin configuration, 205–6
when to update, 20
and Windows, conflicts, 8–11
workgroup parameter, 40
Samba command and configuration option reference, 273–319
client tools, 275–76
rpcclient utility, 275
smbclient utility, 276
smbmnt utility, 276
smbmount utility, 276
smbprint utility, 276
smbspool utility, 276
smbtar utility, 276
smbumount utility, 276
configuration options, 277–315
configuration options, 277–315
Globals, 277–305
Printers, 315–19
Shares, 305–15
daemons, 273–75
NMBD daemon, 274
SMB/CIFS daemon, 273–74
WINBINDD daemon, 275
diagnostic utilities, 276–77
nmblookup utility, 277

smbstatus utility, 277
testparm utility, 277
testprns utility, 277
Samba suite, 273
Samba configuration optimization, 247–55
filename handling, 253
Hide Files setting, 253
Veto Files option, 253
Veto Oplock Files option, 253
locking options, 253–55
Blocking Locks, 299, 312
Fake Oplocks option, 312
Kernel Oplocks, 299
Level2 Oplocks, 254, 312
Locking setting, 299, 312
Oplock Break Wait Time setting, 299
Oplock Contention Limit setting, 299, 312
Oplocks, 253–54, 312
Posix Locking option, 299–300, 312
Share Modes option, 300, 313
Strict Locking, 254–55, 300, 313
write cache size, 255
logging options, 248, 309
miscellaneous options, 255, 301–4
Add Share Command, 301
Change Share Command, 301–2
Default Service, 302
Delete Readonly option, 304
Delete Share Command, 302
Dfree Command, 302
Dos Filemode option, 304
Dos Filetime Resolution option, 304
Dos Filetimes option, 304
Fake Directory Create Times option, 304
Follow Symlinks option, 303
Hide Local Users option, 304
Homedir Map option, 303
Lock Dir option, 302
Message Command, 302
NIS Homedir option, 303
Panic Action option, 304
Preload option, 302
Remote Announce option, 303
Remote Browse Sync option, 303
Socket Address option, 303
Source Environment option, 303
Time Offset option, 303
Valid Chars setting, 302
Wide Links option, 255, 303
protocol options, 248–49
max xmit setting, 249, 289
Read Raw setting, 248–49, 288
Write Raw setting, 249, 288

tuning options, 249–52
Change Notify Timeout, 249
Dead Time setting, 249–50
getwd cache setting, 250
Keepalive setting, 250
lpq Cache Time, 250
Max Disk Size setting, 250
Max Open Files setting, 251
Read Size setting, 251
socket options, 251–52
Samba domain controller:
configuring Samba, 269–70
domain logon options, 272
Logon Drive option, 272
Logon Home option, 272
Logon Path option, 272
Logon Script option, 272
machine accounts:
adding, 270–71
creating, 270–72
domain administrators, 271
netlogon, setting up, 270
setting up, 268–72
Samba fax server, 128–31
fax printer, setting up, 130
fax server software, setting up, 129–30
HylaFAX, 129
mgetty+sendfax, 129
modem, selecting, 129
Windows clients, setting up, 130–31
Samba file server, 53–84
application sharing, 84
homes share, 54–58
Available option, 56
Browseable option, 56
Comments option, 54
Guest account option, 55
Guest OK option, 55
Hosts Allow option, 55
Hosts Deny option, 55
Path option, 55
Read Only option, 55
securing, 56–58
Samba lists, 322–23
Samba newsgroup, 323
Samba printer server, 85–102
Add Printer Wizard, 96–97
automatic printer services, 98–102
configuring Samba for, 98–100
installing printers/drivers, 100–102
customizing printers, 94–95
Network Neighborhood/My Network Places, installing printers from, 97
Printers configuration:
Browseable option, 94

Hosts Allow option, 94
Hosts Deny option, 94
Path option, 94
Printable option, 94
printer sharing:
  choosing a connection, 91
  configuring, 88–94
  creating a spool directory,
    91–92
  naming the printer share,
    90–91
  WebMin Printer Administration
    tool, 88–90
printer support configuration,
  92–94
  Load Printers option, 92
  lpq command, 93
  lprm command, 93–94
  Printcap Name, 92–93
  Print command, 93
  Printer Admin, 92, 185
  Printing option, 93
print sharing, how it works, 86–87
Samba print shares, accessing
  from Windows, 96–97
spool permissions, setting, 86–87
Samba print shares, accessing from
  Windows, 96–97
Samba-related problems, 186–91
  Samba is not running, 186–89
  SWAT can't be opened, 189–91
Samba server, 9–10
  administration of, 8
  configuring, 10
  creating a certificate for, 114
Samba shares:
  accessing using the Net com-
    mand, 163
  basic group share, 68–69
  browsing options, 73
  CD-ROMs, sharing, 80–82
  creating directories for, 61–63
  file locking options, 73–74
    Blocking Locks option, 73
    Level 2 Oplocks, 74
    Locking option, 73–74
    Oplocks option, 74
    Share Modes option, 74
    Strick Locking option, 74
  filename handling options, 72–73
    hidden attribute on dot files, 72
    Hide Files option, 72
    Map Archive option, 72–73
    Veto Files option, 72
  guest access, adding, 79–80
  guest account, 79–80
  Microsoft Access database, shar-
    ing, 82–83
  miscellaneous options, 74–75

public directory, 77–79
  basic, 78
  limited, 78
  secured, 78–79
removable drive share, 82
secure group share, 76–77
security options, 69–72
  Admin Users, 69–70
  Create Mask option, 71
  Directory Mask option, 71
  Force Create Mode, 71
  Force Directory Mode, 71
  Force Group, 70
  Force User, 70
  Hosts Allow option, 71–72
  Hosts Deny option, 71–72
  Invalid Users, 69
  Read List, 70
  Read Only option, 71
  Valid Users, 69
  Write List, 70
setting up, 68–76
shortcut to creating, 65
Samba time server, 126–28
  setting the time on Windows
    clients, 128
Samba virtual servers, 118–22
Samba Web Administration Tool
  (SWAT), 8
Scheduled Cron Jobs module, Web-
  min, 209
Scope IDs, 143
SCSI disk drives, 233–34, 236–37
Secure connections, 224
Secured public directory, 78
Secure group share, 76–77
SecureID, 224–25
Security, 103
Security Mask option, 285
Security options, 69–72, 306–9
  Admin Users, 69–70, 306
  Create Mask option, 71, 307
  Directory Mask option, 71, 307
  Directory Security Mask, 308
  Force Create Mode, 71, 307
  Force Directory Mode, 71, 308
  Force Directory Security Mode,
    308
  Force Group option, 70, 307
  Force Security Mode, 307
  Force User option, 70, 307
  Guest Account option, 306, 316
  Guest Ok option, 308, 316
  Guest Only option, 308
  Hosts Allow option, 71–72, 308,
    316
  Hosts Deny option, 71–72, 309, 316
  Inherit Permissions setting, 308
  Invalid Users, 69, 306

Only User option, 308
Print Admin option, 318
Read List, 70, 306
Read Only option, 71, 307
Security Mask option, 307
Username option, 306
Valid Users, 69, 306
Write List, 70, 306
Security setting, 280–81
Security tips, Linux, 221–24
  changing permissions using octal
    numbers, 223–24
  file permissions, 222–23
  firewalls/secure connections, 224
  monitoring the system, 224
  password protection, 221–22
Sendmail Configuration module,
  Webmin, 210
Server certificate, creating, 115–16
Server Messaging Block (SMB) proto-
  col, 134
Server optimization, Linux, 241–47
Server programs, 27–29
  nmbd, 27–28
  smbd, 27
  winbindd, 29
Servers Index module, Webmin, 209
Server String option, 280
Set Directory setting, 314
SGID ("set group ID"), 60–61
Shared code, 2
Shared directories, Linux, 63
Share-level security, 147
Share Modes option, 74, 300, 313
Shares page of SWAT in Advanced
  View, 305–15
  base options, 305–6
  browse options, 311
  filename handling options, 309–11
  locking options, 312–13
  logging options, 309
  miscellaneous options, 313–15
  security options, 306–9
  tuning options, 309
  VFS options, 315–16
Sharity, 111
Shell, defined, 211
Shortcuts, Linux, 15
Short Preserve Case option, 294, 310
Short version, basic group share,
  75–76
Show Add Printer Wizard, 293
skey-2.2.tar.gz, 224
SMB/CIFS daemon, 273–74
smbclient utility, 276
smb.conf, 29
smbd, 27
smbmnt utility, 276
smbmount utility, 276

smbpasswd, 29–30
Smb Passwd File option, 282
smbprint utility, 276
SMBserver, 3–4
smbspool utility, 276
smbstatus, 30, 287
smbstatus utility, 277
smbtar utility, 276
smbumount utility, 276
smbusers, 29
Socket Address option, 303
Socket options, 43, 251–52, 290
Software Management module, Web-
    min, 208
SO_KEEPALIVE, 253
SO_RCVBUF, 253
SO_SNDBUF, 253
Source code, for Samba, 21
Source Environment option, 303
spool permissions, setting, 86–87
Squid Proxy Server module, Webmin,
    210
SSL, setting up on Samba, 111
SSL options, 300–301
    configuring, 117
    Ssl ca Certdir, 300
    Ssl ca Certfile, 300
    Ssl Ciphers, 300
    Ssl Client Cert, 300
    Ssl Client Key, 300
    Ssl Compatibility, 300
    Ssl Hosts list, 300
    Ssl Hosts Resign, 301
    Ssl Require Clientcert, 301
    Ssl Require Servercert, 301
    Ssl Server Cert, 301
    Ssl Server Key, 301
    Ssl setting, 300
    Ssl Version, 301
SSL proxy server, starting, 117
Startup files, Linux, 14
Stat Cache option, 295
Stat cache size, 253
Stat Cache Size setting, 291
Status setting, 287, 309, 316
Sticky Bit, 60–61, 87, 223–24
Strict Locking option, 74, 254–55,
    300, 313
Strict sync setting, 309
Strip Dot option, 293
stunnel, 111, 113
SUID ("set user ID"), 60–61
Swap space, 239
SWAT, 29, 34–39
    accessing, 34
    Globals, and printer support, 92
    home page, 34, 37
        help on, 50
    home page icons, 34

no display on port 901, remedy
    for, 35–36
options, 37–39
    Globals, 37–38
    Home, 37
    Password, 39
    Printers, 39
    Shares, 38
    Status, 39
    View, 39
Printers, 94
Sync Always setting, 309
Syslog Only option, 286
Syslog option, 286
System administration essentials,
    Linux, 195–226
System Logs module, Webmin, 209
System policies, adding, 107–9
System Time module, Webmin, 210
SysV Init Configuration module, Web-
    min, 209

T

tail command, 220
tape backup:
    creating, 334
    restoring, 335
    with tar utility, 333–34
tar utility, 331, 334
    tape backup with, 333–34
TCP/IP timeout settings, 245
TCP_NODELAY, 252
TCP ports, 246
Telnet Login module, Webmin, 210
testparm utility, 29, 277
testprns utility, 277
Text editors, Linux, 215–17
Time command, 220
Time Offset option, 303
Time Server setting, 289
Timestamp Logs setting, 287
Tom's rescue disk, 226
Tomsrtbt, 226
Tools, Linux, 14
Total Print Jobs setting, 291
tracert utility:
    and Windows 9x/Me configura-
        tion, 149
    and Windows NT configuration,
        154
Tridgell, Andrew, 4–5, 325
Troubleshooting, 169–93
    general guide for, 172–74
    checking the logs, 173
    checking the network wiring,
        172
    checking Windows client con-
        figuration, 173

connection-related problem
    areas, 172
network connection problems,
    174–78
    checking the configuration,
        174–75
    checking WINS and DNS name
        services, 178
    reaching other computers on
        the network, 176–77
new server connection problems,
    169–71
    check networking, 170
    check Samba configuration,
        170–71
printer problems, 191–93
Samba-related problems, 186–91
    Samba is not running, 186–89
    SWAT can't be opened, 189–91
Windows problems, 178–86
    file access problems on Samba
        server, 182–85
    logon problems, 185–86
    Samba server and Network Neigh-
        borhood or Computers Near
        Me icon, 178–82
Tuning options, 249–52, 289–91,
    316–17
    Change Notify Timeout option,
        249, 289
    Dead Time setting, 249–50,
        289–90
    Getwd Cache setting, 250, 290
    Keepalive setting, 250, 290
    Lpq Cache Time, 250, 290
    Max Connections setting, 309
    Max Disk Size setting, 250, 290
    Max Open Files setting, 251, 290
    Max smbd Processes setting, 290
    Min Print Space option, 317
    Read Size setting, 251
    Socket options, 251–52, 290
    Stat Cache Size setting, 291
    Strict sync setting, 309
    Sync Always setting, 309
    Write Cache Size setting, 309
Tuning settings, 43

U

Ultra Direct Memory Access (UDMA)
    drives, 234
Unicode, 122
UNIX Networking module, 205
Unix Password Sync option, 283
Update Encrypted option, 281
Updating Linux, 21–23
User home directories, 53
Use Rhosts option, 284

User-level security, 147
User management, 46–50
Username Level option, 283
Username Map option, 283
Username option, 284
User's home directory, Linux terminal, 211–12
Using Samba (Eckstein/Collier-Brown/ Kelly), 50
Utility programs, 29–30
  nmblookup, 30
  smbpasswd, 29–30
  smbstatus, 30
  SWAT, 29
  testparm, 29

▼ **V**

Valid Chars option, 124–26, 302
Valid Users option, 69, 284
Van Vleck, Tom, 221–22
Vendor independence, 7
Veto Files option, 72, 294, 310
Veto Oplock Files option, 294, 311
VFS options, 304–5, 315
  Host msdfs option, 305
  Msdfs Root setting, 315
  VFS object, 315
  VFS Options settings, 315
View All Connections link, 206
vi text editor, 215–17
  command-line mode, 216
  command mode, 216
  defined, 215
  entering text in, 216
  insert mode, 216
  quitting in, 216–17
  saving in, 216–17
  searching in, 216
  undo in, 216
Volume setting, 313

▼ **W**

Webmin, 30–34
  Bootup module, 201
  configuration page tabs, 31–32
  help, 323
  modules, 208–10
    Apache Webserver module, 209
    BIND DNS Server module, 210
    Configuration module, 209
    Custom Commands module, 210
    DHCP Server module, 210
    Disk and Network Filesystems module, 209

Disk Quotas module, 209
File Manager module, 210
FTP Server module, 210
Help module, 209
Internet Services and Protocols module, 210
Linux Bootup Configuration module, 210
Linux RAID module, 210
Majordomo, 210
MySQL Database Server module, 210
Network Configuration Controls module, 210
NFS Exports module, 209
Partitions on Local Disks module, 210
Postfix Configuration module, 210
PostgreSQL Database Server module, 210
PPP Accounts module, 210
Running Processes module, 209
Scheduled Cron Jobs module, 209
Sendmail Configuration module, 210
Servers Index module, 209
Squid Proxy Server module, 210
System Logs module, 209
System Time module, 210
SysV Init Configuration module, 209
Telnet Login module, 210
printer administration, 206–8
Samba adminstration page, 46
Samba modules, 205–6
  Authentication module, 205
  File Share Defaults module, 206
  Miscellaneous Options module, 206
  Printer Share Defaults module, 206
  UNIX Networking module, 205
  Windows Networking module, 205
  Windows to UNIX Printing module, 206
setting up for Samba administration, 31–34
Shutdown module, 201
software management, 208
Software Management module, 208
and user account management, 32
using, 198–201
Webmin File Manager, 87
WebMin Printer Administration tool, 88–90

Wide Links option, 255, 303, 314
Winbindd, 29, 33
WINBINDD daemon, 275
Winbind options, 305
  Template Homedir option, 305
  Template Shell option, 305
  Winbind Cache Time option, 305
  Winbind gid, 305
  Winbind Separator option, 305
  Winbind uid, 305
Windows 9x/Me configuration, 137–50
  client configuration for Microsoft Windows, 144–45
  connection-checking utilities, 147–50
    ipconfig utility, 148–49
    nbstat utility, 150
    netstat utility, 149
    net utility, 150
    ping utility, 147–48
    tracert utility, 149
    winipcfg utility, 148
  machine/workgroup names, selecting, 145–46
  multiuser profiles, enabling, 137–38
  security and access control setting, 146–47
    share-level security, 147
    user-level security, 147
  TCP/IP networking:
    configuring, 138–44
    Gateway and DNS settings, 143–44
    IP address DHCP, 141–42
    WINS configuration and LMHOSTS, 142–43
    TCP/IP panel tabs, 140
Windows 2000, and print servers, 85
Windows 2000 configuration, 155–67
  checking the connection, 158–59
    netdiag utility, 159
    net utility, 159
    ping utility, 159
  TCP/IP network configuration, 155–58
    assigning the NetBIOS name, 156–57
    configuring the CIFS client and TCP/IP, 157–58
    configuring DNS, 158
    setting the IP address, 158
    WINS and NetBIOS compatibility, 158
Windows:
  access control, 10
  access control list (ACL), 259

Windows (*continued*)
  compared to Samba, 5–11
  hardware support, 10
  and Linux, 11–16
  servers, 9–10
  standards, 9
  Windows 2000, 9
Windows clients, setting up for
  Samba fax server, 130–31
Windows file server:
  eliminating, 259
  passwords, 259
  replacing, 258–68
    adding group directories with-
      out Webmin, 266
    adding users with Webmin,
      261–63
    adding users without Webmin,
      263–65
    configuring Samba server,
      265–67
    configuring shares on Samba,
      266–67
    creating user/group accounts
      on Samba server, 260–61
    getting user/group/file/printer
      sharing information, 259–60
    group shares, 267
    homes share, 266–67

    moving files to the Samba
      server, 268
    other uses shares, 267
    printers, 267
    testing the Samba server, 267–68
Windows Internet Naming Service
  (WINS), 135–36
Windows Networking module, 205
Windows NT configuration, 150–55
  checking the connection, 153–55
    ipconfig utility, 153–54
    nbstat utility, 154
    netstat utility, 154
    net utility, 154
    ping utility, 153
    tracert utility, 154
  TCP/IP network configuration,
    150–53
    assigning the NetBIOS name, 151
    checking the CIFS client, 151
    DNS configuration, 152
    installing/setting up TCP/IP, 152
    setting up the IP address,
      152–53
    WINS configuration, 152
Windows-related problems, 178–86
  file access problems on Samba
    server, 182–85
  logon problems, 185–86

Samba server and Network Neigh-
  borhood or Computers Near
  Me icon, 178–82
Windows to UNIX Printing module,
  206
winipcfg utility, and Windows 9x/Me
  configuration, 148
Wins Hook option, 298
WINS options, 298
  Dns Proxy option, 298
  Wins Hook option, 298
  Wins Proxy option, 298
  Wins Server option, 298
  Wins Support option, 298
Wins Proxy option, 298
WINS server, configuring, 106
Wins Server option, 298
Wins Support option, 298
Workgroup option, 279
Write Cache Size setting, 255, 309
Write List option, 70, 285
Write permission, 59
Write Raw setting, 249, 288

▼ **X**

Xwindows:
  reasons not to use, 197–98
  and terminals, 196–97

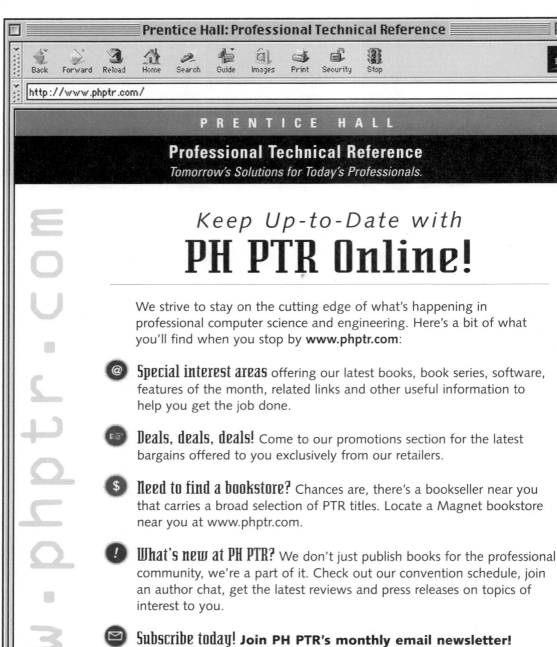